T0301653

The Evolutionary Analysis of Economic Policy

NEW HORIZONS IN INSTITUTIONAL AND EVOLUTIONARY ECONOMICS

Series Editor: Geoffrey M. Hodgson
Research Professor, University of Hertfordshire Business School, UK

Economics today is at a crossroads. New ideas and approaches are challenging the largely static and equilibrium-oriented models that used to dominate mainstream economics. The study of economic institutions – long neglected in the economics textbooks – has returned to the forefront of theoretical and empirical investigation.

This challenging and interdisciplinary series publishes leading works at the forefront of institutional and evolutionary theory and focuses on cutting-edge analyses of modern socio-economic systems. The aim is to understand both the institutional structures of modern economies and the processes of economic evolution and development. Contributions will be from all forms of evolutionary and institutional economics, as well as from Post-Keynesian, Austrian and other schools. The overriding aim is to understand the processes of institutional transformation and economic change.

Titles in the series include:

Institutions and the Role of the State
Edited by Leonardo Burlamaqui, Ana Celia Castro and Ha-Joon Chang

Marx, Veblen, and Contemporary Institutional Political Economy
Principles and Unstable Dynamics of Capitalism
Phillip Anthony O'Hara

The New Evolutionary Microeconomics
Complexity, Competence, and Adaptive Behaviour
Jason D. Potts

National Competitiveness and Economic Growth
The Changing Determinants of Economic Performance in the World Economy
Timo J. Hämäläinen

Conventions and Structures in Economic Organization
Markets, Networks and Hierarchies
Edited by Olivier Favereau and Emmanuel Lazega

Globalization and Institutions
Redefining the Rules of the Economic Game
Edited by Marie-Laure Djelic and Sigrid Quack

The Evolutionary Analysis of Economic Policy
Edited by Pavel Pelikan and Gerhard Wegner

The Evolutionary Analysis of Economic Policy

Edited by

Pavel Pelikan

Professor of Economics, Department of Economic Policy, Prague University of Economics, Czech Republic and the Ratio Institute, Stockholm, Sweden

Gerhard Wegner

Professor of Economics, University of Erfurt, Germany

NEW HORIZONS IN INSTITUTIONAL AND EVOLUTIONARY ECONOMICS

Edward Elgar

Cheltenham, UK • Northampton, MA, USA

Published by
Edward Elgar Publishing Limited
Glensanda House
Montpellier Parade
Cheltenham
Glos GL50 1UA
UK

Edward Elgar Publishing, Inc.
136 West Street
Suite 202
Northampton
Massachusetts 01060
USA

A catalogue record for this book
is available from the British Library

Library of Congress Cataloging in Publication Data
The evolutionary analysis of economic policy / edited by Pavel Pelikan, Gerhard Wegner.
p. cm.– (New horizons in institutional and evolutionary economics series)
1. Evolutionary economics. 2. Economic policy. I. Pelikán, Pavel. II. Wegner, Gerhard. III. New Horizons in institutional and evolutionary economics

HB97.3E9 2003
338.9–dc21

2003040788

ISBN 978 1 84376 225 6 (Hardback)
ISBN 978 1 84542 133 5 (Paperback)

Printed and bound by CPI Group (UK) Ltd, Croydon, CR0 4YY

Contents

List of figures and tables   vi
List of contributors   vii
Preface   x

1. Introduction: evolutionary thinking on economic policy   1
    Gerhard Wegner and Pavel Pelikan
2. Why economic policies need comprehensive evolutionary analysis   15
    Pavel Pelikan
3. Evolutionary markets and the design of institutional policy   46
    Gerhard Wegner
4. Knowledge and economic policy: a plea for political
    experimentalism   67
    Stefan Okruch
5. Democracy as an evolutionary method   96
    Michael Wohlgemuth
6. Ideologies, beliefs, and economic advice –
    a cognitive–evolutionary view on economic policy-making   128
    Tilman Slembeck
7. Equilibrium and evolutionary foundations of competition and
    technology policy: new perspectives on the division of labour
    and the innovation process   162
    J.S. Metcalfe
8. Institutional evolution, regulatory competition and path
    dependence   191
    Wolfgang Kerber and Klaus Heine
9. The German *Neuer Markt* as an adaptive institution   223
    Helge Peukert
10. Understanding and the mobilisation of error: eliminating
    controls in evolutionary learning   245
    Hansjörg Siegenthaler

Index   261

Figures and tables

FIGURES

3.1 Economic policy as institutional design   51
5.1 Competition as a feedback-driven interaction process   103
6.1 A comparison of countries   134
6.2 Why politics?   141
6.3 A cognitive–evolutionary model of the political process   143
6.4 Two approaches to economic advice   150
6.5 Fiscal equivalence   154
8.1 Technological competition and lock-in   199
8.2 Competition among legal paradigms and lock-ins in corporate law in the case of dynamic economies of scale   212

TABLES

6.1 Economic 'fallacies' and possible implications   139
6.2 The two worlds of economists and politicians   148

Contributors

Klaus Heine, born 1970, received his Diploma (M.A.) in Economics from the University of Marburg. He was Research Fellow at the Department of Economics at the Universities of Bochum and Marburg where he received his Ph.D. His dissertation thesis deals with problems of institutional competition with respect to US corporate law. His research interests are: law and economics, evolutionary economics, official statistics, economic psychology.

Wolfgang Kerber, born 1958. Professor of Economics, Philipps University Marburg. Fields of research: evolutionary economics, institutional economics (particularly law and economics), industrial economics, competition policy, European integration. The following monographs have appeared in German: *Evolutionary Market Processes and the Problem of Demand Power* (Nomos, 1989) and *The Practice of European Merger Control* (Bayreuth, 1994).

J.S. (Stan) Metcalfe is Executive Director of the ESRC Centre for Innovation and Competition at the University of Manchester and UMIST. He is a past President of the International J.A. Schumpeter Society. His recent work is focused on questions related to the application of evolutionary ideas to the study of innovation, competition and economic change more generally. Among his recent publications are *Evolutionary Economics and Creative Destruction*, Routledge, 1997; 'Institutions and Progress', *Industrial and Corporate Change*, 2001; 'On the Optimality of the Competitive Process: Kimura's Theorem and Market Dynamics', *Journal of Bioeconomics*, 2002.

Stefan Okruch is Visiting Professor at the University of Kassel (Germany) and Senior Research Fellow at the Max Planck Project Group 'Common Goods: Law, Politics and Economics' in Bonn; he holds a Ph.D. in economics from the University of Bayreuth. His main fields of research are evolutionary and institutional economics with a strong interdisciplinary bias; theory and history of political-economic thought; philosophy of law and of economics. His latest monograph is *Innovation and Diffusion of Legal Norms* (Berlin) in German in 1999.

Pavel Pelikan obtained his Ph.D. in economics from Charles University in Prague for work on information problems in different economic systems, which he continued as a post-doctoral research fellow at the University of California in Berkeley and Carnegie-Mellon University in Pittsburgh. After having been professor of economics at the University of Toronto and the University of Paris 1-Sorbonne, he became a research professor at the Institute for Industrial Economics, Stockholm, before taking up his current position as research professor at the Royal Institute of Technology, also in Stockholm. His first two books appeared in Czech; his first publication in English was 'Languages as a limiting factor of centralization' in *American Economic Review* (1969). His contributions to evolutionary economics include 'Evolution, economic competence, and the market for corporate control' in *Journal of Economic Behavior and Organization* (1989), 'The dynamics of economic systems, or how to transform a failed socialist economy' in *Journal of Evolutionary Economics* (1992), and 'The forming of successful organizations: self-organizing and Darwinian evolution as sources of organizing information', in J. Foster and J.S. Metcalfe (eds) *Frontiers of Evolutionary Economics* (2001).

Helge Peukert is Reader in Public Finance and Fiscal Sociology at Erfurt University. His research interest are in the fields of critical institutional economics, economic sociology, economic history and history of economic thought. His publications include *The Action Paradigm in Economics* (Marburg, 2000, in German) and 'The Schmoller Renaissance', *History of Political Economy, 2001*.

Hansjörg Siegenthaler is Emeritus Professor of Economic History at the University of Zürich; he was formerly a Fellow at the Institute for Advanced Studies, Berlin, where he was in charge of a project devoted to the cultural foundations of rational behaviour. At the beginning of his academic career he spent two years at Harvard University doing research on the American textile industry in the nineteenth century. Later he taught 'New Economic History' at the Universities of Münster (Germany) and Zürich. His research fields encompass the empirical study of recent economic history, institutional change and epistemology. His main field of interest concerns the impact of ideological and institutional change on long run economic development and economic fluctuations. Amongst his many publications, his *Confidence in Rules, Prosperity and Crises* appeared in 1993, and *History and Economy After the Cultural Turn* in 1999 (both in German).

Tilman Slembeck is Professor of Economics and holds posts at the University of St. Gallen (Switzerland), University of Applied Sciences Winterthur (Switzerland), European Business School (Germany). Between 1996 and 1998 he was a Visiting Scholar at Harvard University, University of Pittsburgh, University College London. His fields of interest include evolutionary economics, economic policy, applied microeconomics and experimental economics. His publications include 'The formation of economic policy', *Constitutional Political Economy*, 1997; 'How to make scientists agree: an evolutionary betting mechanism', *Kyklos*, 2000.

Gerhard Wegner is Professor for Institutional Economics and Economic Policy in the Faculty of Economics, Law and Social Sciences at Erfurt University, Germany; he was formerly Professor for Economic Policy in the Economics Department at Bochum University. His current research interests include evolutionary economics and the design of economic policy based on an evolutionary concept of the market economy. He also works on liberal economic theories, methodological issues in economic theory and the design of institutions in open market economies, for example with respect to European integration and environmental policy. He has published three books in German: *Economic Policy Between Self-organisation and Intervention* (Mohr, 1996), *Welfare Aspects of Evolutionary Markets* (Mohr, 1991), *Environmental policy between decisionism and self-organisation* (Nomos, 1996) as well as numerous articles in both English- and German-speaking journals.

Michael Wohlgemuth is Managing Research Associate at the Walter Eucken Institut in Freiburg (Germany) and teaches at the University of Witten/Herdecke and at Freiburg University. He has also held posts as a Research Fellow at the Max-Planck-Institute for Research into Economic Systems in Jena (Germany), Affiliate Assistant Professor at George Mason University and Visiting Scholar at New York University. Major research interests: new institutional economics, public choice theory, Austrian economics, constitutional economics.

Preface

Sometimes the development and production of a book mirrors its theme. This is the case with this edition. The volume we present to the reader, which deals with economic policy and evolution, itself emerged from an evolutionary process set into motion by its editors. Some time ago we felt the need to investigate the impact of evolutionary processes on the conditions and consequences of different economic policies. This investigation promised a double payoff: making theoretical policy analysis safer for practical applications, and increasing the status of evolutionary analysis among economists. Both appeared to us to be of great importance: on the one hand, standard (non-evolutionary) theories have produced a great variety of policy implications, of which only some have proved helpful, whereas many others have turned out to be grossly mistaken; and on the other hand, evolutionary economics has been regarded by a majority of the profession as a pastime of a few enthusiasts, to which no one was obliged to pay serious attention. If we could show that evolutionary analysis is necessary for producing reasonable policy implications and distinguishing them from unreasonable ones, the situation would clearly improve on both points.

To acquire the help of colleagues interested in related problems, we organised a conference on the topic in Bochum, Germany in May 2000. Our first debt of acknowledgement is to the Volkswagen Stiftung which generously supported our project. The conference participants consisted of scholars from diverse branches of economics who had hitherto worked on evolutionary economics and/or institutional economics and were interested in exploring the fruitfulness of different approaches to economic policy. However, the conference itself was nothing more than a starting point. After the conference, an intellectual evolutionary process, which has included much variation and selection, began. We examined the original contributions to the conference in order to seek their underlying thematic coherence. We then linked other authors to this debate and solicited further contributions related to our topic. These contributions, like those presented at the conference, have undergone intensive discussion and revision, a process which lasted well into 2002, in the summer of which the volume was complete.

We thank our authors for their patience and perseverance in writing and rewriting their articles until they suited the specific purpose of this book. Likewise we thank those who contributed to the debates around our theme but whose papers, despite their often high quality, we judged did not suit this purpose. We would also like to thank Edward Elgar, who without hesitation supported our project and offered to publish our book at a relatively early stage of its preparation, and to Geoff Hodgson, who generously invited us to place it in his series *New Horizons in Institutional and Evolutionary Economics* – which we appreciate so much more knowing that several contributions in this volume, to begin with our own, are not entirely congruent with his own views on economic policy. A large portion of our thanks goes to the staff of Edward Elgar Publishing Limited, in particular to Nep Athwal, Dymphna Evans and Alison Stone, who have been most professional, efficient and understanding throughout the entire process of preparing our book for publication. Brigitte Klink, Sven Meth, Sebastian Schäfer and Birgit Schöppe deserve our thanks for help in arranging and completing the manuscript in the required form. Last, but by far not least, we thank Mark Peacock for his incessant and invaluable help during the entire evolution of this volume, from the initial variety of potential contributions, through the difficult selection process, to the final form of what we hope is a relatively coherent book.

Pavel Pelikan and Gerhard Wegner,
Stockholm and Erfurt, November 2002

1. Introduction: evolutionary thinking on economic policy

Gerhard Wegner and Pavel Pelikan

Evolutionary economics is a relatively young but rapidly developing field, concerned with economic processes that can in some sense be considered 'evolutionary'. Its development has largely been motivated by the dissatisfaction of a growing number of economists with static equilibrium analysis which has virtually monopolized mainstream economics during the last half-century. Although this analysis has obtained several rigorous results, they have been limited to selected aspects of simplified economies, and thus only partially relevant to actual problems of real-world economies. Static equilibrium analysis has indeed been able to throw useful light on many narrow policy issues, but it has proved unable properly to cope with any of the major economic problems of the last half-century – including stagflation, the collapse of socialist economic systems, the growing deficits of welfare states, and the Japanese financial crisis. It not only failed to see these problems coming, but was until the last minute producing formal models proving the social optimality of many of the policies which caused these problems, including Keynesian overspending, national planning, government ownership of firms, and selective industrial policies.[1]

These failures can be traced in part to the static character of this analysis which limits its attention to the potential existence of equilibria without examining the processes that might lead to them, and in part to its strongly simplifying assumptions, which make it blind to many important causes of real-world economic problems. These assumptions usually limit analysis to an idealized economy which consists of a constant set of idealized (perfectly optimizing) agents interacting through a constant mixture of markets and firms, using well-known technologies with a given assortment of inputs and outputs, and respecting a constant set of institutional rules (such as property rights and ethical norms). In fact, the last assumption is usually only implicit, as the agents are assumed to trade honestly, and not to steal or cheat, but the institutions required to guarantee such behaviour are rarely explicitly mentioned. Thus, whenever it is important to consider that some of these features change, or are in less ideal states than assumed – as in problems involving technological or organizational innovations, institutional reforms, or system transformation – static equilibrium analysis must lose relevance, and its results may become misleading.

Evolutionary economics can be considered to enter the second stage in the search for less limited analyses, the first stage being reserved to the dynamics of processes by which some equilibria might be obtained whilst maintaining most of the simplifying assumptions of equilbrium analysis. The distinctive mark of evolutionary economics is to drop at least some of these assumptions – in other words, to recognize as variable at least some of the features of economies that equilibrium analysis of both static and dynamic kinds usually assumes constant – such as agents' characteristics, available technologies, market structures, organization of firms, or institutional rules – and to study their changes over time.

But today's evolutionary economics also has limitations of its own. Some of them follow from the fact that among the many different types of economic change which may be considered evolutionary, most evolutionary economists usually deal only with some, without realizing the importance, and sometimes even the existence, of the others. Thus, for example, Nelson's and Winter's *An Evolutionary Theory of Economic Change* (1982), which has had the great merit of convincing many modern economists of the importance of evolutionary processes, and on which many evolutionary economists still continue to build, concentrates on changes of firms' routines, and in particular of their technologies, while saying much less about other evolutionary processes and nothing about institutional change. Somewhat symmetrically, the economists who do study institutional change – for instance, in the directions indicated by Hayek (1967) or by North (1990) – usually pay little or no attention to technological change and the evolution of industries.

Another important limitation of evolutionary economics is that most of it has been concerned with depicting and explaining real-world economies in more realistic ways, with attention to more of their actual aspects, than standard (non-evolutionary) economics, but without making it clear what policy implications the greater realism may have, and in which sense these implications would be superior to those of standard analysis. To be sure, the book by Nelson and Winter does contain a section on economic welfare and policy, but it is largely limited to industrial policies and policies concerning research and development, under simplifying and idealizing assumptions about the motivations and abilities of government policy-making agencies. In assessing economic policies, such a partial evolutionary analysis may not do any better than standard analysis: it may also overlook important policy failures, and thus give support to the wrong policies. Indeed, the evolutionary economists using it in studies of the then highly admired Japanese industrial policies proved as unable to foresee the crisis to which these policies were bound to lead as their non-evolutionary colleagues.

This limitation of today's evolutionary economics is especially bothersome to those of its adherents who feel concerned by the fate of the economies in which they live, and who would therefore like to produce knowledge that in addition to being theoretically interesting would also be practically useful. But to develop a systematic analysis of policy issues from the perspective of evolutionary economics is far from easy. Difficulties start when we think from this perspective about any potentially active role of economic policy with respect to welfare – a role which was (at least theoretically) not questioned from a static theoretical angle. To see how difficult it may be to identify this role, a glance at the two distinctive strands of evolutionary economics – the (neo-) Schumpeterian, of which the leading representatives are Nelson and Winter, and the Austrian, or more precisely Hayekian – is instructive. Both emphasize the evolutionary nature of markets and distinguish themselves sharply from standard static analysis. Nevertheless, they hold opposing views on economic policy. Neo-Schumpeterians more or less advocate an active role for the state and they stress the possibility of inferior allocative states, that is resource wastage which governments can (and ought to) overcome. In contrast, theorists supporting the Hayekian strand of economic thought deem economic policy by definition to be an evil which cannot but detract from the functioning of markets and which, consequently, needs to be diminished as far as possible. The critical attitude towards economic policy has occasionally gone so far that Hayekians have avoided labelling themselves evolutionary economists – in spite of the fact that the very concept of spontaneous order is deeply rooted in an evolutionary understanding of markets.

Thus, neo-Schumpeterians have been inclined to expand on the catalogue of cases of market failure, whereas Hayekians interpret unsatisfactory courses of economic development to be either the unavoidable price of market evolution or the consequence of detrimental economic policy. Hayek's well-known phrase that a spontaneous order defies end-state criteria has been used in a negligent manner and has often been taken to be a blanket apology for any non-desired attributes of market evolution (concerning income distribution in particular), a position which implies that any search for welfare-improving opportunities by the state are a priori futile. But the practical relevance of evolutionary economics will hardly profit from controversy at this level. In the present volume even those who sympathise with Hayek's general perspective on markets – in particular the editors – hesitate to accept this radical view and generally acknowledge a *potential* positive role for the government, which means that a welfare-improving role for the government should not be excluded a priori. Conversely, neo-Schumpeterians have become more sceptical of their former pro-interventional tendency and have absorbed some 'Hayekianism' into their theoretical efforts (see, in particular, the chapter by Metcalfe in this volume).

Nevertheless, it is important to note that consistent evolutionary thinking on economic policy rejects a careless use of the term 'market failure' and in principle agrees, as Pelikan's chapter explains in more detail, with Demsetz's (1969) early critique of the traditional one-sided market-failure analysis for using a 'nirvana approach' and falling victim to 'the grass-is-always-greener' fallacy. But this does not make the notion of market failure easier to define, as illustrated in the chapter by Metcalfe, where market failure is diagnosed with respect to the frequently stated underproduction of innovation in markets. In general, evolutionary approaches suggest a more generous assessment of the waste of resources which is the concomitant by-product of a discovery procedure and cannot be (totally) avoided without suspending that process; additionally, and unfortunately, its appearance is not foreseeable ex ante. In many (but not all) cases the notion of market failure depends on our preconception of what market competition should engender. Yet, the more concrete this preconception is, the less we have to rely upon market competition to discover 'what things are wanted', to paraphrase a well-known Hayekian argument.

Evolutionary economists such as Hayek have continuously stressed that welfare improvements in a market society depend on appropriate institutions which foster the discovery procedure in markets. This idea has inspired more in-depth research into the interaction of institutions and new economic (spaces of) activities. Hence this strand of economic thought acknowledges the impact of institutions on market development and consequently on economic welfare. In so doing it invites scrutiny of the best design of *institutions* with respect to welfare and the potential role of economic policy in such a process of institutional refinement (the two questions are not identical; see Wegner on this topic). In the following chapter, Pelikan delineates a general theoretical framework for discussing distinctive levels of evolutions including the evolution of institutions (in the sense of rules) as an essential part. This paves the way for a more detailed discussion of institutions which can be provided either by the state or by market participants (including hybrid forms). Of much interest in this concern is the respective adaptability in response to changing market interactions among individuals. Although state activity is far from being the best solution for the institutional needs of the market sphere, evolutionary economists admit a potential positive impact of the state on the institutional framework of the market process.

An important difference from standard policy recommendations remains: evolutionary thinking waives guarantees of an inevitable welfare improvement even when it allows room for intervention. As long as the market is not completely abolished, the impact of intervention on it must remain indirect by nature, for the salient feature (and driving force) of evolving markets is entrepreneurship. Although the alertness as well as the success of market participants is provoked by a competitive environment, it is not automatically generated by altered institutional conditions. Neither the occurrence nor the extent of a rise in welfare can be guaranteed as a consequence of economic policy; lacking a yardstick to make ought–is comparisons, normative arguments can only rely on improving *chances* which emerge from a revised institutional framework. Contrary to standard welfare theory, even an ideal economic policy must relinquish the exclusive responsibility for an evolving economy's welfare which results from a synthesis of public decisions and private success.

One must note, here, that evolutionary thinking on normative questions concerning economic policy does not necessarily exclude standard theory. If the latter's conditions are more or less fulfilled in certain special cases, for example the constancy of demand and supply conditions in markets as well as the borders of markets (one may think of agricultural markets), the abstractions of a standard welfare-loss analysis are empirically justified. From this perspective evolutionary thinking amounts to a generalization of welfare analysis which includes textbook tools as a special case. However, a check of the adequacy of abstractions has to be made. In this volume, Metcalfe deals with this question when he analyses the appropriateness of the market failure diagnosis, in particular the assertion of a public good feature of economic knowledge 'incorporated' into novelties. In this case a careful check of the assumptions demonstrate the inappropriateness of the market failure approach.

All this indicates that developing a systematic evolutionary analysis of economic policies is a difficult task, on which little has been done so far. It is our aim with this book to start the task of discussing some of the basic questions which need to be clarified if the development of an evolutionary approach to policy-making is to make progress. Some main types of question are of theoretical interest which indicate where to look for the most important contributions to their answers that evolutionary analysis can be expected to make.

First, however, it should be noted that all the questions discussed, just as the entire evolutionary policy analysis that is the distant aim of this book, are limited to the realm of positive economics – in the sense that they are free of any normative intention to prescribe which economic policies a given society should choose, and only seek knowledge that could help the society's members to make wise policy choices of their own, or at least avoid what they would themselves later recognize to be policy errors. But there is an important qualification which the usual division of economic theories into normative and positive appears to ignore. To make sure that the knowledge found will actually be helpful, and not misleading – as part of the knowledge produced under the standard simplifying assumptions by standard positive analysis turned out to be – the questions and the analysis must belong to a special kind of positive economics. Labelling this kind 'for normative uses', the following chapter by Pelikan distinguishes it from the more usual normative economics 'for academic uses', and shows that among other things, it must indeed be in a well-defined sense 'evolutionary'.

Positive questions about economic policy-making can be divided into three main types:

- *the real effects of different policy alternatives;*
- *the consistency of the choice of policy objectives (set of preferences over policy outcomes);*
- *the political process forming economic policy.*

The following sections summarize what the present authors believe, and to some extent by their contributions also demonstrate, that evolutionary analysis can do to improve our knowledge of the answers.

THE REAL EFFECTS OF ECONOMIC POLICIES

The main contributions of evolutionary analysis can be expected to concern the unintentional and often negative side-effects of policies which are caused by the evolutionary nature of markets and governments and, in particular, by the creative behaviour of market participants. They typically materialize only in the long run and thus escape the attention of policy-makers at the time of policy formulation. The failure of taking them properly into account is one of the most important, but in modern economics least studied, type of government failure.

If such side-effects accumulate, future economic policy will increasingly be occupied with the effects of former measures. In the end the economy will become covered with a blanket of intervention, which would doubtlessly represent a less-desired version of 'third way capitalism'. Evolutionary approaches endeavour to obtain a more in-depth understanding of such inadvertent side-effects which typically emerge from interventions into complex systems, as experience from eco-systems has taught us.

With respect to this point, evolutionary thinking continues a strand of economic thought which can be traced back to Adam Smith who devoted much attention to the often-neglected aftermath of even benevolent measures. Smith criticized politicians of his time for their limited understanding of the complexity of a market society and the counterreactions engendered by purposeful measures; this limited understanding concerns, on the one hand, the inability to identify endogenous forces of the market which may overcome less-desired states of the economy alone (or only require some indirect assistance still to be identified); on the other hand, it concerns the overlooking of long-term effects upon the coordinative forces of the market society, in particular, the over-taxing of these endogenous forces.

Although it is of a great social importance to learn from such government failures, only few systematic attempts have been undertaken so far, most of them belong to the history of economic thought rather than modern economics. They include a study by Mises in the 1920s and the political–economic contributions of the ORDO-liberal school in Germany. As Gerhard Wegner explains in more detail in Chapter 3, an important aspect of governmental interventions in markets that the evolutionary approach points out is the ability of market participants to react to policy measures when these have an impact on economic data. The effects of policy can be boosted or counteracted by entrepreneurial behaviour of agents. This may be the result of learning which consists both of the search for new information concerning profit opportunities, and also activities to act against the intentions of the policy makers (if they run counter to individual interests). Because information costs are sunk, learning on the part of private agents can easily make for irreversibilities which occasionally leave policy-makers even worse off if they decide to withdraw their measures in order to avoid the negative side-effects which their own policies have evoked. Hence, one central idea for coping with side-effects in theory is to conceive private agents as entrepreneurs when policy-makers change the set of economic data. Private agents' intention to revise their plans in accordance with political targets depends on the way in which private agents make use of their alertness towards policy making. Of course, this abstract description underscores the fact that policy-making is challenged by a special type of principal–agent problem.

Its intensive attention to innovative behaviour allows evolutionary policy analysis to highlight the riskiness of interventionism and opens the way for a more general theory of intervention in markets. Its scepticism against untrammelled activism in economic policy results from the essentially unpredictable nature of innovation which nevertheless, in some ways, has to be taken into account a priori. However, the risky nature of interventionism does not generally militate against political attempts to overcome 'market failure' but should stimulate the search for alternatives in order to hedge its non-desired side-effects. In this regard evolutionary thinking on economic policy represents a practically useful tool for policy-making.

THE CONSISTENCY OF THE CHOICE OF POLICY OBJECTIVES

It is in dealing with these questions that evolutionary analysis appears to come closest to normative propositions. It not only tries to produce knowledge about the best means to achieve given ends, as it does when examining the effects of different policies, but constrains the very choice of the ends, and may thus give the impression of prescribing what the policy-makers should strive for. In itself, however, this is nothing new: even the fully positive standard welfare economics does so when it hinders policy-makers from choosing inconsistent policy objectives implying an inconsistent preference ordering – such as the classical case of A preferred to B, B to C, and C to A. Far from prescribing specific policy objectives, this only slightly constrains the choice set from which rational policy-makers, to remain rational, can choose.

In principle, evolutionary analysis does no more than increase the number and/or the severity of such constraints by taking into account intertemporal relationships between short-term and long-term policy objectives. Yet this increase may be substantial. When the long-term evolutionary consequences of policies are taken into account, the choice of short-term policy objective may turn out to be so constrained that analysis suggests a redefinition of goals in view of so-far unknown trade-off relationships; the final choice, of course, is left to the politician.

For example, evolutionary analysis may thus substantially narrow the variety of rational preferences for wealth and income redistribution, and that at both extremes. The evolutionary effects of different redistributive policies, for instance, are likely to be increasingly deleterious as both tendencies to equalization and inequality become more severe. The former not only because of the oft-noted weakening of incentives for work, but even more so because of the decrease of both the incentives and the resources for innovations and entrepreneurship, which is bound to have cumulatively negative effects on the evolution of industries and the entire organization of production. The latter for at least two reasons: one is the emergence and growth of an underclass whose participation in both production and consumption is allowed to wane, and is thus increasingly likely to become source of real threats – both criminal and sanitary – to the productivity and stability of the entire economy; the other reason is political and stems from the limited tolerance to material inequalities which all known human cultures, some more and some less, appear to harbour: an economy which produces increasing wealth and income inequalities is bound to grow politically unstable, not only because of a possible revolt of the poor but also because of its rejection by the compassionate rich.

Evolutionary policy analysis thus admits short-term redistribution objectives, but points out that they are severely constrained by the rather universal long-term objective of avoiding future crises. It thus differs both from standard welfare economics, which sees few limits to voters' sovereignty in choosing the preferred level of redistribution, and from Hayek's argument which excludes redistribution objectives altogether, claiming that policy should only strive for 'just rules', and not for 'just outcomes'. In contrast to both, it realistically recognizes that in all known human cultures, people do value outcomes and have more or less strong preferences against large wealth and income inequalities, and thus can hardly be prevented from trying to diminish them by political means. But it promises to produce knowledge about the limits to which the redistribution can go without undermining the future of the economy.

THE FORMATION OF ECONOMIC POLICY

Explanations of the empirical moulding of economic policy represent a well-established part of economics, but scholars of public choice theory have recently stressed the importance of following new avenues in this realm (see, for example, Frey, 1993). From our point of view a fresh attempt at positive theory seems promising if one recalls the origin of public choice theory established by Downs (1957). Although the idea of self-interested politicians competing for votes in a democratic system was a path-breaking idea half a century ago, the operationalization of this idea has continuously provoked objections amongst theorists in social sciences. From the beginning this approach paralleled Walrasian thinking on competition within the realm of policy. If this concept turns out to be too restrictive even with regard to market theory, the criticism can be generalized when the concept is transferred to politics. Interestingly enough, Downs spoke frankly of a generalization of equilibrium theory which had to include the political sphere in the Walrasian system so that the data of the economy are 'endogenized'. However, the theoretical presumptions again turn out to be too restrictive for an analysis of economic policy.

To be more precise, the basic condition of given voter-preferences implies a rigid starting point for public choice analysis, which means a rather passive (vicarious) role for policy-makers. Essentially theory fails to construe the latter as political entrepreneurs in the proper sense of the word. Whilst this may be an appropriate assumption for the case of a non-evolving economy in which novelty is absent, it can hardly be maintained when new economic activities emerge from the market order and become arguments in preference orders (a refusal of individuals to change their preferences would even be irrational here).

Taking into account that market evolution is naturally combined with intransparency, we are required to conceive the scope of political activity in a more complex way. Even if policy makers are expected to concentrate on the median voters alone, their preferences have first to be identified; on the other hand, in many cases politicians do not know in advance which instruments represent an expedient response to the identified demand. This twofold uncertainty leaves room for an active influence upon the formation of voters' preferences. Additionally, if means–ends relationships are exposed to that uncertainty, too, the means themselves might attain to the status of a preferable good, that is an end. Lacking knowledge about expedient instruments, voters will form beliefs about best political action. Political success will then come to depend much more on the accordance of policy-makers with prevailing beliefs on means–ends relationships than on the objective expediency of their actions, whether or not the beliefs hold true. (In the present volume, Slembeck concentrates on the role of beliefs and ideology guiding economic policy.)

If we still adhere to an economic approach to public choice, the very meaning of entrepreneurship should play a key role in the realm of political competition. Rather like entrepreneurs in the market place, the central task of politicians is to identify and influence the demand side, while the final success of the political programme remains uncertain. In this way, knowledge gathering represents an important part of entrepreneurial activity in the political sphere as well as in the market sphere. When politicians, like entrepreneurs in the market place, try to influence those who control them via competition, they widen the scope of activities and become, in a more active sense, competitors. As it stands, a more complex perspective on competition which evolutionary economists favour will also stimulate the analysis of political competition (Wohlgemuth in this volume pursues this avenue).

THE CONTRIBUTIONS IN THIS VOLUME

In the next chapter Pavel Pelikan begins by recalling the monumental lacunae and mistakes of static equilibrium analysis, which not only failed to see that many once popular policies – such as national planning, Keynesian government overspending, and selective industrial policies – were bound to become harmful and unsustainable, but was even producing formal proofs of their social optimality. He finds an important reason for these failures in lack of attention paid to processes which he defines, in agreement with what this term usually means, as 'evolutionary', and shows that they strongly influence the constraints upon and/or the effects of virtually all policies. This allows him to argue that policy analysis, to avoid similar mistakes in the future, must be comprehensively evolutionary, in the sense that it must strive to take all the policy-relevant evolutionary processes into account. While recognizing that this is a difficult task which may never be fully completed, he outlines a structural model of an evolving economy which makes it possible to work on it in a well-ordered way. He indicates some of the imperfections of both markets and governments that such a comprehensive evolutionary analysis can discover, and examines how to proceed safely from these imperfections to policy implications, without falling victim to the still widespread 'grass-is-always-greener' fallacies.

In his chapter on 'Evolutionary markets and the design of institutional policy', Gerhard Wegner focuses on institutional policy as the type of economic policy that, from the viewpoint of evolutionary analysis, has the greatest chance of helping rather than hindering an economy in difficulty. He deals with Hayek's analysis of the knowledge problem which, according to Hayek, excludes rational interventions and bears the risk of destroying a market order. Wegner reformulates this knowledge problem but, unlike Hayek, does not conclude that successful intervention be a priori impossible. His distinction between top down (state initiated) and bottom up (decentralized) types serves as a guideline for improving the performance of governmental activities. In particular the process of institutionalization which emerges from the market sphere itself largely escapes the attention of ambitious policy-makers as a potential alternative. Following this, Wegner asks whether the bottom up approach to institutional policy is suitable for maintaining the required rules of a market economy whilst, at the same time, avoiding less-desirable states of allocation. Stefan Okruch adds to this general perspective in his discussion of the selection of policy goals from an evolutionary perspective. Unlike Hayek, Okruch argues that the experimental character of policy-making cannot be avoided even if politicians follow the Hayekian recommendations of the attributes of rules constituting a market order. In general, the Hayekian perspective overlooks the need for the fine-tuning of even abstract and negative rules. In order to bring Hayekian arguments down to earth and to overcome their apodicticity, Okruch discusses procedures which are likely to cope with the practical needs for institutional change in a society learning the evolutionary impact of economic policy.

Two chapters dealing with positive questions follow. Michael Wohlgemuth criticizes the static character of economies theories of politics and develops an alternative. Of particular interest are the hitherto disregarded dynamic aspects of democracy, for example interactive processes of political competition, which lead to the creation, change and communication of political opinions and allow for the testing of alternative political solutions. Accounts of these (and other) institutional and epistemological aspects of democracy aim at a more accurate model of political processes which focus on the process of knowledge gathering within political institutions. Hence, Wohlgemuth identifies both the shortcomings of static theories of public choice as well as some key concepts of an evolutionary alternative for coping with political competition. He concludes with reflections on the normative account of democracy. Tilmann Slembeck presents 'A cognitive–evolutionary view on economic policy making' and stresses the role of cognition for real policy-making. While public choice theorists so far have adhered to a view which perceives 'ideologies' as nothing more than obstacles to rational policy, Slembeck emphasizes the ambiguous role of cognitions which can also contribute to a more rational policy. No theory of policy formation can ignore the influence of cognition, nor can policy recommendations ignore the practical influence of shared mental models. It becomes apparent that economists have to acknowledge this fact of political life if they want to establish growth enhancing policies in society.

The three chapters which follow analyse both normative and positive questions but also address a number of specific topics in empirical economic policy. 'Equilibrium and evolutionary foundations of competition and technology policy: new perspectives on the division of labour and the innovation process' is the title of Stan Metcalfe's chapter. Metcalfe highlights the relationship between science, technology and innovation as the core of modern capitalist dynamics, a theme which has been attracting growing theoretical interest. Metcalfe shows that theoretical insight has at least partly been obscured by the standard market failure approach founded by Arrow. For a long time the latter has served as a guideline for policy recommendations in the realm of innovation policy and, for want of an alternative, is still referred to today. Metcalfe gives a flavour of a more nuanced and institutionally grounded systems perspective on the innovation process which involves dropping the idea of market failure as well as any conception of optimal policy. Instead he conceives the idea of innovation systems failure as the basis for policy engagement and carefully probes alternatives for welfare-improving policies.

As indicated in the first three chapters of this volume, market evolution depends also on the evolution of institutions (in the sense of rules such as law or regulation in a broader sense). At present this evolution also occurs as a consequence of the ability of market agents to avoid institutions of one nation-state and, instead, to opt for more preferable institutions provided by some other country. This fact has inspired a debate around the theme of institutional competition and its consequences for the wealth of nations. Some (though not all) evolutionary economists regard this institutional competition as a phenomenon which can prevent economies from becoming locked into an institutional framework which slows down economic growth. Wolfgang Kerber and Klaus Heine refer to this debate and discuss the dynamics of institutional competition in their chapter dealing with 'Institutional evolution, regulatory competition and path dependence'. To a large extent, the authors sympathize with the Hayekian idea of institutional competiton and tend to regard it as an effective device for the revitalization of the forces which drive growth in modern economies. Their empirical study of the competition concerning US corporate laws encourage them to lower the expectations expressed by the Hayekian party. The authors conclude with thoughts on the prospects of regulatory competition in the European Union.

Helge Peukert scrutinizes one of the most dynamic markets in Germany – the 'New Market' (the German equivalent of the NASDAQ) which comes closest to fulfilling the function of providing liquidity to Schumpeterian entrepreneurs. The New Market is also an example of innovation in the economy. After a promising start, the New Market has been subject to much criticism in light of the crash which it suffered in the year 2000, the aftermath of which is still being felt. In his chapter 'The German *Neuer Markt* as an adaptive institution' Peukert shows how the German stock market company (Deutsche Börse AG) attempted to cope with the ongoing crisis by introducing new regulations. This analysis demonstrates that even highly dynamic markets rely on rules (here in the sense of regulations) which can sometimes, as in this case, be identified only by trial and error. Evolutionary analysis is vital for the analysis of emerging markets, for it underlines the fact that markets require a framework of rules which is itself the subject of a process of evolution and which, as in the case of the New Market, was established by market agents themselves.

The volume concludes with a methodological chapter written by Hans-Joerg Siegenthaler: 'Understanding and the mobilisation of error-eliminating controls in evolutionary learning'. Standard public choice theory is pessimistic about the ability of modern democratic societies to organize political reforms in light of collectively recognized errors of the past. Scepticism towards collective rationality may be seen to be part of a more general suspicion regarding collective concepts of rationality in the current methodological mainstream. Economists rarely notice the relevance of these widely held sceptical method-ological arguments for the ability of the polity to learn from policy errors and to launch an economic reform: Is collective learning ruled out once and for all because interest groups are involved in the thought habits of their 'sub cultures'? Siegenthaler gives a negative answer and concludes with a more positive view on the learning ability of a 'Great Society'.

NOTES

1. That these policies were the main causes of the above-mentioned economic problems is now broadly agreed upon by a majority of both theoretical and practical economists. The breadth of this agreement is also reflected in the changed policy views even of those parties by which these policies used to be supported: today, budgetary discipline, market competition, privatizations, and general rather than selective industrial policies belong to the economic programs of virtually all political parties, regardless of their position on the left–right political spectrum. In theory, however, this agreement can still be put in doubt – just because of the lack of solid theoretical arguments in the area of policy analysis that is the purpose of this book to point out and try at least partially to remedy. The readers are therefore not required to accept this agreement now, but may wait and see how their possible objections to it may be modified after the reading of this book.

REFERENCES

Demsetz, H. (1969), 'Information and efficiency: another viewpoint', *Journal of Law and Economics*, **12**, 1–22.
Downs, Anthony (1957), *An Economic Theory of Democracy*, New York: Harper & Row.

Frey, B.S. (1993), 'From economic imperialism to social sciences inspiration', *Public Choice*, **77**, 95–105.

Hayek, F.A. (1967), 'The evolution of the rules of conduct', in F.A. Hayek (1967), *Studies in Philosophy, Politics and Economics*, Chicago: The University of Chicago Press.

Mises, L.V. (1929), *Kritik des Interventionismus*, Jena: Gustav Fischer.

Nelson, R.R. and S. Winter (1982), *An Evolutionary Theory of Economic Change*, Cambridge: Harvard University Press.

North, D.C. (1990), *Institutions, Institutional Change, and Economic Performance*, Cambridge and New York: Cambridge University Press.

2. Why economic policies need comprehensive evolutionary analysis[1]

Pavel Pelikan

1. INTRODUCTION

Theoretical economics is still far from offering reliable guidance to practical policy-making. While relatively successful in assessing economic policies in the short run, it has often been blind to their long-run consequences. In particular, it has repeatedly failed to warn against approaching crises caused by policies that at first appeared advantageous, but in the long run proved detrimental. Examples of such policies, on which more will be said below, are national planning of both socialist and development varieties, Keynesian government overspending, monetarist therapies neglecting structural rigidities, and selective industrial policies à la Japanese. Although all these policies also had opponents, their warnings were receiving little attention: the most respected theorists were building formal models proving these policies to be socially optimal.

Here I will show that one of the main causes of such misleading assessment of policies has been insufficient attention to processes that Section 3 below will define, in agreement with what this term usually appears to mean, as 'evolutionary'. This will imply that theoretical economics, if it is to help and not mislead practical policy-making, must develop, and in policy applications actually use, a comprehensive evolutionary analysis. I will then examine which evolutionary processes must be comprehended and outline how this can be done. Without aspiring to develop such analysis in detail, my present objective is limited to indicating some of the steps that theoretical economics must take to become a more reliable guide to practical policy-making, and to increasing the status of evolutionary analysis by showing it to be an obligatory part of these steps.

Why, in economics, evolutionary analysis is still considered at best optional is due to the weakness of the arguments with which it has been advocated. Its main merit has usually been claimed to be greater realism in descriptions of real-world economies, compared to the grossly simplified models of standard equilibrium analysis. But this is far from convincing: as all theories must more

15

or less simplify, its opponents can rightfully object that the degree of realism of economic theories, much like that of paintings, is a matter of subjective taste. In contrast, if evolutionary analysis is shown to be indispensable for reliable policy advice, this analysis proves *objectively* necessary: no policy analyst can then ignore it, whatever his or her tastes for different theories.[2]

My argument is based on two elementary requirements – obvious in engineering and medicine, but often violated in economics – which *any* theoretical analysis, to be a reliable guide to practical actions, must meet: (1) *No* condition on which the success of the actions considered may critically depend should be omitted or wishfully assumed more favorable than it might actually be. (2) Efforts must be made to take into account *all* the success-relevant effects, including the possibly negative side-effects, that the actions might sooner or later bring about. It is indeed obvious to engineers that they must not wishfully assume their construction materials unrealistically strong, if their constructions are not to collapse, and to physicians that they must not ignore any important side-effect of their therapies, if they are not to cure diseases while killing their patients.

To be sure, these requirements are not easy to meet, and neither engineers nor physicians can boast about always meeting them. But at least they try. Collapsed constructions and deceased patients are typically used for learning more about the possibly unfavorable conditions and the negative side-effects that must be taken into account. Theoretical economists, in contrast, often violate these requirements systematically, without even noticing it, in the basic assumptions on which they build their entire analysis.[3] All the above examples of their blindness to important policy failures can indeed be linked to such violations. While details of these links will gradually become clear below, a brief look at the failure of Keynesian theory to foresee the difficulties caused by Keynesian policies may convey a first idea. The theory violated requirement (1) at least twice: (a) the government was wishfully assumed so smart as to always correctly recognize, and promptly react to, the actual phase of the business cycle, and (b) all the other agents were not less wishfully assumed so obtuse as never to learn the difference between nominal and real values. Requirement (2) was violated by neglecting, among other things, the perverse effects that encouraging governments to overspend is bound to have in terms of inefficient and difficult to reverse growth of government bureaucracy. Since the real world disobeyed both the assumptions (for 1b see also the subsequent theory of rational expectations) and inefficient growth of government bureaucracy proved to be a real and still largely unsolved problem, much of this failure of Keynesian theory can indeed be ascribed to these violations.

As requirement (1) may appear to clash with Friedman's (1953) classical argument that a positive theory is free to make any unrealistic assumptions as long as its final results reasonably agree with empirical data, a comment on this argument is in order. The crucial but apparently overlooked point is that positive theories may have two different uses – academic, or as help in practical policy-making – and it is only when limited to the former uses that they are as free as Friedman argues. The authors of such theories can indeed choose any partial aspects of the economy they like to study, make simplifying assumptions about everything else, and yet their results may be deemed correct and published in prestigious journals if their analysis is logically consistent and their predictions *concerning the chosen aspects* are reasonably accurate.

The special status of *positive theories for policy uses* deserves therefore emphasis. First, it may be useful to spell out that theories for policy uses need not be normative, but may indeed be purely positive, provided only that they abstain from prescribing which policies should be implemented and limit themselves to producing knowledge about the policies considered for implementation.[4] But they cannot freely mix with other positive theories because of their obligation to meet the reliability requirements, which significantly limit their freedom to make assumptions and choose the problems studied. Although they may draw on results of other positive theories, they must first critically assess these results under assumptions which meet requirement (1), and not blindly accept the original assumptions under which the results were obtained.

How positive theories can help practical policy-making may need explanation. That their task is not to prescribe policies, but only produce knowledge about policies, was just noted. What may need to be explained is in which ways and to what extent such knowledge can help. This may be unclear, as existing political theories usually focus on conflicts of interest (values, preferences) among the actors involved, under the assumption that everyone fully knows all the relevant effects of all the policies over which the conflicts take place. This unrealistic assumption must first be dropped, in order to recognize that such effects may at least partly be ignored or subject to false beliefs. Positive theories then emerge as important tools for increasing the actors' knowledge about the true links between policy means and policy ends, and between policy ends in the short run and those in the long run. They can thus avoid two types of costly mistake, still widespread among both politicians and the electorate at large: to support policies that fail to lead to the objectives desired, and to pursue objectives which appear desirable in the short run but prove detrimental in the long run. As many real-world policy conflicts are still caused by lack of such knowledge, positive theories can increase the level of social consensus and cooperation, and thus help to find economic policies which minimize unpleasant surprises and maximize political support.

To make my point about the need for a comprehensive evolutionary analysis, I must explain – and this is what most of the following pages are about – why the reliability requirements cannot be met without it. That the analysis must not only be evolutionary, but moreover comprehensively so, deserves emphasis.

In theories for policy uses, the freedom to choose the problems studied is also limited for evolutionary economists, and not only for their non-evolutionary colleagues. They also may, and many indeed do, choose to study only certain evolutionary processes and not others – for instance, the evolution of technologies, but not the one of government bureaucracies – and this may also give support to unreasonable policies. On the other hand, while emphasizing the need for comprehensiveness, I cannot promise to satisfy it myself. As is well known in medicine, one can never be sure to take into account all the important effects of a therapy, especially not the long-term ones. A sufficiently comprehensive policy analysis, taking into account all the important evolutionary processes which policies may influence and/or on which their welfare-relevant effects may depend, must thus be regarded as an objective to strive for, without ever being sure to fully attain it.

The explanation is organized as follows. Section 2 outlines a conceptual model of an evolving economy, aimed at comprehending all of its policy-relevant features. Section 3 considers the economic processes involved and defines which of them will be termed 'evolutions'. Section 4 surveys the evolutions that may be of importance for economic policy-making – by affecting its constraints, or its effects, or both – and that policy analysis, to be safe, must therefore take into account. Section 5 introduces the notion of evolutionary efficiency, relates it to the standard allocative efficiency, and prepares the ground for considering how evolutionary policy analysis can contribute to the existing lists of market and government imperfections. Sections 6 and 7 use this ground to indicate in more detail what the evolutionary contributions to the two lists will be. Section 8 concludes by considering the ways from imperfections to policy implications, and by enhancing the old, but still often forgotten, Demsetz's (1969) warning against the 'grass is always greener' fallacy.

2.   HOW TO VISUALIZE ALL POLICY-RELEVANT FEATURES OF AN EVOLVING ECONOMY

Whereas positive theories for academic uses may be limited to quantitative changes of a few selected economic variables, reliable policy analysis must often take into account more variables and more kinds of changes, including those of forms (structures, institutions, organizations). One reason is that even quantitative policies may have important side-effects on organizational or institutional features of an economy, which must be carefully considered before such policies can be cleared as safe to use. Moreover, just as cancer cannot be cured by blood transfusion, so the crises of many economies cannot be remedied by quantitative policies alone, but require more sophisticated qualitative policies

– such as institutional reforms or system transformations. This demands a model in which all the quantitative and qualitative variables that may matter for the success or failures of some policies could be orderly accommodated.

That such a comprehensive model in spite of lacking mathematical solutions can nevertheless be precise and useful may have to be made clear, as many of today's economists, specialized in purely mathematical modeling, may fail to see it. To make the model precise it suffices, as usual, to clearly define all its ingredients. But to make it useful, it is necessary to have in mind a somewhat different purpose than formulating a solvable mathematical problem: comparable to the models of human body meant to help to search for the causes of and the remedies for various diseases, its main use is to be seen in searching for the causes of and the remedies for various cases of unsatisfactory (inefficient, suboptimal) performance of economies.[5]

Although the model is somewhat unusual, virtually all of its ingredients are familiar. The main novelty is that many of them, instead of being assumed to be constants in certain perfect states – such as a constant set of perfectly competitive markets, or a constant collection of perfectly optimizing agents – are recognized as variables, outcomes of certain ongoing processes, with no a priori guarantee to be perfect in any sense. It will prove fruitful to partition them into four broad notions:

R: institutions, consisting of formal laws and informal custom;
S: organizational structure, including both individual agents and multipersonal organizations – such as firms, markets, and government agencies – into which the agents are arranged, through which they interact (transact), and to which they confer some of their non-transferable abilities ('tacit knowledge');
Y: output stocks and flows of transferable resources;
X: exogenous conditions, including initial stocks of transferable resources and the terms of trade with other economies and nature.

Note that the term 'institutions' is limited, in agreement with modern institutional economics, to humanly devised constraints shaping human interactions, comparable to 'rules of the game' (North, 1990, p. 3). This term is thus sharply distinguished from that of 'organizations', which denotes interconnected sets of agents interacting under certain institutions. This distinction is important, as in most common languages and older institutional economics, 'institutions' may also mean 'organizations' – such as banks, ministries, and universities – which has caused much confusion. The importance of this distinction also explains why S is defined so broadly, including organizations of such different origins and natures: first it is important to distinguish between rules and agents, and only then among different kinds of agents.

This partition makes it possible to see an economy materialized by its S, containing a mixture of markets and private or government hierarchies, whose functioning exploits X to produce and allocate Y – while both the functioning and further organizing or reorganizing of S is shaped (channeled, constrained) by the prevailing R. Alternatively, an economy can be visualized as a game, R as its rules, S as the possibly changing configuration of its actual players, and Y as the things with which and for which it is played, under the constraints of R and X.[6]

There are interesting links between this partition and Hayek's and Schumpeter's terminologies: Hayek's (1973) 'order of rules' and 'order of actions' correspond to R and Y, whereas Schumpeter's (1942/1976) 'creative destruction' is about changes of S. These links make it possible to remind Hayek and his followers of the importance of S – possibly termed, in his spirit, the 'order of *actors*' – without which rules could not effectively generate actions. On the other hand, Schumpeter and his followers may be reminded of the importance of R, whose rules concerning freedom of enterprise and private property rights in general determine how much, if any, of 'creative destruction' can actually take place.

More clarifications are in order. The rules of R, to be effective, must be internalized in the agents, which means that R is also a part of S. But this is a very special part, which justifies its separate status: it shapes both the functioning and the evolution of S, and, as explained below, its evolution is largely independent of the evolution of S. In particular, if R contains rules providing for high structural adaptability, S may keep evolving (developing, adapting to changing X), while R can stay put as a kind of rigid core, on which all the S-adaptability ultimately reposes.[7]

In addition to rules concerning all agents – such as property rights and competition laws – R also defines the rights and/or the duties of government to conduct certain types of economic policies (use certain policy instruments). The form of R thus determines the institutional type of the economy ('economic system') – such as 'laissez-faire' with a minimum of government intervention, or various forms of 'mixed economies' with different types and degrees of government control and welfare and/or industrial policies. In consequence, as will be considered in more detail below, policy questions can be divided into those concerning *institutional design*, or the form of R, including design of the policy instruments that R allows or requires government to use (the government economic agenda), and those concerning *policy conduct*, about the best ways of using these instruments.[8]

Another clarification may be needed about the place of technologies. What should be made clear is that the borderline between S and Y divides them into two parts: the transferable pieces, which agents can buy, sell, or otherwise exchange, are kinds of resources included in Y, whereas the inherent ('tacit'), and therefore non-transferable, technological abilities of the transferring and receiving agents are considered internalized in S. These internalized abilities are basic in the sense that they set limits to which parts of technologies can effectively be transferred and used, and thus be included in Y.[9]

As a first approximation, S may be regarded in a standard way as a certain mixture of markets, firms, and government agencies, together with their intrinsic properties, such as preferences (objectives) and abilities. For the purposes of evolutionary analysis, however, a more complicated view is often necessary. While in standard analysis, S is studied as a one-level entity, either as a set of of interacting individuals or as a set interacting organizations, evolutionary analysis may have to consider both, and thus admit S to contain several organizational levels. One reason is that different organizational levels may evolve in substantially different ways. For instance, the births and deaths of firms rarely imply births and deaths of individuals, and vice versa. Thus, markets, firms, and entire industries may be created, developed, or destroyed, while the individuals involved may remain the same or change at a different pace. Another reason is that different organizational levels may be differently responsive to policies – for instance, a policy that improves *external* conditions of incumbent firms may help to perpetuate or even increase their *internal* inefficiency.

As multilevel analysis is facilitated if its different levels can be handled in formally analogous ways, it is useful to have the possibility to characterize each agent, be it an individual or an organization, by analogous properties. All the important ones appear possible to concentrate into two broad notions: the objective(s) pursued (U), possibly including a utility function, preferences, values or interests; and the cognitive abilities (Q) with which available information is perceived and processed, and decisions on how to use available resources for the pursuit of U are taken, possibly meaning rationality, competence, or internal efficiency.

These properties are again familiar, although ascribing both of them to both individuals and organizations is less so. More usually, individuals are admitted to have different U, but assumed unbound in Q (perfect rationality, abundant optimizing abilities), whereas organizations are admitted to be limited in Q (internally inefficient) but denied to have any U of their own.

The problem of individuals with differently bounded Q plays an important role in evolutionary policy analysis and will be considered in more detail below. The problem of organizations' own U is here of lesser importance, but a brief note on it may clarify the logic of building multilevel models from formally analogous levels, likely to be increasingly important in studies of increasingly complex national and supranational economies. The main point is the irrelevance of whether a given entity *really has* a U, as may be argued by advocates of teleology, or whether it responds to its environments in a causal fashion according to an internal program (possibly with ingredients of chance and/or chaos), as is believed, even about human individuals, by today's natural scientists. It suffices *to view it as if it had* a U, even if its working is clearly causal. The reason is that referring to such a *virtual* U often facilitates the description of behavior.[10] It is in this virtual, or teleo*nomical* sense that economic organizations, including entire economies, may be seen to have a U of their own, possibly different from the U of any of their individual members. All policy problems may even be thought of as concerning differences between the virtual U of an economy – which may currently behave *as if it aimed at* keeping a high unemployment, a low growth, or a polluted environment – and the U of some of its agents, such as a political majority or a ruling elite.[11]

The multilevel view of S requires a corresponding multilevel view of R. Here, it will suffice to distinguish the overall R of an economy, including the formal laws and the informal cultural norms of a nation, from the internal Rs of its organizations, including the rules of corporate governance, the explicit and implicit employment contracts, and the internal culture of a firm. Note that the institutions which can be directly influenced by public policies are limited to the overall R and the internal Rs of government agencies and state-owned firms (if any). Other internal Rs may be influenced by public policies only indirectly, by overall institutional rules (laws) that constrain other agents in *their* choice of these Rs. For example, the overall R of an economy may, and often does, contain a corporate law constraining the choice of the corporate governance of firms. Problems of corporate governance may thus concern two different, but not always well distinguished, levels: the laws which constrain its permissible forms across an entire national (or supranational) economy, and its specific forms within specific firms.[12]

3.   ECONOMIC PROCESSES AND EVOLUTIONS

When all the main concepts of the model are put in place, the next step is to identify the processes which may be changing their states and to explain which of these processes will be considered 'evolutionary'. As this term is frequently used, but still lacks a clear, generally accepted definition, let me suggest the following one, which I believe expresses what this term is most often intended to mean.

To be considered 'evolutionary', or in short an 'evolution', a process must: (a) produce or qualitatively modify forms ('patterns', 'arrangements', 'organization'), *and* (b) produce novelty, in the sense that at least some of the information determining its outcomes did not initially exist.[13]

Property (a) means that the process must not be limited to quantitative changes of a given variable or variables – such as changes of prices and quantities of given types of goods. Processes which do no more than that are more suitably called 'non-evolutionary dynamics'.[14] Property (b) means that the process must not be fully determined by pre-existing routines. A process which has property (a) but not (b) can suitably be called 'pre-programmed development'. Note that such routines need not blindly lead to rigidly predetermined outcomes, but may very well provide for flexible continuations by means of conditional pre-programmed responses to different environmental conditions.[15]

Property (b) implies that economic evolutions must at least partly be experimental, involving some trial-and-error search. More precisely, they must involve an incompletely informed (more or less 'random', or 'Monte Carlo') generation of trials and a systematic elimination of errors. Such a trial-and-error search is the only way to proceed when relevant information is missing and to produce such information while proceeding. A biological example is Darwinian evolution by random mutations and natural selection; an economic example is the evolution of industrial structures by imperfectly informed entry and market-selection enforced exit of firms.

All this makes it possible to stratify economic processes into three layers, of which two correspond to the present definition of 'evolutions':

Y-allocation by a given S under a given R;
S-evolution under a given R;
R-evolution.

This stratification provides a useful frame where all the causal relationships which policy analysis may need to consider can orderly be arranged. It also provides clear links to different strands of existing economic literature, which facilitates the search for useful references, and moreover helps to clarify some so far poorly understood links among these strands themselves.

Each layer can indeed be seen to have its own strand of literature in which it has been studied, at least to some extent. For Y-allocation (which, as usual, also includes production, consumption, and inter-agent transactions of goods and services), this is the standard non-evolutionary economics, whose extent is usually limited in two ways: (i) what is studied are not allocation processes as such, but only their possible or conceivable equilibria; (ii) the equilibria are examined only for certain idealized types of S, such as those in which all agents are perfectly competent (rational) optimizers, or, in present terms, have abundance of Q.

For S-evolution under a given R (which includes product innovations and thus also *qualitative* changes of Y), the corresponding strand is the neo-Schumpeterian evolutionary economics, studying how technologies, firms, and industries evolve by means of market competition and selection (often likened to natural selection), with Schumpeter (1912/34, 1942/76), Alchian (1950), and

Nelson and Winter (1982) among the most frequent sources of inspiration. The extent of these studies is usually limited by the assumption that the given R is of the standard capitalist type. This assumption is often only implicit, for institutions are usually ignored. This ignoring also explains why selection by market competition is usually taken for granted and mistakenly considered 'natural', while its strong dependence on the prevailing institutions, such as the form of property rights, competition law, and bankruptcy law, is overlooked.

The strand studying R-evolution is not yet very developed, and therefore somewhat more difficult to identify. Although knowledge of the possibilities of, and the constraints upon, R-evolution is urgently needed for the problems of economic development and system transition, relatively little has been done to obtain it. To be sure, components and variants of R have been extensively studied in the growing fields of law and economics, constitutional economics, and new institutional economics, but it is their effects on Y-allocation, and not their origins and possible evolution, that have been there in the focus. Important exceptions are Hayek (1967, 1973), North (1990), and Vanberg (1992).[16] From outside economics, Boyd and Richerson (1985) examine the cultural evolution producing the informal part of R.

The two layers of economic evolutions can be more finely divided along the following lines. According to the distinction between formal and informal institutions, R-evolution can be divided into 'legislative evolution', which changes formal laws and contains the main policy inputs, and 'cultural evolution', which changes informal custom (ethical norms) and is more difficult to influence by policy. S-evolution can be divided into 'organizational evolution', which changes the internal organization of firms and government agencies, 'structural evolution', which changes their interrelationships, such as the number and the degree of competitiveness of markets, and 'technological evolution', which changes products and production processes.[17]

The stratification of R- and S-evolutions into several levels depends on the level of the point of view. The manager of a firm must often clearly distinguish the evolution of its internal R from the evolution of its internal S. For a public policy-maker, in contrast, both these evolutions belong to the economy's S-evolution, while R-evolution is limited to changes of the economy's R.

4.   EVOLUTIONS AROUND ECONOMIC POLICIES

After these rather long, but for clarity necessary, preliminaries, it is now possible to start addressing the central issue: How do economic evolutions relate to economic policy-making, and why must policy analysis, to be reliable, take them into account?

As usual, economic policies are seen to be made by politically selected policy-makers, who intervene in their national (or supranational) economy by certain uses of certain policy instruments, in order to make it attain, or at least approach, certain policy objectives. Right now, it does not matter whether the policy-makers are benevolent, pursuing some democratically chosen notion of common good, or predatory, trying to extract the highest rents for themselves. The present task is to provide a rough survey of all the evolutions which may influence, and/or be influenced by, some of the policy instruments that the policy-makers use or consider to use.

The initial observation is that each use of a policy instrument intervenes at a certain moment in a continuous stream of possibly several evolutions. Hence the first dividing line: in relation to a given instrument used at a given moment, the relevant evolutions can be divided between the *upstream* ones that condition and constrain this use, and the *downstream* ones that are influenced by it, while at the same time influencing the effects that it will eventually have.

This division, of course, is only relative to a given moment. During longer periods which contain sequences of several policy interventions, the two kinds of evolutions intertwine: some of the downstream ones influenced by past uses of certain policy instruments become the upstream ones conditioning and constraining the future uses of the same or other instruments. As has often been observed, much of present policy-making is indeed constrained by effects of past policies, which may even be the main causes of the difficulties with which present policy-making has to struggle.

In spite of its relativity, the upstream–downstream division appears useful for ordering the survey. Beginning with the upstream evolutions, they can be described as including all the branches of the past S- and R-evolutions that have contributed to determining the currently available technologies and the actual behavioral characteristics (U and Q) of the economy's agents, both individuals and incumbent organizations. The available technologies and the agents' U and Q constitute indeed the main conditions of, and constraints upon, the uses of virtually all policy instruments.

It can now be made clear why standard policy analysis so often violates Reliability Requirement 1: the main reason is that instead of examining the relevant upstream evolutions, it only makes simplifying and more or less wishful assumptions about their outcomes. A particularly important case is the standard assumption of perfect optimizing abilities (abundant Q) of all agents, whatever the difficulty of the problems they may have to solve. As will become clear below, many practical failures of theoretically optimal policies can be ascribed to the wishful character of this assumption.

An early hint that this assumption is only a substitute for the outcome of an upstream S-evolution is Friedman's (1953) classical argument that the presently existing (surviving) firms can reasonably be assumed able to maximize their expected returns, because all those that were not very able to do so, although they also initially existed, have been eliminated by market competition and selection. While this argument may be accepted, at least as a first rough approximation, for successful firms in developed markets with a long history of reasonable competition, it cannot be extended to firms in emerging markets, where market selection has not yet had enough time to eliminate all the grossly suboptimal competitors, nor to government agencies, which escape market competition and selection altogether. Yet in standard analysis, such illegitimate extensions are widespread. The optimization assumption is made there for all agents, whether selected by market competition or not. Perhaps the only exception was the Keynesian assumption of permanent inability of market participants to distinguish between real and nominal values, but this was not very happy either, for it concerned precisely those agents for whom the optimization assumption was the least misplaced.

The illegitimate extensions of this assumption have led to at least two types of mistaken policy implications: false alarms about failures of privatization and market reforms, and overestimation of sophisticated policy instruments as means of alleviating market imperfections. The importance of taking into account the relevant upstream S-evolutions now clearly appears: this is indeed the way in which these mistakes can be explained and avoided. The false alarms then turn out to be caused by impatience stemming from lack of understanding of the dynamics of market competition and selection. In the short run, there cannot indeed be any guarantee that newly privatized firms or new private firms will perform any better than the previous government-owned or government-protected monopolies; they may even begin by performing worse. It is only after a more or less long period of reasonably working market competition and selection that truly superior firms may be expected to emerge and eventually prevail. The overestimation of the potential of sophisticated policy instruments – such as fine macroeconomic tuning and selective industrial policies – is related to government imperfections in S-evolution and its consequently severe Q-constraint, on which more will be said in Section 7.

The downstream evolutions relative to the use of a certain policy instrument at a certain moment can be described as including all the branches of the following S- and R-evolutions that this use would affect – in other words, cause to take a different course than they would take without it. To identify them with more precision, it is fruitful to stratify policy instruments into Y-, S-, and R-layers. Y-instruments consist of ways of directly intervening in the consumption or production of existing consumers or producers – such as taxes, subsidies, price controls, rationing of consumption, and political planning or control of production. S-instruments include the means for intervening in the creation, the growth or the dissolution of firms, markets, and government agencies – such as credit rationing, selective industrial policies, government entrepreneurship, and organizing or reorganizing of government-owned firms and agencies. R-instruments consist above all of legislation of formal institutions (laws), including those defining the scope of the allowed or required uses of other policy instruments, but may also comprise government educational campaigns or ideological propaganda, aimed to influence informal institutions, such as moral norms and business ethics.[18]

In general, hardly any instrument can be used without some effects on both S- and R-evolutions. But it is interesting to distinguish between direct effects, by which an instrument influences processes of the same layer, and indirect effects, which concern processes of another layer or layers. Thus, all evolutionary effects of Y-instruments are indirect, whereas those of S- and R-instruments may be both direct and indirect. What makes this distinction interesting is that direct effects typically work faster and are easier to see and predict than indirect effects, which are often hidden and start to be felt only in the long run, although then, possibly, with an increasing force. Another point of interest is that direct effects are mostly intended, whereas most unintended effects are indirect. Discrepancies between rapidly working positive direct effects and slowly but surely growing negative indirect effects appear indeed to be the main reasons why so many policies successful in the short run proved detrimental in the long run.

An important example is the decline of extensive welfare states. Much of their current problems can be found to be caused by their excessive use of redistributive Y-instruments, aimed to decrease not only poverty, but income inequalities in general. While they appeared to be successfully approaching this aim, their indirect effects on both S- and R-evolutions were increasingly negative. S-evolution was increasingly impeded by diminished incentives for work and, even more importantly, by both diminished incentives and diminished resources for entrepreneurship. As this caused underdevelopment of S – in the previously industrialized economies relative and in the Third World absolute – the poor ended up by being more numerous and/or poorer than what they would have been with a more moderate income redistribution. R-evolution was increasingly damaged by a combination of high taxes for the self-declared rich with high benefits for the self-declared poor. This increased the incentives for cheating in both self-declarations, and eventually also made much of cheating socially acceptable. As a result, extensive welfare states not only became economically unsustainable – which is relatively easy to correct by making them less extensive through fiscal reforms – but their informal institutions were moreover eroded by a higher level of socially acceptable dishonesty, likely to increase their transaction costs and thus handicap their economies for a much longer time in the future.

That both policy-makers and policy analysts have paid most attention to direct effects, while often overlooking the indirect ones, can at least partly be explained by the influences that the logic of mechanics and mechanical engineering has had on economic thinking. In this logic, the most effective method to make a certain variable or parameter assume a certain state is indeed to get hold of a direct control over it and then simply force it to do so. This logic can indeed be found at work in all the old but still far from extinct arguments that if a certain outcome is politically demanded, then its realization must also be politically organized and controlled – for example, that obligatory primary education requires government schools, or that development of modern industries requires government enterprises or at least government-directed investment in these industries.

Although many indirect effects are now known, it is mostly the negative ones, and the knowledge was often obtained the hard way, from the growing difficulties they started to cause. What is claimed here to be an important merit of evolutionary analysis is that it is able, when suitably developed, to comprehend all the important indirect effects in a systematic way. The expected payoff is double: in addition to helping to predict and avoid negative indirect effects, such analysis would help to exploit more extensively the positive ones. This is of great importance, as doing so appears to be the only promising strategy for approaching many generally desired policy objectives that are difficult or impossible to attain directly.

For this purpose, the most important indirect effects appear to be those of R-instruments (institutional policies) on S-evolution and Y-allocation.[19] The main reason is, in essence, that the high complexity of modern economies and the Q-constraint on real-world governments (on which more will be said in Section 7) make most of Y- and S-instruments prohibitively difficult to use. In other words, such instruments challenge governments with prohibitively large competence–difficulty gaps in the sense of Heiner (1983), so that using them is likely to be beset by errors which would cause them to do more harm than good. This is not to say that R-instruments are very easy to use, but only easier enough to be often the only promising means of pursuing policy objectives concerning growth and distribution of Y, and what may be for these objectives needed states of S – such as creation and development of highly productive firms and industries. What makes R-instruments relatively easier to use than Y- and S-instruments is that general laws, however sophisticated they might have to be, are nevertheless informationally simpler, and therefore easier to formulate or imitate, than specific firms, and even more so than detailed resource-allocation. In addition, theoretical analysis can be expected to provide more help with the formulation of laws of desired effects than with the creation of firms of desired performance: the feasible ratio 'science/art', or 'explicit knowledge/tacit knowledge', is indeed much higher for the former than for the latter.

Admittedly, this survey of policy-relevant evolutions is only very rough, but rather than refining it, let me turn to the more substantial question of what new results can be obtained by an analysis which takes these evolutions into account.

5. EVOLUTIONARY EFFICIENCY AND IMPERFECTIONS

A suitable ground for considering what evolutionary policy analysis can accomplish that a non-evolutionary one cannot appears to be the lists of what is usually called 'imperfections' (or 'failures') of markets and governments. As, in these lists, 'imperfection' is related to the norm of 'efficiency', meaning inefficient (suboptimal, wasteful) allocation of scarce resources for the pursuit of given policy objectives (possibly expressed as maximization of an objective function), it is first necessary to clarify what this norm can mean in evolutionary analysis.

Up to a point, this meaning can remain quite standard. In particular, the efficiency norm can continue to be considered value-free, for virtually all possible differences among voters' and politicians' values can again be expressed in the choice of the objectives – for example, in the extent and content of the politically chosen demand for public and merit goods. Its status can even be considered increased: instead of a norm subjectively chosen by analysts, its usual status in standard economics, it becomes an objectively important evolutionary advantage – although only if the objectives chosen are 'wise' in the sense of promoting, and not undermining, the sustainability ('survival') of the economy.[20]

But in evolutionary analysis, efficiency cannot be limited to the standard 'allocative efficiency'. The reason is that this analysis sees both markets and governments doing more things than just allocating resources. This allows it to see both to suffer from more imperfections, but also makes it necessary to clarify what such additional imperfections may mean. As these imperfections concern the roles of markets and governments in S- and R-evolutions, both they and the efficiency norm to which they need to be related may suitably be denoted as 'evolutionary'.[21]

At low levels, both 'allocative efficiency' and 'evolutionary efficiency' can first go a long way together: improving one also improves the other. In other words, S and R, not to be evolutionarily too inefficient, must also be able to secure a not too inefficient Y-allocation. For purely market economies, many of the properties that such S and R must have follow from well-known standard results: the markets of such S must be sufficiently competitive, or at least sufficiently open to competition ('contestable'), and populated by technologically and economically competent sellers and buyers; and the private property rights of such R must be well-defined and enforceable for all the goods and resources that may be of value, positive or negative, for some agents.

But when allocative efficiency becomes high, it starts to clash with the evolutionary one: some of it must be sacrificed if the latter is not to deteriorate. To see why, consider that allocative efficiency is limited to the *functioning* of an assumedly constant S under an assumedly constant R. Now, however, when S and R are admitted to be variable, it is moreover necessary to consider the S- and R-evolutions which could *make and keep* them allocatively not too inefficient, and the resources that these evolutions need to consume. It is most of these resources that in the usual perspective on allocative efficiency appear wasted.

The consumption of resources by evolutions is easiest to explain in the case of S-evolution, whose task is making and keeping S acceptably efficient. What makes this task difficult is that, typically, an efficient S can remain efficient only for a limited range of environmental conditions, such as a limited scope of technological innovations and a limited variety of relative price changes. When the conditions change beyond this range, as they now appear to do frequently for both exogenous and endogenous reasons, then S, to remain efficient, must also change – for example, by opening, developing or closing markets, and/or by entry, reorganization or exit of firms.

Why such changes of S may have to consume important resources is the inevitable lack of a priori information about what changes of S will prove successful – for example, which firms and which technologies will turn out to be the future winners that may or must be parts of an efficiently evolved S. This implies that S-evolution cannot proceed without a likely large number of incompletely informed trials, including many seemingly duplicated efforts, most of which may turn out to be errors – for all of which R must make room through institutional rules that allow and encourage such trials to be made and force the errors committed to be corrected or eliminated.[22] It is the resources used up by erroneous trials that in static analysis appear wasted, whereas evolutionary analysis discloses many of them to be the necessary price to pay for gaining the initially missing information on how, under the changing conditions, an efficient S will have to be organized.[23]

An optimal trade-off between allocative and evolutionary efficiencies is difficult to determine with any precision. But it appears safe to say that an economy in frequently changing environments, to secure its long-term prosperity or just to avoid disruptive crises, needs a certain minimum of evolutionary efficiency, even if the required losses of allocative efficiency appear relatively high.[24] In consequence, both S and R must make room for such losses, although ideally not more than required by this minimum. For example, S may have to maintain a higher variety of firms in each industry than justified by consideration of allocative efficiency, and R may thus have to contain a correspondingly more severe protection of competition ('antitrust').

To facilitate the following discussion, the term 'efficient' will sometimes be used without an adjective, to refer to a favorable mix of both types of efficiency, which may be thought of as containing the necessary (possibly high) minimum of the evolutionary one, and the maximum of the allocative one for which this minimum leaves room.

6. EVOLUTIONARY IMPERFECTIONS OF MARKETS

As market imperfections started to be studied earlier and still appear to attract more of economists' attention than government imperfections, let me consider them first. The additional tasks that evolutionary analysis sees markets performing, and in which it may therefore find them imperfect, is guiding S-evolution towards forming and maintaining a reasonably efficient market S, and R-evolution towards forming and maintaining a reasonable efficient market R.[25] The imperfections of both these evolutions can be divided into three broad types: an evolution may be (i) blocked, (ii) excessively wasteful, (iii) misdirected.

A blocked S-evolution results in S which either remains chronically under-developed, or, if already developed, becomes unable to restructure and adapt to changing environmental conditions. Examples of possible causes are: lack of industrial and/or financial entrepreneurship, unfair competition ('predation') of incumbent producers, retarded or blocked exit of inefficient producers, insufficient supply of public producer goods (for example, roads, general education), and insufficient complementary production and consumption (for example, underdeveloped or absent networks). The last cause, however, is less serious than some authors believe it to be. More precisely, it is serious only if protectionist policies hinder access to world markets. Otherwise, if economic globalization is not hindered, local industrial networks can develop from a single firm, which begins by importing most of its inputs and exporting most of its outputs.

An excessively wasteful S-evolution produces necessary structural changes at unnecessarily high social costs – such as those of hopeless new entries, unnecessary duplication of efforts, winner-takes-all competition, hit-and-run competition, and overambitious takeovers. Such imperfections have two basic causes: unavailability of information, or low Q for using the information available. For example, the entrepreneurs who waste scarce resources on hopeless trials (including overambitious acquisitions and fusions) would hardly do so if they had more of relevant information or a higher Q allowing them to better use the information they have. These causes are basic even in cases which appear due to misdirected incentives, such as when the managers of a firm, striving for more power and prestige, expand it well beyond its socially efficient size: this is again possible only if its owners lack relevant information or have a low Q.

In concrete cases, however, it is often difficult to determine when this type of market imperfection really occurs. The problem is, as follows from the above discussion of evolutionary efficiency, that some waste of resources on unsuccessful trials is always necessary, and the limit to which the waste is necessary and over which it becomes excessive is usually difficult to estimate. Grossly mistaken estimation can be avoided only by considering which relevant a priori information and which relevant Q may be available to the best informed and most competent agents within the economy, and by considering, as will be done below, whether government could do a better job at finding such agents and effectively using their Q and their information. Otherwise, if market outcomes are judged with hindsight information or from the standpoint of an assumed omniscient Planner or Creator, the limit can be grossly underestimated and this type of market imperfection correspondingly overestimated.[26]

Misdirected S-evolution means convergence toward the wrong S – for example, efficient only locally and myopically, but not globally and lastingly – which is subsequently difficult to change. An often quoted example is the QWERTY keyboard pointed out by David (1985). The causes of this imperfection have been given different names – such as path dependence, increasing returns to adoption, or lock-in effects. In principle, however, all these names refer to basically the same phenomenon: a feedback that is initially positive, in the sense that it amplifies deviations from a future optimum, but later becomes negative, counteracting deviations from, and thus making it difficult to leave, the initially taken wrong direction. Interesting mathematical models of this phenomenon are offered by the well-known urn processes.[27]

But before concluding that a market S-evolution is really misdirected, the positive and the negative stages of the market feedback must be assessed for their relative importance, to see which of them will prevail in the long run. The problem is that the two have rarely been considered with equal attention: while neoclassical economists have traditionally focused on the nice negative feedback, which can make markets converge towards a stable general optimum, many of their evolutionary colleagues now emphasize the troublesome positive feedback (sometimes also called 'the butterfly effect'), which can allow a small initial disturbance to push markets towards far less favorable and possibly unstable states. When both are properly taken into account, they turn out to counteract each other in complex ways, in which the initially subdued one may eventually prevail. This often appears to be the case of a negative feedback, which may for a long time remain dormant, but then energetically counteract, possibly by means of a crisis, the cumulating deviations of a positive, 'path-dependent' feedback, when these have reached a certain more-or-less high threshold.[28]

Such a delayed negative feedback may nevertheless cause a market imperfection: if the threshold is high, the reign of the positive feedback may be long and its possibly growing deviation from an efficient S may cause growing social losses; moreover, when the negative feedback finally hits, the required adjustment may be large and its costs therefore high. But this imperfection is not of the misdirected type – after all, S-evolution does eventually get back closer to an efficient track – but rather of the previously discussed excessive waste type. But, to recall, whether or not such a market imperfection really takes place can be decided only after estimating the limit to which the waste is not excessive, but necessary, given what relevant information and what Q for using it are effectively available to at least some of the economy's agents.

Note that all this makes the QWERTY path-dependence example weigh less as evidence of market imperfection. In part, the discounted losses from the continued use of the QWERTY keyboard, compared to the best imaginable keyboard, may have well remained far below the threshold needed to activate the costly switch. And in part, as considered in more detail below, governments are hardly superior, and most likely inferior, to markets in defining and rapidly adjusting technical norms. That market participants may not, and indeed can hardly afford to, hesitate to change a widespread norm when a critical threshold is reached is illustrated by IBM's abandoning its own standards for personal computers in the early 1990s, in spite of the use of these standards by most of the computer industry. On the other hand, there appear to be numerous examples of the rigidity with which government bureaucracies remain 'locked-in' even on such no longer (or never) efficient standards that would be easier to change than the QWERTY keyboard.

As market imperfections in R-evolution are part, be it under a different name, of the 'bottom-up evolution of institutions' which is one of the main themes of the following chapter by Gerhard Wegner, they will be only briefly considered here. In general, there seems to be widespread agreement that markets alone cannot produce and maintain all the rules of an evolutionarily efficient and allocatively not too inefficient R. To be sure, many such rules, including basic property rights, appear to be conventions spontaneously evolved by markets, along the lines explained by Hayek (1967). But political actions are usually needed, especially in large societies where many economic transactions take place among strangers, to guarantee their stability and to legislate additional rules that are required by efficiency, but which markets alone would take too long, or even be unlikely, to produce. Corporate law, patent law, antitrust law, and laws limiting insider trading in capital markets appear to be examples of such additional rules, although the question of what precisely such rules should be, to serve social efficiency and not particular group interests, is still far from closed.

Whatever the correct answer to this question might be, the present question is: can it be provided and maintained by markets alone, and if not, why? In general, the main obstacles appear to be cultural constraints and the fact that many institutional rules have the character of collective goods, which, as is well known, markets alone can rarely demand in efficient quantities and qualities. Considering again the three types of evolutionary imperfections, the following comments appear of interest. Market R-evolution may be blocked because some rules needed for efficiency would violate some prevailing cultural norms, so that no market participant dares to try them, or because experimentation with these rules cannot be individual, but requires politically coordinated collective action.[29]

Excessive waste may be caused by the unnecessarily long time which markets often appear to take to eradicate inefficient rules (norms, habits) and spread instead efficient ones. But, while it is again important not to confuse excessive waste with the necessary one, an important difference is that parts of R are often easier to imitate than parts of S. For instance, it is usually easier to copy and reasonably enforce a successful law – even if it may take time before agents learn fully to exploit it – than to duplicate a successful firm. Hence how much waste is necessary depends on whether an efficient rule is being evolved for the first time or whether it is already known in another observable economy, so that the local R-evolution could benefit from imitating it: the necessary waste is clearly much higher in the former case. This difference is of particular importance in the study of transition economies.

To be misdirected – in other words, to develop and lastingly lock-in on inefficient rules – market R-evolution usually needs a combination of two factors: a culture with low standards of honesty and trust, and a non-transparent market with rarely repeated transactions between the same partners, so that neither reputation effects nor tit-for-tat strategies can help. Examples of this imperfection, particularly serious in transition economies, are taxicab transportation and emerging financial markets: even the most radical pro-market reformers ended up by admitting that competition in both these markets, to reward and select for efficiency and not dishonesty, needed some legislated rules.[30]

7. EVOLUTIONARY IMPERFECTIONS OF GOVERNMENTS

Turning to government imperfections, recall first the two basic types found by non-evolutionary analysis: imperfect information (knowledge of particular facts), and imperfect motivation. The study of the former can be said to begin with Hayek (1945), who showed that no centralized collection and processing of information could possibly comprehend all the information needed for efficient coordination of economic activities in society. The latter has been the focus of the public choice and rent-seeking theories, pioneered by Buchanan and Tullock (1962), and Buchanan et al. (1980). Their premise is the elementary, but previously largely ignored truth that governments consist of politicians and bureaucrats pursuing their own objectives, which may be very different from any notion of common good. An important illustration of this truth is in Niskanen (1971), who shows that a typical leading objective of government bureaucrats, which causes much of government inefficiency, is maximizing under all circumstances the budget of their bureaux.

As is natural in the evolution of sciences, however, these attacks have not been left without objections. The most serious ones can globally be characterized as references to very large private firms, some larger than many national economies, where similar informational and motivational problems with their top management are being solved well enough – through informational decentralization and various incentive schemes – to allow them to prosper. This has been taken for evidence that these problems do have satisfactory solutions, and that, therefore, they cannot be insurmountable obstacles to government successfully conducting policies at least as complex and sophisticated as top management decisions in large private firms. Although these objections stop short of giving support to detailed national planning – on this point Hayek's argument remains intact, and can even be seen corroborated by the fact that detailed central planning has been found inefficient already in firms of relatively modest size – they can justify a large government agenda, including ownership of firms and extensive technological and industrial policies.

It is at this point that evolutionary analysis appears to be the only compelling way to demonstrate that, in spite of these objections, government organizations do differ from, and on average cannot be as efficient as, private firms exposed to market competition. The problem with this difference is that, although strongly significant, it is only probabilistic: there is indeed no deterministic reason why government could not solve the informational and motivational problems equally well as such firms. Although rare, some government firms and agencies can indeed be claimed highly efficient, while at any given moment it is usually possible to observe private firms that are quite inefficient. This raises hopes that such rare cases of efficient government organizations could be multiplied, and thus make the entire government sector as efficient as the best private firms. A new argument has been that even if a government agency is currently not very efficient, it can organize a learning process by which its efficiency can approach this ideal.[31] But evolutionary analysis strongly limits these hopes as it can demonstrate that the learning of government agencies, however helpful, is also bound to be, on average, far inferior to the learning of an entire population of competing, and possibly entering or exiting, private firms.

This demonstration, which can be here only briefly outlined, is based on comparison of S-evolution within governments with that in reasonably competitive markets.[32] It admits that even for large organizations, reasonably efficient solutions to the informational and motivational problems do exist, but with the qualification that the larger the organization the more difficult they are to find, to implement in all relevant details, and to protect from deterioration – and therefore also the more likely it is to commit, while trying to do all this, increasingly costly errors. Because of the above-mentioned low 'science/art' ratio in the creation of successful firms, only a market S-evolution, after a long experimentation with many mostly unsuccessful trials, can be expected, in a few exceptional cases, to get all of this right.

Note that the usual ex post observation of existing successful large firms hides the true difficulty of these solutions and the low a priori probability of finding and keeping them: it allows such firms to be taken for granted, without realizing how exceptional creatures they really are. Evolutionary analysis is needed to disclose the crucial fact that they are the rare survivors of market S-evolution, during which many firms tried to survive and grow, but only few have succeeded, while there was no solid a priori knowledge of which ones these will be.[33]

The main implication is that the expected quality of these solutions, and thus the expected efficiency of the organizations using them, depends on properties of the S-evolution from which they have resulted. It can be said, in a first approximation, that the more trials the evolution allows to be made and the faster it forces the errors committed to be corrected or eliminated, the better the results. The fundamental evolutionary difference between politico-administratively organized government agencies, including government-owned firms, and private firms resulting from market competition and selection, thus begins to be seen: the evolution of the latter is clearly superior on both accounts.

A more precise view can be obtained by considering that what matters about the trials allowed is not only their quantity, but also their quality – meaning the probability of each of them to prove successful – which depends on the relevant Q of the agents allowed to conduct them. Comparison of the politico-administrative selection of such agents within governments with their selection by competitive markets – especially if selection of entrepreneurs by product markets is complemented by selection of investors by financial markets – shows that the latter, provided it takes place under an evolutionarily efficient R, tend in the long run to select exceptional agents with the highest relevant Q, whereas the former cannot be expected to select much better than run-of-the-mill experts, regardless of the diplomas they might be required to have.[34] In consequence, the difference turns out even larger than the first approximation indicates.

Another reason why this difference is and will remain large appears when government and private firms are compared for their abilities to prevent their bureaucracies from deteriorating. As is well-known in practice, but still little studied in theory, both public and private bureaucracies have internal 'bottom-up' tendencies to increase inefficiency – for example, through excessive growth, diminished effort, excessive complication of procedures, and misdirected selection criteria, which may promote agents of low relevant Q, provided they have high competence for pleasing their superiors, who may have themselves been promoted in similar ways.[35] But there are important differences in the limits to which their inefficiency is allowed to increase, and in the speed and the force with which it is counteracted. While both have several 'top-down' feedback loops by which such counteractions can be generated, those of private firms are more powerful and consist of more levels, including top managers, owners, product markets, financial markets, takeovers, bankruptcies and liquidations. These loops, through their increasingly powerful sanctions, can indeed be expected to work faster, sharper, and more reliably than the loops of government organizations which consist of top public officials, to them often loyal politicians, and by elections separated by several years in which the efficiency of government organizations is often only a secondary issue.[36]

In sum, evolutionary analysis shows that informational and motivational problems are bound to cause on average more inefficiencies in governments than in large private firms. It also shows that governments, moreover, suffer from a stronger competence constraint, as their politico-administrative Q-selection proves in the long run inferior to the market one. It thus excludes from government agenda – in addition to the tasks which *no* human mind can successfully handle, such as national planning excluded by Hayek – also many of those which *some* human minds can successfully handle, but need for it an exceptionally high Q that is unlikely to be found otherwise than by market competition and selection. An important example is recognizing future winners among firms and technologies, the central task in all selective R&D and industrial policies: it proves to be, especially over long periods of time, much better performed by the variable population of successful private investors, continuously selected from many more candidates on competitive risk-capital markets, than by any government bureaucracy.

8. FROM IMPERFECTIONS TO POLICIES: THE GRASS IS NOT ALWAYS GREENER

Although discoveries of market and government imperfections are important, the way from them to policy implications is not as short and direct as many economists appear to believe, but requires careful analysis if serious errors are to be avoided. The required analysis may suitably be denoted as 'balanced two-sided', and contrasted with unbalanced analyses, which can be divided into 'one-sided' and 'biased two-sided', both of which can further be divided into 'anti-market' and 'anti-government'. The lack of balance may often be ascribed to an a priori preference for one of the 'anti' varieties which many economists appear, perhaps depending on their early youth experiences, to harbor. As the unbalanced analyses have a long history and many misleading policy implications are still being produced by them, they call for a few comments and a warning.

One-sided anti-market analysis was widespread in the old-fashioned ('Pigouvian') welfare economics, whose search for allocative imperfections was indeed limited to markets. Whenever such an imperfection was found, it was automatically implied that government should intervene by corrective policies, without examining how these policies should or could actually be conducted. More recently, somewhat surprisingly, this kind of analysis has been rejuvenated by some evolutionary economists, who find markets imperfect in the area of inventions, innovations and technological change, and imply the need for government intervention with similar automatism.

Anti-market analysis of the biased two-sided kind has grown in popularity with the mathematization of theoretical economics, which has been producing an increasing number of increasingly sophisticated optimization methods. This analysis does examine how optimal corrective policies could be calculated, and implies the need for them only when a suitable optimization method is found and formally proven correct. But – and this is what makes it biased – it idealizes governments by means of various simplifying and wishful assumptions about their U and Q, and thus builds on the illusion that real-world politicians and government bureaucrats are perfectly both willing and able to use theoretically suitable optimization methods in practical policies. Examples of its results are the earlier mentioned proofs of optimality of socialist planning, fine macro-economic tuning, and selective industrial policies.

Admittedly, this analysis has since then made progress by weakening some of its wishful assumptions. In particular, it has recognized that the amount of information that can be centrally collected and processed is limited, and that government agents may need specially designed incentives to align their personal objectives with the policy ones. The results consequently obtained – for example, about optimal informational decentralization, or optimal incentives schemes with incentive-compatible signalling – can also be seen as part of the above-mentioned objections to the criticism of governments for their informational and motivational imperfections.

In spite of this progress, however, a substantial part of the bias remains undiminished. The reason is that the wishful standard assumption that all government agents are always perfectly able to optimize (have an abundant Q) has been maintained in its original strength, and indeed cannot be weakened without making most of this sophisticated analysis worthless. The fundamental error in making this assumption about government agents can be seen by recalling the above-mentioned classical argument by Friedman (1953), which can justify this assumption, in the best case, only for agents selected by a long-lasting market competition. How far from the best available Q the Q of politico-administratively selected government agents is likely to be was at least partly made clear in the previous section.[37]

Although in modern economic literature, most of the one-sided and biased two-sided analyses are of the anti-market variety, and most of the actual difficulties of real-world economies can be ascribed to 'too much' of government, rather than 'too much' of markets, it should be noted that both these types of analysis also exist in anti-government versions. Their policy implications may be misleading in symmetrical ways: whenever government is found imperfect – be it because of its imperfect information, selfish motivation, or limited competence – it is automatically, and sometimes therefore mistakenly, implied that markets alone can always do better.

There is an obvious necessary condition that policy analysis, to be balanced two-sided, must meet: it must consider both markets and governments without idealizing either, or, in other words, take into account all possible imperfections of both lists. Such analysis can approve of a policy aimed at correcting a market imperfection if and only if the expected social losses of this imperfection exceed those of the imperfections of the policy. In spite of being obvious, however, this condition still appears only seldom met. Its early advocate is Demsetz (1969), who answers Arrow's (1962) biased analysis of the imperfect market allocation of resources for invention. Demsetz denounces the 'nirvana viewpoint' and the 'grass is always greener fallacy', which he shows hidden in Arrow's implicit assumption that whenever markets are imperfect, government can do better. An interesting attempt to develop a balanced two-sided analysis more systematically is in Wolf (1987).

That policy analysis, to be reliable, must be of the balanced two-sided type is easy to see. If it is blindly assumed that government is and will remain able to conduct socially optimal policies, both reliability requirements are clearly violated. The first because this is a wishful assumption about a critical initial condition, and the second because it hides possibly important side-effects of today's policies which might diminish government's policy-making abilities in the future.[38] Analogously, both reliability requirements are also violated if it is blindly assumed that all markets are and will remain efficient.

But to consider a balanced mix of imperfections of both sides does not suffice. As noted, reliable policy analysis must be able to take into account *all* the market and government imperfections that may be critical for the success or failure of some of the policies under consideration. This calls for exhaustive lists of both types of imperfections, which, however, may never be fully known. The best that can be done is to work on discovering as many imperfections of both types as possible.

That policy analysis must be evolutionary can now be seen to follow from the fact that there are many important imperfections of both markets and governments – of which the previous two sections gave a foretaste – that only studies of evolutionary processes can discover. And to be comprehensively so is a necessary condition for being balanced two-sided, which in turn is a necessary condition for meeting the reliability requirements. That being balanced two-sided is of particular importance just for evolutionary analysis deserves emphasis. One-sided or biased two-sided evolutionary analysis, which would keep discovering more imperfections only of markets, or only of governments, while continuing to ignore or to idealize the other side, would suffer even more from the 'grass is always greener' fallacies, and thus give even more support to the wrong policies, than the less sharp-sighted static analysis of the same types.

NOTES

1. Acknowledgements: I thank Pontus Braunerhjelm, Dan Johansson, Douglass North, Mark Peacock, Viktor Vanberg, Gerhard Wegner, Ulrich Witt, and Michael Wohlgemuth for helpful comments on earlier drafts.
2. As noted in more detail below, evolutionary analysis has sometimes been accompanied by policy implications, but they were usually limited to industrial and R&D policies. The rare attempts to develop an evolutionary perspective on policy issues in general include Pelikan (1994), Wegner (1997), and Witt (2001). But as yet no one appears to have it made entirely clear that policy analysis *must* be evolutionary if grossly mistaken policy implications are to be avoided.
3. A satirical illustration of such violations is the old joke about a group of hungry scientists with cans of food on a desert island: while other specialists try to find how to use available materials to open the cans, the economist suggests that they assume they have a can-opener.
4. To avoid misunderstanding between economists and jurists, whose cooperation on policy issues is increasingly needed, it may be useful to point out that when denoting an economic theory, 'positive' has the connotation of 'passively descriptive or predictive', whereas when denoting a law, it means what economists would rather call 'normative'.
5. That in medicine, complete mathematical modeling of the human body, whose complexity is comparable to that of a national economy, is considered neither possible nor particularly useful is instructive to note. Although quantitative relationships are there also important, most of the useful medical knowledge consists of logical models of forms, which interrelate a great number of causes and consequences in structural ways. The fundamental relationships between genetic messages and forms of proteins, on which both the forming and the working of the human body ultimately repose, and which are the basis of modern genetic therapies, are indeed basically structural. As will become clear below, the relationships between forms of institutions and the organizing and functioning of an economy, a good understanding of which is needed for solving the most difficult policy problems of economies in crises, is of a similar structural nature.

6. Note that this is a more complex game than those studied by evolutionary game theory: they are usually limited to pairwise matches under given rules between different given strategies, with results concerning the growth or the decline of the populations of these strategies over time. In contrast, the presently visualized game is more generally about the organizing and working of an economy's S, under a possibly changing R, which may involve both competition and cooperation, often among more than two agents at a time. While evolutionary game theory may throw useful light on some aspects of this game, many important aspects remain outside its reach.

7. The comparison with medicine (and more generally biology), mentioned in footnote 3 above, can now be made a little clearer. The relationship between the S and the R of an economy resembles the one between the genes (genotype) and the body (phenotype) of an organism in that the genes are also part of the body, of which they also shape both the forming and the functioning (see Pelikan 1988, 1992). But of course, there are also important differences: one of them is that there are several ways in which S can in return influence the shaping of R – for example, firms may lobby legislators, or introduce new informal habits – whereas there is no known feedback channel through which a phenotype could influence the shaping of its genotype.

8. The difference between 'institutional design' and 'policy conduct' may be seen to correspond to the one between 'constitution-making' and 'policy-making within a constitution' made by Buchanan (1975), and to the one between *Ordnungspolitik* and *Prozesspolitik* made in German 'Ordo-liberalism'. Note that formal policy analysis has often been limited to questions of policy conduct, with misleading implications for institutional design: namely, when an optimal way of using a given policy instrument by an idealized government in an idealized economy was found – which proved possible to do for virtually all imaginable instruments, including highly centralized socialist planning – it was often naively implied that this instrument may also be optimal to use by a real-world government in a real-world economy.

9. Michael Polanyi (1962) appears to be first to point out that communicable technological knowledge cannot be effectively transferred to and used by agents who lack the corresponding tacit knowledge.

10. For example, even an ordinary thermostat may be ascribed a virtual U: the one of maintaining a stable temperature. Far from denying that the thermostat is in fact a simple causally working device, this only simplifies the description of its behavior, compared to giving details of its switching programs.

11. It may be enlightening to consider that similar interlevel differences in U may also arise between a multicellular organism and its individual cells. For instance, if some of our cells become cancerous, their U is to grow and divide without limits, whereas our U includes preventing it, in order to keep our entire organism in a workable state.

12. A consistent multilevel view of institutions is still far from developed. Yet this seems to be the only way to clearly interrelate the two main branches of modern institutional economics: studies of institutions of entire economies, such as North (1990); and studies of institutions of firms, with implications for corresponding segments of national institutions, such as Williamson (1985).

13. That production of novelty is an important feature of evolutionary processes is emphasized by Witt (1993).

14. Economists studying non-evolutionary dynamics are kindred with evolutionary economists in that they also depart from the static equilibrium analysis of standard economics, but to a somewhat shorter distance.

15. Biological examples of such flexible, but nevertheless pre-programmed, development are the genotypes which can result in different phenotypes in function of environmental influences – for example, differences in food determine whether the genotype of a bee will develop a queen or a worker. Nevertheless, contrary to what is sometimes argued, the outcome is not *determined* by the environment: the development follows one out of a limited set of genetically pre-programmed paths, while the environment only determines which one.

16. Much like most of evolutionary economists have ignored institutions, most of institutional economists have ignored evolutions. I tried to build bridges between the two in Pelikan (1987, 1988, 1992).

17. In current policy discussions, however, these terms are not always well defined and clearly distinguished from each other; in particular, the term 'structural change' has often been employed to include, or even to mean, 'institutional change'. Compared to the rigorous conceptual framework that economists have for dealing with quantitative policies, their conceptual tools for dealing with qualitative policies – such as economic reforms and system transformations – are still largely underdeveloped. This is also an important reason why such policies still lack a good theory.

18. Readers with interdisciplinary interests may find it enlightening to note that medical therapies remedying a low level of a certain chemical can be seen stratified into three analogous layers: supplying the chemical, transplanting the organ producing it, and repairing the genes which can induce the organ to properly develop by itself.

19. The argument that institutional policies are the most important kind of policies is reflected by their central position in the following chapter by Gerhard Wegner.

20. The relationship between the wisdom of objectives and the efficiency with which they are pursued is discussed in Pelikan (1995).

21. 'Evolutionary efficiency' includes what I used to call, borrowing the term coined by Marris and Mueller (1980), 'adaptive efficiency' (Pelikan, 1987, 1989, 1992). Although this term was later also used by North (1990) and several other authors, I now see it insufficient in that it only conveys the idea of responses triggered by exogenous changes, whereas successful evolution often also requires acts of creation producing endogenous innovations. Adaptation abilities lose nothing of their importance – they are also needed for responses to such innovations – but they are disclosed to be only part of the story. Note also the difference from 'dynamic efficiency', which is limited to programmable developments, whereas 'evolutionary efficiency' concerns above all the generation of, and the adaptation to, novelties.

22. Compare also property (b) of evolutionary processes defined in Section 2.

23. The clash might conceivably be resolved by counting the information produced by S-evolution as part of the economy's useful output, and thus count the resources lost by the inevitable errors as its efficient cost, and not a waste. The problem is that both the information and its cost are difficult to estimate. What can be said about the cost is not much more than that it will often be enormous. For an intuitive feeling of how costly the information produced by an evolution might be, try to imagine all the resources used by the enormous number of unsuccessful mutations during the estimated four billion years of evolution of life – astronomically many times more frequent than the successful mutations – without which the complex information in the genes of today's well-adapted species could not have been found out.

24. That, at this margin, evolutionary efficiency has a much higher social value than the allocative one is in line with the classical argument by Schumpeter (1942/76) that the competition which introduces new technologies and concerns the very existence of firms ('creative destruction') contributes much more to economic development than price competition among existing firms.

25. The classical references for the tasks of markets in S-evolution and R-evolution is Schumpeter's (1942/1976) discussion of 'creative destruction' for the former, and Hayek's (1967) discussion of the evolution of the rules of conduct for the latter.

26. The mistaken logic of using hindsight information is nicely illustrated by the old story about the greedy person who bought two lottery tickets, won a million on one of them and regretted the waste of money on the other.

27. See, for example, Arthur et al. (1987) or Arthur (1990). As the principle of these processes is simple, but not always well understood, let me recall it. There is an urn with one white and one black ball. Draw randomly one of them and return it to the urn together with an extra ball of the same color. Keep repeating random draws, returning the ball drawn together with an extra ball of the same color. The questions are: (1) Will the two colors converge towards an equilibrium ratio? (2) If so, what will this ratio be? The answers that often cause surprise are: (1) yes; (2) *any* ratio between zero and infinity. The point is that after very many draws, when very many balls are already in the urn, any ratio becomes self-reproducing ('locked-in'), while it is the initial draws that weigh the most in determining which ratio this will be, out of the infinite number of a priori possible equilibrium ratios.

28. A familiar example of negative feedback which intervenes only when the deviation from a potential equilibrium has reached a certain threshold is the thermostat in a refrigerator.
29. The role of cultural constraints is clearly exposed by North (1990), who points out that some cultures, probably due to initial good luck, are highly conducive to efficient institutions, whereas in others efficient institutions are difficult to implement even with the help of legislation and formal enforcement, as competent legislation and honest enforcement are also difficult to obtain. A pioneering inquiry into the limits to which efficient institutional rules can be produced by individual experimenting and selecting as considered by Hayek (1967), and beyond which collective actions are required, is in Vanberg (1992).
30. On the other hand, however, the widely publicized imperfection of the market for used cars proves less serious, as reputation effects could there induce many sellers voluntarily to institute warranties. A clear empirical refutation of the famous argument by Akerlof (1970) is that this market still exists, and even thrives, with a large number of buyers getting what they themselves regard as fair deals. Akerlof has certainly the merit of pointing out the theoretical possibility of what is called here 'misdirected market R-evolution', but his empirical example is somewhat misplaced.
31. For an interesting variant of this argument see Metcalfe in this volume.
32. The difference between market S-evolution and government S-evolution is still relatively little explored for the simple facts that standard economics pays little attention to evolutions in general while evolutionary economics has mostly been limited to market S-evolution. The few studies which try to compare this evolution with government S-evolution include Forte (1982), and Pelikan (1988, 1993, 1999), where the presently outlined demonstration is elaborated and discussed in more detail.
33. This argument is compellingly presented and empirically documented in Eliasson (1988).
34. A simple mathematical model of the selection principles resulting in this difference is in Pelikan (1999).
35. Inefficiencies of bureaucracies appear to be more frequent topics of satirical essays and cartoons – such as Parkinson's Laws, Peter's Principle, and Adam Scott's Dilbert – than of serious economic literature. Ironically, most of these satires are aimed at bureaucracies of large private firms. Without denying that private bureaucracies may indeed grow and for a certain time remain quite inefficient, the present argument claims that government bureaucracies are likely to grow more inefficient and remain so for a longer time.
36. Kerber and Heine (2000) interestingly argue that the corrective feedback on the government side can be strengthened, and government inefficiencies thus decreased, by means of competition among governments.
37. How unrealistic it is to expect that the sophisticated optimization methods in question would be correctly used by real-world government bureaucrats in real-world conditions can also be seen by considering that correct application of these methods in simplified theoretical cases often challenges even the most advanced and mathematically most talented students.
38. For an illustration of both violations, see the introductory example of Keynesian policy analysis. The negative side-effects by which present policies may worsen conditions for future policy-making are pointed out and examined by Wegner (1997).

REFERENCES

Akerlof, G.A. (1970), 'The market for "lemons": qualitative uncertainty and the market mechanism', *Quarterly Journal of Economics*, **84**, 488–500.
Alchian, A.A. (1950), 'Uncertainty, evolution, and economic theory', *Journal of Political Economy*, **58**, 211–22.
Arrow, K.J. (1962), 'Economic welfare and the allocation of resources for invention', in National Bureau of Economic Research, *The Rate and Direction of Inventive Activity: Economic and Social Factors*, Princeton, NJ: Princeton University Press.

Arthur, W.B. (1990), 'Positive feedbacks in the economy', *Scientific American*, 80–85.
Arthur, W.B., Y.M. Ermoliev and Y.M. Kaniovsky (1987), 'Strong laws for a class of path-dependent urn processes', in V. Arkin, A. Shiryayev and R. Wets (eds), *Stochastic Optimization: Proceedings of the International Conference*, Berlin: Springer-Verlag.
Boyd, R. and P.J. Richerson (1985), *Culture and the Evolutionary Process*, Chicago: University of Chicago Press.
Buchanan, J.M. (1975), *The Limits of Liberty: Between Anarchy and Leviathan*, Chicago: University of Chicago Press.
Buchanan, J.M. and G. Tullock (1962), *The Calculus of Consent*, Ann Arbor, MI: University of Michigan Press.
Buchanan, J.M., R.D. Tollison and G. Tullock (eds) (1980), *Toward a Theory of the Rent-Seeking Society*, College Station, TX: Texas A&M University Press.
David, P. (1985), 'CLIO and the economics of QWERTY', *American Economic Review Proceedings*, **75**, 332–37.
Demsetz, H. (1969), 'Information and efficiency: another viewpoint', *Journal of Law and Economics*, **12**, 1–22.
Eliasson, G. (1988), 'Schumpeterian innovation, market structure, and the stability of industrial development', in H. Hanush (ed.), *Evolutionary Economics: Applications of Schumpeter's Ideas*, Cambridge, UK: Cambridge University Press.
Forte, F. (1982), 'The law of selection in the public economy as compared to the market economy', *Public Finance*, **27**, 224–45.
Friedman, M. (1953), *Essays in Positive Economics*, Chicago: University of Chicago Press.
Hayek, F.A. (1945), 'The use of knowledge in society', *American Economic Review*, **35**, 519–30.
Hayek, F.A. (1967), 'The evolution of the rules of conduct', in F.A. Hayek (1967), *Studies in Philosophy, Politics and Economics*, Chicago: University of Chicago Press.
Hayek, F.A. (1973–79), *Law, Legislation, and Liberty*, Chicago: The Chicago University Press London: Routledge and Kegan.
Heiner, R.A. (1983), 'The origin of predictable behavior', *American Economic Review*, **83**, 560–95.
Kerber, W. and K. Heine (2000), 'Institutional evolution, regulatory competition and path dependence', paper presented at the Workshop on Evolutionary Analysis of Economic Policy, University of Bochum.
Marris, R. and D.C. Mueller (1980), 'The corporation, competition, and the invisible hand', *Journal of Economic Literature*, **18**, 32–63.
Nelson, R.R. and S. Winter (1982), *An Evolutionary Theory of Economic Change*, Cambridge: Harvard University Press.
Niskanen, W.A. (1971), *Bureaucracy and Representative Government*, Chicago and New York: Aldine & Athertone.
North, D.C. (1990), *Institutions, Institutional Change, and Economic Performance*, Cambridge and New York: Cambridge University Press.
Parkinson, C.N. (1957), *Parkinson's Law and Other Studies in Administration*, New York: Ballantine Books.
Pelikan, P. (1987), 'The formation of incentive mechanisms in different economic systems', in S. Hedlund (ed.), *Incentives and Economic Systems*, London and Sidney: Croom and Helm.

Pelikan, P. (1988), 'Can the imperfect innovation system of capitalism be outperformed?', in Dosi et al. (eds), *Technical Change and Economic Theory*, London: Pinter Publishers.

Pelikan, P. (1989), 'Evolution, economic competence, and the market for corporate control', *Journal of Economic Behavior and Organization*, **12**, 279–303.

Pelikan, P. (1992), 'The dynamics of economic systems, or how to transform a failed socialist economy', *Journal of Evolutionary Economics*, **2**, 39–63, reprinted in H.J. Wagener (ed.), *On the Theory and Policy of Systemic Change*, Heidelberg: Physica-Verlag and New York: Springer-Verlag.

Pelikan, P. (1993), 'Ownership of firms and efficiency: the competence argument', *Constitutional Political Economy*, **4**, 349–92.

Pelikan, P. (1994), 'Evolutionary analysis of economic policy', paper presented at the 1994 Meeting of the International J.A. Schumpeter Society, Münster.

Pelikan, P. (1995), 'Competitions of socio-economic institutions: in search of the winners', in L. Gerken (ed.), *Competition among Institutions*, London: Macmillan and New York: St. Martin's Press.

Pelikan, P. (1999), 'Institutions for the selection of entrepreneurs: implications for economic growth and financial crises', Working Paper 510, Stockholm: The Research Institute of Industrial Economics.

Polanyi, M. (1962), *Personal Knowledge: Towards a Post-Critical Philosophy*, New York: Harper & Row.

Schumpeter, J.A. (1912/1934), *The Theory of Economic Development*, Cambridge, MA: Harvard University Press.

Schumpeter, J.A. (1942/1976), *Capitalism, Socialism, and Democracy*, New York: Harper and Row.

Vanberg, V. (1992), 'Innovation, cultural evolution, and economic growth', in U. Witt (ed.), *Explaining Process and Change: Approaches to Evolutionary Economics*, Ann Arbor, MI: The University of Michigan Press.

Wegner, G. (1997), 'Economic policy from an evolutionary perspective: a new approach', *Journal of Institutional and Theoretical Economics*, **153**, 485–509.

Wegner, G. (2000), 'Evolutionary markets and the design of institutional policy', paper presented at the Workshop on Evolutionary Analysis of Economic Policy, University of Bochum.

Williamson, O.E. (1985), *The Economic Institutions of Capitalism*, New York: The Free Press.

Witt, U. (1993), 'Emergence and dissemination of innovations: some principles of evolutionary economics', in R.H. Day and Ping Chen (eds), *Nonlinear Dynamics and Evolutionary Economics*, Oxford, UK: Oxford University Press.

Witt, U. (2001), 'The evolutionary perspective on economic policy-making: does it make a difference?', *Papers on Economics and Evolution 0101*, Jena: Max Planck Institute for Research into Economic Systems.

Wolf, C. Jr. (1987), *Markets or Governments*, Cambridge, MA: MIT Press.

3. Evolutionary markets and the design of institutional policy

Gerhard Wegner

1. INTRODUCTION

In the following I start from the empirical fact that within democracies policy-makers attempt to correct market performance in various ways, or, if you like, that economic policy exists. Choosing this point of departure I leave open whether policy-makers act in accordance with recommendations of theories of market failure, but nevertheless I will not, a priori, exclude a more benevolent view of policy-makers attempting to improve economic welfare – provided that such a term can be operationalised if we abandon the static view on markets.[1] Of course, economic policy has in the past demonstrated a change of confidence concerning the ability of the state to intervene successfully in markets. The formerly enthusiastic attitude of the early post-war period, in particular with respect to macroeconomic policy, has been superseded by a more sober and critical view in the past years. Not only liberal economists but also policy-makers themselves have become sceptical with regard to the possibility of devising market outcomes (on the macro-level as well as on the micro-level) according to political targets, whether or not these targets are justified from the perspective of economic welfare. The abandonment of ambitious political targets appears to characterise current economic policy and has recently given rise to the worry that the state might become too weak to correct market failure, namely with respect to the new phenomenon of institutional competition driven by nation states.

This phenomenon of political failure calls for a theoretical investigation. It was Hayek who reflected upon the limitation of economic policy in a fundamental way and put it down to the essentially evolutionary character of markets (Hayek, 1973, 1976). Although his view is somewhat biased for his exclusive concentration on distributional policy, Hayek's general argument appears convincing in that evolutionary, self-organising systems such as markets defy control from the outside. In particular, the phenomenon of decentralised knowledge erects a barrier to policy designed at particular allocational and distributional outcomes. The cost of crossing this barrier is the subversion of the principle of self-organising social system such as markets in their ability to allow for the production of knowledge. From this point of view, the older theory of economic policy posed by Tinbergen, with its suggestion that a decision-maker in the political sphere be capable of determining outcomes in the market sphere, appears to be a fundamental misunderstanding of the market order.

I will not engage in a detailed discussion of Hayek's social philosophy but maintain the evolutionary view on markets as a promising starting point to analyse the limitations of economic policy. Modifying the notion of 'catallaxy' which Hayek frequently uses, I concentrate more explicitly on the concept of innovation and innovativeness as the cornerstone of an evolutionary market view. I will show that such a revised view is appropriate in analysing the consequences of economic policy. Although I reinforce Hayek's sceptical view with respect to the riskiness of economic policy, I do not conclude that ambitious policy leads inevitably to the destruction of the market order. Nor do I agree that policy-makers have no chance to influence the market performance in accordance with their goals. Rather, the explicit consideration of the phenomenon of innovativeness is suitable for a modified analysis and, in particular, indicates that political failure can materialise in various ways (although even this is not a necessary consequence). Among these ways, the erosion of the market order represents one single possibility.

The chapter will proceed as follows: in Section 2 I conceptualize the term economic policy which is used here as the setting of institutions or rules in order to correct market outcomes. Some illustrations are given which demonstrate the impact of institutions on individual choice and the potential relationship between individual choice and political targets. In Section 3 I elaborate what is referred to as the top-down approach to institutional policy, that is the attempt to achieve market outcomes by the (re-) setting of rules. At first I analyse the precondition of a successful institutional policy and then shift to such an institutional policy which undermines the working condition of a market order (3.2). Finally, I discuss a third possible outcome of economic policy which provokes innovativeness directed to work against political targets (3.2). My examples of institutional policy do not support the view that policy-making itself represent the vice of modern democracies which needs to be hedged by appropriate constitutional reforms in the sense of Buchanan (1975) or Hayek (1981), although the potentially illegitimate use of the monopolistic power of the rule-setting state is not denied. Hence, I put forward a less-biased view on economic policy which questions how markets can be corrected in order to improve economic welfare. In response to this question I suggest a bottom-up approach of institutional policy. In doing so I follow the basic insights of New Institutional Economics which analysed how institutions can emerge from markets without the involvement of the state. Section 4 gives indications as to how the emergence of institutions from the market sphere may be instrumentalised or linked with political targets so that the negative consequences of conventional (top-down) institutional policy do not materialise. Indeed, practical examples underscore that this approach to economic policy has already been practised, something which has been widely ignored by economists. Section 5 concludes that the evolutionary features of the market order challenge the concept of policy-making in the conventional sense: on the one hand, the top-down approach necessarily implies development risks, while the bottom-up approach, on the other hand, cannot escape from its accidental nature.

2.   ECONOMIC POLICY AS INSTITUTIONAL DESIGN

In this chapter a particular concept of economic policy will be applied which in some respect has affinities to that of Buchanan (1975): only those forms of economic policy which concern the purposeful setting of rules or, if you like, the choice of rules are taken into consideration here.[2] Rules, in turn, define 'limits of liberty' but leave room to choose alternatives which are allowed by the rules. In this respect economic policy is identical with institutional policy and represents an indirect form of regulating market behaviour in so far as the selection of alternatives is not controlled by rules.[3,4] (The freedom of choice would be repressed if policy-makers were to prescribe the choice of opportunities. Cases of this type of interventionism also exist in reality, for example in the realm of environmental policy and also in some kinds of competition policy.)

I presume here that policy-makers are not interested in the existence of rules as such but intend to influence market outcomes by setting rules. Nor do I presuppose that economic policy only deals with the constituent institutions of the market order without regard to market performance in more concrete terms (see below). In this respect, a difference exists between constitutional (or institutional) policy, on the one hand, and economic policy, on the other. Economic policy is supposed to be successful, if the selection of alternatives leads to a market outcome which is in line with some political targets concerning that outcome.[5] Since it is a common feature of rules that they (explicitly or implicitly) exclude some behaviour, policy-makers have at least the chance of bringing individual choice into line with political goals. The following examples are representative:

(1) Environmental laws which prohibit environmentally harmful activities (without prescribing pro-environmental activities in a concrete manner) such as emissions; this limitation of economic freedom is designed to encourage the production of environmental public goods such as clean water or non-toxicated soil.

(2) Product regulations prohibiting the selling of goods which violate some standards of consumer safety or product quality, for example minimum levels of toxic standards or the exclusion of non-desired substances to produce food stuff due to some 'cultural' quality standards.[6] Prescribed warranties can also be included here.
(3) Competition laws which exclude cartels, quotas, the abuse of a dominant market position, binding contracts or mergers beyond a certain level of market power.

These types of rule-setting doubtlessly go beyond constituent rules of the market economy such as the freedom of trading, property rights or the right of abode, since they represent attempts on the part of policy-makers to align private behaviour with *some* political design of preferred market performance or, alternatively, to avoid non-preferred market outcomes (see below). On the other hand, economic policy as rule-setting does not go so far as abandoning economic freedom. By the same token, institutional policy differs from older versions of interventionism such as price controls (Mises, 1929/1976). Rather, the aforementioned examples can be interpreted as negative rules in a Hayekian sense (Hayek, 1969). However, this characteristic does not guarantee that rules will match the target of policy-makers.[7]

The term economic policy is used in a highly abstract way: I speak of economic policy or policy-makers whenever a parliament or the government or a democratically legitimated authority pursues a goal with respect to the economy; hence, an environmental authority or competition policy authority represents a case of economic policy. I skate over the problem of multi-level governmental co-ordination (Scharpf, 1993) and apply the abstraction of a unique decision-maker whose actions are orientated to economic outcomes. Although political scientists as well as sociologists (such as Luhmann) object that this concept of a unique decision-maker fails to capture the complexity of the state, I will stick to this abstraction for it enables us to focus on the interaction between the state and the market.

Furthermore, the aforementioned examples of institutional policy leave open whether policy-makers select their targets in accordance with recommendations of the theory of market failure in a broader sense. At first glance an orientation to 'economic welfare', that is a more benevolent orientation, is not excluded a priori, if external effects are supposed to be internalised or allocational distortions due to asymmetric information call for regulatory activities. Hence, I do not presuppose a purely rent-seeking character of institutional setting, that is the exclusive application of institutions to redistribute income (Knight, 1993). Practically, political decision-making will be inextricably driven by interest group behaviour attempting to correct market outcomes on their own behalf. Ultimately, institutional setting will overlap with distributional policy but here it will not be identified with the latter in a straightforward sense. In some cases it may be even futile to draw a sharp distinction between the distributional and the allocational aspect if the notion of market failure itself lacks precision.[8] Furthermore competition policy is difficult to assess in a normative way if the collective good of unrestricted competition coincides with the particular interests of competitors who profit when their rivals are put into their place by competition laws. For these problems of operationalising market (or co-ordination) failure it has become obvious that most kinds of institutional policy will be interlaced with (re-)distributional aspects in practice (North, 1990; Knight, 1993), although this does not mean that systematic problems of institutional policy can be derived from that fact alone.

Apart from that, the aforementioned examples of institutional policy reflect different kinds of target which economic policy can pursue. As a consequence, the 'narrowness' of institutions or their exclusive character will vary, depending on the concreteness of political targets. With respect to environmental laws this characteristic can easily be illustrated: environmental policy can define some collective good the attainment of which necessitates the exclusion of a plethora of opportunities at the micro level of the firm. This is the case if, for example, the political definition of 'clean water' encompasses chemical and biological requirements which restrict the use of particular techniques or input resources. On the other hand, environmental policy can be sparing with the catalogue of requirements that makes up the collective good 'clean water'. In this case, only a small number of opportunities of firm behaviour need to be excluded by environmental laws. But in either case institutional policy will desist from defining opportunities in a positive manner or from issuing 'commands', to put it in Hayekian terms.

With regard to product regulation, the idea of the varying degree of narrowness pertaining to institutions can be – mutatis mutandis – transferred analogously, since regulators can define product quality or safety standards to different degrees of concreteness. But apart from that, institutional policy can envisage targets which refer to allocational outcomes in a rather indirect way. A case in point is competition policy if it sets the rules for market participants in order to ensure unrestricted competition. Here, the market outcome is of minor importance in so far as allocational terms (such as product quality, prices, technical progress or even market structure) are concerned. If competition policy aims only at unrestricted competition (which means a non-Harvardian conception of competition policy), those types of private behaviour which give rise to a restriction of competition have to be excluded. Effectively, this will also make for a restriction of private opportunities, if for example mergers or cartels are excluded from the private set of opportunities. But this kind of institutional policy concentrates on the micro-level of private behaviour while the consequential market performance itself is of minor interest to policy-makers: a wide range of market outcomes may be accepted if it is the result of unrestricted competition (see Figure 3.1).[9]

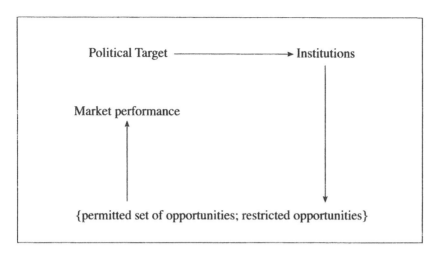

Figure 3.1   Economic policy as institutional design

In a preliminary sense we can reiterate that institutional policy as being a part of economic policy concerns the choice of rules while market participants remain free to choose within rules. In this respect institutional policy exclusively concerns 'negative rules' in a broader interpretation of Hayek. This holds true irrespective of the restrictiveness of institutions, in so far as we do understand freedom in a purely formal sense here. In doing so we assume that the state uses its power to (re)set institutions as a monopolist. Of course, the restrictive character of institutions may vary something, which depends on the character of the target of policy-makers and – if they are interested in particular market outcomes – on the concreteness of the definition of market outcomes. Narrowly defined regulatory targets call for more restrictive institutions and affect 'material freedom' in a negative way, to put it in Weberian terms.

3.   TOP-DOWN INSTITUTIONAL POLICY, INNOVATION AND ECONOMIC POLICY

Two main issues are of special interest in our context: (1) Is the top-down approach to institutional policy well-suited to harmonise with an evolving economic order and how can its potential limits be theorised, in so far the market order is concerned? (2) What determines the success and the failure of institutional policy, if there is no negative impact on the market order? In a sense, both questions are closely related with the phenomenon of innovation.

3.1   Institutional Policy and Economic Evolution

In his essay on 'Principles of a liberal society' Hayek (1969) took it for granted that economic policy could rely on negative rules which were supposed to harmonise well with an evolving market economy. Denying the possibility that economic policy could be orientated towards end-states (particularly in the realm of distributional policy), Hayek came to the conclusion that negative rules, that is rules which leave the freedom to choose open, represent the most adequate instrument of economic policy. Apart from those rules which are constituent for a market order, Hayek gave the impression that negative rules principally accord with the working conditions of an evolving market order: inasmuch as negative rules permit all opportunities which are not explicitly excluded, the remaining set of permitted opportunities is principally indefinite. In particular, all innovating activities which enlarge this set are allowed by negative rules. From a Hayekian point of view one would conclude that innovation as the driving force of economic evolution cannot come to a halt by any attempt to (re)set institutions: *whenever a change of relative prices incites the search for new opportunities (innovations), negative rules permit such behaviour since they permit everything which is not explicitly excluded.* This would definitely not be the case if economic policy were to 'prescribe' micro-behaviour.

But this literal interpretation of Hayek orientating economic policy towards negative rules cannot be maintained if economic policy pursues targets which go beyond the constitution of an economic order. Here, the restrictive character of rules needs to be assessed in each individual case. Our aforementioned examples of governmental targets suggest that narrowly defined targets (for example in the field of environmental policy) require more restrictive rules. If those rules exclude a subset of private opportunities from the freedom of choice, innovations are not only permitted but simply required in order to offset this reduction. Yet, whether market participants are able to cope with a restrictive institutional policy depends on the private capability to innovate, and it would be erroneous to deduce such a capability from the freedom of choice. If this capability is deficient, even negative rules may impede economic evolution. In other words: *what matters is the extent to which institutions exclude private opportunities and not the negative type as such.* For that reason the private capability to innovate has to be taken into consideration if the impact of negative rules on economic evolution is to be ascertained.

Theoretically it may be helpful to distinguish between two ideal-typical cases (see below). Both of them are characterised by the fact that regulatees at least attempt to enlarge their private set of opportunities if it has been restricted by institutional policy.[10] But in the one case they succeed to innovate and find new opportunities within the new institutional setting, while in the other they fail, something which leads to economic stagnation on the macro-level.

(1)   Hence, institutional policy which harmonises with an evolving economic order shifts the path of innovating activity instead of 'stifling' innovation altogether (Kirzner, 1978/1983). A case in point would be the innovativeness of firms which have to cope with environmental laws (including discharge permits or ecological taxes). If firms successfully shift their innovative efforts towards environmentally beneficial products or techniques they may 'lock into' a new 'technological trajectory' which furthers innovative activity in future. This implies that later innovative activities naturally follow a line of techniques or products by accumulating human skills which are favourable to that type of innovative activity (David, 1985; Dosi, 1982). Thus, the restrictive character of an institutional rule may be overcome by the existence or the emergence of path-dependencies guiding innovative behaviour. If the lock-in effect is strong enough, the institution may even be cancelled without redirecting the innovational path towards environmentally harmful products and techniques (compare Erdmann, 1993). A similar effect can materialise in the case of competition policy; as we have seen above, this type of rule-setting is much more directed to exclude some individual courses of action (which may hamper unrestricted competition) than it is to achieving certain allocational results. Hence, changing the rule of the market game may perfectly harmonise with economic evolution. This is the case if market agents have to cope with the exclusion of mergers (beyond some certain size) or the ban of price cartels but are nevertheless able to innovate under this changed institutional setting.

Indeed, one important argument in favour of competition policy is its allegedly beneficial effect towards economic development, insofar as economic agents are forced to innovate rather than enjoy the absence of competition. Taking into account some Chicago-critics who have questioned this effect, one would carefully conceptualise competition policy as a change of the path of innovation. Thus, innovative activities which require considerable size effects might be excluded if mergers are forbidden; instead these activities will occur within medium-sized plants. But as in the former example it is conceivable that the restrictive character of institutions is limited to an initial period and will be overcome if rule-followers have successfully shifted their path of innovative activities.

Although it is a matter of empirical evidence whether these effects materialise, there exists at least the possibility that institutions reshape economic evolution instead of blocking it at the micro-level. What matters is the relationship between institutions and innovative capability which makes up the restrictiveness of institutions.

(2) The opposite effect is possible, too, and needs no further elaboration for it derives directly from the foregoing. Innovative activities may be blocked by the prevailing institutions since the market agents fail to find innovative paths or niches which are not excluded. In this case the innovativeness has been 'stifled' by institutional policy and hence the driving force of an evolving economy is crippled. Product regulations, for instance, may be designed in such a way that innovations cannot pass the regulatory regime, thus retarding innovations substantially. This effect may be enhanced by institutional policy if it readapts the prevailing rules in order to regulate innovations anew which would otherwise find a loophole. Apart from that, the blocking effect will be strengthened if institutions prevent innovation in a whole sector of the economy. This has been the case in the German economy with respect to the bio-technological sector which was intensively regulated – in the first place for ethical reasons – during the 1980s. Although many of these rules have been withdrawn in order to sharpen the competitive edge of the German economy, the negative impact on the growth of an innovative pharmaceutical sector is only gradually fading away.

Because of limited space the ideal-typical effects of institutions are not analysed in more detail here; in particular, case studies with respect to single institutions would shed more light on the interdependence between institutions and their impact on innovations. Nevertheless, the central idea has been conveyed; in particular, it is obvious that this interdependence matters when the impact of rules on economic evolution is to be analysed. With regard to Hayek's work on this issue, the negativity of rules offers only some clues in this respect.

Note again that these ideal-typical effects may be established regardless of whether the target of economic policy can be justified from a normative point of view, in particular with reference to some concept of market failure. *Hence, the blocking effect of institutional policy may even occur if institutional policy is guided by the attempt of overcoming market failure*. For that reason an additional assessment of institutional policy from an evolutionary perspective appears to be highly recommended for policy-makers, since the opportunity costs of successful institutional policy may be paid in losses of dynamic welfare; normally the latter will be of much greater importance than potential welfare improvements in static terms which are to be attained by economic policy. However, one may speculate that policy-makers will not stick to an over regulating institutional policy in the long-run if they cannot afford its economic consequences, in particular a downsizing economy as the most negative result.

In that case economic performance itself incites policy-makers to correct their initial targets of institutional policy, that is to check its appropriateness with regard to the working condition of a market order and to free the economy from the burden of too restrictive rules.[11] Then a negative feedback loop between overtaxing institutional policy and economic performance would materialise which can partially explain the phenomenon of deregulating economic policy.

3.2 Innovative Activity as an Attempt to Evade Institutional Policy

So far I have dealt with the impact of rule setting on the development of an economy. I implicitly assumed that successful innovative activities – to the extent that they take place – harmonise with the target of economic policy more or less automatically. The above examples of shifted paths of innovation indicate this fact. For that reason one may conclude that economic policy is interested in an evolving economic order in a twofold sense: firstly, for the dynamic welfare gains and secondly for its congruence with political success. On the other hand, this perspective appears to reiterate the vision of a Leviathan-like state which is capable of annulling economic development if policy utilises the monopolistic power to (re)set institutions by overtaxing the economy. In the following I will modify this view and thereby our former result. Thus we enter into a more detailed discussion with regard to the preconditions of successful institutional policy in an evolving economy. On the other hand, I will explain the fact that an economy may evolve whilst policy-makers simultaneously fail to achieve their targets – in my view an indisputable fact about modern societies.

Again, innovativeness is the key concept. So far we have seen that innovativeness is to be taken into account because the functioning condition of an evolving economy depends on it. But it also impinges on the question of whether policy-makers can achieve their targets at all. To be more precise, the ability to innovate may also give rise to a problem for policy-makers even if that ability is not hindered by institutional policy.

This becomes more obvious if we take into account that innovative activities can occur which lead to non-desired market outcomes from the policy-makers' point of view. The resetting of institutions to achieve certain market outcomes can make for inadvertent effects as a result of the very fact of innovativeness. Since the prevailing institutions only record experiences from the past (Vanberg, 1998), novelties may emerge from the market sphere which are not included by them. This can occur even if the inconsistency of novelties with the 'sense' or the 'intentions' of institutions is obvious so that a readaption is required or, if you like, innovations have been placed in a blind spot of the prevailing institutional setting – whether intentionally or not (see below). But if innovations emerge as a result of institutional policy which are inconsistent with the intentions of policy-makers, the latter encounter a systematic problem.

To some extent this phenomenon overlaps with the very fact of asymmetrical information, but note an important difference: asymmetrical information pertains to the fact that policy-makers (principal) do not know the private set of opportunities which are only known by market agents. Hence one would search for a mechanism design which induces market participants to reveal their private information in order to avoid unintentional incentive effects. Furthermore, the capability to innovate aggravates the difficulty for policy-makers to direct private reallocation in accordance with political targets. Successful innovative activities enlarge the private set of opportunities from which the optimal alternative is to be selected. Even if policy-makers were fully informed about the original set of private opportunities, they will be – by the very definition of innovation – surprised by its enlargement via innovation. The character of innovation itself excludes that policy-makers can predict its emergence in concrete terms, let alone some sort of 'rational expectations'. Thereby the steering problem of economic policy is aggravated because the private set of opportunities – usually treated as a fixed one – undergoes a change if market agents succeed in innovating.

To some extent the phenomenon of path-dependencies will facilitate the task of policy-makers to foresee the extension of private opportunities in future. In the realm of environmental policy, for instance, policy-makers may justifiably rely on the proceeding of emission-reducing techniques or the emergence of economically feasible techniques due to prior research. In spite of the necessarily shaky grounds for technological forecasts, economic policy can improve its knowledge base by taking path-dependencies into consideration. Yet, one point turns out to be an issue: innovative activity results from search efforts (including technological research) combined with the allocation of resources due to new knowledge. Consequently any forecast about the results of innovative efforts has to be based on information about potential search directions of the innovator. Such information, in turn, is closely related to information about private intentions regarding how to react to institutional policy. Different types of reaction are possible:

(1) Market participants can guide their innovative efforts in line with the intentions of policy-makers or, if you like, with the 'sense' of their acts (to put it in terms of Max Weber). A case in point would be the search for innovations which promise to reduce emissions as a consequence of pro-environmental institutions (for example the introduction of discharge permits). Here innovative behaviour supports the realisation of political targets and outperforms the policy record if the set of opportunities has been left unchanged (the static case). Another example would be represented by competition policy if restricted anti-merger laws were to induce innovative strategies and thus sharpen the competitive edge via internal

growth strategies, while external growth strategies are not possible. Such innovations that result from the new institutions are embraced by the rule-setters for they have intended them to be a part of intensive competition.

(2) Contrary to these examples, market participants can direct their search efforts to work against the target of policy-makers. Whilst institutions limit the available set of opportunities, they leave open innovations which create new opportunities to circumvent political targets on the behalf of market participants.[12] If policy-makers motivate regulatees to thwart the targets of policy – for example if they disapprove of these targets altogether – the incentive to create anti-policy innovations will be strengthened yet more. The field of competition policy offers a lot of examples of the ingenuity of market agents to avoid competition by finding loopholes in the current set of rules. Firms embarking on mergers, for instance, may rearrange their product range or engage in new geographical markets or find similar practices which are promising to widen the boundaries of the relevant market so that competition authorities are prone to accept mergers. Particularly in the realm of competition policy, we have experienced much creativity in circumventing current competition laws where the political target of competition is typically at variance with private intentions of the regulatees. (Hence, an update of competition laws is required for systematic reasons.) For limited space I will omit a detailed illustration here, but the reader may imagine that a plethora of infringements of competition laws are possible since the latter simply invite market agents to search innovatively for loopholes (namely, many kinds of vertical restrictions including the abuse of market power within vertical relations can be disguised as means of *intensifying* competition, while it is difficult to expose the opposite effect).

The realm of environmental policy offers similar outcomes, although private intentions will probably not be directed to circumventing political targets. But regulatees can also redirect their research efforts if they face restrictive institutions which limit their set of opportunities. Effectively they may find novelties such as new techniques or chemical products which are just as harmful to the environment (including the health of consumers) as former techniques and products as well but which are not captured by the prevailing environmental laws. In particular with regard to highly innovative sectors such as the chemical industry, one can conceive of the difficulty for policy-makers to cope with the private innovativeness.[13] For that reason, successful institutional policy would encounter the problem of synchronising the institutional setting with the innovativeness of the industrial sector, that is to update institutions permanently. This requirement of readaption results from the unintentional effects (insofar as the policy-makers' perspective is concerned) of an initial attempt to exclude non-desired opportunities and ends up in a chain of interventions.

Obviously policy-makers encounter a problem if they base their instruments on governmental institutions completely (that is the top-down approach of institutional policy). In the worst case strategic interaction sui generis could arise, the consequences of which can rarely be calculated because the 'moves' of the game, in particular the reactions of market participants, are not given a priori but will be revealed sequently. If policy-makers refuse to acknowledge this interaction, they could easily get involved in a game against the innovativeness of market participants. Hence they may be well-advised to take this peculiar interaction into account and check the willingness of market participants to direct their innovative efforts in line with governmental intentions.[14]

Note that this phenomenon of provoking inadvertent innovations differs from the result in the section above. Insofar as policy-makers fail to 'stifle' private innovativeness altogether, the economy as a whole will not lose the driving force of evolution. Rather, policy-makers alone will fail to correct market performance via institutions and will have to take note of the fact that the economy shields itself against the political sphere, as it were. Doubtless, such a phenomenon is missing in liberal theories developed by Hayek or Buchanan who both focus solely on the deleterious effects on the market whenever the political sphere attempts to intervene. Political failure with minor negative effects on the market has been more or less ignored by these far-reaching theoretical contributions.

Although these remarks remain rather sketchy, I hope to convey one central idea of an essentially evolutionary approach of institutional policy. If policy-makers intend to check the potential success of their efforts, they have to take intangible factors into account which can be justifiably ignored if the analysis remains static (but then lacks relevance). The private willingness to innovate in accordance with, or alternatively against, political targets does not matter from a static point of view. Here, even the acceptance of a political target on the regulatees' side is of no concern, for market participants react to institutional restrictions only passively instead of finding a better reply by innovative activities. This prompts the thought that some sort of communication between the players is necessary; for the political sphere can only avoid a pointless resetting of institutions (which is typically combined with inflating bureaucracy) if it is informed about the private willingness (and capability) to innovate in accordance with political targets. Conversely, private agents, too, have an interest in knowing the intentions of institutional policy, whether or not they concur with it (in case they concur and are able to innovate in correspondence with it, they can cut short the process of institutional readaptation).[15] As it stands, such subjective factors are of greater importance and require an appropriate theoretical framework which standard theory fails to offer. Our reflection supports the well-known misgivings about rational-choice theory which presumes that private behaviour can be directed in a quasi-mechanical sense by resetting restrictions (here: institutions) in view of 'objective' information (private cost curves, prices); from that perspective further information concerning the private 'valuation' of restrictions (institutions) remains redundant and need not to be taken into account by policy-makers. But if such valuation influences the direction of change concerning objective data (here: private opportunities) and the willingness to innovate, it cannot be ignored by rational principals.

3.3 Preliminary Conclusion and Reformulation of the Problem

So far I have explored the ambivalent impact of institutional policy on innovation:

- on the one hand, institutional policy may restrict both the innovativeness of market participants and economic evolution via overregulation; this effect will occur if the private ability to innovate falls short of political intentions to correct market outcomes;
- on the other hand, private agents may cope with new institutions: in that case, one has to distinguish whether innovation in the market harmonises with political targets. If they refuse and succeed to withdraw from political ambitions, political failure coincides with economic evolution, or, if you like, the economy evolves in spite of a restrictive institutional policy, which signifies a growing autonomy of the economy from the state. Note that this fact emanates only from the ability to innovate and does not require that private agents are able to withdraw from the nation state altogether, although the very fact of institutional choice weakens the efficacy of institutional policy even more (Wohlgemuth, 1995; Vanberg and Kerber, 1995; Wegner, 2000).

For the time being one can reformulate the problem of institutional failure as a potential non-correspondence of innovativeness with political targets; in my view this appears to be a more adequate description of the principal–agent-problem which challenges economic policy and represents a generalised case of 'asymmetric information'. In the remainder I will discuss a potential solution of this knowledge-problem.

4. THE BOTTOM-UP APPROACH OF INSTITUTIONAL POLICY

The aforementioned description of the problem suggests that institutions be brought into line with the private ability and willingness to innovate. Although a variety of solutions might be considered in this context – the idea of intensifying communication has already been mentioned – I will confine myself to one concept which is of much interest to institutional economics. In doing so I will leave aside the top-down approach of institutional policy which relies upon the monopolistic power of the state to (re)set institutions. Instead, I will address an approach to institutional policy which could be labelled as a 'bottom-up' approach and which could be able to overcome the knowledge problem of economic policy, although the concept of policy itself will thereby undergo a substantial change. But note that the following reflections are less hypothetical than it may appear; to some degree they articulate what is already being practised in economic policy (although economists as well as jurists widely ignore this phenomenon or tend to underestimate its relevance).

To be more precise, self-regulatory mechanisms which emerge from the economy are germane in our context. By this we mean legally non-binding norms or institutions which control private behaviour according to commonly shared interests. Although agents may contract to follow such norms and are committed to such contract a posteriori, they are principally free to codify their behaviour a priori. As we know from recent economic history, such norms or institutions can emerge without any state involvement. Some examples are

- the international lex mercatoria which codifies customary norms and practices of international trade in order to warrant transactional security;
- the industrial norm setting such as the German Institute of Technical Norms (DIN) which has been created by all sectors of the German industry or
- the Committee of European Normalization (CEN), the International Organisation for Standardisation (ISO) the European Committee for Electrotechnical Standardisation (CENELEC) or the European Telecommunication Standard Institute (ETSI).[16]

Such 'internal' institutions (Lachmann) typically emerge in the absence of state authority, because groups have an interest to codify their behaviour in order to lower transaction costs.[17] Hence, empirical evidence has taught that state activity is not necessary to bring forth institutions even if the production of a collective good is involved. But while private norm setting has characterised the market order for a long time and represented a form of self-governance, it can also – at least to some extent – be utilised by the state in order to achieve targets of economic policy. It is the delegated character of authority which transforms such decentralised norm setting into a version of institutional policy (Lehmkuhl, 2000). In particular those internal institutions which tend to correct some form of market failure are germane (provided that the creators of these institutions have an interest to do so). In addition to the aforementioned examples the following institutions (among others) are of special interest:

- norm-setting by private associations of industry which also concerns standards of consumer safety or environmental standards;
- voluntary labelling of products which informs consumers about product qualities (e.g. ISO 9000), the impact of product on the environment (for example the application of techniques or raw materials);
- codes of conduct concerning warranties or standards of fairness which restrict cheating behaviour of firms (for example in the case of long-term contracts);
- private courts of arbitration beyond official courts which strengthen the right of customers towards sellers.

The delegation of public policy towards such institutions of self-governance can take place in various forms (see also Engel, 2001). On the one hand, the state can simply do without 'external' institutions or political instruments in the conventional sense and assign the fulfilment of some targets to private associations. For instance, standards of consumer safety (for example pertaining to toxic chemical products) can be determined by such private associations alone, while the public authority only generally demands that consumer safety be guaranteed. It is then left up to private associations to put this public instruction into practice.[18] On the other hand, the state can also combine the setting of law with delegation to private association. A case in point is the German environmental law concerning emissions. Here, the state defines quality standards in a rough sense and co-operates with private associations to define environmental standards in concrete terms. Interestingly enough, the state utilises institutions of private norm-setting for its own political interest.

Eventually, the state can completely waive political activities even though it desires a correction of market performance. In this case, policy-makers rely upon the operation of self-regulatory institutions in order to improve market results in accordance with political visions. Thus, if policy-makers wish to spread regulated products (for example with respect to product quality) in order to overcome allocational distortions due to asymmetric information, they can leave this task to the device of self-governance alone. In this case, public authorities would rely upon the emergence of private norm generation and probably support this emergence via public information pertaining to the content of such norms. If a variety of self-regulation measures compete with each other (for example in the case of environmental labelling), public information could improve the identification of goods which correspond with preferences on the demand side. But apart from this potential informational support, government will totally desist from public regulation.

Economically, self-regulation resembles governmental regulations since private agents restrict their opportunities through regulations. As empirical evidence indicates, such voluntary commitment may be even more restrictive than public regulations (Majone, 1994, p. 166; see also Peukert in this volume). Generally, the bottom-up type of institutionalisation offers a number of advantages in comparison to the top-down approach as analysed above.

- First, with respect to the capacity to innovate one would expect private agents to avoid overtaxing by overly restrictive institutions. Since private associations have better access to decentralised information, they will ensure that firms can adapt efficiently to the reduced set of opportunities required by regulation.
- Secondly, whilst the improved access to information may not necessarily give rise to soft regulations, private associations can identify new technologies or paths of innovation earlier than governmental bureaucracies; for that reason, regulations may emerge which, although stricter than public regulations, do not have a substantial impact on cost curves. Conversely, governmental regulators might be too cautious due to a lack of knowledge with respect to technological paths, in particular if they are aware of the development risk of ambitious institutional policy. In that case, a private involvement in rule-setting can better exhaust the ability to innovate.
- Thirdly, regulatees will be more willing to innovate in accordance with the intentions of those who design institutions, if the bottom-up approach of institutional policy is applied. External institutions might lack legitimacy, in particular if those who incur their costs do not participate in the decision process of rule setting. In that case, regulatees will be more inclined to ignore the intention of policy-makers and avoid their targets by evading innovative activities. Conversely, participation will improve the legitimacy as well as the acceptance of targets.[19] In practice it has also transpired that private regulations up-date the list of cases for intervention more rapidly than governmental bureaucracies.[20]
- Fourthly, one will expect that self-governance enables rule-setters to learn much better from experience. If cases for regulation have become unnecessary (for whatever reasons), rule-setters can deregulate without involving decisions of a parliament. Regulations with a poor record as well as a disadvantageous cost–benefit relationship will probably be abandoned much earlier. For this reason the flexibility of regulations will be improved compared to the top-down approach to institutional policy.

Of course, one should not be naive with an assessment of the applicability of self-governance. Note again, that a group interest directed to regulation must be presupposed, for otherwise no incentive for self-regulation exists and hence no alternative to external rule-setting. The group-interest, in turn, may issue from different sources. A strong incentive can be assumed if it is the common interest of a group (of firms) to signal product quality, where the latter needs regulation so that it can be screened by consumers. In such a case, advertisements (for example as to consumer safety) will not suffice in convincing consumers of product quality whereas some general standard will convey more credible information. Consequently, suppliers or a group of suppliers will have an incentive to create regulations and possibly correct a particular kind of market failure as a non-intentional by-product. On the other hand, regulations lower transactions costs so that customers can orientate their decision towards regulations. If preferences are heterogeneous, suppliers will have an incentive to establish different regulations which coexist with each other.[21]

Self-regulations may be also inspired by an alternative incentive which is closely linked to governmental regulations and can be observed in recent economic policy in Germany. In this case, policy-makers make credible threats to regulate the economy by external institutions but give the private sector a chance to implement self-regulations before putting threats into practice.[22] If regulatees appreciate the advantages of self-regulation (for example more flexible regulations with lower costs compared with external institutions), they will establish standards, regulations, codes of conduct and so on, on their own. Prudent market agents will even anticipate potential targets of economic policy in order to forestall disadvantageous rules or to keep the political agenda small. As a side effect, such 'learning' will contribute to relieve the state from tasks which can also be accomplished by groups.

I will not engage into a more detailed discussion here, for the potential applicability of the bottom-up approach needs a reflection. Above all, one must ensure that a new type of rent-seeking behaviour is not engendered (Lehmann, 1999). Elsewhere I have examined that mechanisms can be devised which limit such non-desired effect (Wegner, 1998), but it may also have become obvious that some tasks of economic policy have to be kept in the realm of governmental rule setting. In particular, encompassing public good problems (such as unrestricted competition as well as global environmental quality) belong to this indispensable part of economic policy in the conventional sense. But besides this core of economic policy, self-governance holds out the possibility to regulate markets independently of the state. If you like, a new type of capitalism will emerge.

5. CONCLUSION

The essentially evolutionary feature of markets challenges the efficacy of economic policy, even if political targets can be justified from a point of normative economics. Theoretically, this calls for the task of describing the riskiness of economic policy. Although I have not outlined a fully-fledged evolutionary market theory here, concentrating on the innovativeness of a market economy offers many indications as to how political failure can materialise (a by-product of our reflection is a modification of earlier reflections of Hayek on this issue). The distinction between the development risk on the one hand, and the failure to attain political targets without such a development risk appears to be of much importance. Practically, one obtains a more balanced view of the determination of successful institutional policy. But it may have become obvious that external institutional policy, that is policy in the conventional sense, cannot guarantee avoiding the sources of failure identified. This, again, gives rise to the need to re-conceptualise economic policy along the lines of a bottom-up approach. The knowledge problem of policy-makers with regard to the innovativeness speaks in favour of relieving the state of its rule-setting duties whenever possible. In particular, policy-makers will be well-advised to identify group interests which promise to undertake the correction of market performance. As a consequence, the notion of 'state' undergoes a change when institutional policy is partly 'privatised'. Furthermore, the experimental character of this new type of policy should likewise not be overlooked.

NOTES

1. For a discussion of this issue see Cordato (1992).
2. The terms 'rule' and 'institution' are used synonymously here.
3. The term 'regulation' is used in a broad sense here.
4. Buchanan himself was not aware of the consequence of this fact, which provokes a comparison between Buchanan's and Hayek's concept of rule.
5. In so far as we follow an older view of the theory of economic policy which can be traced back to Tinbergen.
6. This alludes to Belgium standards of high quality chocolate or the German standard of high quality beer, both of which occupied the European Commission for a long time.
7. For experts of Hayek one should add that the term 'political design' differs from the term 'design' in Hayek's sense, since Hayek thought of concrete, micro-level targets of an organisation and transferred this concept to the political realm.
8. Who will decide whether an environmental group lobbying for pro-environmental laws eliminates market failure or pursues its own environmental preferences and charges the whole collective? (see Noll, 1989).
9. Note, that the Harvard School pursued a more positive definition of the targets of competition policy which comes close to a positive design of competitive markets.
10. In Wegner (1997) I analyse the rationality of this sort of behaviour from a market process view. The most important point here is that evolutionary markets are characterised by a permanent tendency to devalue the current set of private opportunities in the sense of Schumpeter's 'creative destruction' (Schumpeter, 1942/1987). The survival of market participants depends largely on their ability to offset this devaluation by innovating (Of course, via side effects on rivals or spill over effects in other markets, market participants fuel this creative destruction unintentionally).
11. Recent activities of deregulation in Germany can be interpreted in this manner.
12. Sometimes this sort of evading innovative behaviour overlaps with an erosion of 'intrinsic motivation' (as Frey put it) which gives the circumvention effect a boost (Frey, 1992; Frey and Oberholzer-Gee, 1997).

13. For instance, the German Ministry of the Environment reported on 500 marketed new substances in the chemical industry from 1983 to 1986.
14. Here one may think of the role of informal institutions as a signal of private intentions; I will come to this problem below.
15. Environmental policy in Germany has established this communication in order to avoid real-location which would give rise to new environmental laws.
16. see Lehmkuhl (2000) for a detailed discussion from a legal point of view.
17. Peukert in this volume devotes his analysis to the regulative capacity of internal institutions with respect to the Neuer Markt in Germany (equivalent to the NASDAQ of the New York Stock Exchange).
18. It should not be overlooked that norm-setting behaviour in such a case offers the opportunity to protect markets against entry; in this case, private norm-setting overlaps with rent-seeking behaviour. Of course, this problem also arises if norm-setting is left to governments which are captured by interest groups.
19. Regarding German environmental policy, in which industrial associations take part in the operationalisation of environmental targets, the acceptance of environmental targets could be substantially improved. Furthermore, it is rather surprising to see how most ambitious targets were accepted as a consequence of participation, that is the semi-public character of politics (see especially the 'Kreislaufwirtschaftsgesetz').
20. Compare Majone (1994) who reports that a private regulation association in the US outperformed public regulations with respect to the speed in identifying new toxic substances that require regulation.
21. I do not discuss the problem of revealing and sanctioning defective behaviour in the case of self-regulation. For a detailed discussion compare Eisenberg (1999).
22. A case in point is the German environmental law concerning emissions (Bundesimmissionsschutzgesetz).

REFERENCES

Buchanan, J.M. (1975), *The Limits of Liberty – Between Anarchy and Leviathan*, Chicago: University of Chicago Press.

Cordato, R.E. (1992), *Welfare Economics and Externalities in an Open Ended Universe: A Modern Austrian Perspective*, Boston et al. Dordrecht, Netherlands and Boston, MA: Kluwer.

David, P.A. (1985), 'Clio and the economics of QWERTY'. *American Economic Review*, **75**, 332–7.

Dosi, G. (1982), 'Technological paradigms and technological trajectories: a suggested interpretation of the determinants and directions of technical change'. *Research Policy*, **11**, 147–62.

Eisenberg, A. (1999), 'Die Lösung sozialer Dilemmata und der Wandel informeller Institutionen', Max-Planck-Institut zur Erforschung von Wirtschaftssystemen, Diskussionsbeitrag 04–99, Jena.

Engel, C. (2001), 'Institutions between the state and the market (Institutionen zwischen Markt und Staat)'. *Die Verwaltung*. **34**. 1–24.

Erdmann. G. (1993), *elemente einer Evolutorischen Innovationstheorie*, Tübingen: Mohr.

Frey, B.S. (1992), 'Tertium datur: pricing, regulating and intrinsic motivation', *Kyklos*, **45**, 161–84.

Frey, B.S. and Oberholzer-Gee (1997), 'The cost of price incentives: an empirical analysis of motivation crowding-out', *American Economic Review*, **87**, 746–55.

Hayek, F.A.v. (1945), 'The use of knowledge in society', *American Economic Review*, **35**, 519–30.

Hayek, F.A.v. (1969), 'Grundsätze einer liberalen Gesellschaftsordnung', in F.A.v. Hayek (ed.), *Freiburger Studien*, pp. 108–25.

Hayek, F.A.v. (1973), *Law, Legislation, and Liberty. Vol. 1 – Rules and Order*, Chicago and London: Routledge.

Hayek, F.A.v. (1976), *Law, Legislation, and Liberty. Vol. 2 – The Mirage of Social Justice*, Chicago and London: Routledge.

Hayek, F.A.v. (1981), *Law, Legislation, and Liberty. Vol. 3 – The Political Order of a Free People*, Chicago and London: Routledge.

Kirzner, I.M. (1978/1983), *The Perils of Regulation: A Market-Process Approach*, Law and Economics Center, Coral Gables: University of Miami.

Knight, J. (1993), *Institutions and Social Conflict*, Cambridge: Cambridge University Press.

Lehmann, M. (1999), *Private Institutions in Waste Management Policy and their Antitrust Implications*, Bonn: Reprints aus der Max-Planck-Projektgruppe Recht der Gemeinschaftsgüter.

Lehmkuhl, D. (2000), *Commercial Arbitration – A Case of Private Transnational Self-Governance?*, Bonn: Reprints aus der Max-Planck-Projektgruppe Recht der Gemeinschaftsgüter.

Majone, G. (1994), 'Comparing Strategies of Regulatory Reprochement', in OECD (ed.), *Regulatory Co-operation for an Interdependet World*, Paris, pp. 155–77.

Mises, L.v. (1929/1976), *Kritik des Interventionismus*, Darmstadt: Wissenschaftliche Buchgesellschaft.

Noll, R.G. (1989) 'Economic Perspectives on the Politics of Regulation', in R. Schmalensee and R.D. Willig (eds), *Handbook of Industrial Organization*, vol. 2, Amsterdam etc.: North-Holland, pp. 1253–87.

North, D.C. (1990), *Institutions, Institutional Change and Economic Performance*, Cambridge.

Scharpf, F.W. (1993), 'Positive und negative Koordination in Verhandlungssystemen', *Politische Vierteljahresschrift*, Sonderheft 24, 57–83.

Schumpeter, J. (1942/1987), *Kapitalismus, Sozialismus und Demokratie*, Tübingen.

Vanberg, V. (1998), 'Rationale Wahlhandlung, Regelorientierung und Institutionen: Eine evolutorische Perspektive', in G. Wegner and J. Wieland (eds), *Formelle und informelle Institutionen. Genese, Interaktion und Wandel*, Marburg, pp. 379–422.

Vanberg, V. and W. Kerber (1995), 'Competition among institutions: evolution within constraints', in L. Gerken (ed), *Competition among Insititutions*, Basingstoke: Houndsmill, pp. 35–64.

Wegner, G. (1997), 'Economic policy from an evolutionary perspective – a new approach', *Journal of Institutional and Theoretical Economics (JITE)*, **153**, 485–509.

Wegner, G. (1998), 'Entstaatlichung der Umweltpolitik durch innere Institutionen? – Verhandlungslösungen als Komplement regulativer Umweltpolitik', in G. Wegner and J. Wieland (eds), *Formelle und Informelle Institutionen – Genese, Interaktion und Wandel*, Marburg, pp. 35–68.

Wegner, G. (2000), 'Zur Funktionsfähigkeit des institutionellen Wettbewerbs – Ein Beitrag zur Theorie des Systemwettbewerbs', *Diskussionsbeiträge des Instituts für Europäische Wirtschaft, Fakultät für Wirtschaftswissenschaft der Ruhr-Universität Bochum*, 29, Bochum.

Wohlgemuth, M. (1995), 'Institutional competition – notes on an unfinished agenda', *Journal des Economistes et des Etudes Humaines*, **6**, 277–99.

4. Knowledge and economic policy: a plea for political experimentalism

Stefan Okruch

1. INTRODUCTION: THE NEED FOR AN ALTERNATIVE POLITICAL ECONOMY

> The proliferation of competing articulations, the willingness to try anything, the expression of explicit discontent, the recourse to philosophy and to debate over fundamentals, all these are symptoms of a transition from normal to extraordinary research. (Kuhn 1996, 91).

Economics seems to be in a state of planned or unplanned irrelevance for political decisions. Either the advice given by economists is neglected, or the economists eschew policy recommendations for the sake of scientific purity.

The case of unintended irrelevance is not, at a first glance, a problem of economics. It can be attributed to the 'deaf ears' of politicians that, unlike the benevolent scientific advisors, are not interested in the common good, but motivated only by their success in the political marketplace. However, explaining the failure of scientific advice-giving with 'wrong' structures of the political system or the ignorance of political decision-makers, leads to the question of whether economic science is actually unable to adapt its recommendations to these structures.[1] This might be a question of rhetoric and thus of form, but it can also be a problem of content, or matter.[2] Recommendations of standard economics may be especially inappropriate for the governance of complex systems because of their exclusive focus on static criteria such as allocative efficiency and their notorious underestimation of complexity. In this respect, the politicians' ignorance for 'wrong' prescriptions is absolutely rational. The poor demand for economic expertise in the political arenas is, in other words, only one side of the 'marketplace for ideas' (Holmes 1992).[3] Improving the supply is an equally promising strategy.

The simplest way to evade these difficulties, however, is to avoid any policy recommendations. This is the case of planned irrelevance. Such inner emigration may be favourable for the internal consistency and the scientific rigour of economics, but it produces the 'explicit discontent' of those who do not perceive their discipline as separated from political economy. The dissatisfaction is not only apparent with books and essays that proclaim economics' 'decline' (Cassidy 1996) and 'end' (Perelman 1996) or its 'disease' (Blaug 1998) and 'death' (Ormerod 1994). Economists' 'debate over fundamentals' with regard to economic policy recently became especially visible with the relaunch of the German Economic Association's journals, one of them entitled *Perspectives of Economic Policy*. Although the journal's mission statement emphasises better communication between theory and practice and the contribution of theoretical research for problems of practical economic policy, the longest lasting and most prominent discussion has been about fundamentals, starting in the very first issue with two contributions (Frey 2000; Weizsaecker 2000) which referred to the famous epilogue of Keynes's *General Theory* and scrutinized the political and societal relevance of economics – with quite sceptical results (Frey 2000, 26).

Apparently, there is a need for a new approach. Douglass North (1999, 80) expects evolutionary economics to be a remedy for the 'sickness' of modern economics: 'Economic theory is static; and in the world of dynamic change in which we live a static body of theory consistently and persistently yields the wrong policy prescriptions. ... The recent interest in evolutionary economics is, however, a heartening development'. Ironically, also evolutionary economics is not too well prepared to give policy prescriptions. Most of evolutionary economists' energy has been directed toward positive economics (Pelikan, in this volume). Their analyses, emphasising processes and dynamics instead of final states, the fragmentarity of knowledge instead of certainty, only touch implicitly on the difficulties evolutionary political economy may face.

As many of those scholars who are the exception to the rule are contributors to this volume, the modest ambition of this chapter is to add an interdisciplinary view on the subject. The focus will be on institutional policy and the recommendations to be derived from an evolutionary point of view in order to establish a set of adaptively efficient institutions. As this is apparently a task of both law and economics, the starting point of my analysis is the concept of *Ordnungstheorie* which not only aims directly at normative statements that could inform the lawyer but has indeed been an extremely influential concept for shaping important parts of the law. This is especially true for the Freiburg school of law and economics and its protagonist, Walter Eucken. Friedrich Hayek, which can be seen as another central figure of *Ordnungstheorie*[4] contributed the evolutionary dimension to the interdisciplinary research programme. His scepticism towards economic policy is still the point of departure for any evolutionary analysis of economic policy.

My conjecture is that Eucken's rejection of political experimentalism cannot be upheld as far as it is not assumed that the knowledge necessary for the political governance of a complex evolutionary market system is 'given'. With respect to the knowledge dimension I further conjecture that beyond Hayek's ([1949] 1976, 33 ff.) exploration of 'Economics and Knowledge' with respect to economic theory there is more to be said about knowledge and economic policy. In the intersection of these two conjectures I will scrutinize the role of experiments for the generation of knowledge in both the economic and political sphere. In this context, I will refer to the tradition of philosophical pragmatism and to recent attempts to give more (institutional and legal) substance to the pragmatist idea of experimentally determining the proper scope of government. I conclude by pointing to tendencies towards a system of political experimentalism in different policies.

2. LEGITIMATE ECONOMIC POLICY: THE QUALITATIVE SOLUTION

In order to explore the common ground of *Ordnungstheorie*, I will summarize the concepts of Eucken and Hayek. Most basically, they share the view that the solution to the problem of (legitimate) economic policy for dynamic economies is a qualitative one. Thus, the scale and scope of legitimate state action should be delineated by recourse on the (legal) form of state action.

2.1 The Primacy of *Ordnungspolitik*

According to Eucken ([1952] 1990, 6), economic policy in advanced economies faces one central problem that lies in the high degree of complexity. Eucken juxtaposes two ideal types of governance and argues that neither of them, if used in a pure form, can meet his criteria for a satisfactory management of economic complexity. These criteria are described by the goal of *Ordnungspolitik*, that is the implementation of an economic order that is both efficient ('workable') and just ('humane', 'fair') (Eucken [1952] 1990, 166). Laissez-faire as the first ideal type cannot solve the social problems of industrialised countries (Eucken [1952] 1990, 55); the second type dubbed experimental economic policy ('Wirtschaftspolitik der Experimente') tries to eliminate the cause of those social problems, but thereby jeopardizes the functioning of a market economy (Eucken [1952] 1990, 149). Eucken presents a taxonomy of different forms of experimental economic policy, but most of his criticism is directed towards its furthest-reaching version, an economic policy that aims at a centrally administered economy (Eucken 1948; [1952] 1990, 58).

It is important to note that Eucken has such large-scale experiments in mind when he criticises experimental economic policy. More specifically, he observes as a result of experimental economic policy a dangerous trend towards national monopolies which also induces, with necessity, a centralization of political control (Eucken [1952] 1990, 55, 151). This agglomeration of both economic and political power, he argues, is often promoted by policy-makers (and public managers) that believe they could command a firm, an economy, and the society as a whole like a machine. Eucken ([1952] 1990, 56, 211) argues against such a social technology and the mechanics of the economics behind it and points to the limited knowledge about the effects of large-scale economic experiments. In sum, his rejection of experimental economic policy is based on two arguments: first, the problem of uncontrolled power, which is not restricted to economic power but comprises – in contrast to a laissez-faire system – also concentration of political power; second, the limited knowledge of the experimenter, as an additional problem that is relevant only for experimental economic policy.

Following Eucken's rejection of both extreme types of economic policy, it is clear that a 'middle way' is needed. As some of those intermediate forms that only vary the quantity of state interventions fall under the verdict of being experimental (Eucken ([1952] 1990, 140), Eucken (1952, 95) finally presents a qualitative criterion, the 'primacy of *Ordnungspolitik*':

> The question whether there should be more or less state activity evades the essential issue which relates to quality, not quantity. ... the state should influence the *forms* of economy, but not itself direct the economic process.

According to Eucken's interpretation the historical experience shows that only one order can meet the criteria of workability and justice, that is the competitive market order (*Wettbewerbsordnung*). After the unsuccessful age of political experimentation (Eucken [1952] 1990, 241) the goal of economic policy can, in other words, only consist in the implementation of a workable price system, a system of complete competition (Eucken [1952] 1990, 254).[5]

2.2   Rule of Law

Similar to Eucken, Hayek's argument starts from the high complexity of modern economies. He argues that (different types of) rules are crucial for the governance of such an 'extended order of human cooperation' (Hayek 1988). In Hayek's view, there exists an exact correspondence between (types of) orders and different 'systems of rules' (Hayek 1978, 72): while an 'organization' (*taxis*) is built upon 'commands' (*theseis*), a spontaneous order (*cosmos*) can only be guided by 'the universal rules of just conduct' (*nomoi*). The potential complexity of an organization is always lower vis-à-vis a spontaneous order, because an organization is deliberately constructed to serve a specific purpose of its makers and necessarily reflects their cognitive limitations. A spontaneous order, in contrast, allows the pursuit of a great variety of different purposes, the use of the dispersed knowledge of all elements of which the order consists and may thus achieve any degree of complexity (Hayek 1973, 38). As the merits of the modern economy lie exactly in its ability to generate and use knowledge, it is clear that such a catallaxy is one – and the most prominent – example of a spontaneous order (Hayek 1978, 91).

Given these two types of orders, together with the implication of their different 'knowledge management' capabilities, Hayek further elaborates on the different systems of rules. He specifies *nomos* and *thesis* in legal terms and postulates that public law is the realm of commands, while private law contains the universal rules of just conduct. He explicitly includes constitutional law in his concept of public law and thus conceptualises the constitution as a set of rules that aim at the construction of an organisation (Hayek 1978, 78). As Hayek (1978, 80) sees a dangerous confusion of these distinct legal spheres and especially the permeation of public commands into private law, he further elaborates on the (legal) characteristics of the rules of just conduct and stresses four criteria that allow the proper distinction of rules of private law. Rules must be abstract, only 'referring to yet unknown cases and containing no references to particular persons, places, or objects' (Hayek 1960, 208). At the same time true laws are required to be certain, in the sense that 'the decisions of the courts can be predicted'[6] (ibid.). 'The third requirement of true law is equality' (ibid.), the fourth that its rules do not prescribe (positively) a certain behaviour, but only (negatively) exclude some actions from the range of allowed behaviour (Hayek 1960, 216).

It is clear, then, that economic policy for an extended or spontaneous market order can only operate within rules of private law. It is less clear, however, whether such institutional policy is restricted to the enforcement of rules or whether – and to what extent – it could also deliberately modify the universal rules. In other words, the question of the origin of rules is crucial. In Hayek's view (1988, ch. I), there are three layers of rules inherited from the past, the oldest genetically fixed and shaped by biological evolution, the most recent represented by 'constructivist' legislation. The most important layer, however, is the intermediate one 'between instinct and reason', that is rules that are the cultural heritage of mankind, often learned implicitly by individuals and emanating from an evolutionary process of trial and error (Hayek 1967, 87; 1973, 18). In the course of this evolution 'more experience and knowledge has been precipitated [in the rules] than any one person can fully know' (Hayek 1967, 92).

As instincts are obviously irrelevant for institutional policy, the interesting point is the relative importance of cultural evolution vs. deliberate implementation of rules. However, Hayek's analysis in this respect is somewhat ambivalent. Although he (1978, 74) concedes that 'a spontaneous order may rest in part on regularities which are not spontaneous but imposed', he seems to eventually limit the necessity of deliberate legal innovations to cases where cultural evolution is locked into a detrimental path of development, apparently assuming that these cases are quite rare (Hayek 1973, 88, 100). For an important part of private law he welcomes 'improvements' of universal rules that could possibly made with the help of a NIE analysis (Hayek 1988, 36, 69), but generally it is the process of cultural evolution that brings about the appropriate rules. The most important argument in favour of the spontaneous emergence of rules is that they 'of necessity' comply with the stated criteria for rules of just conduct (Hayek 1973, 85).

Summarizing, Hayek's analysis of rules and orders and its policy conclusions can be seen as an elaboration of the primacy of *Ordnungspolitik* that specifies the legal form of economic policy. While his arguments against interventionism and for an institutional policy are similar to Eucken's, Hayek's additional argument of the evolutionary origins of institutions substantially changes the role of the state. Hayek, like the Freiburg School, makes this out to central problems of interventionism, namely the lack of knowledge and the danger of uncontrolled power. For Hayek, however, a strong government that could limit the accumulation or at least the abuse of private power would only replace one problem with another, because public power, too, is difficult to control and could easily be abused. Even the state that refrains from interventionist experimentation and confines itself to institutional policy constitutes an 'exclusive, monopolistic power to experiment in a particular field – power which brooks no alternative and which lays a claim to the possession of superior wisdom' (Hayek 1960, 70) and is generally inferior to an evolutionary improvement of rules that is the result of numberless small and individual deviations from existing rules. In this sense Hayek (1988, 53) is indeed 'in favour of experimentation'. As the outcome of the process of cultural evolution is generally in accordance with the rule of law as specified by the characteristics of the rules of just conduct, Hayek's (1960, 222) qualitative delineation of the proper scope of government implicitly limits state actions also substantially: 'the rule of law provides the criterion which enables us to distinguish between those measures which are and those which are not compatible with a free system'.

2.3   A Critique of the Qualitative Solution

2.3.1   Economic order as an equilibrium?

The ordoliberal approach can be interpreted as an attempt to balance the dynamics of both the economic and the legal order. Note that Eucken's ([1952] 1990, 180) interdependence of orders (*Interdependenz der Ordnungen*) is a dynamic one: on the one hand there is the rapid change of industrialized countries' economic order, on the other hand the change of the legal order is accelerated by experimental economic policy to an extent that must, according to Eucken's analysis, be appeased by appropriate institutional policy. From an evolutionary point of view it is important to ask whether this dynamic interdependence can indeed be interpreted as a statement about the different speed of change of evolving orders or whether either the economic or the political order is conceptualized in a way that implicitly rules out creative change.

With respect to the economic order it is important to note the central role that the idea of equilibrium plays for Eucken's concept of complete competition. Subsequent research in the line of the Freiburg School replaced this view with a more dynamic, Schumpeterian concept of competition and thereby introduced novelty and evolutionary change into the market order.[7] For Eucken the importance of equilibrium is, however, not limited to the economic sphere: 'The task is always the same: The establishment of a workable and just order. This double task can clarify the meaning of equilibrium. Workability is a matter of equilibrium. To the same extent is justice [a matter of equilibrium]. Thus, the meaning of equilibrium exceeds economics and its technique' (Eucken [1952] 1990, 166; my translation). But what does equilibrium mean more precisely for the legal framework of a competitive market order? Eucken ([1952] 1990, 373) describes the equilibrium first as a state of harmony between the social macrocosms and the microcosms of 'human nature'. Therefore the social order can 'in a certain sense' be seen as 'a natural order or Ordo'. A second characterization (ibid.) refers to the correspondence between social order and historical trends. The competitive market order is meant to reflect the 'strong tendencies that strive for complete competition'. Eucken stresses the fact that these tendencies do not bring about the appropriate order automatically. As the order that is in correspondence with historical trends must be deliberately established, it is 'in this sense no natural order, no ordre naturel' (ibid.).

There is an obvious ambivalence in Eucken's statement about the naturality of orders, but apart from this, each characterization is problematic in itself. First, it is questionable whether the micro–macro correspondence can be operationalized, that is whether human nature can instruct institutional policy. The second characterization has a flavour of historicism, although Eucken ([1952] 1990, 200; 1952, 89) rejects, for example, the Marxian philosophy of history and its idea of inevitable institutional developments.[8] It seems as if for Eucken the co-evolution of economic and political order could come to an end once the appropriate legal framework is scientifically determined. The subsequent implementation of a stable legal order appears to be a 're-creation of reality' (Eucken 1938, 198) leading to the desirable end-state of historical development. Further experimentation is in this perspective indeed meaningless. Such an 'end-state-liberalism' (Barry 1989, 112)[9] is necessarily incompatible with an evolutionary theory of institutional change, which would focus on open-ended processes.

2.3.2   Are the qualitative criteria reliable?

(1) *Institutional policy vs. regulation*   Even if the legal framework of the competitive market order could be specified and legitimized in a way that avoids the problematic concept of equilibrium, an evolutionary perspective on the interdependence of economic and legal order has important consequences for the qualitative statement concerning the scope of government, that is the primacy of *Ordnungspolitik*. Whatever legitimation and whatever delineation for the institutional arrangement is chosen, this choice can never be interpreted as a final state but only as a provisional one (Hesse 1979, 218; Koch 1996, 141). The institutional arrangement will always and necessarily undergo changes, because – unlike the metaphor of a framework suggests – the legal order, that is, in Eucken's words the 'form of economies', is not only an exogenous restriction for the economic process but is endogenously co-determined by the process (Budzinski 2000, 224 ff.). From an evolutionary point of view it is clear that within the economic process novelty can occur as a result of the actors' creativity. With respect to the interdependence of institutional arrangement and economic process this also implies that actors can react creatively to legal rules, even if the law remains absolutely unchanged (Okruch 1999), and that it is impossible to calculate the actors' reaction to a modification of the legal order. Therefore the beneficial effect of a political measure cannot be determined by the qualitative criterion of form. Although some forms of interventionism are obviously incompatible with a competitive order this statement relies on the probable effects and not on the form of the measure. This is true for such crude interventionism as price controls or quotas, as the addressees' creativity is directed toward the evasion of the regulation, so that these interventions are both futile and obviously anti-competitive. But in contrast to these blatant cases it is far more difficult to foresee reactions to the modification of the more general rules of the economic game.

Given this co-evolution of economic and legal order, the distinction between *Ordnungspolitik* and direct intervention into the process becomes less clear. Potentially, however, the Hayekian specification of the legal form of *Ordnungspolitik* could deliver more reliable criteria for the forms of institutional policy that are beneficial for the (spontaneous) market order.

(2) Nomos *and* thesis *in a legal perspective*   Hayek's legal theory consists first of his legal systematic that links the two kinds of rules to public vs. private law and secondly of his criteria that rules of just conduct have to meet and that are connected with the theory of cultural evolution.

With respect to the first part it is surprising not only from the standpoint of continental constitutional law that Hayek confines the constitution to commands for the organization of government. Consequently, general civil or human rights that are laid down in a constitution should be seen as being part of private law. Whereas this might be a minor problem of taxonomy, there is a more general problem with the strict dichotomy of public (and especially administrative) law as a sphere of command and coercion and private law as the domain of liberty. Within legal science this traditional concept has been contested and substantially modified. Although many lawyers share Hayek's scepticism vis-à-vis over-regulation by public law and some legal scientists were even in search of a 'post-interventionist law', the growing intermixture of the public and private law is no longer perceived only as an apostasy from legal purity but also as a result of and a chance for a 'learning law' (Trute 1996; Zumbansen 2000). Ladeur (1997, 191) convincingly argues that the classical liberal model of law for a 'society of individuals' must undergo changes given 'the rise of organizations ... as the primary actors', so that legal theory has to ask 'how the model ... has to be varied in conditions of the society of organizations, by looking for sup-plementation and functional equivalents for the market's knowledge-generating function' (ibid.).

The second part can be seen as an elaboration of Hayek's (1978, 250) 'twin ideas of evolution and of the spontaneous formation of an order'. Hayek argues that the rules which are necessary for the maintenance of a spontaneous order are mostly the result of an evolutionary process, that is cultural evolution. The cultural evolution produces, in other words, the universal, abstract and certain rules of just conduct. As Hayek (1973, 94 f.; 1978, 100 f.) further is convinced that these beneficial rules could only emerge in a common law system, the central agent within the process of cultural evolution is the judge (Okruch 2001).

There are, to my point of view, two (interdependent) shortcomings of Hayek's concept: first, with the criteria that every single rule must cumulatively meet, Hayek sets a utopian standard (Weinberger 1992, 270), especially with respect to the assumed harmony between the abstract universality and the certainty of rules. Secondly, his view of adjudication's role in cultural evolution does not fully reflect the complex interplay of rules, decisions and principles that guide them. This, ironically, results in viewing the legal order as quite rigid.

The common cause of both deficits lies in some terminological confusions about rules and principles: on the one hand it is not clear whether rule means the factual uniformity of behaviour ('is') or whether it signifies a prescription for behaviour ('ought'). On the other hand rule can either mean a prescription for behaviour or a legal principle ('principles as rules', Hayek 1978, 101; 'principles as inchoate rules', Hayek 1973, 119). This vagueness leads to the described shortcomings: the characteristics of or the criteria for rules (as pre-scriptions) are internally inconsistent because these requirements can only be met by the interplay of both legal norms (rules) and legal principles that finally leads to a judicial decision. Law as only a 'model of rules' (Dworkin 1996, 14) without principles can be certain, but is unable to cope with novel conflicts

('Hard cases make bad law', Holmes 1992, 130). A model of principles (Steiner 1976, 143, 150) without rules can be abstract as it is able to cope with potentially every conflict, but cannot yield certainty; the concrete judicial decisions cannot be foreseen.[10] The balancing of certainty and flexibility is the task of judicial procedures. Only a legal system that contains rules, principles and procedures can produce both reliability and flexibility (Dworkin 1996; Alexy 1996). Without focussing on principles and procedures the change of legal norms is explained in a way that confuses the basic distinction between 'is' and 'ought', because the change of factual (individual) behaviour is linked directly to the change of (collectively binding and beneficial) norms (Vanberg 1986).

The direct causal link from behaviour to norms, which ignores the effects of principles and procedures, also results in an overestimation of the certainty of judicial decisions. According to Hayek the judge can easily make this step from 'is' to 'ought', and it is interesting that Hayek (1967, 166; 1978, 79) refers to this decision making process in terms of a 'discovery' or 'finding' of rules. The innovative potential of adjudication is thereby underrated (Okruch 1999). Eventually Hayek – similar to Eucken – refers to the idea that the change of legal orders is guided or even determined by the 'nature of things' (Hayek 1973, 106).

(3) Nomos *and* thesis *as different forms of governance*   Hayek claims that a spontaneous market order needs the abstract and certain universal rules of just conduct or that, the other way round, the enforcement and cautious modification of those rules can guarantee the spontaneity and workability of a market order. Any attempt to govern the economic system more directly is impossible, as it requires the use of commands for a specific purpose and would ultimately transform the economic order into an organization.

This impossibility-theorem of governance, however, underrates the creative potential of the addressees of any political measure (Wegner 1996, 1997, see also in this volume). Even if economic policy does only operate with general and abstract prohibitions that narrow the addressees' set of possible actions it is not guaranteed that the economic actors react in a way that supports the spontaneity of a market order. Universal rules can be, in other words, so strict that they ultimately destroy a spontaneous order. This leads to the conclusion that, once again, the beneficial or detrimental effect of a political modification of the institutional arrangement cannot be qualified along formal criteria, but only on the basis of an economic analysis that must – from an evolutionary perspective – take into account the creativity of actors.

Such an analysis (Wegner 1996, 1997) has to differentiate, first, whether either the actors can expand the set of potential actions creatively or whether they lack the innovative potential to do so. It is clear that, secondly, it should be analysed, whether the addressees' actions ultimately help in reaching the goal of the measures taken. This two-dimensional analysis results in a classification of four possible cases, and it appears that Hayek's impossibility theorem describes only one of them. This case is characterized by the failure to reach the political goal, because the creative actors do not find ways to creatively substitute the prohibited action by an innovative option that conforms with the goal. Additional attempts to reach the goal ensue and finally lead to stagnation. Note that this consequence crucially depends on the lack of ability to innovatively expand the set of possible actions. As far as actors are endowed with creativity there is, in other words, a potential for the political governance of the economic system. Whether a deliberate modification of the institutional arrangement, that is the set of prohibited actions, depends on the innovative potential in the specific case and is irrespective of formal legal criteria Hayek views as decisive.

The potential success of institutional policy can only be assessed for a specific situation and has to estimate the innovative potential in relation to a considered measure. Given the creativity of the addressees and the possibility of unanticipated novelty, an optimal measure can never be determined. Institutional policy therefore is always a venture that political entrepreneurs have to answer for. As knowledge about the reaction to a political measure can never be certain but is necessarily fallible and subject to future learning, an 'evolutionary policy maker adapts rather than optimises', his attention 'shifts away from efficiency towards creativity' (Metcalfe 1995, 418). As there is, in other words, 'a strong case for experimentation and policy learning' (Metcalfe and Georghiou 1997, 7) in order to improve the knowledge about governance, it should be asked how the experimental and learning process is to be designed so that most knowledge can be used for institutional policy.

3.   LEGITIMATE ECONOMIC POLICY: PROCEDURAL CRITERIA

The procedural analysis can be structured along the distinction between institutional choice and institutional change. The dichotomy is analogous to Eucken's ([1952] 1990, 375) notion of grown vs. made orders and can also be related to Hayek's differentiation of *nomos* vs. *thesis*, as the former is consciously chosen, while the latter is for the most part the result of evolutionary change.

As has been shown above, Eucken and Hayek take a similar starting point, that is the problem of an appropriate institutional arrangement for a dynamic economy. Their solutions, however, differ substantially in setting the focal point within the continuum between choice and change. While Hayek mainly relies on the gradual change of institutions by adjudication, ordoliberalism aims at the choice and implementation of a workable and just order. Note that this choice, according to Eucken, is not the choice of the people concerned, but it is a scientific decision on the basis of historical experience derived from past experiments. As this historical substantiation, as argued above, is questionable, the institutional choice must be legitimized in another way.

The legitimation Hayek gives for the rules that are the outcome of cultural evolution is their superior problem solving capacity. As there is no choice to be made, it is once again not the individual decision of the people concerned that is decisive, but the beneficial function of evolved rules, that is to 'help to make the members of the society in which they prevail more effective in the pursuit of their aims' (Hayek 1976, 21). Beside the foregoing critique of Hayek's view on the process of judicial change of rules, one may ask whether there could be other mechanisms that produce rules that promote the success of societies.

3.1   Input-legitimation in Institutional Choice

The legitimatory deficit of ordoliberalism can be cured, if and when the institutional choice is explicitly based on a decision of those who will be affected by the institutional arrangement (Vanberg 1988, 1997). Hence institutional choice is seen as an agreement on a social contract that reflects the preferences of all people concerned. As it is important that each contractor voluntarily assents to the contract, the institutional choice has to be taken unanimously. Unanimity is a central requirement of the contractarian approach and can be interpreted as analogous to the Pareto-criterion (Brennan and Buchanan 1985, 135). Given this analogy also the contractarian interpretation of ordoliberalism uses the idea of equilibrium for the legitimation of order. This provokes two questions: First, whether factual consensus could be a utopian normative standard, an ideal norm that – similar to Pareto-efficiency – could only be reached in nirvana ('Pareto-illusion', Albert 2001, 32). Secondly and interrelated, whether consensus can fruitfully be used as an explanatory principle, too. This means using it for a positive constitutional economics (Voigt 1999) that explains institutional change. The latter question can be answered in two ways. Either empirical modifications of the institutional arrangement are rationalized by describing a hypothetical consensus, or institutional change is explained by the change of preferences that could be expressed in a new actual consensus. The first solution is highly problematic in that it only alleges the voluntary agreement of individuals, that is it assumes preferences that could never be revealed by actual choice. The second solution is plagued by the described problem of actually reaching a consensus.

In order to avoid the difficulties of the potential nirvana approach that the principle of unanimity represents, a comparative institutional approach is to be taken. This means, I argue, not to focus on consensus or on majority rules (as deviations from consensus), but to take into account the complex system of democratic institutions. 'It is not the majority rule alone, that is meant to "substitute" consensus, but it is the system of parliamentary-democratic institutions. [This system] is to be evaluated as to whether and to what extent it offers the protection against discrimination the consensus offers' (Homann 1985, 59; translation by author).

This version of democratic legitimation has in common with a contractarian approach the reference made to the people's preferences that ought to be actually expressed. Basically both approaches use – from the point of view of the individuals that make the institutional choice – an internal criterion for the quality of choice, that is the correspondence with people's preferences (Vanberg 1994, 208). Below perfect consensus it can be asked to what extent preferences flow into the 'production' of the institutional framework. Therefore this kind of legitimation can be dubbed 'input-legitimation' as 'government by the people' (Scharpf 1999). Scharpf (1999, 8 f.) points to an important prerequisite for input-legitimation, namely the high degree of common identity that limits the possible number of people involved. This can be illustrated by examining the institutional preferences more closely.

Following the argument of Vanberg and Buchanan (1994a, 168 ff.) concerning constitutional preferences, two dimensions can be distinguished, namely constitutional interests and constitutional theories. Theories in this context mean 'predictions (embodying assumptions and beliefs) about what the factual outcomes of alternative rules will be' (Vanberg and Buchanan 1994a, 169). Vanberg and Buchanan argue that a consensus on theories could be approached by discourse and deliberation, whereas the conflict of interest would persist. The probability of an agreement on theories, however, will first depend on the number of people involved. Secondly and decisively, it depends on the cultural homogeneity of the participants of the discourse (Scharpf 1999, 9). The more people from different 'epistemic communities' are involved, the lower the probability of consensus will be for the theory dimension, too (Hegmann 2001).

From an evolutionary point of view, at least two interesting features of this approach should be stressed:

- The theory dimension in institutional choice introduces knowledge as an important factor (Vanberg and Buchanan 1994b, 180 f.). Note that theory does not mean to make a scientific statement about the best of all possible worlds (like the described end-state liberalism), but theories consist of the fallible knowledge of people involved (what comprises, of course, scientific advisors).

– Secondly, mechanisms of using knowledge are described, that is mechanisms of mutual learning about theories. This procedural view is able to perceive democracy not only as the application of the majority principle but as a 'process of forming opinions' (Hayek 1960, 108).[11]

One additional distinction, however, has to be made with respect to the knowledge encapsulated in theories, in order to better specify the conditions under which a consensus of theories can be reached by discourse. According to Vanberg and Buchanan (1994a, 169) 'theories are about matters of fact', but as Hayek repeatedly argues, 'the rules of fact which one knows' (Hayek 1967, 80) are only one part of the knowledge necessary to act in way so that an order of actions can be sustained (Hayek 1960, 25). The formal institutions that are deliberately chosen are, in other words, embedded in a system of informal institutions. As one cannot assume that a change of formal institutions is always in harmony with the informal constraints, but the latter also influence the effect of a change of formal institutions, one may argue that the individual knowledge about outcomes of institutions is partly 'knowing that', partly 'knowing how' (Ryle 1949). These two kinds of knowledge differ in the way they can be communicated. While knowing that can be expressed by means of language, so that it can be exchanged in a discourse, knowing how cannot be expressed in words and is best acquired by imitation, that is learning by doing or learning by using. If an individual has acquired such practical knowledge about the working properties of a specific institutional arrangement (containing both formal and informal institutions), it is not at all certain that she is convinced by theoretical (that is knowing that) arguments about the superior quality of another institutional setting. Given that knowing that cannot be transformed into knowing how and vice versa, the discourse will have difficulties reaching an agreement, if the participants' theories also embody knowing how. This problem is aggravated by psychological effects that have been long neglected by both economics and the philosophical tradition that focuses on discourse and deliberation (Kahneman et al. 1991). A strong status quo effect will plausibly also prevail in institutional choice. This status quo effect needs not be viewed as an irrational anomaly only, given the high degree of uncertainty about the performance of an institutional innovation (Fernandez and Rodrik 1991), that is the utility derived from the 'consumption' of a changed institutional arrangement (Rabin 1998). Theoretical arguments will not be sufficient to overcome inertia of this kind.

Both arguments – the distinction of different kinds of knowledge as well as the status quo effect – hint at difficulties a discourse will have in reaching an agreement. In other words: learning by discourse, that is the theoretical examinations of different options in institutional choice, is only one learning mechanism. Beside these thought experiments there might be the need for real world experiments, in order to give the opportunity for learning by using and overcoming the uncertainty that induces the status quo orientation (Heinemann 2000). This is, of course, already an argument related to output legitimation.

3.2 Output-legitimation in Institutional Change

Input-legitimation focuses on the collective institutional choice in a 'constitutional moment'. A change of the institutional arrangement is possible – no institutional setting could be qualified as the end-state – but has to wait until the next constitutional moment. This also means that an individual that is discontented by the institutional arrangement cannot make an individual institutional choice that would express her preferences, as long as only input-legitimation prevails. Introducing the possibility of individual choice of orders, according to the 'output' the relevant institutions 'produce' for the individual, can be seen as one mechanism of 'output-legitimation' (Scharpf 1999, 10 ff.).[12] This means that the individual can choose among different international orders (institutional/systems competition),[13] among different intranational orders (federalism)[14] or among different functional equivalents (functional federalism).[15] In any case there is no longer a monopoly for the institutional supply, but different suppliers make their institutional offers in a competitive process. This implies competitive control but also the incentive to generate and use new knowledge. Institutional competition, too, is a discovery procedure, a 'constitutional exploration, for the inventing of and experimenting with new solutions to constitutional problems' (Vanberg and Buchanan 1994b, 188).

Although the limits to these different forms of institutional competition must not be overlooked, the very idea of competitive supply of institutions should not be rejected a priori. Such fundamental criticism would, as Oates (1999) recently pointed out, once again imply the pretence of knowledge about a desirable end-state. With respect to the economic theory of (fiscal) federalism he points to a neglected dimension dubbed 'laboratory federalism': 'In a setting of imperfect information with learning-by-doing, there are potential gains from experimentation with a variety of policies for addressing social and economic problems. And a federal system may offer some real opportunities for encouraging such experimentation and thereby promoting "technical progress" in public policy' (Oates 1999, 1132).

Oates refers to the US welfare reform in 1996 which 'replaced the long-standing federal entitlement programs with a new system under which the states have broad scope both to determine the form and levels of their programs to assist the poor' (Oates 2001, 141). Simultaneously, however, 'the federal government continues to provide extensive financial support to the states ... in the form of substantial block grants with few strings attached to them' (Oates 2001, 142). This example is interesting in that it combines the competition of jurisdictions ('laboratories') with a federal 'supervisor' that seeks 'to find out what sorts of programs can work' (Oates 1999, 1132). There is, in other words, not only a competitive feedback that works among the different states, but also the potential of horizontal or vertical cooperation and learning (Oates 1999, 1133).

4. THE NECESSITY OF INSTITUTIONAL EXPERI-MENTS AND POLITICAL EXPERIMENTALISM

Both input-legitimation and output-legitimation of institutional arrangements concern, I argue, institutional experiments:

- Either thought experiments that are examined in a discourse or experiments 'in the field' that are evaluated by the actual choice in institutional competition.
- Either sequential experiments from one constitutional moment to another or parallel experiments, that is the spatial or functional coexistence of different orders at one moment of time.
- Either experiments that are shaped by 'voice' or experiments that fail by 'exit'.
- Either the 'market place for ideas' is what Holmes (1992, 320) had in mind, or the realizations of ideas compete in institutional competition.

It is by experiment that an evolutionary economic policy can acquire the knowledge that is necessary for its adaptation to ever-changing circumstances. In order to clarify my argument, I will first examine the meaning of experiments more closely and then try to generalize the different suggested ways of organizing the experimental process.

4.1 The Meaning of 'Experiments'

Social experiments can never result in the certainty a laboratory experiment in natural science yields. This also means that economic theories differ substantially from, for example, explanations in physics with respect to their explanatory content and precision. One possible methodological reaction to the peculiarities of social sciences has been proposed by Hayek (1967, 11) and Watkins (1992), who claim that social science can at best reach an 'explanation of the principle' or an 'explanation in principle'. Such explanations do not allow predictions with quantitative precision, but can be used for 'pattern prediction' (Hayek 1967, 31). A social experiment can therefore test the pattern prediction, that is the applicability of a pattern for a certain situation. This test cannot falsify the pattern definitely as it could in natural science, but this does not mean that a social experiment could not contribute to more and better knowledge.[16]

Popper ([1961] 1976, 83) distinguishes two classes of social experiments, namely piecemeal experiments and holistic experiments, and rejects the idea that only large-scale experiments could be valuable. While holistic experiments 'can be called "experiments" only in the sense in which this term is synonymous with an action whose outcome is uncertain', piecemeal experiments are indeed 'a means of acquiring knowledge, by comparing the results obtained with the results expected' (Popper [1961] 1976, 85). Historicism's and Utopianism's exclusive preference for holistic experiments, Popper argues, overlooks 'the fact that we possess a very great deal of experimental knowledge of social life. There is a difference between an experienced and an inexperienced business man, or organizer, or politician, or general. It is a difference in their social experience; and in experience gained not merely through observation, or by reflecting upon what they observed, but by efforts to achieve a practical aim'.

Note that Popper depicts quite clearly what above has been conceptualised as the know-how component of knowledge. As Popper's research programme aimed at criteria for scientific know-that and its progress, he consequently hastens to add 'that the knowledge attained in this way is usually of a prescientific kind' (ibid.), but nevertheless points out 'that the knowledge in question is based on experiment rather than on mere observation'.

Popper's arguments can be easily expanded to the acquisition of practical knowledge in the market. Entrepreneurial actions can be conceptualized as tests of hypotheses – and the competitive process discovers which hypothesis can stand the test (Kerber 1997). The social experiments I am pledging for are, in contrast, institutional experiments, and there might be peculiarities that would be against the extension of the experimental logic. Note, however, that many approaches yet described are in favour of market-like competition and use a kind of goods–institutions analogy.

Institutional experimentalism, the argument goes, would deprive institutions of their most fundamental function of shaping human interaction (North 1990, 3) in a stable and reliable way. But the stability of institutions can only be relative stability, for example the stability of the legal framework vis-à-vis the market process. In transferring the idea of competition as a discovery procedure to the realm of institutions or economic systems it is clear that there must be a relatively stable framework for experimentation. This also becomes clear with the analogy of market competition and institutional competition. As has been pointed out by Heuss (1965) in an important contribution to market process theory, both innovations (experiments as 'mutations') and learning ('iteration') are necessary within the market process. While Heuss focused on the supply side of the market, most recently Loasby (2000, 307) argues with the idea of 'variation in a stable ambience' with regard to the demand side.[17]

Hence, the relative stability of institutions must not lead to the conclusion that the legal order is or ought to be absolutely rigid. This conclusion is not clearly avoided, I argued, by ordoliberalism. Furthermore, the discussion of Hayek's legal theory showed that the claim for certainty of rules must not be exaggerated, that legal principles are the means by which creativity is introduced in legal reasoning and, finally, that legal procedures channel the potential legal innovations within the legal system.

4.2   The Pragmatist View on Political Experimentalism

Although Popper is known for his falsificationism this 'mechanical test' is only one possible methodological consequence that can be drawn from the impossibility of certainty ('methodological revisionism', Albert 2001). It is only one possible solution for the basically pragmatic problem of how to organize the inquiry or how to guide research in praxes so that it reflects the fallibility of knowledge (Albert 1998, 20). At least for the technological (and instrumental) knowledge of the know-how type, which in Popper's classification is pre-scientific, one can avoid the discussion of different concepts of truth that seem to be the controversial point with respect to scientific know-that. To this background, I argue, it is promising to introduce pragmatism as an approach that expands the experimental search for knowledge to the realm of politics and conceptualises politics as a discovery procedure that delineates the proper scope of government experimentally. Basically Popper's plea for experimentalism, too, relies on the three central features of pragmatism (Knight 2001, 30), namely *fallibilism* (*experimental* knowledge) and *anti-scepticism* (experimental *knowledge*), and is connected with an institutional *meliorism*: progress of our knowledge is possible dependent on the organization and institutional framework of the experimental process.

John Dewey's (1954, 33) classical exposition of the pragmatist approach to the delineation of the legitimate scope of government brilliantly depicts this experimental discovery:

> In concrete facts, in actual and concrete organization and structure, there is no form of state which can be said to be the best: not at least till history is ended, and one can survey all its varied forms. The formation of states must be an experimental process. The trial process may go on with diverse degrees of blindness and accident, and at the cost of unregulated procedures of cut and try, of fumbling and groping, without insight into what men are after or clear knowledge of a good state even when it is achieved. Or it may proceed more intelligently, because guided by knowledge of the conditions which must be fulfilled. But it is still experimental. And since conditions

of action and of inquiry and knowledge are always changing, the experiment must always be retried; the State must always be rediscovered.

Even if the experimental process is not 'blind' but 'guided by knowledge', the outcome with respect to the appropriate economic policy is not determined (Dewey 1954, 74):

> At one time and place a large measure of state activity may be indicated and at another time a policy of quiescence and *laissez-faire*. ... There is no antecedent universal proposition which can be laid down because of which the function of a state should be limited or should be expanded. Their scope is something to be critically and experimentally determined.

This is obviously not the kind of experimentalism Frank Knight ([1935] 1997, 343) criticized following a blatant misinterpretation of Dewey's intention: 'In an age of experimental science, he [the reformer] also rather typically advocates experimental procedure – with himself as experimenter and society as experimented upon'.[18] This criticism does not touch a concept that cannot imagine society as experimented *upon*, because the experiments are always internal, coming from *within* society. This view, however, provokes another critique. The pragmatist concept of the democratic society is that of a 'Great Community' (Dewey 1954, 143 ff.) and it is doubtful whether a complex society as a whole can reach the autonomy that prevails in communities. In Dewey's exposition of the discovery of the state the two concepts of input-legitimation and output-legitimation eventually collapse: the experience derived from the practical experiments directly flow into an ongoing discourse within the Great Community, leading easily to a consensus on a new and improved experimental design.

4.3 Competition and Cooperation in Markets and Politics: the 'Order of Actors'

Scrutinizing Dewey's idealization of democracy as an ongoing discourse and of society as an ever-cooperating community, must not lead to the conclusion that cooperation does not matter. With regard to the cultural evolution and to its most important mechanism – the competition of systems of rules – Hayek (1960, 37) makes the following important statement:

> The competition on which the process of selection rests must be understood in the widest sense. ... To think of it in contrast to co-operation or organization would be to misconceive its nature. The endeavour to achieve certain results by co-operation and organization is as much a part of competition as individual efforts. ... The relevant distinction is not between individual and group action but between conditions, on the one hand, in which alternative ways based on different views or practices may be

tried and conditions, on the other, in which one agency has the exclusive right and the power to prevent others from trying. It is only when such exclusive rights are conferred on the presumption of superior knowledge of particular individuals or groups that the process ceases to be experimental ....

This paragraph provokes the question whether the cooperative element only prevails in institutional competition. If this question is answered negatively – that is, if there is possibly an analogy between market competition and competition among rules – then a more fundamental problem arises for both kinds of competition. Given the importance of organization of actions and of voluntary cooperation one may ask what Hayek's theory of the spontaneous market order has to say about it.[19] Analysing organization and cooperation would mean to introduce a third layer in between the 'order of actions' and the 'system of rules': the order of actors.[20] 'Order of actors' can, in principle, mean two different things. It can refer to the intermediate level between individual actions (and their competitive order) and general rules or, within this intermediate level, the internal organization of entities like firms, governments or bureaucracies. The first meaning locates 'cooperation and organization' logically between autonomous individual action and heteronomous general rules, the second focuses on the governance rules that, as Hayek directly connects 'cooperation and organization' apparently need not be (only) the coercive 'rules of organizations'. Both dimensions are interrelated: in order to understand the action of corporate actors one needs to know the internal governance structure. To the extent that corporate actions show peculiarities, it is necessary to introduce an intermediate level. Then it is impossible to reduce the 'society of organizations' (Ladeur 1997, 190) to a 'society of individuals' (Elias [1939] 1991) (and an order of individual actions). Hayek (1988, 37) notes that 'as the overall spontaneous order expands, so the sizes of the units of which it consists grow. Increasingly, its elements will not be economies of individuals, but of such organizations as firms and associations, as well as of administrative bodies', but it is debatable whether the difference between the elements is only one of size.

Concerning the internal governance structure the vast literature on the theory of the firm can be used to fill the gap – as far as the underlying theory is compatible with Hayek's evolutionary approach.[21] The same caveat applies to the Public Choice literature that analyses bureaucracy and government.[22]

Interestingly, a deeper analysis of the cooperative element in competition for a knowledge-based economy has been advocated by Helmstaedter (2000, 2001), who elaborates on the institutional implications of Hayek's cursory reference to the 'division of knowledge'. Helmstaedter points to the need for institutions that promote the cooperative sharing of knowledge. In a similar vein, recent contributions to innovation theory stress the importance of a cooperative element in R&D, because the process of invention regularly exceeds the boundaries of a single firm (Hippel 1987). Both empirically and theoretically it has paid special attention to the role of informal networks for the generation of such 'collective inventions' (Silverberg 1990).

4.4 The New Pragmatism of Firms and Political Design

An important contribution to network analysis has been made in the spirit of pragmatism, describing the innovative process within a firm (as a network of working teams) or within a network of firms as 'pragmatic method of economic coordination' (Sabel 1994, 1997). According to Sabel firms often 'operate on pragmatist, not principal–agent principles. Instead of trying to resolve ambiguity by creating clear goals (the province of the principal) and clear roles for achieving them (the responsibilities of the agent), these firms accept that ends and means are mutually defining' (Sabel 2001, 124).[23] Benchmarking, simultaneous engineering or targeting are seen as mechanisms of 'disciplined comparison' in a process of 'learning by monitoring' (Sabel 1997, 124 f.).

The 'New Pragmatism of Firms' (Sabel 1997) has inspired a reformulation of the pragmatic theory of democracy that avoids the idealization of democratic discourse and fills the institutional vacuum that surrounded it in Dewey's depiction. This approach, for which the notion 'democratic experimentalism' was coined. seeks to make more precise proposals for the organization of the experimental process of 'rediscovering the state' and is, I argue, a promising approach for the never-ending task of the management of complex economic phenomena in 'real time' (Dixit 1996).[24] In other words: for an evolutionary economic policy.

The basic idea is again to establish an order of actors that allows innovation and learning not in contrast to but *by* monitoring. A 'design through learning-by-monitoring provides a model for public rule making when the solution to collective problems can only be found by experiment' (Sabel 1997, 140). The intermediate character of this form of governance – between autonomy and heteronomy – as well as the modifications of informal networks with respect to public and political problem-solving are characterized as follows (Sabel 2001, 123):

> The role of the administrative centre in this experimentalist democracy is not to set rules and police compliance. Rather, with local units, it defines broad projects and fixes provisional general standards. In addition, it provides infrastructure by which local units can achieve their own goals, and pools measurements of performance to allow refinement of the general standards as well as the particular local strategies in the light of the results. The resulting organisation is neither a formal bureaucracy nor an informal network, yet it combines the capacities for super-local learning characteristic of the former with the access to local knowledge characteristic of the latter.

Summarizing, this model makes use of local units as 'laboratories' like in laboratory federalism and interjurisdictional competition, but does not leave the division of knowledge that ensues only to coordination in a competitive process or to voluntary learning, because both mechanisms are limited in their workability. With respect to interjurisdictional competition it has often been remarked that the limited mobility of factors together with the territorial 'bundling' of institutions sets limits to the workability of competition (Vanberg and Kerber 1994; Wohlgemuth 1995). Empirical studies of voluntary mutual learning among the different local units in a federal system and between local units and the federal level also point to some substantial limitations of workability (Oates 1999, 1133).

As the proof of the cake, ultimately, is in the eating, it is interesting that there is indeed a tendency towards democratic experimentalist models within nation states (and their federalist structure) as well as among nations (that is within interjurisdictional competition). Beside the examples presented by Sabel (2001) (as school reform in the US or administrative reform in the Whitehall countries) or the US welfare reform of 1996, recent modifications in the German social security system, especially in health care, can be interpreted as a first, albeit modest step towards a decentralized 'learning' system (Okruch 2001). On the supranational level there is a remarkable trend towards learning by monitoring models in the European Union. The Luxembourg, Cardiff and Cologne processes, which all function with the central instrument of benchmarking/best practice, are relevant for a broad and constantly expanding range of economic policies with special emphasis on social policy and the labour market (Hodson and Maher 2001).

5. CONCLUSION

I have argued that ordoliberal and Hayekian answers to the question of legitimate economic policy for a complex and dynamic economy point to the central knowledge dimension inherent in the governance of an evolving system. The formal solutions for the knowledge problem, however, are based on assumptions that are problematic both from the perspective of evolutionary economics and legal theory. As the procedural solutions, that is the legitimation of institutional choice and the legitimation of institutional change, ultimately encapsulate the idea of institutional experiments, the meaning of social experiments has been further elaborated, referring to Popper's piecemeal experiments and to the pragmatist view on experimental inquiry. I argue that political experimentalism, especially in its recent 'New Pragmatist' form, is a promising contribution to an evolutionary economic policy that has to consider the use of knowledge, the fallibility and fragmentarity of governance knowledge and the opportunity for policy learning. As the pragmatist 'democratic experimentalism' focuses on the organization of the political process so that 'learning by monitoring' is possible, it reveals an intermediate level, the order of actors, as an important dimension for political intervention that has been neglected with the Hayekian dichotomy of actions and rules. The idea of a disciplined experimentalism thereby re-opens the horizon of economic policy beyond Hayek's 'impossibility theorem'.

NOTES

1. This dilemma can be resolved on a constitutional (meta-) level by proposing an institutional design 'so that politicians who seek to serve "public interest" can survive and prosper' (Buchanan, 1993). This, however, provokes the question of how to establish the superior constitution within the existing political structures. This problem of 'self-reference' (Witt, 1992) can only be avoided by referring to the rare 'constitutional moments' in the course of 'constitutional revolutions' (Buchanan, 1975; Brennan and Buchanan, 1985).
2. Slembeck (in this volume) analyses the interplay of both form and content in a cognitive-evolutionary framework.
3. The metaphor of the 'marketplace for ideas' goes back to a dissenting vote of Judge Holmes (1992, p. 320) concerning freedom of speech: 'the ultimate good desired is better reached by free trade in ideas – that the best test of truth is the power of the thought to get itself accepted in the competition of the market. ... It is an experiment, as all life is an experiment'.
4. Wohlgemuth (2001, p. 214) explicitly compares 'Hayekian and ordoliberal *Ordnungstheorie*'. For a detailed discussion of the common ground and the major differences of both concepts compare Streit and Wohlgemuth (2000).
5. For a description of Eucken's concept of complete competition in contrast to the strict notion of perfect competition and for a summary of the principles of the competitive market order, see Streit and Wohlgemuth (2000, p. 231); Gerber (1998, p. 248).
6. Hayek apparently alludes to Holmes's (1992, 163) famous sentence, which is often conceived as describing the programme of legal realism: 'The prophecies of what the courts will do in fact, and nothing more pretentious, are what I mean by the law'. Whether Hayek's legal theory is compatible with legal realism is, however, debatable.
7. Mantzavinos (1994) offers an excellent survey on German *Wettbewerbstheorie*, see for a short summary Mantzavinos (2001, 191).
8. As Eucken ([1952] 1990, 27) notes, laissez-faire was equally convinced of having 'finally discovered the one and only right, natural and divine order' (translation by author).
9. 'An end-state doctrine ... supposes that a particular pattern or form of economic or social organization is desirable on ethical or metaphysical grounds and that it may be imposed. Thus whereas procedural or process theory directs attention towards how things come about, end-state theory tries to demonstrate the intrinsic desirability of things as they are, or could be'; (Barry 1989, 112).
10. 'General propositions do not decide concrete cases' (Holmes 1992, 306). A principle 'states a reason that argues in one direction, but does not necessitate a particular decision' (Dworkin 1996, 26).
11. Hayek (1960, 109) points out that '[i]t in its dynamic, rather than in its static, aspects that the value of democracy lies', that is 'democracy is the only effective method of educating the majority'. Wohlgemuth (in this volume) gives a lucid account of Hayek's theory of democracy.
12. Scharpf (1999, 11) characterizes output-legitimation as 'government for the people' that derives legitimacy from its capacity to solve problems requiring collective solutions.
13. See for an evolutionary theory of institutional competition Vihanto (1992), Vanberg and Kerber (1994), Wohlgemuth (1995). Compare Voigt (1999, 182) for a short summary of the competing views on institutional competition.

14. Compare Dye (1990), Oates (1999).
15. See especially the concept of 'functional overlapping competing jurisdictions' advocated by Frey (1996) and Frey and Eichenberger (1996).
16. Hayek (1967, 7) argues that 'the problem will not be whether the model as such is true, but whether it is applicable (or true *of*) the phenomena it is meant to explain'. Concerning the applicability of patterns he further notes '[t]he selection and application of the appropriate theoretical scheme thus becomes something of an art where success or failure cannot be ascertained by any mechanical test'.
17. Loasby (2000, 307) argues: 'Without variation there is no experience to act as a basis for learning; without a stable framework there is no assurance that any valid connections can be made between actions and outcomes that will have any future relevance'.
18. In a footnote Knight adds: 'every democratic country has been flooded, especially during the depression period, with propaganda of innumerable kinds as contradictory among themselves as most of them are foolish from any sound critical standpoint. (Among the worst in America is that put out over the signature of Professor John Dewey ...)'.
19. Compare Foss (1998): 'It has often been observed that Austrian economics does not feature a theory of the firm. ... Austrians have next to nothing to say about pricing, buyer–seller relations, vertical integration and other aspects of economic organization; in other words, one of the most important constituent mechanisms of the market process, namely firm behaviour, is simply not theorized in Austrian economics'.
20. Pelikan (in this volume) theorizes the issue of organizations as economic agents and conceptualizes the economy as 'an organization of organizations'.
21. See for an extensive survey Foss (2000).
22. Wohlgemuth's article (in this volume) is obviously a contribution to the burgeoning field evolutionary Public Choice.
23. Sabel (1997, 124) introduces pragmatisms as 'at bottom a theory of the relation between means and ends, where ends take the place of theory in practical reason, means the place of practice, and their relation, again as in practical reason, is one of reciprocal or mutual causality as a consequence, in turn, of the ambiguities of each. In pragmatism it is only in pursuing our ends, be they projects of administrative reform or efforts to explain the natural world, that we come to understand the implications of the original goal or idea; and this experimental understanding furnishes the knowledge with which we revise or abandon that first declaration of intent, and set the stage for further experimentation'.
24. Dixit (1996, 19) analyses the 'policy process in "real time"', characterizing 'economic policymaking is a dynamic game, whose conditions are uncertain and changing, and whose rules are at least partially made by the participants as they go along' (ibid., 30).

REFERENCES

Albert, Hans (1998), 'Pragmatismus und kritischer Rationalismus: Zur Rolle pragmatischer Tendenzen im modernen Denken', in Volker Gadenne (ed.), *Kritischer Rationalismus und Pragmatismus*, Amsterdam/Atlanta: Rodopi, pp. 19–36.
Albert, Hans (2001), 'Zum Problem einer adaequaten sozialen Ordnung', in Hans G. Nutzinger (ed.), *Zum Problem der sozialen Ordnung: Beitraege zur Ehrenpromotionsfeier von Hans Albert an der Universitaet Gh Kassel*, Marburg: Metropolis, pp. 23–34.
Alexy, Robert (1996), *Theorie der Grundrechte*, Frankfurt/Main: Suhrkamp.
Barry, Norman P. (1989), 'Political and economic thought of German neo-liberals', in Alan Peacock and Hans Willgerodt (eds), *German Neo-Liberals and the Social Market Economy*, Basingstoke: Macmillan, pp. 105–24.

Blaug, Mark (1998), *The Disease of Formalism in Economics, or Bad Games That Economists Play*, Jena: Max-Planck-Institute for Research into Economic Systems (Lectiones Jenenses/Jena Lectures, vol. 16).

Brennan, Geoffrey and James M. Buchanan (1985), *The Reason of Rules: Constitutional Political Economy*, Cambridge: Cambridge University Press.

Buchanan, James M. (1975), *The Limits of Liberty: Between Anarchy and Leviathan*, Chicago/London: University of Chicago Press.

Buchanan, James M. (1993), 'How can constitutions be designed so that politicians who seek to serve "public interest" can survive and prosper?', *Constitutional Political Economy*, 4 (1), 1–6.

Budzinski, Oliver (2000), *Wirtschaftspolitische Implikationen evolutorischer Ordnungsoekonomik. Das Beispiel ordnungskonformer öekologischer Wirtschaftspolitik*, Marburg: Metropolis.

Cassidy, John (1996), 'The decline of economics', in *The New Yorker* (December 2, 1996), pp. 50–60.

Dewey, John (1954), *The Public and Its Problems*, Denver: Alan Swallow.

Dixit, Avinash K. (1996), *The Making of Economic Policy: A Transaction-Cost Politics Perspective*, Cambridge, US/London: The MIT Press.

Dworkin, Ronald (1996), *Taking Rights Seriously*, 8. impr. (new impression with a reply to critics), London: Duckworth.

Dye, Thomas R. (1990), *American Federalism: Competition Among Governments*, Lexington: Lexington Books.

Elias, Norbert ([1939] 1991), 'Die Gesellschaft der Individuen', in Norbert Elias, *Die Gesellschaft der Individuen*, Frankfurt/Main: Suhrkamp, pp. 15–98.

Eucken, Walter (1938), 'Die Üeberwindung des Historismus', *Schmollers Jahrbuch*, 62, 191–214.

Eucken, Walter (1948), 'On the theory of the centrally administered economy: an analysis of the German experiment', *Economica*, 15 (58/59), part I: 79–100, part II: 173–93.

Eucken, Walter ([1952] 1990), *Grundsaetze der Wirtschaftspolitik*, 6th ed., Tuebingen: Mohr Siebeck.

Eucken, Walter (1952), *This Unsuccessful Age, or The Pains of Economic Progress*, Oxford/New York: Oxford University Press.

Fernandez, Raquel and Dani Rodrik (1991), 'Resistance to reform: status quo bias in the presence of individual-specific uncertainty', *American Economic Review*, 81, 1146–55.

Foss, Nicolai J. (1998), 'Austrian and Post-Marshallian Economics: the bridging work of George Richardson', in Nicolai J. Foss and Brian J. Loasby (eds), *Economic Organization, Capabilities and Co-Ordination: Essays in Honour of G.B. Richardson*, London/New York: Routledge, pp. 138–62.

Foss, Nicolai J. (ed.) (2000), *The Theory of the Firm: Critical perspectives on business and management*, London/New York: Routledge.

Frey, Bruno S. (1996), 'A directly democratic and federal Europe', *Constitutional Political Economy*, 7, 267–79.

Frey, Bruno S. (2000), 'Was bewirkt die Volkswirtschaftslehre?', *Perspektiven der Wirtschaftspolitik*, 1, 5–33.

Frey, Bruno S. and Reiner Eichenberger (1996), 'FOCJ: competitive governments for Europe', *International Review of Law and Economics*, 16, 315–27.

Gerber, David J. (1998), *Law and Competition in Twentieth Century Europe: Protecting Prometheus*, Oxford: Clarendon Press.

Hayek, Friedrich A. ([1949] 1976), *Individualism and Economic Order*, London/Henley: Routledge & Kegan.

Hayek, Friedrich A. (1960), *The Constitution of Liberty*, London: Routledge & Kegan.

Hayek, Friedrich A. (1967), *Studies in Philosophy, Politics and Economics*, Chicago: University of Chicago Press.

Hayek, Friedrich A. (1973), *Law, Legislation and Liberty: A new statement of the liberal principles of justice and political economy, vol. I: Rules and Order*, London: Routledge & Kegan.

Hayek, Friedrich A. (1976), *Law, Legislation and Liberty: A new statement of the liberal principles of justice and political economy, vol. II: The Mirage of Social Justice*, London: Routledge & Kegan.

Hayek, Friedrich A. (1978), *New Studies in Philosophy, Politics, Economics and the History of Ideas*, London/Henley: Routledge & Kegan.

Hayek, Friedrich A. (1988), *The Fatal Conceit: The Errors of Socialism*, Chicago: University of Chicago Press.

Hegmann, Horst (2001), *Die Verfassung einer kulturell fragmentierten Gesellschaft: Zur wissenssoziologischen Grundlegung eines verfassungsoekonomisch formulierten Sozialvertrags*, Marburg: Metropolis.

Heinemann, Friedrich (2000), *Die Psychologie irrationaler Wirtschaftspolitik am Beispiel des Reformstaus*, ZEW-Diskussionspapier, March 2000.

Helmstaedter, Ernst (2000), 'Arbeitsteilung und Wissensteilung – Zur Institutionenoekonomik der Wissensgesellschaft', in Hans G. Nutzinger and Martin Held (eds), *Geteilte Arbeit und ganzer Mensch: Perspektiven der Arbeitsgesellschaft*, Frankfurt/New York: Campus, pp. 118–41.

Helmstaedter, Ernst (2001), 'Wissensteilung: Thüenen-Vorlesung bei der Jahrestagung 2000 des Vereins füer Socialpolitik, Berlin 20. September 2000', *Perspektiven der Wirtschaftspolitik*, **2**, 445–65.

Hesse, Guenter (1979), *Staatsaufgaben: Zur Theorie der Legitimation und Identifikation staatlicher Aufgaben*, Baden-Baden: Nomos.

Heuss, Ernst (1965), *Allgemeine Markttheorie*, Tuebingen.

Hippel, Eric von (1987), 'Cooperation between rivals: informal know-how trading', *Research Policy*, **16**, 291–302.

Hodson, Dermot and Imelda Maher (2001), 'The open method as a new mode of governance: the case of soft economic policy co-ordination', *Journal of Common Market Studies*, **39**, 719–46.

Holmes, Oliver W. (1992), *The Essential Holmes*, ed. by Richard A. Posner, Chicago/London: The University of Chicago Press.

Homann, Karl (1985), 'Legitimation und Verfassungsstaat – vertragstheoretische Interpretation der Demokratie', *Jahrbuch füer Neue Politische Öekonomie*, **4**, 48–72.

Kahneman, Daniel, Jack L. Knetsch and Richard H. Thaler (1991), 'Anomalies, the endowment effect, loss aversion and status quo bias', *Journal of Economic Perspectives*, **5**, 193–206.

Kerber, Wolfgang (1997), 'Wettbewerb als Hypothesentest: Eine evolutorische Konzeption wissenschaffenden Wettbewerbs', in Karl von Delhaes and Ulrich Fehl (eds), *Dimensionen des Wettbewerbs: Seine Rolle in der Entstehung und Ausgestaltung von Wirtschaftsordnungen*, Stuttgart: Lucius & Lucius, pp. 29–78.

Knight, Frank H. (1935), *The Ethics of Competition*, Transaction edition with a new introduction by Richard Boyd (1997), New Brunswick/London: Transaction Publishers.

Knight, Jack (2001), 'A pragmatist approach to the proper scope of government', *Journal of Institutional and Theoretical Economics*, **157**, 28–48.

Koch, Lambert T. (1996), *Evolutorische Wirtschaftspolitik: Eine elementare Analyse mit entwicklungspolitischen Beispielen*, Tuebingen: Mohr Siebeck.

Kuhn, Thomas S. (1996), *The Structure of Scientific Revolutions*, 3rd ed., Chicago/London: University of Chicago Press.

Ladeur, Karl-Heinz (1997), 'The liberal legal order and the rise of economic organizations – towards a legal theory of proceduralization', in Karl-Heinz Ladeur (ed.), *Liberal Institutions, Economic Constitutional Rights, and the Role of Organizations*, Baden-Baden: Nomos, pp. 169–99.

Loasby, Brian J. (2000), 'Market institutions and economic evolution', *Journal of Evolutionary Economics*, **10**, 297–309.

Mantzavinos, Chrysostomos (1994), *Wettbewerbtheorie: Eine kritische Auseinandersetzung*, Berlin: Duncker & Humblot.

Mantzavinos, Chrysostomos (2001), *Individuals, Institutions, and Markets*, Cambridge etc.: Cambridge University Press.

Metcalfe, J. Stan (1995), 'The economic foundation of technology policy: equilibrium and evolutionary perspectives', in Paul Stoneman (ed.), *Handbook of the Economics of Innovation and Technological Change*, Oxford: Blackwell, pp. 409–512.

Metcalfe, J. Stan and Georghiou, Luke (1997), *Equilibrium and Evolutionary Foundations of Technology Policy*, CRIC Discussion Paper, Manchester.

North, Douglass C. (1990), *Institutions, Institutional Change and Economic Performance*, Cambridge: Cambridge University Press.

North, Douglass C. (1999), 'Hayek's contribution to understanding the process of economic change', in Viktor Vanberg (ed.), *Freiheit, Wettbewerb und Wirtschaftsordnung: Hommage zum 100. Geburtstag von Friedrich A. von Hayek*, Freiburg/Berlin/Munich, pp. 79–96.

Oates, Wallace E. (1999), 'An essay on fiscal federalism', *Journal of Economic Literature*, **37**, 1120–49.

Oates, Wallace E. (2001), 'Fiscal competition and the European Union: contrasting perspectives', *Regional Science and Urban Economics*, **31**, 133–45.

Okruch, Stefan (1999), *Innovation und Diffusion von Normen: Grundlagen und Elemente einer evolutorischen Theorie des Institutionenwandels*, Berlin: Duncker & Humblot.

Okruch, Stefan (2001), 'Der Richter als Institution einer spontanen Ordnung: einige kritische Bemerkungen zu einer zentralfigur in Hayeks Theorie der kulturellen Evolution', *ORDO: Jahrbuch fuer die Ordnung von Wirtschaft und Gesellschaft*, **52**, 131–53.

Ormerod, Paul (1994), *The Death of Economics*, London: Faber & Faber.

Perelman, Michael (1996), *The End of Economics*, London: Routledge.

Popper, Karl R. ([1961] 1976), *The Poverty of Historicism*, London/Henley: Routledge & Kegan.

Rabin, Matthew (1998), 'Psychology and economics', *Journal of Economic Literature*, **36**, 11–46.

Ryle, Gilbert (1949), *The Concept of Mind*, London: Penguin Books.

Sabel, Charles F. (1994), 'Learning by monitoring: The institutions of economic development', in Neil J. Smelser and Richard Swedberg (eds), *The Handbook of Economic Sociology*, Princeton/New York: Princeton University Press/Russell Sage Foundation, pp. 137–65.

Sabel, Charles F. (1997), 'Design, Deliberation, and Democracy: On the New Pragmatism of Firms and Public Institutions', in Karl-Heinz Ladeur (ed.), *Liberal*

Institutions, Economic Constitutional Rights, and the Role of Organizations, Baden-Baden: Nomos, pp. 101–49.

Sabel, Charles F. (2001), 'A Quiet Revolution of Democratic Governance: Towards Democratic Experimentalism', in OECD (ed.), *Governance in the 21st Century*, Paris, pp. 121–48.

Scharpf, Fritz W. (1999), *Governing in Europe: Effective and Democratic?*, Oxford/New York: Oxford University Press.

Silverberg, Gerald (1990), 'Adoption and diffusion of technology as a collective evolutionary process', in Christopher Freeman and Luc Soete (eds), *New Explorations in the Economics of Technical Change*, London: Pinter, pp. 177–92.

Steiner, Joseph M. (1976), 'Judicial discretion and the concept of law', *Cambridge Law Journal*, **35**, 135–57.

Streit, Manfred E. and Michael Wohlgemuth (2000), 'The market economy and the state: Hayekian and ordoliberal conceptions', in Peter Koslowski (ed.), *The Theory of Capitalism in the German Economic Tradition: Historism, Ordo-Liberalism, Critical Theory, Solidarism*, Berlin etc.: Springer, pp. 224–69.

Trute, Hans-Heinrich (1996), 'Wechselseitige Verzahnung zwischen Privatrecht und öeffentlichem Recht', in Wolfgang Hoffmann-Riem and Eberhard Schmidt-Aßmann (eds), *Öeffentliches Recht und Privatrecht als wechselseitige Auffangordnungen*, Baden-Baden: Nomos. pp. 167–223.

Vanberg, Viktor (1986), 'Spontaneous market order and social rules: a critical examination of F.A. Hayek's Theory of Cultural Evolution', *Economics and Philosophy*, **2**, 75–100.

Vanberg, Viktor (1988), '"Ordnungstheorie" as constitutional economics – the German conception of a "social market economy"', *ORDO: Jahrbuch füer die Ordnung von Wirtschaft und Gesellschaft*, **39**, 17–30.

Vanberg, Viktor (1994), 'Individual choice and institutional constraints: the normative element in classical and contractarian liberalism', in Viktor Vanberg (ed.), *Rules and Choice in Economics*, London/New York: Routledge, pp. 208–34.

Vanberg, Viktor (1997), 'Die normativen Grundlagen der Ordnungspolitik', *ORDO: Jahrbuch füer die Ordnung von Wirtschaft und Gesellschaft*, **48**, 707–26.

Vanberg, Viktor and James M. Buchanan (1994a), 'Interests and theories in constitutional choice', in Viktor Vanberg (ed.), *Rules and Choice in Economics*, London/New York: Routledge, pp. 167–77.

Vanberg, Viktor and James M. Buchanan (1994b), 'Constitutional Choice, Rational Ignorance and the Limits of Reason', in Viktor Vanberg (ed.), *Rules and Choice in Economics*, London/New York: Routledge, pp. 178–91.

Vanberg Viktor and Wolfgang Kerber (1994), 'Institutional competition among jurisdictions: an evolutionary approach', *Constitutional Political Economy*, **5**, 193–219.

Vihanto, Martti (1992), 'Competition between local governments as a discovery procedure', *Journal of Institutional and Theoretical Economics*, **148**, 411–36.

Voigt, Stefan (1999), *Explaining Constitutional Change: A Positive Economics Approach*, Cheltenham, UK/Northampton, US: Edward Elgar.

Watkins, John W. (1992), 'Ideal Types and Historical Explanation', in John O'Neill (ed.), *Modes of Individualism and Collectivism*, reprint Aldershot: Gregg Revivals, pp. 143–65.

Wegner, Gerhard (1996), *Wirtschaftspolitik zwischen Selbst- und Fremdsteuerung – ein neuer Ansatz*, Baden-Baden: Nomos.

Wegner, Gerhard (1997), 'Economic policy from an evolutionary perspective – a new approach', *Journal of Institutional and Theoretical Economics*, **153**, 485–509.

Weinberger, Ota (1992), 'Oekonomismus im politischen Denken', in Ota Weinberger and M. Fischer (eds), *Demokratie und Rationalitaet: Internationales Jahrbuch fuer Rechtsphilosophie und Gesetzgebung*, Wien: Manz pp. 259–76.

Weizsäecker, Carl C. v. (2000), 'Üeber die Schlußpassage der *General Theory* – Gedanken zum Einfluß Öekonomischer Theorie auf die Politik', *Perspektiven der Wirtschaftspolitik*, **1**, 35–52.

Witt, Ulrich (1992), 'The endogenous public choice theorist', *Public Choice*, **73**, 117–29.

Wohlgemuth, Michael (1995), 'Economic and political competition in neoclassical and evolutionary perspective', *Constitutional Political Economy*, **6**, 71–96.

Wohlgemuth, Michael (2001), 'The Present Relevance of *Ordnungstheorie* for the Politics and the Economics of the Social Order', in Agnès Labrousse and Jean-Daniel Weisz (eds), *Institutional Economics in France and Germany: German Ordoliberalism versus the French Regulation School*, Berlin etc.: Springer, pp. 200–243.

Zumbansen, Peer (2000), *Ordnungsmuster im modernen Wohlfahrtsstaat: Lernerfahrungen zwischen Staat, Gesellschaft und Vertrag*, Baden-Baden: Nomos.

5. Democracy as an evolutionary method

Michael Wohlgemuth

1. INTRODUCTION

> The insights offered by some of the analyses of spontaneous order that occurs outside
> of equilibrium settings may prove useful in applications to politics as well as to
> economics. (James M. Buchanan 1993, 70)

Economic theories of politics are mostly static. This is most obvious for theories
of democracy such as spatial voting models in the Downsian tradition which
view politics as an equilibrium state, with voter preferences readily distributed
over a given issue-space and vote-maximising parties passively adapting to
these given conditions. Similarly, models in the Arrowian Social Choice
tradition view democracy as a mechanism that is to aggregate given preferences as consistently and permanently as possible, thus guaranteeing the
satisfaction of given majority preferences.

These models are able to highlight some important aspects of public choice.
But they face grave difficulties in accounting for the most important aspects of
the democratic process.[1] The latter include interactive processes that lead to
the creation and change of political opinions, and the creation and selection of
political problem solutions. Accounting for these aspects of democracy should
not only provide a more accurate representation of political processes. It should
also lead to a more convincing account of democracy as a valuable method if
compared to realistic political alternatives, while still being a rather deficient
method for the discovery and social use of knowledge if compared to evolutionary market processes.

The aim of this chapter is to show that, combining various contributions to
evolutionary, institutional and Austrian economics, these issues can be
addressed.

In Section 2, different views of the meaning of democracy are discussed. As
an illustration, Arrow's view of democracy as a mechanism for the aggregation
of given preferences on given issues is contrasted with Hayek's view of
democracy as a process of forming opinions.

In Section 3, political competition is described as a compound of two interactive processes: a process involving political entrepreneurs who compete for

citizens' attention, compliance and, finally, votes and a process involving voters who select among political alternatives. While on this abstract level, the model resembles the general structure of evolutionary market processes, fundamental differences between market competition and political competition are quite obvious. Their effects on the evolutionary potential of democratic systems are analysed in Sections 4 and 5.

Section 4 focuses on elections' lack of convincing equivalents to voluntary market exchange. Under these conditions low incentives to acquire knowledge and to invest in co-operative efforts, and problems allocating resources to competent users, are to be expected as comparative shortcomings of political methods of co-ordination.

Section 5 focuses on processes of political rivalry, which also display important differences to market competition – although basic similarities in terms of rivalry, rewards and repercussions exist. The effective realm of political rivalry is, however, largely reduced to the periodic 'competition for the field' of an essentially monopolistic provision of political goods. Under these conditions opportunities to learn are restricted to a consecutive (instead of parallel) testing of single bundles of (instead of various independent) potential problem solutions. In addition, several barriers to entry prevent political entrepreneurs from acting like capitalist entrepreneurs as prime movers of progress. And finally, political innovation as such by no ways warrants political 'progress'.

The above arguments refer to democracy as compared to capitalistic market processes. Compared to realistic alternatives of political organisation, however, important advantages of democracy can be shown when using an evolutionary approach. In Section 6 it is argued that democracies provide better protection of freedom of expression which, in turn, allows political information to travel faster and wider, thus enhancing the scope for knowledge creation. In addition, competitive elections create valuable incentives for politicians and citizens to supply and demand information about alternative political problem solutions. It is concluded that democracy can be analysed and appreciated as a special kind of discovery procedure.

Section 7 gives a summary of the methodological and political conclusions and an outlook for further research.

2.   DEMOCRACY AS A METHOD

Schumpeter is commonly regarded a precursor of the economics of democracy and of evolutionary economics. How far such claims are justified remains a debatable issue that cannot be taken up here.[2] Suffice to mention that Schumpeter's ([1942] 1987) 'another theory of democracy' is not, as may be expected, much of an evolutionary economic theory of democracy. Apart from stressing the role of leadership, he does not apply his 'theory of economic development' ([1912] 1934) to the realm of democratic decision making. In fact, he uses sociological and psychological, rather than an economic approaches, trying to demystify the democratic ideal. Some of his arguments will be used later in this chapter. At this stage, Schumpeter's definition of democracy may serve as a starting point:

> the democratic method is that institutional arrangement for arriving at political decisions in which individuals acquire the power to decide by means of a competitive struggle for the people's vote. (Schumpeter [1942] 1987, 269)

While most scholars in the economics of politics would have no problem accepting this definition so far, differences arise in how far 'institutional arrangements' of democratic systems are really accounted for and how the 'competitive struggle' is being perceived. It is mostly in the latter respect that traditional disagreements between static-neoclassical and evolutionary views reappear in the field of respective theories of democracy (see Wohlgemuth 2002).

2.1   The Static and the Dynamic View: Arrow vs. Hayek

Neoclassical economics and with it mainstream Public Choice concentrate on a representative agent's logic of maximising utility subject to given preferences. Its construction manuals forced many model builders to reduce economic and political competition in the same way to pure aggregation mechanisms, each being, as Arrow (1951, 2) put it, a 'procedure for passing from a set of known individual tastes to a pattern of social decision-making'. There could hardly be a more radical contrast to Hayek's understanding of competition as a procedure for the discovery of such preferences, knowledge and abilities 'as, without resort to it, would not be known to anyone, or at least would not be utilised' (Hayek [1968] 1978, 179). This is obvious for both authors' view of the market order. But the same opposing views reappear in an Arrowian and Hayekian understanding of the meaning of democracy.

   In an Arrowian perspective (and in large parts of mainstream Public Choice) democracy is assessed according to its ability to work as an aggregation-mechanism which transforms given preferences into a collective 'will' or social welfare function. Especially Arrow's 'impossibility theorem' (Arrow 1951) has induced some of the most ingenious thinkers to discuss the virtues of democracy predominantly under the spell of logical puzzles within a closed static system in which there was no room for purposeful human action, social interaction or the creation of novelty. These aspects of the democratic process are also kept from view if the pure logic of choice is applied to locational equilibria of party positions within a given issue space, along which given and known voter preferences are assumed to align themselves.

The political philosophies of Hayek or Popper and the theoretical work of Boulding and Kuran lead to very different questions. The virtue of democracy is here predominantly assessed according to its ability to serve as a rule-guided procedure for the formation, discovery and testing of opinions and conjectural problem-solutions. Thus, for Popper ([1945] 1966) the distinguishing features of a good system of government cannot be judged according to preconceived end states of maximised happiness or welfare. Rather, they depend on institutions and processes that allow for open criticism and thus, as a political analogue to scientific conjectures and refutations, lead to the articulation of alternatives and the peaceful replacement of bad rulers. In a similar vein, Hayek (1960, 108f.) argues:

> Democracy is, above all, a process of forming opinion . ... It is in its dynamic, rather than in its static, aspects that the value of democracy proves itself . ... The ideal of democracy rests on the belief that the view which will direct government emerges from an independent and spontaneous process. It requires, therefore, the existence of a large sphere independent of majority control in which the opinions of the individuals are formed.

These dynamic aspects of democracy can be summarised as three major propositions, all of which entail strong differences to the neoclassical perspective: (1) political preferences and opinions build on fallible conjectures and theories; (2) democratic opinion-formation results from an open-ended process of interactive learning and discovery: (3) the important element in this process is not the supremacy, but the contestability of current majority opinions.

2.2 The Micro-level: from Tastes to Opinions

As Vanberg and Buchanan (1989, 50) pointed out, preferences depend on interests in results (what one wants) as well as on theories about the effects of certain actions (what one thinks). After all, 'man is a "theoretical animal", an animal. fabricating, adopting, and using "theories" that are effective in action' (Albert 1979, 23). The combination of idiosyncratic, subjective tastes and interests with equally subjective, but fallible and possibly erroneous expectations or theories, holds for preferences for economic as well as for political alternatives.[3]

In some respects the creation of political preferences relies even more strongly on theories. Preferences for daily consumption-goods (food, clothes, leisure activities) can mostly be a matter of taste, unreflective and not affording much justification (*de gustibus* ...). The formation of political preferences, however, cannot dispense with 'speculative or explanatory views which people have formed about ... society or the economic system, capitalism or imperialism, and other such collective entities, which the social scientist must regard as no more than provisional theories' (Hayek [1952] 1979, 64). The citizen who wishes to express a political opinion does this with reference to some conjectures about cause and effect (however inappropriate they may seem to 'expert' observers). Some form of more or less reasoned expectations is needed to justify expressed political preferences. A citizen may use his narrow self-interest or some broader understanding of a common weal as guidelines for what he wants – in both cases her preferences concerning political alternatives (candidates, parties, laws, regulations) rely on theories or conjectures about the suitability of these alternatives to serve these respective interests. Political preference formation is thus predominantly conjectural theory formation.

This is most important when the static view on the aggregation of pure preferences (or tastes) is abandoned in favour of a dynamic view on the creation and change of opinions (tastes *and* theories). The doctrine which Boulding (1970, 118) called the 'Immaculate Conception of the indifference curve' is a major barrier in the way of an adequate account of democracy as an opinion-building process, where 'by far and away the greater number of human preferences are learned, again by means of a mutation-selection process' (ibid.).

2.3   The Macro-level: Political Opinion Formation and Social Interaction

In the process of political communication, opinions are shaped above all through their conjectural components. To be sure, there is no implication that political opinions would result from meticulous and painstaking theory formation. This is most obvious in view of the weak incentives for the ordinary citizen-voter to think about political issues. The basic point has been made already by Schumpeter ([1942] 1987, 261):

> the private citizen musing over national affairs ... is a member of an unworkable committee, the committee of the whole nation, and this is why he expends less disciplined effort on mastering a political problem than he expends on a game of bridge. ... At the bridge table ... we are prevented from behaving irresponsibly because every mistake we make will not only immediately tell but also be immediately allocated to us. These conditions, by their failure to be fulfilled for the political behavior of the ordinary citizen, show why it is that in politics he lacks all the alertness and the judgement he may display in his profession.

Most people, however, do entertain some 'theoretical' ideas about how the world of politics works, and how it should work to make them better off. The major reasons for this can not be directly related to instrumental qualities of adequate voting. Rather, one would have to look at intrinsic and extrinsic incentives in terms of self-esteem and a reputation of having sound opinions. Hirschman (1989) presents these two reasons for having opinions as elements of individual well-being: 'not to have an opinion is tantamount to not having individuality, identity, character, self' (ibid., 75), and: 'vacillation, indifference, or weakly held opinions have long met with utmost contempt, while approval and admiration have been bestowed on firmness, fullness and articulateness of opinion' (ibid., 76). Hence, while the Downsian instrumental 'vote value' of making the right choice provides no incentives for citizens to elaborate on the theory-component of their political opinions, it is the 'reputational value' of having an opinion that motivates at least some learning about policy issues. As a consequence of the dominance of reputational utility in the sense of Kuran (1995),[4] the citizen is 'more dependent on society in political contexts than in the realm of ordinary consumption' (ibid., 162). This dependence, in turn, begs recognition that political opinions rest to a large extent 'on beliefs shaped by *public discourse*, which consists of the suppositions, facts, arguments, and the theories that are communicated publicly' (ibid., 18).

It is with these premises that the meaning of democracy as a knowledge-creating process can be established. As will be shown in more detail in Section 6, even if the ballot box *as such* provides poor incentives for voters to engage in political theory-building and poor signals about the content of citizens' political views, there are several reasons why democracy provides incentives for political opinion-formation which includes an interactive process of creation and change of individually held 'theoretical' views about political means, ends, and constraints:

- Freedom of speech, press and assembly are more effectively safeguarded in democratic societies than in most non-democratic ones; hence the openness of the process of opinion-formation for new and opposing views has a better institutional backing.
- Political entrepreneurs, in order to win elections, are forced to permanently engage in the creation of public issues, the formulation of alternatives, the rebuttal of critique and the 'selling' of plausible reasons for potential actions.
- As a consequence, citizens in democratic societies are more naturally confronted with different, often conflicting opinions than citizens in non-democratic societies; hence more people are compelled to form political opinions on pertinent issues if they want to avoid social isolation and a loss of self-esteem.

2.4 A Normative Conclusion: on the Role of Minority Opinions

In evolutionary economics, heterogeneity and variability of products or preferences are not regarded as imperfections but as elementary preconditions of social development. The same should be true for an evolutionary economics of democracy. The evolutionary theme could not be the construction and warranty of a consistent rule of the majority; it would have to be the contestability of current opinions and policies. In a straightforward critique of Arrow (1951), Buchanan (1954) quickly made the point that preference-aggregation aiming at unambiguously and permanently ruling majorities may be equivalent to an unambiguous and permanent exploitation of minorities. The majority principle, Buchanan argues, could only be a workable instrument of political control and knowledge-creation. if Arrow's 'problem' of cycling majorities does in fact occur:

> It serves to insure that competing alternatives may be experimentally and provisionally adopted, and replaced by new compromise alternatives approved by a majority group of ever changing composition. This is democratic choice process, whatever may be the consequences for welfare economics and social welfare functions. (Buchanan 1954, 119)

From an evolutionary perspective of the political process, therefore, democracy is not about the most exact, comprehensive and permanent realisation of given majority preferences. It is about the chances of minorities to change majoritarian views and practices (Hayek 1960, 109). The fact that new ideas necessarily start to emerge from minorities stresses the importance of giving entry opportunities to minority views to an extent which only prevails in democratic systems under the rule of law. This entails more than just universal expressive rights. It requires extended spheres of private autonomy and freedom to act, which allow groups to pursue different aims and test different practices as long as they do not violate the freedom of others to do so as well. Indeed the growth of civilisation depends on minorities' freedom to act:

> The conception that the efforts of all should be directed by the opinion of a majority or that society is better according as it conforms more to the standards of the majority is in fact a reversal of the principle by which civilisation has grown ... Advance consists in the few convincing the many. New views must appear somewhere before they can become majority views ... it is always from a minority acting in ways different from what the majority would prescribe that the majority in the end learns to do better. (Hayek 1960, 110)

Hayek himself, however, has not contributed much more than that to an evolutionary theory of democracy. But much of the democratic process can be analysed in terms of a theory of competition inspired by market process theory and evolutionary themes rather than neoclassical equilibrium logic. Our approach will provide strong reasons why the evolutionary potential of the democratic process must remain below that of market processes (Sections 4 and 5). However, an evolutionary view of democracy as a valuable method of opinion formation, experimentation and knowledge creation can still be established if it is compared to alternative methods of *political* co-ordination and control (Section 6).

3. A SIMPLE MODEL OF POLITICAL COMPETITION AS A PROCESS

Competition can be modelled as a compound of two interrelated processes, both of which depend in their thrust on the actors' incentives and willingness to incur transaction costs (Streit and Wegner 1989, 197). This general structure not only applies to market competition. It also describes political competition in a democracy, where one can distinguish a selection process (voters selecting among parties and candidates) and a process of rivalry (political rivals competing for attention and votes). Both economic and political selection processes create rivalry through gain-and-loss feedback. And in both cases, the intensity and quality of the processes of selection and entrepreneurial rivalry depend on information and skills that actors on both sides are willing to invest in (see Figure 5.1).

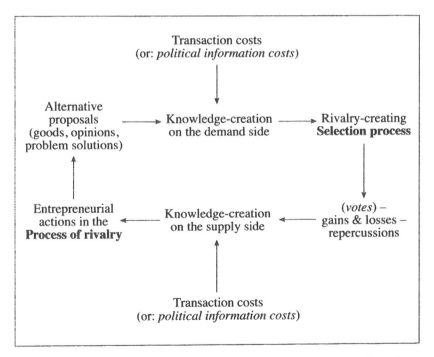

Figure 5.1 Competition as a feedback-driven interaction process (based on the model of Streit and Wegner 1989, 197)

Although political and economic competition share these very general similarities in structure, in their substance the respective processes of selection and rivalry differ dramatically. Political selection does not mean individual selection in the sense of a reciprocal exchange of property rights. It can only mean collective choice, which may occasionally change political leadership. Also, political rivalry does not involve producers of alternative political goods (laws and regulations) competing in the same jurisdiction at the same time. Both substantial differences limit the evolutionary potential of democracy as a method of competitive creation and selection of political problem solutions. These limitations will be discussed in the following two parts.

4. POLITICAL SELECTION WITHOUT MARKET EXCHANGE

The intensity of competitive selection processes depends critically upon the freedom of the actors on the demand side to choose, using their individual knowledge and pursuing their individual goals. General, open and secure rules allow an open range of alternatives to be substituted by an open range of actors, which is a major prerequisite of the knowledge-creating and power-restricting quality of competitive selection. In addition, the citizens' propensity to invest in transaction costs critically affects the intensity and quality of the selection processes (Streit and Wegner 1989, 194). The more substitutes with differing price–quality combinations can be chosen according to individual preferences and needs, the more are actors on the demand side exposed to high-powered incentives and opportunities to discover these differences and benefit through mutually advantageous transactions.

The spontaneous co-ordination of individual plans on the market is greatly supported by the price system in at least three important respects: (1) As a signalling device, it reflects changes in market conditions and supports the social use of local and temporal knowledge (information function, see Hayek 1945). (2) As a sanctioning device, it provides the feedback (profits and losses) that acts as an incentive for market actors to adapt to changed environments (control function) and to introduce new products and technologies (development function). (3) As a consequence, the price system supports a permanent reallocation of resources into uses that reflect changed preferences, scarcities and competence levels (allocation function).

Selection processes of *political* competition hardly provide convincing equivalents to these characteristics of open market processes. The exchange between voters and politicians provides no sufficient analogy to market transactions, in which personal preferences are not only revealed, but also satisfied through the voluntary exchange of property rights. As a consequence, one has to expect functional deficiencies of political selection processes in the following respects, to which we now turn:

(1) the creation, communication and use of information about citizens' opinions;
(2) the allocation of resources to competent users and
(3) the creation and use of potentials for voluntary co-operation.

4.1 Low Incentives and Opportunities to Acquire and Communicate Knowledge

A consumer of market goods only receives goods she actually demanded and for which she is willing to pay. A political subject receives a complete bundle of political goods and services, regardless of his personal preferences, demands or any form of reciprocal action. Note that the act of voting does not involve an act of exchange: the voter for the winning coalition, the voter for the losing party and the non-voter equally end up with the same election result. Not surprisingly, therefore, her incentives to search, store and interpret information on political offers (programmes, candidates), political products (laws, regulations) or political systems (rules of the game) are very low indeed. This lack of high-powered incentives for knowledge-creation on the political demand side reduces the ability of the political selection process to discover comparative qualities of political alternatives.

But this is only one reason why aggregated voter judgements do not reflect much of the contents and structures of political opinions (interests and views). Other reasons relate to the limited articulateness of the ballot itself. General elections do not *continuously* signal citizens' opinions on *particular goods and services*. They are only meant to voice and be capable of voicing bold aggregate judgements about bundles of promises as incorporated in parties and candidates – thus changing their relative political power positions every four or five years. These conditions would reduce the ability of electoral selection to communicate structures and changes of political opinions even in the absence of the above-mentioned deficits of voters' incentives to gather information about political alternatives. Public choice theories usually recognise the latter aspect and content themselves with deducing a representative voter's 'rational ignorance' from the low pay-off from a better informed voting decision. From an evolutionary point of view, it may be more important to note that political selection processes lack an equivalent to the system of relative prices, and thus to devices for the discovery and use of a diversity of local knowledge and skills in society.

Consequences arise also on the supply side. For political agents, elections are not capable, in the same measures as markets, to indicate opportunity costs of political action in such a way as to enable them to discover how their particular goods and services are valued by the respective users. Since government officials deliver their services at zero or less-than-cost prices, they cannot learn about the values citizens place on their services. Nevertheless, incumbent politicians are at least exposed to some feedback, which is somewhat similar to price-signals and pecuniary sanctions. The permanent exposure of political agents' performance to opinion polls may signal the popularity of political actions as judged by their 'consumers'. And through the 'principle of anticipated reactions' (Sartori 1987, 152) on election day, these signals often do have some commanding power. Again, it is mainly from a 'political consumer's' perspective that analogies to market signals and market selection are utterly misleading. The electoral selection process provides no means for citizens to compare alternative uses of political goods and act as 'producers of consumption activities' (Loasby 2000, 306) who adapt to new circumstances in entrepreneurial and responsible ways.[5]

4.2 'Socialist' Problems: Political Apathy

Already the above-mentioned problems of democracy to provide incentives to develop and discover personal knowledge and skills, and make them socially productive through processes of spontaneous co-ordination, recall systemic shortcomings of socialist economies. More 'socialist' elements result from the fixed distribution of political resources among voters.

In modern democracies, the political 'purchasing power' is distributed on a strictly egalitarian basis: One man – one vote. Democratic societies have not yet found generally accepted procedures that would allow the distribution of voting power, for example according to differences in voters' competence, efforts, or needs. One may dislike the outcomes of the market's distribution of income. But markets for labour, capital and goods, which spontaneously create income distributions as a result of personal skill and luck are today widely preferred to the attribution of fixed relative income positions: only the former provide powerful external stimuli for economic actors to increase their 'per-formance', using their personal knowledge and skills in efforts to provide attractive market services for unknown others. And only incomes earned on markets reflect satisfaction and/or trust of other market participants in one's ability to serve the needs of others. Thus, economic resources tend to be directed to those who are expected to make best use of them (see Pelikan 1997).

To be sure, the 'socialist' distribution of votes as political resources is no instance of 'policy failure'. There just seems to be no convincing procedure to 'earn' unequal budgets of votes without destroying the general acceptance of the democratic method as a means of solving conflicts peacefully and of regulating the use of the monopoly of force which, after all, creates conditions that apply about equally to everyone (Dahl 1998, Weber [1917] 1988). But this justification of egalitarian voting rights does not preclude the identification of weaknesses of voters' property rights. Like in socialism, so in politics, egalitarianism and apathy go hand in hand. Whereas the market's lure of income earnings, linked with the basic mechanism of 'do ut des', drives actors to provide valuable services for others, the electoral context gives no such opportunities and incentives. Again, the differences are most pronounced at the 'demand' or 'consumption' side of political goods and services.

A concrete example would be citizens' 'paying morale'. The political goods' typical lack of reciprocity makes it that taxpayers' willingness to pay has to be secured through the state's threat of coercion. The reliance on coercion has, however, serious drawbacks: because coercion only entails punishment for the case of non-compliance with prescribed actions, it cannot encourage initiatives to develop mutually beneficial (new) modes of behaviour. Because coercion drastically reduces the ability to use one's own knowledge and skills for the pursuit of self-selected goals, the citizen–taxpayers' ingenuity and skills are rather directed at finding ways to avoid coercion or detection of unwarranted behaviour. And, finally, because coercion does not rely on the consent and self-interest of those affected, it has to be made effective through an expensive apparatus of control and punishment. Taken together, it seems fair to conclude with Boulding (1970, 10) that voluntary exchange has 'much more evolutionary potential than threat'.

Positive incentives to engage in mutually beneficial adaptive and innovative modes of behaviour are hard to find within any political system. Free-riding and prisoners' dilemmas are not accidentally defining properties of collective decision-making. True, defection and fraud can also be found in market settings. However, where services rendered are well defined and clearly reciprocal in nature, and where mutual self-interest in upholding business relationships prevails, co-operation tends clearly to be the dominant strategy (Sugden 1986; Klein 1991).

We summarise: compared to market competition, democratic selection processes are poorly equipped to discover individual opinions and satisfy individual preferences according to their diversity, intensity and variability, and they provide much less opportunities and remuneration for co-operative efforts of the actors involved. But again, these comparative shortcomings are not 'policy failures'. They are mostly necessary consequences of collective action in general and of democratic decision making under the rule of law in particular. The equality before the law and the quality of the law both demand that laws and policies are not individually 'selected', and that particular political favours and services are not 'exchanged' in a market-like fashion. The same activities one usually welcomes on markets attain negative connotations (horse-trading, favouritism, bribery) when observed on political 'markets'. Hence, we are not yet discussing the virtues of democracy as compared to alternative *political* methods. This caveat also applies to the following part, which discusses fundamental differences between the processes of entrepreneurial rivalry under conditions of economic and political competition.

5.   POLITICAL RIVALRY WITHOUT MARKET COMPETITION

In the process of entrepreneurial rivalry we find actors who (depending on the level of information costs) are perceived as suppliers of alternative problem solutions. In addition (and depending on the level of barriers to entry), new rivals can enter this process and compete for customers' resources, or create 'potential competition' by threatening entry. This process is driven by entrepreneurs who, by creating new variety, typically reduce profits of competitors, who are thus induced to react by ways of adaptation or innovative initiatives of their own.

In the same way as social selection processes depend on knowledge-creation on the demand side, the intensity and quality of the process of entrepreneurial rivalry depends on the rivals' willingness and incentives to engage in knowledge creation and to bear information costs, in order to interpret market signals and assess potentials of new courses of action (Streit and Wegner 1989, 197). Because the market price system not only sends out informative signals, but also pecuniary sanctions, rivals in economic competition are exposed to strong material incentives to incur information costs, permanently seeking to improve their performance. It is in this context that processes of political rivalry have comparable mechanisms to offer.

5.1   Some Basic Analogies: Rivalry, Rewards, Repercussions

Democracies, like markets, are characterised by the peaceful rivalry for the attainment of scarce rewards. Business firms compete for customers and shares of their purchasing power; political parties compete for voters and shares of their voting power. Pecuniary gains and losses provide signals and incentives for entrepreneurial reactions in market settings, and quite similarly (expected) gains and losses of votes inform and incite political entrepreneurs. Whereas high-powered incentives to engage in costly search for and interpretation of information are lacking for voters, they exist at least for politicians who compete for votes as means to attain personal power, prestige and income.

In particular information about voters' feelings and beliefs is in high demand and continuously supplied by professional polling agencies. Indeed, market research on behalf of businesses is not crucially different from opinion research on behalf of political parties. The search for (new) profit opportunities and the search for (new) voter potentials are both driven by profits or gains acting as 'stimuli to attention' (McCain 1992, 5). And like profits and losses, election results signal success and failure of political offers, and at the same time redistribute power resources in favour of the successful contenders.

By rewarding successful political rivals with votes as a means for the attainment of power, prestige and income, democracy also creates incentives to *supply* information. Competing for voters' favour makes it necessary for incumbents to spread information about the advantages of their actions and intentions, thus creating favourable attitudes and enhancing the citizens' compliance upon which a policy's success often depends. Even more importantly, it is the primary task of members of the opposition to discover flaws in the government's policies and make them known to the public, but also to develop alternative strategies and push them on the agenda of public opinion.

As mentioned, most economic models of political competition ignore political entrepreneurs' attempts to acquire opinion-leadership. The dominant assumption is 'that citizens' political tastes are fixed' (Downs 1957, 47), or 'preferences are given ... advertising, political speeches, etc. do not affect voters' preferences' (Wittman 1989, 1396). In radical contrast to that, Schumpeter ([1942] 1987, 263) takes for granted that politicians 'are able to fashion and, within very wide limits, even to create the will of the people'. The political reality, as empirical research suggests, confirms neither extreme position (Zaller 1992). But following Schumpeter, political entrepreneurship should at least be granted a role. One of the most important and indispensable roles of political entrepreneurs is discussed in the following section.

5.2 Political Entrepreneurs and the Creation of Issues

Just as goods (the objects of interactive price-evaluation) are not given in a market process, political issues (the objects of interactive opinion-formation) are not given. Pertinent issues have to be discovered or created and then pushed on the agenda. This activity entails costs and affords skills because the 'political agenda evidently has a limited "carrying capacity"' (Kuran 1995, 46). The public's attention is necessarily scarce and ephemeral; it cannot deal with many issues at a time. And that is where political entrepreneurs enter the stage as major actors in the competition of ideas and opinions (Wohlgemuth 2002, 235).

As Sunstein (1996) shows empirically, many political movements owe the sometimes unexpected attention to their cause, often associated with a surprisingly strong and sudden change of attitudes of the general public, to so-called 'norm entrepreneurs', to opinion leaders who induce a swing in opinions and values. In Kuran's theory, a similar role is attributed to 'activists' with 'extraordinarily great expressive needs' (Kuran 1995, 49) who do not shy away from formulating dissenting views and introducing new issues in face of an apparently hostile or indifferent public. In Boulding's (1956) chapter on the 'Sociology of Knowledge', changes in private and public images come about 'through the impact on society of unusually creative, charismatic, or prophetic individuals' (ibid., 75); as 'bearers of viable mutant images' – they are 'the true entrepreneurs of society' (ibid., 76).

All these roles of political opinion leadership are not only performed by rivalling party politicians, but also by interest group leaders, media figures or other intellectual agitators. They all take advantage of the fact that on many issues no strong and articulated opinions (preferences and theories) exist to begin with. Knowledge about most issues is quickly devaluated in the course of time and new problems may arise, which cannot easily be judged by referring to established knowledge or ideological shortcuts. With the increasing complexity of political activities and environments the number of issues increases for which there is no public opinion ready at hand.

Hence, political entrepreneurship cannot, as implied in mainstream public choice, consist of mere adaptations to given voters' preferences. Rather, it has to entail creating issues, attracting attention and, as a consequence, framing opinions (tastes and theories) which in the end might be expressed as votes.

5.3 Democracy as Bidding for Natural Monopoly

In spite of similar incentives for political and economic entrepreneurs to engage in communication with their 'customers', processes of political rivalry are subject to particular institutional structures which, again, differ substantially from typical market competition. Most importantly, political competition in a democracy does not entail parallel rivalry of simultaneously acting producers of political alternatives within the same jurisdiction. Democracy is competition for the field of monopolistic production (Wohlgemuth 1999b, 2000a). It resembles Demsetz's ([1968] 1989) auction solution for natural monopolies in the following respects:

- based on declarations and *promises*
- made by *potential* producers
- *one* (group of) candidate(s) is given the
- *exclusive* right to provide certain goods and services
- for a specified *period of time* and a specified *area*.

Democracy does not abolish the state's monopoly of legitimate coercion. But, instead of 'competition within the field', it introduces 'competition for the field' of political production, in order to make incumbents contestable and accountable. This restriction of the realm of actual competition, of course, translates into restrictions of the available means of entrepreneurial action. Most importantly, new political 'products' (laws and regulations) or 'production methods' (modes of political organisation) cannot be exposed to market-like tests of viability.

The evolutionary potential of political competition is therefore restricted in two major respects: (1) In one jurisdiction or 'natural' monopoly of government, there is only one set of political problem solutions being tested at a time; hence political evolution is basically limited to learning from consecutive trials and errors (Vanberg 1993, 15). (2) The forward-pushing and variety-creating entry of political innovators is severely hampered by barriers to entry to the field of political production. And, finally, we will find that (3) associations with positive notions of 'progress' or 'development' cannot be established for the case of political innovations. We now discuss these three peculiarities of the process of political rivalry in more detail.

5.4   Limited Potentials of Consecutive Learning

Hayek formulated one of the most fundamental evolutionary hypotheses as follows:

> Only when a great many different ways of doing things can be tried will there exist such a variety of individual experiences, knowledge and skills, that a continuous selection of the most successful will lead to steady improvement. (Hayek 1978, 149)

Hence, the knowledge-creating and problem-solving capacities of social learning processes critically depend on the continuous creation and parallel testing of alternative courses of action. Variety and variability of trials, together with the effective selection of errors are essential for the discovery of problem solutions that are regarded superior by their users. These conditions are not present on the level of government-produced 'deliberately imposed coercive rules, which can be changed only discontinuously and for all at the same time' (Hayek 1960, 63).

Individuals (in economic, academic or political contexts) act on the basis of fallible, hypothetical knowledge about their environment. Competition creates favourable conditions for the generation and selection of these hypotheses. Both generation and selection, however, are limited in degree and thrust if alternative hypotheses do not meet on the same field of experimentation. This argument is neglected by neoclassical models of both 'contestable markets' (for example Baumol 1982) in industrial economics and 'efficient political markets' in the new Public Choice literature (for example Wittman 1995). Both concepts claim that 'potential competition' or the threat of market entry can lead to market results not much different from those to be expected under polypolistic competition. While it can be argued with Schumpeter ([1942] 1987, 85) that potential competition 'disciplines before it attacks' to the effect that an incumbent producer 'feels himself in a competitive situation even if he is alone in his field', the important difference is that potential competition does not really test alternatives before it attacks. Potential rivals make no actual contribution to an ongoing process of trial and error, and hence to a process of knowledge creation, which would send out valuable or signals for others (Kerber 1997, 60).

The ability of political systems to discover and correct errors is further reduced by institutional peculiarities of collective decision making 'within the field'. As Hayek (for example 1973) explained at great length, evolutionary processes that support the detection and use of knowledge in society depend on a system of abstract and open rules of behaviour that protect individual freedom to choose among alternative means to pursue self-chosen individual aims. The realm of political action, however, is in major parts not defined by the abstract rules of the spontaneous order but by rules that prescribe specific (and mostly uniform) modes of behaviour, directed at predefined collective purposes. To be sure, rules of public and administrative law mostly have to be prescriptive and concrete in order to control and co-ordinate public officials. Accountability and uniformity of the public bureaucracy, however, comes at a cost. Public officials (but also citizens forced by public law to serve predefined collective purposes) are discouraged to make use of their local knowledge and skills; they are unable to experiment with new modes of behaviour; and they are kept from reacting promptly and independently to perceived risks and errors.

Political competition's ability to generate useful trial-and-error experiences is further restricted by several limits on substitutability. One aspect has already been discussed: voters only engage in an occasional selection of the group of producers, but not an ongoing selection of particular products. In representative democracies political problem solutions are exposed to valuation by their users only indirectly and only as complex bundles. But also political 'producers' are constrained by various indivisibilities. The production of laws and regulations is confronted with structural interdependencies (such as demands on legal consistency) and path-dependencies (such as habituation and network effects), both of which act as barriers to the diversification and variation of political problem solutions. In the following part, even more restrictions on political entrepreneurship remain to be shown.

5.5   Entry Barriers and Political Entrepreneurship

From an evolutionary perspective, the quality of competitive market processes depends much more on the dynamics of entry and exit of alternative suppliers than on the sheer number of existing firms. In some respects, this also holds for political competition. The sheer amount of political actors (for example parties in parliament) does not create evolutionary potential. What seems far more important is the ability of the opposition to enter the political arena with alternative views and proposals and to present a sufficient challenge to the incumbent.

If Schumpeter's ([1912] 1934, 66) observation that 'new combinations are, as a rule, embodied ... in new firms which generally do not arise out of the old ones but start producing beside them' also applied to political innovators, one would have to infer that political competition hardly ever allows new political combinations to see the light of day. And indeed, the contestability of the political 'market' is rather low in comparison to typical economic markets. Within the field of party politics, new 'firms' rarely appear and, even among the few established parties, one party can dominate political production for a considerable time.[6]

One obvious reason relates to differences of award criteria. If a business firm gains, say, 20 per cent, or as a newcomer some 4 per cent market share, this can often be called a success. By contrast, only with a 'market share' of over 50 per cent of the seats in parliament can a group of political entrepreneurs enact new policies. In this respect problems of entry of political innovators are very similar to those of admitting innovative producers in socialism, where the 'man with the new idea will have no possibility of establishing himself' (Hayek [1940] 1994, 247) and put his new idea to the market test until he has convinced the central planners that his way of producing or his new product is worth the trouble of rewriting the central production plans. Similarly, the political 'man with the new idea' cannot start producing new politics until he has convinced a majority of voters to elect him to office.[7]

And finally, capitalist markets promise considerable rewards for entrepreneurs as a premium for personal risk-taking. Political entrepreneurs, by contrast, are exposed to a high risk premium. To the contrary, political agencies seem to reward and thus create and/or attract people with high levels of risk-aversion .

But again, these arguments do not lend themselves to a critique of democracy. This is just the way politics works under the rule of monopolised legitimate coercion and how it should work if we take into account that the risks of failed political innovations are borne by their users (citizens) collectively (Wegner 1997, 507). And indeed, barriers to entry and change in politics serve most important functions (Wohlgemuth 1999b, 187). A certain amount of protection of incumbents (for example incumbency periods of several years or representation thresholds for small parties) is needed to secure governability and the stabilisation of citizen' expectations. Private investors and partners in long-term contracts have a need for stable political 'data'. Also, incumbency protection may enhance political entrepreneurs' propensity to invest in structural reforms, which often 'pay-off' in terms of economic performance (and votes) only in the long run, while in the short run – like all investments – involving sacrifices (deeply felt and loudly deplored by the special interests affected). In such situations, long-term incumbency periods or plurality voting schemes create a more reliable power base and a longer time-horizon, which may nourish incumbents' hopes to profit from their investment.[8]

Barriers to entry, however, do not generate investments, but only *opportunities* to invest. And they do this by reducing opportunities to oust incompetent cabinets and reflect changing voter opinions. Hence, democracy is confronted with a fundamental 'trade-off' between (a) institutional conditions that support reliable, consistent and sustainable policies, but do this by restricting competitors' ability to enter the field and the voters' ability to choose and (b) political rules of the game that would support more political novelties or adaptations to new views and conditions, but at the same time may reduce the accountability and consistency of political actions. Trade-offs such as these are, of course, not peculiar to politics. They can be regarded as a special case of the general problem of balancing variability and stability in an effort of finding, as Loasby (2000, 307) put it, 'variation within a stable ambience':

> Without variation there is no experience to act as a basis for learning; without a stable framework there is no assurance that any valid connections can be made between actions and outcomes that will have any future relevance. The appropriateness of institutions ... to the maintenance of this balance is a major determinant of evolutionary pathways. (Ibid.)

However, the case of political innovation remains special. Collective decision-making procedures can endure much less variations than market processes, which are able to expose an amazing amount of alternatives to ongoing social selection processes without putting the stability of the system at risk. In addition, as will be argued in the following part, innovation and variation are much more ambivalent notions in the realm of politics than in the realm of economics.

5.6   The Ambivalence of Political 'Innovations'

Economists tend to agree that the permanent creation of new products and procedures is a fundamental trait of prospering societies. In spite of losses afflicted to 'old economies', innovation-driven economic development is commonly regarded as a 'positive-sum game' for society at large. In evolutionary terms, innovations are needed to attain the systems' necessary variety and complexity, which support the problem-solving capacity of the variation–selection interplay. Similarly strong links between new governments, laws, or regulations and social values such as progress, development or enhanced problem-solving capacities cannot be taken for granted. The basic reason relates to the fundamental differences between political and economic selection environments. On competitive markets, novelty creates additional variety and thus increases the pool of alternatives, which can be, but do not have to be, chosen. This is a central element of the concept of cultural evolution as a

> process in which individuals, by their very choices of adopting or not adopting, of imitating or not imitating, particular practices constantly select among the various alternatives that are tried out – by themselves or others – those which to them, at any given time and measured against whatever purposes and interests they pursue, appear to be the most advantageous ones. (Vanberg 1992, 110)

In the realm of political competition, however, most new practices are strict substitutes: the new government, law, and policy takes effect by replacing the old. Whether these novelties are regarded superior by their users is not subject to the test of parallel use and voluntary selection. Since new policies remain subject to monopolistic provision and forced consumption, they do not increase variety and citizens' freedom to choose. And because of strong indivisibilities and redistributive intentions or effects, any new political combination (reform) typically produces winners *and* losers – without, however, providing reassurance that the 'creative destruction' of old political structures would in general be of a positive-sum type. Hence, a general assumption of progress for 'innovative' policies is unfounded. To sum up the comparison between political and economic processes of entrepreneurial rivalry, there is, again, a twofold result.

Democracy introduces rivalry for incumbency; but it produces no convincing analogy to the entrepreneurial rivalry of simultaneously competing firms. Thus, its evolutionary potential must fall short of capitalistic market processes. These peculiarities of political competition, however, do not lend themselves to a critique of democracy as a method of political decision making. As Lowell (1913, 54) put it: 'The presence of such matters involves no condemnation of democracy, but a consideration of its mode of operation'. The comparative evolutionary merits of democracy as a political mode of operation are discussed in the following section.

6. THE COMPARATIVE EVOLUTIONARY ADVANTAGES OF DEMOCRACY AS A POLITICAL METHOD

6.1 Assessing the Evolutionary Potential of Political Competition

The above-mentioned shortcomings of the democratic method may be a major reason why economists such as Hayek (for example 1979) defended markets against interference of political forces. To most observers Hayek is known only for his critique of the prevailing forms of democracy, and his political opponents are fond of denouncing him to be an anti-democratic conservative. What is mostly ignored, however, is Hayek's eloquent defence of democracy as the best available political method of opinion-formation and social control – provided that democratic decision-making is subject to the supremacy of the rule of law (Hayek 1960, ch. 7).

And indeed, there are many arguments that Hayek and others made in more general contexts of evolutionary social theory, which can be used to assess advantages of democracy as a political method – advantages that static neo-classical models of public choice are unable to reflect. Again, the basic reason is that the 'meaning of competition' (Hayek [1946] 1948) is different. In an evolutionary or market-process perspective, as opposed to a neoclassical or welfare-economic approach the following methodological principles are much more naturally endorsed:

- 'Not the approach to an unachievable and meaningless ideal but the improvement upon the conditions that would exist without competition should be the test' (Hayek [1946] 1948, 100) and
- 'competition is the more important the more complex or "imperfect" are the objective conditions in which it has to operate' (ibid.,103).

In the two preceding parts, it has been shown how complex or imperfect the conditions of political competition are when compared to competition on cap-italistic markets. In this part, it remains to be shown that democratic processes improve upon the conditions that would not exist without the competitive struggle for votes.

As indicated in Section 2, a major field in which the evolutionary potential of the democratic method can be shown relates to the concept of democracy as a process that helps create, change and discover political opinions, mostly in their 'cognitive' dimension (that is the hypothetical knowledge which guides the actions of citizens and politicians). This contrasts sharply with the neo-classical view of democracy as a mechanism that aggregates given preferences in a given 'issue space' to something like a common will of the omniscient majority, which serves as the 'unachievable and meaningless' ideal of a democratic state of affairs.

The question remains: how can Hayek's claim that the value of democracy proves itself in its dynamic aspects as a process of forming opinions be sub-stantiated? After all, David Hume's 'First Principle of Government' ([1777] 1987, 32), that it is 'on opinion only that government is founded' not only applies to democratic systems.[9] And, indeed, many revolutionary overthrows of autocratic systems demonstrate how powerful public opinion can show itself in an openly hostile manner against autocrats who seemed immune from pressures of public opinion.

Democratic regimes usually do not face equally dramatic outbursts of public anger and comparable personal risks of 'hostile take-overs'. And indeed, the peaceful resolution of political conflicts is a major achievement of the democratic method.[10] What is more important in the present context, is that democratic rules of the game also yield better prospects to embrace and encourage changes in public beliefs and opinions, since they support the permanent creation, discovery and testing of political preferences and (relational) images. The main reasons have already been mentioned. Together with some additional arguments, they can be subsumed under two categories: (1) more secure and effective rights to express and broadcast diverging opinions and (2) stronger incentives to make use of these rights.

6.2 Democracy and the 'Strength of Weak Ties' in Communication Networks

In autocratic regimes freedom of speech, the press and assembly are no necessary components of the political constitution. And even if they are part of the constitutional text, they tend to be less reliably safeguarded than in democratic systems of government, where incumbents – feeling that they may find themselves voted out of power – have an interest in securing those rights for a future, when they may need them most badly. The 'freedom of speech, or of the press; or the right of the people peacefully to assemble' (1st Amendment to the US Constitution) meet at least the following minimal requirements for a knowledge-creating political process:

> (1) make generally available knowledge that alternative perspectives exist over an issue; (2) make easily available representative alternative perspectives to those wishing to investigate further; and (3) provide a means by which those arguing for alternative views can continue reaching others who are interested. (diZerega 1989, 219)

From a systems perspective, the freedom of the individual to express her opinion on any issue she likes offers a better prospect for the creation, discovery and dissemination of political information and thus to enlarge the cognitive (knowledge-) component of public opinion. This basic relationship can be formulated in terms of the communication model by Granovetter (1973). Social communication networks are, inter alia, characterised by the strength of inter-personal connections which depend on 'the emotional intensity, the intimacy (mutual confiding), and the reciprocal services which characterize the tie' (ibid., 1361). The diffusion of information and opinions is negatively related to the strength of these ties, because:

whatever is to be diffused can reach a larger number of people, and traverse greater social distance ..., when passed through weak ties rather than strong. If one tells a rumor to all his close friends, and they do so likewise, many will hear the rumor a second and third time, since those linked by strong ties tend to share friends ... the rumor moving through strong ties is much more likely to be limited to a few cliques than that going via weak ones; bridges will not be crossed (ibid.).

Granovetter himself offers no explicit political application of his theory. His basic idea, however, can be used to clarify differences between the effects of safeguarded and of suppressed or fragile freedom of expression on the diffusion of political information. In societies (and organisations like clubs, firms, religious groups and so on) in which the rights to express and broadcast diverging opinions are less generally or reliably established, the channels of communication are predominantly reduced to 'strong ties'. This leads to a frag-mentation into local communication groups and thus reduces the 'publicness' of political opinions. In open societies information and opinions about political issues and alternatives travel faster and longer. More individuals are members of several overlapping and comparatively open circles of communication; bridges between different groups can be crossed more easily. At the end, more information reaches more recipients, because free expression and free utilisa-tion of independent media facilitate the diffusion of information and opinions through 'weak ties'.

In closed societies with barred freedom of expression and action, the autocrats themselves are most seriously cut off from reliable signals of changing public preferences and beliefs. As Boulding (1956, 100) points out, the central weakness of the authoritarian structure lies 'in the inadequate amount of feedback to the higher roles' because the authorities surround themselves with 'yes men' or breed a surrounding of men who have no incentives to reveal their 'true' individual opinion and no means to report the 'true' opinion of the public. Thus, comparative institutional analysis of political systems suggests that there is more to the socialist 'calculation problem' than just the planning authorities' inability to acquire the necessary knowledge about changing economic envi-ronments and consumers' preferences. There is also the autocrats' inability to acquire knowledge about changing political environments and citizens' opinions. As the sudden overturns produced by a momentous withdrawal of public support showed in 1989, socialist political leaders were unable to calculate the dramatic shifts of public opinions and moods (Kuran 1995, ch. 16). Socialism, thus, is not only unable to co-ordinate economic plans in the absence of capitalist markets. Its leaders are also unable to anticipate and react to the threat of a complete destruction of their political system in the absence of democratic pluralism and discourse.

To be sure, I am not arguing that 'preference falsification', the misrepre-sentation of private opinions under social pressure, does not also occur in free, liberal, societies. After all, the creation of public opinion builds on social pressures to conform to widely shared attitudes (Noelle-Neumann 1993, Kuran 1995). However, 'the proclivity to engage in preference falsification depends crucially on the institutional context' (Kuran 1995, 15). This context not only includes constitutional rights of expression, but also and even with priority, cultural traditions and value systems. The open society is above all a matter of tolerant attitudes towards dissenting minorities. At the same time, the dynamics of the process of political opinion formation is also a matter of the self-understanding and self-confidence of crucial groups of potential dissenters. The taming of preference falsification depends on the presence of a critical mass of vocal dissenters (Kuran 1998, 525). This condition is more likely to be met in pluralistic systems where intellectuals (and not least economists), journalists and other political entrepreneurs take pride in expressing disagreement and in putting unheard-of issues on the agenda. These dissenters highly value the 'expressive utility' of their own view (based on self-respect and self-assertion), and often their courage and independence is rewarded with 'reputational utility' (based on respect from their peers or even from an admiring general public). Both benefits can compensate for the risks of expressing disagreement and introducing innovation.

6.3 Democracy and the Marketplace of Opinions

To be sure, one can imagine and occasionally observe political systems with a high legal and cultural acceptance of the freedom of political expression, but without general elections as a means to select political leaders. Here, 'weak ties' would not be legally blocked. Still, I would expect less information and opinions about political issues and alternatives to be generated in such systems. In a democracy, rivalry between incumbents and opposition are institutionalised and routinised. This, I argue, creates stronger incentives for more actors to supply and demand competing opinions, critique and alternative proposals.

Politicians who are exposed to institutionalised competition for citizens' support are more readily pressed to explain and justify their actions in front of the general public. But also citizens, the inconsequential nature of their individual vote notwithstanding, are more readily exposed to incentives and occasions to participate in opinion-building processes simply due to the fact that they are allowed to voice their opinion in the expressive act of voting. Even an inconsequential expression of preferences may beg some justification. Especially in conversations with other citizens who are facing the same alternatives and who will experience the same political outcomes, some good arguments why one should prefer some party or policy to another are helpful. Reasonable arguments increase (a socially innocent form of) 'reputational utility' and are thus in demand. Hence, it is not surprising that Huckfeldt and

Sprague (1995), in a number of empirical studies, observe that during election campaigns political opinions and political information are not just passively received from parties and media. They are also interactively 'exchanged' in various forms of social interchange which at other times mostly remain 'unpolitical' (conversations with friends, colleagues, and so on).

In short, elections provide special occasions and incentives for public opinion formation. Most importantly, the democratic struggle for power makes it necessary for rival parties and candidates, but also for rival interest groups and the media to broadcast criticism, dissent and alternative problem solutions in order to be successful. Even if political debates are often staged to camouflage the 'real' power struggle behind the scenes, they may still have (besides a possible entertainment value) some educational effect on the public. Incentives for citizens to build political views based on more sound arguments and sincere views increase in situations where views differ. 'Disagreement between political discussion partners ... furnishes the occasion for new information search' (Huckfeldt and Sprague 1995, 112). In other words, dissenting views tend to sharpen the cognitive component of individually held opinions. In addition, opportunities for open dissent reduce the political realm of 'fundamental attribution errors' (see Kuran 1995, 81) which occur when individuals falsely conclude from a lack of open opposition that there must be ample support for the status quo, and adjust their public positions accordingly to minimise the risk of ostracism – thus reinforcing the status quo even further.

6.4   Democracy as a Discovery Procedure

Democracy and the competition of political ideas can therefore be regarded as a procedure for the generation and critical assessment of political hypotheses. And as a discovery procedure, it is most useful and effective when political opinions are neither fixed nor 'given', but in the process of being formed and open to adapt to new circumstances and experiences (Hirschman 1989, 77). It has, of course, to be acknowledged that political discourse will never be able to perform as a real 'marketplace of ideas' in terms of openness for new ideas and effective criticism.[11] But it also has to be acknowledged that – compared to non-democratic political systems – democracy is the political system most likely to create the evolutionarily essential combination of creativity and criticism.

Competition between political opinions and alternatives (programmes, proposals, parties), like competition as a discovery procedure in general, receives its major justification on the grounds that we do not know in advance which opinions and alternatives exist and which policies under which conditions are considered 'right' or 'acceptable' by those who have to endure them. Thus, very much like Hayek's ([1968] 1978, 179) advocacy of the freedom to compete ('if anyone really knew all about what economic theory calls the *data*, competition would indeed be a very wasteful method of securing adjustment to these data') one could state: if anyone knew all about political opinions and opportunities which most of the economics of politics treats as data (given preferences, given issue-space ...), democracy would be a rather wasteful method and a government by élite consent would be much preferable. Our lack of knowledge and hence the high probability of erroneous perceptions and theories would from this evolutionary-liberal position not represent the problem, but the main justification of democracy and freedom of speech, press and assembly. This argument is summarised by Hayek (1978, 148) as follows:

> The central belief from which all liberal postulates may be said to spring is that more successful solutions of the problems of society are to be expected if we do not rely on the application of anyone's given knowledge, but encourage the interpersonal process of the exchange of opinion from which better knowledge can be expected to emerge .... Freedom for individual opinion was demanded precisely because every individual was regarded as fallible, and the discovery of the best knowledge was expected only from that continuous testing of all beliefs which free discussion allowed.

7. SUMMARY AND OUTLOOK

Evolutionary Economics, Austrian market process theory and the New Institutional Economics have important contributions to make to an economic theory of democracy. Even if prospects of ending the dominance of neoclassical economics in mainstream Public Choice are slim, there is a strong case for supporting Hayek's (1960, 109) claim that democracy should be assessed by 'its dynamic, rather than its static aspects'. And there are no compelling reasons why theories that focus on co-ordination processes, knowledge creation and dissemination, entrepreneurial action, the role of institutions in stabilising expectations, the detection and elimination of errors, evolutionary learning processes, and much more should not also be applied to political systems. Such an application could, paraphrasing Hayek again, serve as a procedure for the discovery of such insights and theories, which, without resort to it, would not be accomplished.

In this chapter only some of the issues could be raised. It was argued that democracy can be analysed as a compound of feedback-linked processes of entrepreneurship and selection, the quality of which depends on the available property rights, and the intensity of which depends on the actors' willingness to invest in skills and information. Thus having established a structural congruence to dynamic models of economic competition, parallels and differences between political and economic processes of competition were identified.

Most importantly, it was shown that the evolutionary potential of political competition is seriously reduced since (a) political selection processes cannot rely on ongoing, decentral and targeted choices of particular alternatives mediated through an informative and incentive-rich price system and (b) the process of political rivalry is not subject to parallel performance-tests of potential problem solutions and to the entry of entrepreneurial creators of variety.

Nevertheless, some evolutionary potentials of democratic competition for the field of monopolistic provision of political goods could be identified. In this chapter, the focus was on the process of public opinion formation. It is here that political entrepreneurship is most important and, in fact, indispensable. And it is here that differences between the neoclassical concept of democracy as an aggregation of, or adaptation to, given preferences within a given 'issue space', and an evolutionary view of the spontaneous formation and change of opinions (that is tastes and theories) in a process of communication and learning can be most distinctly established.

This chapter remains largely suggestive and by no means exhaustive. Its aim was to open new vistas rather than to present a clear-cut model of the democratic process. Before more concrete models and possible policy conclusions can be presented, it will be necessary to reduce the level of abstractness of the discussion and take account of the fact that 'democracy' comes in many different institutional forms. Different forms of democracy should be differently effective as discovery procedures and evolutionary methods for the creation and selection of political problem solutions. But the general characteristics and limits of democracy as an evolutionary method developed here can also inform a comparative analysis of the evolutionary potentials of alternative democratic systems.

One application would be the analysis of various combinations of entry barriers in politics and their effects on political entrepreneurs' incentives and abilities to invest in political reforms (Wohlgemuth 1999b, 2000a). In a similar context, Hayek's (1960, 1979) claim that strict limits to the realm of democratic decision-making set by the rule of law are essential to a free political system and its ability to evolve, finds support in our analysis. Two further amendments of representative majority rule could also be expected to increase the evolutionary potential of political experimentation and opinion formation: popular initiatives formulated by and directly voted upon by the citizens could provoke public discussion and deliberation focused on concrete political problem solutions and at the same time reduce the agenda-setting monopoly of the 'classe politique' (Adamovich and Wohlgemuth 1999; Frey 1994). And inter-jurisdictional competition would introduce forms of parallel instead of consecutive political learning processes as it enables citizens to choose between sets of political alternatives (Wohlgemuth 1995; Vanberg 1993).

Many more fields wait to be discovered by evolutionary political economists.

NOTES

1. This view has gained some ground recently (see Boettke 1994; Buchanan 1989, 1993; diLorenzo 1987; diZerega 1989; Frey 1981; Langlois 1992; Rowley 1994; Wagner 1993; Wiseman 1989, 1990).
2. See Wohlgemuth (2000b) on why Schumpeter is no precursor of mainstream public choice and what a Schumpeterian political economy would be; see Witt (1994), Hodgson (1997), Foster (2000) on Schumpeter's place in the evolutionary economics paradigm.
3. Boulding (1956) captures these arguments with his concept of the 'image'. Preferences 'do not usually have the courtesy to parade themselves in rank on the drill ground of the imagination' (ibid., 84); they depend on a 'highly learned process of interpretation and acceptance' (ibid., 14). In Boulding's terminology, the value image (that is 'the ordering on the scale of better or worse' of given alternatives, ibid., 47), which in most of economics exclusively motivates human action, is only a part of the whole image that guides human action. And it is not a part which can be properly isolated from other aspects of the image, such as, most of all, the 'relational image' (that is subjective hypotheses on causal systems and regularities in the outside world).
4. Kuran (1995, 24) distinguishes three kinds of utility an individual can derive from publicly expressing an opinion: the 'intrinsic utility' which flows from the social outcomes of a collective decision, the 'reputational utility' which is derived from the social approval of others, and the 'expressive utility' which is based on an individual's self-respect and self-assertion. As Kuran (ibid., 41) notes, standard economics tends to regard intrinsic utility as the sole driving force of individual action. Reputational and expressive utilities are rarely integrated into rational choice models.
5. See Mitchell and Simmons (1994, 47): 'When the price of something in the market changes, consumers can alter their consumption – that is, buy less of that which increases in price and purchase more when the price decreases. Given fixed quantities of publicly supplied goods and public sharing of costs, individual citizens cannot follow this eminently sensible course of action. Coerced collective consumption does not permit, let alone encourage, responsible marginal adjustments by the citizen-consumer'. The entrepreneurial role of consumers is stressed by Loasby (2000, 307): 'People do not consume goods or characteristics; they attempt to satisfy needs or solve problems, and in the process they may create new goods for themselves'.
6. See, for example Demsetz ([1982] 1989, 291) on the American experience. Extreme cases can also be found in Europe. In Austria, for almost all of her post-war history, both major parties shared political power and framed all parliamentary decisions beforehand in joint 'coalition committees'. Even more strict and encompassing power sharing rules are typical for the Swiss system – combined, however, with low barriers to citizens' entry in politics as a consequence of direct democracy.
7. Viewed as a multi-stage process it is more realistic to argue that the 'man with the new idea' would first have to convince his party members to adopt the new ideas in a new programme or parliamentary initiative and then convince voters to elect or (re-) elect his party. But now, intra-organisational barriers to the introduction of novelty may dampen this effort.
8. See Wohlgemuth (1999b, 186) and Williamson and Haggard (1994) on the problem of sustainable investments in market-oriented reforms.
9. Hume ([1977] 1987) himself argues that 'this maxim extends to the most despotic military government as well as the most free and popular'. See also Hayek (1960, ch.7) or Kuran (1995, 84).
10. See Hayek (1960, 107): 'whenever it is necessary that one of several conflicting opinions should prevail and when one would have to be made to prevail by force if need be, it is less wasteful to determine which has the stronger support by counting numbers than by fighting. Democracy is the only method of peaceful change that man has yet discovered.' The strong complementarity of democracy and the peaceful settlement of conflicts is also supported by the fact that democratic states have almost never waged war against other democratic states (Dixon 1994).

11.   See Wohlgemuth (1999a, part 7) on practical and psychological limits to 'ideal speech situations' of political deliberation.

REFERENCES

Adamovich, Ivan Baron and Michael Wohlgemuth (1999), '"Exit" und "voice" im Systemwettbewerb: Das Zusammenwirken von Föderalismus und direkter Demokratie in der Schweiz', in Manfred E. Streit and Michael Wohlgemuth (eds), *Systemwettbewerb als Herausforderung an Theorie und Politik*, Baden-Baden: Nomos, pp. 123–49.

Albert, Hans (1979), 'The economic tradition – economics as a research programme for theoretical social science', in Karl Brunner (ed.), *Economics and Social Institutions – Insights from the Conferences on Analysis and Ideology*, Boston: Martinus Nijhoff, pp. 1–27.

Arrow, Kenneth J. (1951), *Social Choice and Individual Values*, New York: Wiley & Sons.

Baumol, William J. (1982), 'Contestable markets: an uprising in the theory of industry structure', *American Economic Review*, 72, 1–15.

Boettke, Peter J. (1994), 'Virginia political economy: A view from Vienna', in Peter J. Boettke and David L. Prychitko (eds), *The Market Process. Essays in Contemporary Austrian Economics*, Aldershot, UK and Brookfield, US: Edward Elgar, pp. 244–60.

Boulding, Kenneth E. (1956), *The Image. Knowledge in Life and Society*, Ann Arbor: University of Michigan Press.

Boulding, Kenneth E. (1970), *Economics as a Science*, New York: McGraw-Hill.

Buchanan, James M. (1954), 'Social choice, democracy, and free markets', *Journal of Political Economy*, 62, 114–23.

Buchanan, James M. (1989), 'The public-choice perspective', in *Essays on the Political Economy*, Honolulu: University of Hawaii Press, pp. 13–24.

Buchanan, James M. (1993), 'Public choice after socialism', *Public Choice*, 77, 67–74.

Dahl, Robert A. (1998), *On Democracy*, New Haven and London: Yale University Press.

Demsetz, Harold ([1968] 1989), 'Why Regulate Utilities' in *Efficiency, Competition, and Policy – The Organization of Economic Activity*, vol. II, Cambridge and Oxford: Blackwell, pp. 75–86.

Demsetz, Harold ([1982] 1989), 'Competition in the Public Sector' in *Efficiency, Competition, and Policy – The Organization of Economic Activity*, Vol. II, Cambridge and Oxford: Blackwell, pp. 280–94.

diLorenzo, Thomas (1987), 'Competition and entrepreneurship: Austrian insights into Public Choice theory', *Review of Austrian Economics*, 2.

diZerega, Gus (1989), 'Democracy as a spontaneous order', *Critical Review*, 3, 206–40.

Dixon, William J. (1994), 'Democracy and the peaceful settlement of international conflict', *American Political Science Review*, 88, 14–32.

Downs, Anthony (1957), *An Economic Theory of Democracy*, New York: Harper & Row.

Foster, John (2000), 'Competitive selection, self-organisation and Joseph A. Schumpeter', *Journal of Evolutionary Economics*, 10, 311–28.

Frey, Bruno S. (1981), 'Schumpeter, Political Economist', in Helmut Frisch (ed.), *Schumpeterian Economics*, New York: Praeger, pp. 126–42.

Frey, Bruno S. (1994), 'Direct democracy: politico-economic lessons from Swiss experience', *American Economic Review*, 84, 338–42.

Granovetter, Mark (1973), 'The strength of weak ties', *American Journal of Sociology*, 78, 1360–80.

Hayek, Friedrich A. (1940), 'Socialist Calculation III: The Competitive "Solution"', reprinted in Israel M. Kirzner (ed.) (1994), *Classics in Austrian Economics – A*

Sampling in the History of Tradition, Vol. III: The Age of Mises and Hayek, London: William Pickering.

Hayek, Friedrich A. (1945), 'The use of knowledge in society', *American Economic Review*, **35**, 519–30.

Hayek, Friedrich A. ([1946] 1948), 'The Meaning of Competition', reprinted in *Individualism and Economic Order*, Chicago: University of Chicago Press, pp. 92–106.

Hayek, Friedrich A. ([1952] 1979), *The Counter-Revolution of Science. Studies on the Abuse of Reason*, 2nd edition, Indianapolis: Liberty Press.

Hayek, Friedrich A. (1960), *The Constitution of Liberty*, London: Routledge.

Hayek, Friedrich A. ([1968] 1978), 'Competition as a discovery procedure', reprinted in *New Studies in Philosophy, Politics, Economics and the History of Ideas*, London: Routledge, pp. 179–90.

Hayek, Friedrich A. (1973), *Law, Legislation and Liberty, Volume 1: Rules and Order*, London: Routledge.

Hayek, Friedrich A. (1978), 'Liberalism', in *New Studies in Philosophy, Politics, Economics and the History of Ideas*, London: Routledge, pp. 119–51.

Hayek, Friedrich A. (1979), *Law, Legislation and Liberty, Volume 3: The Political Order of a Free People*, London: Routledge.

Hirschman, Albert O. (1989), 'Having Opinions – One of the Elements of Well-Being?', *American Economic Review Papers and Proceedings*, **79**, 75–9.

Hodgson, Geoffrey M. (1997), 'The evolutionary and non-Darwinian economics of Joseph Schumpeter', *Journal of Evolutionary Economics*, **7**, 131–46.

Huckfeldt, Robert and John Sprague (1995), *Citizens, Politics, and Social Communication – Information and influence in an election campaign*, Cambridge: Cambridge University Press.

Hume, David ([1777] 1987), 'Of the First Principles of Government', reprinted in Eugene F. Miller (ed.), *Essays, Moral, Political and Literary*, pp. 32–41.

Kerber, Wolfgang (1997), 'Wettbewerb als Hypothesentest: Eine evolutorische Konzeption wissenschaffenden Wettbewerbs', in Karl von Delhaes and Ulrich Fehl (eds), *Dimensionen des Wettbewerbs*, Stuttgart: Lucius & Lucius, pp. 31–78.

Klein, Daniel B. (ed.) (1991), *Reputation. Studies in the Voluntary Elicitation of Good Conduct*, Ann Arbor: University of Michigan Press.

Kuran, Timor (1995), *Private Truths, Public Lies. The Social Consequences of Preference Falsification*, Cambridge and London: Harvard University Press.

Kuran, Timor (1998), 'Insincere deliberation and democratic failure', *Critical Review*, **12**, 529–44.

Langlois, Richard N. (1992), 'Orders and Organizations: Toward an Austrian Theory of Social Institutions', in Bruce J. Caldwell and Stephan Boehm (eds), *Austrian Economics: Tensions and New Directions*, Boston: Kluwer. pp. 165–83.

Loasby, Brian J. (2000), 'Market institutions and economic evolution'. *Journal of Evolutionary Economics*, **10**, 297–309.

Lowell, A. Lawrence (1913), *Public Opinion and Popular Government*, New York: Longmans, Green, and Co.

McCain, Roger A. (1992), *A Framework for Cognitive Economics*, Westport, CT: Praeger.

Mitchell, William C. and Randy T. Simmons (1994), *Beyond Politics – Markets, Welfare, and the Failure of Bureaucracy*, Boulder: Westview Press (The Independent Institute).

Noelle-Neumann, Elisabeth (1993), *The Spiral of Silence: Public Opinion – Our Social Skin*, 2nd edition, Chicago: University of Chicago Press.

Pelikan, Pavel (1997), *Allocation of Economic Competence in Teams – A Comparative Institutional Analysis*, IUI working paper series # 480, Stockholm: The Research Institute of Industrial Economics.

Popper, Sir Karl R. (1945, reprinted in 1966), *The Open Society and its Enemies*, Princeton: Princeton University Press.

Rowley, Charles K. (1994), 'Public choice economics', in Peter J. Boettke (ed.), *The Elgar Companion to Austrian Economics*, Cheltenham, UK and Brookfield, US: Edward Elgar, pp. 285–93.

Sartori, Giovanni (1987), *The Theory of Democracy Revisited*, Chatham, NJ: Chatham House.

Schumpeter, Joseph A. (1912, reprinted in 1934), *The Theory of Economic Development – An Inquiry into Profits, Capital, Credit, Interest, and the Business Cycle*, Cambridge: Harvard University Press.

Schumpeter, Joseph A. ([1942] 1987): *Capitalism, Socialism, and Democracy*, 6th edition, London: Unwin.

Streit, Manfred E. and Gerhard Wegner (1989), 'Wissensmangel, Wissenserwerb und Wettbewerbsfolgen – Transaktionskosten aus evolutorischer Sicht', *Ordo*, **40**, 183–200.

Sugden, Robert (1986), *The Economics of Rights, Co-operation and Welfare*, New York: TJ Press.

Sunstein, Cass R. (1996), 'Social norms and social roles', *Columbia Law Review*, **96**, 903–68.

Vanberg, Viktor (1992) 'Innovation, Cultural Evolution, and Economic Growth', in Ulrich Witt (ed.), *Explaining Process and Change – Approaches to Evolutionary Economics*, Ann Arbor: University of Michigan Press, pp. 105–21.

Vanberg, Viktor (1993), 'Constitutionally constrained and safeguarded competition in markets and politics with reference to a European constitution', *Journal des Economistes et des Etudes Humaines*, **4**, 3–27.

Vanberg, Viktor and James M. Buchanan (1989), 'Interests and theories in constitutional choice', *Journal of Theoretical Politics*, **1**, 49–63.

Wagner, Richard E. (1993), 'The impending transformation of public choice scholarship', *Public Choice*, **77**, 203–12.

Weber, Max ([1917] 1988), 'Wahlrecht und Demokratie in Deutschland', reprinted in Johannes Winckelmann, (ed.) *Gesammelte Politische Schriften*, 5th edition, Tübingen: J.C.B. Mohr (Paul Siebeck), pp. 245–91.

Wegner, Gerhard (1997), 'Economic policy from an evolutionary perspective: a new approach', *Journal of Institutional and Theoretical Economics*, **153**, 485–509.

Williamson, John and Stephan Haggard (1994), 'The political conditions for economic reform', in John Williamson (ed.), *The Political Economy of Policy Reform*, Washington: Institute for International Economics, pp. 527–96.

Wiseman, Jack (1989), 'The Political Economy of Government Revenues', in *Cost, Choice and Political Economy*, Aldershot, UK and Brookfield, US: Edward Elgar, pp. 199–212.

Wiseman, Jack (1990), 'Principles of political economy – an outline proposal, illustrated by application to fiscal federalism', *Constitutional Political Economy*, **1**, 101–24.

Witt, Ulrich (1994), 'Evolutionary Economics', in Peter Boettke (ed.), *The Elgar Companion to Austrian Economics*, Aldershot, UK and Brookfield, US: Edward Elgar, pp. 541–8.

Wittman, Donald A. (1989). 'Why democracies produce efficient results', *Journal of Political Economy*, **97**, 1395–424.

Wittman, Donald A. (1995), *The Myth of Democratic Failure. Why Political Institutions are Efficient*, Chicago: University of Chicago Press.

Wohlgemuth, Michael (1995), 'Institutional competition – notes on an unfinished agenda', *Journal des Economistes et des Etudes Humaines*, **6**, 277–99.

Wohlgemuth, Michael (1999a), *Democracy as a Discovery Procedure. Toward an Austrian Economics of the Political Process*, Max-Planck-Institute for Research into Economic Systems, Jena, Discussion paper 17/99.

Wohlgemuth, Michael (1999b), 'Entry barriers in politics, or: why politics, like natural monopoly, is not organized as an ongoing market-process', *Review of Austrian Economics*, **12**, 177–202.

Wohlgemuth, Michael (2000a), 'Political entrepreneurship and bidding for political monopoly', *Journal of Evolutionary Economics*, **10**, 273–95.

Wohlgemuth, Michael (2000b), Paper prepared for the Annual Meeting of the Joseph Schumpeter Society, Manchester 2000.

Wohlgemuth, Michael (2002), 'Evolutionary approaches to politics', *Kyklos*, **55**, 223–46.

Zaller, John R. (1992), *The Nature and Origins of Mass Opinion*, Cambridge: Cambridge University Press.

6. Ideologies, beliefs, and economic advice – a cognitive–evolutionary view on economic policy-making

Tilman Slembeck[1]

> People act in part upon the basis of myths, dogmas, ideologies and 'half-baked' theories. (A.T. Denzau and D.C. North, 1994, 3)

1. INTRODUCTION

This chapter discusses several aspects of the politico-administrative process from an evolutionary and cognitive perspective with focus on the roles of beliefs and ideologies. While 'ideological beliefs' are often blamed by economists for causing irrational policy decisions, I argue that beliefs and ideologies are at the center of economic policy-making, and can, therefore, not be overcome by simply proposing 'efficient solutions' to policy problems, nor by fostering 'solid analytical knowledge' alone. Such a view would naïvely overlook the very essence of politics. That is, the aim of 'decreasing the influence of ideologies' cannot be achieved solely by putting forward 'rational policies' without taking into account the nature of the game called politics.

Therefore, it seems crucial for economists to understand the roles of beliefs and ideologies in policy-making, and to take them seriously – especially when giving economic policy advice. In this view, economic advisers are themselves part of the game. They are only actors among other actors – many of whom are much more influential in, and knowledgeable about, the political process. Within the rules of the political game, economists are often not equipped with superior knowledge or wisdom. Their views on the economy and the way it functions are not unrivaled. This has, for instance, led to the following complaint by William H. Hutt in 1936:

> Although an expert, no authority attaches to the economist's opinion ... whilst there are few intelligent members of the public who would dare to argue with a professor of mathematics about *his* subject, there are few who would *not* be prepared to question the validity of an economist's teachings. (Hutt, 1936, 36; original emphasis)

Promoting rationality in politics requires understanding the game and knowing how to play it. Otherwise, politicians and economists may well end up blaming each other for being 'ideological'. Note, for instance, that terms such as 'economization of society' or 'economic imperialism' have a negative connotation, and are used to fight the 'ideology of the market'.

But, then, what should economists do? How can they put forward rational policy solutions? The first step is to systematically analyse and understand economic policy-making as an evolutionary process that involves important psychological aspects of perception and interpretation on one hand, and aspects of power and interests on the other hand (Sections 2 and 3).

A second step is to look at the effects and compatibility of economic policy proposals within the system. In Section 4 I will discuss why many seemingly efficient improvements or reforms are not attractive for politicians and are, thus, difficult to implement.

Both steps are outlined in this chapter. In following them economists may be able to judge their own possibilities and limitations more realistically. They may avoid falling prey to fruitless ideological confrontations and be more effective in giving policy advice.

While the public choice school has emphasized the importance of individual and group interests, and has analysed the (maximizing) behavior of politicians and bureaucrats under various restrictions (such as budgets and re-elections), I will focus on the cognitive and evolutionary aspects of policy-making, and those of giving policy advice. This is not to deny the importance of the public choice view. It is to enlarge the analysis in crucial respects, and, hopefully, to make economic advice more successful.

2. IDEOLOGIES AND BELIEFS IN DEMOCRACIES

There seems to be a strong tendency for economists to fight ideologies. At least two battle grounds exist. One is *within* the field of economics where economists aim to keep their science ideology-free, since 'given the economists' desire for status as "scientists" the very notion of ideology is threatening' (Samuels, 1977, 469). I will not enter the discussions on the roles of ideology within economics, but instead focus on the second area where economists fight ideologies from *outside* their field, namely with regard to economic systems and policies.

Until the 1989–91 soft revolutions in Eastern Europe the main ideological enemy was socialism. After the 'factual victory' of capitalism in most countries and in the light of the spreading of democracy throughout the world, however, there still exist 'ideological debates' over economic goals and policies within capitalism. The term ideology, as used by economists in such debates, is in a sense the opposite of rationality.[2] Ideologies are thought to conceal rational argument, and to prevent us from using solid analytical knowledge. Hence the economists' call for 'decreasing the influence of ideologies' in favor of rational solutions that are argued to be non-ideological, but efficient in the sense that goals are achieved at minimal cost or that given resources are put to their maximal use.

I will refrain from discussing to what extent the economists' views involve ideology. It may suffice to say that most of what economists do – like the selection of topics, the definition of problems, the formulation of concepts and theories, the ascription of meaning to phenomena, data and variables, the differentiation between means and ends and so on – is not value-free, and that presenting 'optimality proofs and implications for desirable government policy [is] an inevitably ideology-laden exercise' (Samuels, 1977, 479). Instead, I will try to shed some light on the roles of ideology and beliefs in policy-making. While economists see them as obstacles to rationality, I argue that ideologies serve certain purposes in politics, and that differences in beliefs between political actors are inevitable. Understanding these purposes and learning to deal with these differences may not only make the life of economists easier, but enable them to be more effective in giving policy advice (see Section 4).

2.1 Ideologies vs. Beliefs

Let us start with a tentative and incomplete definition of the term ideology. Broadly speaking an ideology is a 'coordinated and integrated set of ideas, beliefs, and conceptions, which presents a more or less coherent view of the nature and structure of the socio-economic system' (Samuels, 1977, 470; see Denzau and North, 1994, 4, for a similar definition that refers to ideologies as *shared mental models*). By this definition, ideologies are conglomerates of beliefs that are organized in a systematic, possibly coherent manner. This is to define ideology as a social phenomenon that does not *a priori* include the negative connotation it has in public debates. Similarly, Tuchtfeld (1983) uses the more neutral notion 'systems of ideas' (Ideensysteme) for describing and distinguishing the concepts of liberalism or socialism.

Beliefs, as basic elements of ideologies, involve two main aspects (Slembeck, 1997a, 230). *Normative beliefs* define what *ought* to be at a normative level. They include preferences over how the world should work and what outcomes are desirable. In addition to the traditional connotation in economics, preferences in the political context also refer to processes, institutions and outcomes in politics, in the economy, and in other domains of society. In this view, normative beliefs are the individual-based, normative building blocks of ideologies.

The second aspect is *positive beliefs* about what *is* and how the socio-economic world does work. At a positive, though not objective, level positive beliefs identify real-life causalities, dependencies, and restrictions. They define how one perceives the world 'as it is' as an outside observer. The distinction between normative and positive beliefs may seem somewhat artificial, since both types of beliefs tend to influence each other, but it may help to understand the nature and roles of beliefs more clearly. This point will become more lucid when I focus on the content of positive beliefs in Section 2.3.

Taken together normative and positive beliefs have been labeled 'regulative beliefs' in Slembeck (1997a) while the German word '*Ordnungsvorstellungen*' was used in the textbook by Meier and Slembeck (1998). Before discussing their meaning and roles within the *process* of economic policy-making in Section 3, I will now turn to the basic roles of ideologies and beliefs in a more *static* view.

2.2 The Roles of Ideologies

It is typical for established ideologies that they are held not only by individuals, but are shared, formed, promulgated, and actively developed by groups such as political parties. In providing a more or less coherent view of the world, ideology serves several functions for the group or party (see Samuels, 1977, 471). First, ideology provides meaning and attaches value to socio-economic reality. Hence, a fundamental role of ideology is to explain and to rationalize. Second, by providing a definition of system reality, ideology focuses perception, directs analysis, and biases interpretation. Third, by providing a framework of thought *and* behavior ideology serves to promote social cohesion and group identity. Fourth, 'ideology serves as an instrument of social control and rule: an instrument for standardizing and routinizing attitudinal and behavioral responses, a mode of conflict generation and resolution, and a weapon in the struggle for power' (op. cit., 471). Thereby, ideology helps in legitimizing a system and structure of power, status, and privilege.

With regard to policy-making in democracies ideology not only serves as a device for putting forward a group's views and interests, but has properties that may be desirable from a system view.

One property is that ideologies allow the formation of groups of actors that share interests and beliefs. Without the possibility to commit to some ideology it would be difficult for isolated political actors to bring together their resources and find political support. This bundling and coordination of interests and views may be desirable (at least to some degree), because it allows the formation of platforms that are needed for finding the consensus necessary for collective action in a democracy.

A related aspect is that ideology makes political actors and groups identifiable. In a democracy, ideology provides orientation in the political market of ideas, views, and interests. It allows voters to gather information more efficiently, and therefore to take better informed decisions. This has been emphasized, for example, by Downs (1957). Democratic competition between ideologies is to prevent an ideology of the type found in socialist systems from dominating and may bring forward new ideas and solutions to collective problems. The extent of such competition, however, depends on the number of groups or parties that are able to compete for government, and the degree of 'ideological overlap' induced by this number (see below for a short comparison of Switzerland, Germany and the United States).

The predominant aspect of ideology in a democracy is perhaps that it provides an 'anchor' for making commitments that may otherwise not be credible. The advantages of rule-based over discretionary policy-making have widely been acknowledged in the literature (see, for example, Barro 1985). Following rules has the advantage that it makes behavior more predictable and thus reduces the costs associated with uncertainty.[3] Therefore, it can be rational for policy-makers to confine themselves to certain rules and behaviors, rather than have discretion. In their seminal paper Kydland and Prescott (1977, 487) conclude: 'The reason that they should not have discretion is not that they are stupid, or evil, but that discretion implies selecting the decision that is best, given the current situation. Such behavior either results in consistent but suboptimal planning or in economic instability.'

The problem of *time-inconsistency* that emerges here is that a policy that seems to be optimal at a given point in time may no longer appear to be optimal at a later time. Without a binding commitment to the original plan, policy-makers may switch to a new, seemingly better policy. But if economic actors or markets form rational expectations, they will anticipate such policy change and will behave in ways that make the original plan ineffective. Kydland and Prescott (op. cit.) recommend that 'economic theory be used to evaluate alternative policy rules and that one with good operating characteristics be selected. In a democratic society, it is probably preferable that selected rules be simple and easily understood, so it is obvious when a policymaker deviates from the policy.'

The problem of much policy-making, however, is that self-binding to overcome time-inconsistency is not easy to implement. In a dynamic context where policy decisions are taken sequentially over time new coalitions may be formed in parliament or the incumbent government may be replaced by elections. One possibility is to delegate policy-making to institutions that are not directly accountable to voters, and do not depend on majority-voting. This option is used in *monetary policy* by establishing independent central banks. Another way of self-commitment is to anchor policy rules at the constitutional level which makes it more difficult and costly to change the rules at later stages of the political process.

An additional aspect is that policy-makers or governments often lack credibility in their policy-making. This can be overcome only in the long run by forming a *reputation* for sticking to their own rules and policies. The problem of lack of government credibility in macroeconomic policy has been emphasized in the literature especially with regard to monetary and fiscal policy (see Persson and Tabellini, 1997, for an overview of the literature).

In view of these problems there is an important role for ideology in policy-making. Ideologies limit the set of behaviors that are compatible with a given ideology. Hence, for a policy-maker that is known to stand for some ideology it is difficult to change behavior radically or to implement a policy that is not compatible with this ideology without losing credibility and jeopardizing re-election. Therefore, the occurrence of ideologies tends to make behavior of policy-makers more predictable. Ideologies support rule-based behavior and tend to limit discretion. They serve as anchors for implicit rules that cannot easily be violated and make deviations from such rules more easy to detect. Ideologies can also help policy-makers in gaining reputation and implementing policies that are credible not only in the short run.

In this view, ideologies serve as a self-binding device that allow policy-makers to credibly commit to some rules or programs. As noted in the literature mentioned above, rule-based behavior, credibility, predictability, and detectability of deviations from rules are all features that are supposed to be desirable in economic policy-making. Ideologies tend to foster these features. They help policy-makers to overcome the time-inconsistency problem, and can, thus, be understood as a rational device of commitment. This aspect, however, has been ignored by those economists who label ideology as being irrational.

It should be stressed that the favorable features of ideologies are most pronounced in an open democracy where there is competition between political parties and ideologies. For instance in Switzerland there are four leading parties that share responsibility in federal government. In Germany there are two leading parties competing for federal government, each of which forms coalitions with one of two smaller parties. In the United States there appear to be only two parties able to compete for federal government.

Figure 6.1 visualizes the relative positions of the political parties of these three countries according to the common left–right scheme (horizontal axis). The circles depict the size and outreach of the respective ideologies. It is shown that there exists an overlap in ideology between neighboring parties in all countries. What is important to note, however, is that the ideological overlap of the center parties increases with a decrease in the number of parties able to compete for government. In the United States, for instance, there appears to be a large overlap in ideology between Democrats and Republicans.

Hence, it is difficult to distinguish between these two parties or their proponents in terms of ideology or political program, and both design their programs in aim of the median voter. In Switzerland four leading parties are involved in federal government according to a 'magic formula' that assigns a fixed number of seats in the cabinet to each party since 1959 (so-called *Zauber-*

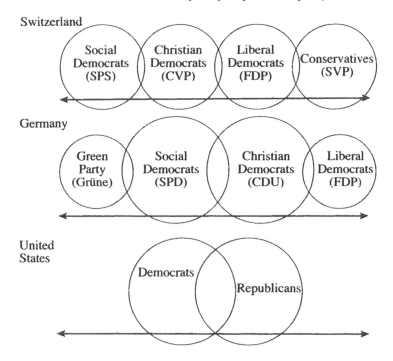

Figure 6.1   A comparison of countries

formel). This allows larger differentiations in ideology (see top of Figure 6.1), since the 'opposition' is always included in government (system of *concordance government*). Such differentiations may also be fostered by the public's need for information induced by the Swiss direct democratic system where citizens are routinely asked to vote over policy proposals. In such a system, different ideologies may be useful or even needed to produce additional information.[4]

In effect, in political systems with only two dominant parties (for example, induced by the single-member constituency currently used in most English-speaking countries) there are fewer 'ideological anchors' available. This makes it less predictable what policy a government will adopt in a specific case or policy field over time. It increases the probability of policy changes within the incumbent government. For instance, some have argued that policy under the Clinton administration over time tended to become more conservative than previously expected. Similar tendencies have been observed in the Blair administration in Great Britain whose economic policy has been found to be more conservative than that of the Tories by commentators. Also, George W. Bush has adopted policies (such as subsidies in farming and protection in the steel industry) that are not strictly in line with 'market ideology', indicating that his ideological anchors are not overly strong. However, since the leading parties do ideologically overlap in the center of the political spectrum, no extremist policies or drastic changes of policies are to be expected.

2.3 The Roles of Beliefs

As mentioned in the previous sections, beliefs fall into two broad categories. Normative beliefs define what *ought to be* while positive beliefs involve concepts about *what is*. The former are the normative building blocks of ideologies, and their social power has long been acknowledged in economics, for example, by John Stuart Mill who finds that 'One person with a belief is a social power equal to ninety-nine who have only interests' (quoted in Hutt, 1936, 63). Similarly, John Maynard Keynes (1936) in one of the most famous quotes in economics finds that ideas are more powerful than interests:

> Practical men, who believe themselves to be quite exempt from any intellectual influences, are usually the slaves of some defunct economist. ... I am sure that the power of vested interests is vastly exaggerated compared to the encroachment of ideas. ... sooner or later, it is ideas, not vested interests, which are dangerous for good or evil.

Given the power of normative beliefs, it seems somewhat surprising how little attention economics has paid to them. Instead, the discipline has focused on *preferences* in the economic realm and on *interests* in the political realm. However, when it comes to economic policy-making there appear to be good reasons to take the normative aspect of beliefs, ideas or views seriously, especially when they emerge in the form of organized ideology. Since I have tried to discuss these normative aspects above, I will now take a closer look at positive beliefs.

Positive beliefs involve mental constructions of real-life causalities and restrictions.[5] They are individual or shared theories about how the world works. Such beliefs are inevitable since they allow us to interpret our environment, understand economic and social relations, and make plans. They are cognitive (though not necessarily conscious) constructions of the world and allow us to communicate with others. As will be discussed in more detail below (Section 3), processes of collective construction and interpretation of the socio-economic world or system play a crucial role in actual policy-making. The point I want to make for now is that the positive beliefs of economists differ from those of politicians and the public in many important respects.

The economists' complaints about how little the public as well as professional politicians understand about the economy and its functioning has some tradition, especially among those who give economic policy advice (see

Schultze, 1996; Stiglitz, 1998). Surveys on economic literacy routinely find that the general public is badly informed about economic processes and institutions.[6]

A somewhat natural reaction of economists is to identify and brandmark so-called 'economic fallacies'. For instance, Wood (1997) has compiled a list of such fallacies in order to demonstrate the many areas in which the public 'mis-understands' basic economic principles. The list presented at the end of this section (Table 6.1) draws on Wood's observations and merges them with cases where the beliefs of policy-makers are at odds with economic wisdom. The latter are in the focus of what Henderson (1986, 3) calls 'do-it-yourself economics': 'Over wide areas of policy the judgements of politicians and their officials, as also of public opinion in general, have been and still are guided to a large extent by beliefs and perceptions about the working of the economic system ... which owe little or nothing to the economics profession.'

Similarly, Buchanan (1993, 10) observes that

> the operation of markets is within the working knowledge of everyone. 'Every man his own economist' or 'do it yourself economics' has been a characteristic feature of policy discourse since the professionalization of the science. ... Even in those national economies that are not, and have never been, organized on socialist principles, there is no general public understanding of the 'principles of economics'.

The fact that economists talk about 'economic fallacies' or complain about the lack of understanding of economic principles implies that economists perceive themselves in the possession of superior knowledge about the economy and the way it works. This observation clearly reveals the normative nature of much economic theorizing.[7] For the purpose of the present chapter, however, it seems unimportant whether one agrees on the existence of fallacies, since the focus is on observing the existence of differences in economic beliefs between economists and non-economists, and on deducing implications for policy-making and policy advice.

2.4 Towards a New Research Agenda

Despite their apparent significance in economic policy-making, the roles of positive beliefs have rarely been studied by economists. While in psychology there exist some attempts to investigate what mental models people have about the economy (for example, Williamson and Wearing, 1996) and how they may affect behavior (for example, Shimp and Sharma, 1987), little work has been done in economics. There exist only few studies that try to explore and assess the positive beliefs (for example, Caplan, 2002) or mental economic models of the general public – though not of policy-makers. Shiller (1996) asks why people do not like inflation. Economists have a long list of reasons why inflation may harm the economy. Lay-people also dislike inflation just as economists, however, for quite different reasons. Shiller (1996, 44) reports that low inflation is an important element of national pride, and concludes from his study that people appear to believe in a 'bad-actor–sticky-wage model'. That is, inflation is seen to be caused by some badly-behaving or greedy people. Inflation hurts the general public's standard of living. Increases in prices, however, are not met with increases in wages. Such a finding may have implications for the making of monetary policy:

> Those who implement national policy towards inflation have to sort out which concerns they share with the public, and which they do not. ... The public's models of the economy are fundamentally different from those of economists. (op. cit. 46)[8]

In the light of such (still preliminary and incomplete) evidence three basic and broad questions arise: (i) What beliefs do citizens and policy-makers actually hold and how do they contrast with economists' beliefs? (ii) To what extent do economic beliefs guide economic behavior and what happens when economic and political actors behave according to their 'deviating' beliefs? And perhaps more fundamentally: (iii) How do people acquire beliefs, mental models or theories, and how do they evolve?

The simple background to the last question is that people do not seem to be equipped with beliefs at birth (that is, a *near tabula rasa situation*, Denzau and North, 1994, 15), and that they live in a world of true (or Knightian) uncertainty that requires them to form mental models in order to act purposefully. This leads to the even more basic question of how people learn about and cope with the world around them. Hence, a solid foundation to answer the third question requires a *theory of human learning under uncertainty*.

While most economists' efforts to develop an economic theory of learning have focused on learning under certainty (and sometimes risk),[9] and have tended to ignore the roles of positive beliefs or mental models, there exist attempts to develop behavioral (not behaviorist) foundations of economic learning (Slembeck, 1998), or to explicitly account for the roles and evolution of 'shared mental models' (Denzau and North, 1994, who refer to Holland et al., 1986, and Arthur, 1992). Somewhat surprisingly, psychologists seem to have only started to study economic socialization (Leiser et al., 1990; Lewis et al., 1995; Lunt and Furnham, 1996), however, without referring to the economic literature or making use of economic thinking (Frey, 1998).

The answer to the second question seems to be taken for granted by most economists. Even Denzau and North (1996) who carefully discuss several aspects of the roles and evolution of mental models (that is of positive beliefs in the terminology of the present chapter) do not address the problem of how these models translate into actual (economic) behavior.[10] Their implicit assumption, like in most standard economics, appears to be that people act according to their mental models or beliefs. However, the basis for such an assumption has been in the center of much debate in social psychology (see for example, Triandis, 1971; Ajzen and Fishbein, 1980; Upmeyer, 1989), and the connections between attitudes, beliefs, and behavior continues to involve many unsolved questions (for example, with regard to ecological behavior, see Kaiser and Fuhrer, in press).

In economics, a potential problem arises from the fact that *homo oeconomicus* is implicitly assumed to hold the same beliefs as his creators. But what if real people hold beliefs different from the model-builders (alias homo oeconomicus) *and* behave according to these beliefs? Does economic theory need to be revised if economic actors do not stand up to the normative implications of this theory? Or should we teach people how to behave rationally until their behavior fits the theory? What if political actors behave according to their economic beliefs (for which there exists much evidence in real-life policy-making)? Is it enough to give them 'rational' economic advice? Should we revise our models, or simply teach laymen until they 'get it right' (Barro, 1996)?

I cannot offer any definite answers to these broad and deep questions. However, I suggest two things: first, we need to revise and enrich our models of economic policy-making to better account for the roles of ideologies and beliefs, and to understand actual policy-making as an evolutionary process. An attempt in this direction has been made in the *cognitive–evolutionary approach* (Slembeck, 1997a; Meier and Slembeck, 1998) as briefly discussed in Section 3. Second, I suggest that studying systematically and empirically the actual beliefs of the general public, policy-makers, journalists and business leaders (as compared to economists) would be a good starting point. Such studies seem largely missing today (with the exception of Caplan, 2002). The odds are strongly in favor of finding significant and systematic differences not only in normative, but also in positive, beliefs between economists and non-economists in many important areas of economic policy-making.[11] Having established such differences empirically, the next step will be to investigate their relevance for economic and political behavior.

That is, if beliefs induce or guide behavior – as implicitly assumed in most economic theory – actors that hold beliefs different from those of economists may behave differently from what is predicted by economic theory. At the level of individual behavior, for instance, people that hold mercantilistic beliefs may prefer domestic over foreign goods. At the political level people may vote in favor of (protectionist) policies that are compatible with their own positive beliefs, but that may appear 'irrational' or inefficient in economic terms. Thus, establishing the link between positive beliefs on one hand, and economic and political behavior on the other hand, may help us to understand why people buy, save or vote the way they do. This may not only improve theory prediction,

Table 6.1 Economic 'fallacies' and possible implications

Economic 'fallacy'	Possible implications	
	Economic/behavioral level	Economic policy level
Economic activity is always a zero-sum-game.	Potential gains from trade or exchange are not recognized. Behavior is more competitive/less cooperative.	Support of policies that redistribute income and/or wealth.
Small firms cannot survive in the free market.	Discouragement of entrepreneurship.	Support of strong antitrust laws and subsidies or tax cuts for small firms.
Markets are created and maintained by the government.	Discouragement of entrepreneurship.	Support of a strong and discretionary government.
Speculation is harmful to the economy. Stock markets are like casinos and thus are not important (or even harmful) to the economy.	Under engagement in market activity and stock markets. Selection bias towards more risky market participants.	Support of restrictive market rules/of taxes on gains from speculation and stock markets.
There is a fixed amount of labor demand in the economy so that unemployment is mainly a problem of labor not being distributed evenly among workers.	Increased willingness to accept reductions in working time and/or early retirements. Negative attitude towards immigration.	Support of policies that redistribute labor (e.g., shorter working week, early retirement) and of restrictions on immigration.
New technologies induce unemployment to rise.	Reluctance to adopt/accept new technologies.	Support of laws that restrict the introduction of new technologies.
A country's economic welfare is increased by exporting as much as possible and importing as little as possible.	Increase consumption of domestic goods at the expense of foreign goods. Reduction of foreign trade.	Support of export subsidies and import restrictions (such as tariffs and import quotas).
Developing countries cannot profit from free trade because they cannot compete with strong and rich nations at international markets.	Favor products from developing countries.	Reluctance to support free trade with developing countries. Support of foreign aid.
A country profits more from exporting finished goods than from exporting raw materials.	Increase of export of finished goods at the expense of raw materials.	Support of industries of finished goods at the expense of raw materials.
Large profits of major companies induce inflation to rise.	Avoidance of major companies by consumers and/or private investors.	Support of high taxes on company profits.
Money holds its value well in times of inflation.	Excessive holding of cash in times of inflation. Reluctance to indexed contracts.	Reluctance to the role of monetary policy.
Inflation does not affect investment and saving behavior.	Reluctance to (expected) inflation in investments. Excessive saving in cash or non-indexed assets at times of inflation.	Reluctance to the role of monetary policy.

but have important implications for economic education (especially of journalists) and the way economists give advice. I will conclude this section with
a tentative list of 'economic fallacies' and their possible implications that may
give some illustrative indications for the direction of the proposed research
(Table 6.1).

As will be discussed in Section 4.1, it follows from the above discussion that
the public, politicians, and economists live in different worlds, not only because
they are subject to different incentive schemes but also because of fundamental differences in *positive* beliefs.

3.   A COGNITIVE–EVOLUTIONARY APPROACH

In the previous section the roles and functions of ideologies and beliefs have
been discussed in a somewhat static manner. I will now discuss them in a more
dynamic context that looks at economic policy-making as a continuous process.
The aim of the *cognitive–evolutionary approach* is to model actual processes
of policy-formation by adding elements from psychology and evolution theory
(see Slembeck, 1997a and Meier and Slembeck, 1998, for elaborated versions
of this approach). While current economic approaches focus on particular
aspects of policy-making (such as rent seeking or vote maximizing) or on the
pros and cons of specific policy instruments, our approach aims to provide a
comprehensive and dynamic view on the real processes of policy-formation.

One main aspect is that political (and economic) actors not only bring their
interests but also their individual perceptions and interpretations to the process.
Therefore, much actual policy-making involves collective interpretations of
socio-economic 'reality' and the definition of problems and goals. The second
main aspect is that the political process evolves in time. This means that
problems are dealt with in a multi-stage process that changes the nature of the
problems and the solutions over time. It means also that political mechanisms
are not fixed, but may change as problems work their way through the system.

The political process itself is characterized by continuous processes of mobilization and negotiation. It is modeled as a problem-solving process that involves
a sequence of filters. Any collective problem (be it 'economic' or not) has to
pass this sequence in order to be solved.

3.1   Why Politics?

In order to analyse the basic properties and characteristics of policy-making, it
seems useful to think about the reasons why politics are needed at all. At a very
general level politics serves to provide collective solutions to a variety of societal

conflicts. In this view, the political process serves as a collective problem-solving device.

There are several sources of such conflict (see Figure 6.2). In a pluralistic society there exists a variety of diverging and possibly conflicting beliefs, ideologies and interests. With regard to the economic realm these divergences are fueled by division of labor and specialization. The latter also induce factual interdependencies within the economic and social system. Interdependencies tend to induce conflicts that need social coordination and can be solved only by collective action. In a world of insatiable needs and scarce resources such interdependencies also arise from economic scarcity. A main theme of economic policy-making, therefore, involves conflicts about the (re)distribution of income and wealth. In sum, much societal conflict emerges from basic economic scarcity and interdependencies between individuals or groups (for example, producers and consumers, or employers and employees).

What has been acknowledged in the economic literature is that politico-economic conflicts arise from the diverging interests of individuals and groups.

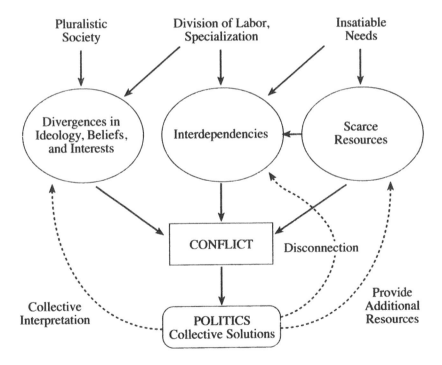

Source: Slembeck (1997a).

Figure 6.2   Why politics?

What has been neglected, however, is the role of divergences in beliefs and ideology. When looking at actual economic policy-making processes it is easy to see how much time and effort is invested in interpreting socio-economic reality, defining goals and evaluating alternative policies.[12] In fact, these processes are not only driven by diverging interests, but by divergences in beliefs and ideology. They are needed to establish a commonly accepted basis for collective action. Without such processes economic policy-making would be reduced to finding a rational solution to some (possibly complicated) socio-economic puzzle, and there would often be a unique, socially efficient solution – just as traditional models of economic policy-making in the Tinbergen tradition suggest (see Tinbergen, 1956). As argued throughout this chapter, such a view would miss the essence of much real-life policy-making.

In the cognitive–evolutionary approach economic policy provides collective solutions to economic and social conflicts. There are three basic ways to ease such conflicts (see the dotted arrows in Figure 6.2). One is to provide additional (collective) resources to reduce scarcity. This may also help to reduce interdependencies that may be disconnected by designing specific policy instruments for specific aspects of an interconnected problem area. For instance, allocative and distributive aspects can be disconnected by designing separate policy instruments for achieving the respective goals. Aside from providing collective resources and disconnecting problem aspects, a third main way of solving societal conflicts through politics is to provide a common platform that allows the balance of beliefs and interests by collective interpretations. Before discussing this latter function of the political process more extensively, I focus on the emergence of economic-policy problems.

3.2   Individual Level: the Emergence of Problems

A basic tenet of the cognitive-evolutionary approach is that problems are not fixed and given, nor do they exist independent of individual perception. *Problems emerge through the perceptions and interpretations of individuals.* With regard to policy-making this means that problems arise at the individual level in that the individual perception of problems initiates the political process.

We distinguish two main sources of problem emergence: discontent and ambiguity. *Discontent* arises from a discrepancy between the perceived state and development of the economy and normative beliefs or preferences (see the top portion of Figure 6.3). That is, actors are dissatisfied with actual economic processes or outcomes compared to how they think 'things ought to be'. Insofar as actors are unable to solve the perceived problem individually they may attempt to promulgate their problem view and seek some sort of collective action. Discontent is the typical motivation of interest groups to start political initiatives.

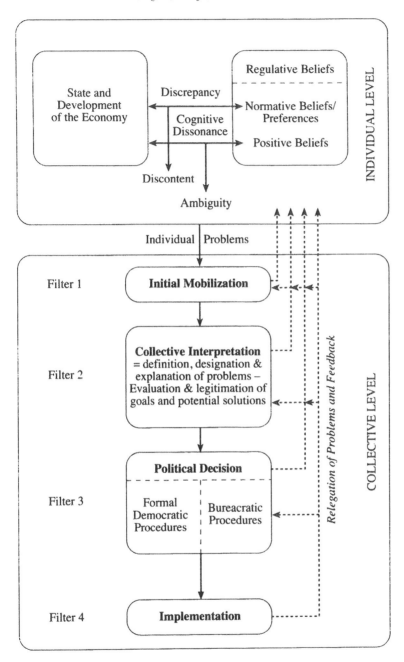

Figure 6.3   A cognitive–evolutionary model of the political process

Ambiguity arises when actual perceptions of economic states or developments do not match with the actors' positive beliefs about how 'things do work'. In this state of cognitive dissonance actors may seek collective interpretations in order to check whether collective action is necessary and to equilibrate their cognitive structures. Many debates in cabinets or parliaments seem to arise from ambiguity. Examples include the heated debates in many parliaments around the world after the stock market crash in 1987 or following September 11 in 2001.

3.3 Collective Level: the Selection of Problems and Solutions

Obviously, not all individually perceived problems do initiate political processes. Problems have to be brought forward to the collective level. The first step toward collective action is to spread the problem view and find economic and political support among those who share the view. This phase of *initial mobilization* is the first filter of a sequence of filters that constitute the political process (see Figure 6.3). The problem has to be acknowledged as being significant by a sufficient number of voters, politicians, parties or opinion leaders in order to be accepted and dealt with at the collective level. For instance, parliaments, committees, or commissions may refuse to discuss policy proposals because they feel that the problem is too insignificant and lacks political pressure. Typically, political bodies are congested by a great number of requests and proposals so that there is a struggle for attention among parties and interest groups. Many individual or group problems may not find political support or public attention. Clearly, attention is one of the scarcest resources in modern societies and getting on the public (policy) agenda can be difficult since the politicians' agenda is always full. In effect, when initial mobilization fails, the problem is relegated to the individual level and may come up at some later time.

Once the problem has been acknowledged at the collective level, its content needs to be *defined* in order to get onto the political agenda. Definition includes deciding which aspects of the problem are relevant to be dealt with and which are not. Problems are also designated by giving them a name or label that allows efficient communication and attaches a connotation.[13] Explanation of the problem involves the formation of chains of causalities that connect the problem with some source or origin.

The processes of definition, designation and explanation are elements of *collective interpretation* (see filter 2 in Figure 6.3). These processes are biased by the actors' regulative beliefs and interests, and involve attempts to persuade others of one's own views and perceptions. They often influence the outcomes of the political process significantly since diagnosis guides therapy. The more ambiguous a situation or problem appears, the more important is collective interpretation.

Before deciding about political measures, alternative courses of collective action have to be *explored and evaluated*. This process is guided by the expected contribution of an alternative to the actual solution of the problem, *and* by its congruity with the regulative beliefs of the actors. This notion goes beyond the focus of most economic theories of politics where commonly only the first aspect is considered. Finally, the agreed course of action has to be *legitimized* by demonstrating its congruity with the dominant interpretation systems, that is, the regulative beliefs of leading parties, politicians, interest groups, or voters.

In all these steps and processes of collective interpretation problems may not survive and be filtered-out due to a lack of consensus, shared interpretation and political support (see filter 2 in Figure 6.3). They may remain at the collective level or be relegated to the individual level (see dotted arrows in Figure 6.3).

What most economic models of politics focus on is the *formal political decision* process. It involves two basic mechanisms. If the problem at hand is considered a 'routine case' the solution will be based on existing patterns of behavior. The issue can then be forwarded to a *bureaucratic procedure* that follows routines or rules of thumb that have emerged through previous treatments of similar cases, so that the decision costs can be lowered and the process may proceed faster. If the problem challenges existing routines significantly, or if legislation necessary to proceed is deficient, a *formal democratic procedure* must be employed. This involves the preparation of a formal proposal in committees or commissions within the administration or parliament, and voting by ministers, parliamentarians or citizens. Obviously, even well prepared proposals may not survive formal voting and therefore be filtered-out at this stage (see filter 3 in Figure 6.3).

Finally, decided policies have to be implemented. *Implementation* is typically delegated to bureaucrats. During the process of implementation, however, bureaucrats and those affected by the policy may re-interpret its content, try to renegotiate the issue, and exert various sorts of passive or active resistance so that the policy is not necessarily implemented as intended by policy-makers (see Slembeck, 1997a, 241, for a more detailed discussion). Resistence and re-interpretation may be substantial so that the policy may not be implemented, but the issue is relegated to earlier stages of the process (see filter 4 in Figure 6.3).[14]

3.4 Evolution

All four phases of the political process described here function as *filters*. Most problems and issues of economic policy that compete for collective action are never 'solved' or implemented the way a rational social planner would. They are relegated or drop out at one or the other stage of the process, and remain unsolved until they come up some time later or vanish due to changes in the social, economic, or technological situation. Since the sources of societal conflicts (see Figure 6.2) that call for collective action seem inexhaustible, the loops that issues take during the political process (see dotted upward arrows in Figure 6.3) are continuously fueled by new problems. These loops involve feedback information that constantly change and renew the way economic policy is formed. By this system-feedback new ideas and policies are developed and tested, and the system evolves as a whole. Hence, the political process not only selects political issues, it also selects patterns of thinking and behavior, and institutions.

At the level of individual regulative beliefs and behavior, evolution signifies changes in patterns of thinking and behavior in response to changes in the environment. Internal variation of these patterns is induced by external variations *and* flawed application of existing patterns; that is, existing patterns are internally varied, and external patterns from other circumstances outside the political field are incorporated to produce new patterns. Together with existing successful patterns, these new patterns are applied in the political process where they are *selected* in practice. Selection leads to modification (that is, internal variation) of futile patterns and preservation of successful patterns. Due to this individual learning process the repertoire of patterns of thinking and behavior is increased so that new problems may be treated in a more sophisticated way.

At the collective level, evolutive effects occur when the selection of patterns influences the political constellation.[15] This will be the case, at least in the long run, because successful actors – that is, actors equipped with effective patterns who have successfully managed to promulgate their beliefs and to pursue their interests in the political process – can often improve their position in that process and increase their influence, thereby shifting political constellation over time. In effect, the ongoing changes in political constellation continuously influence current and future processes of collective treatment of problems. This way the system often evolves smoothly to adjust to changes in the relative influence of actors. It may explain why radical changes are seldom observed in democratic systems (Slembeck, 1997a, 246).

Overall, the fuel of evolution in the polity is the continuous emergence of individually perceived problems that are due to ambiguity and discontent. In the approach presented here, problem views are brought forward to and filtered-out (or selected) by the actual political process. Similar to biological processes of variation or mutation, new views, ideas, problems, and potential solutions are produced by political actors, and are tested and selected in the political realm. Those views, ideas, and solutions that survive the selection process are (at least for some time) preserved and condensed into new rules, laws, and institutions.

4.   ON THE ART OF GIVING POLICY ADVICE

The above discussion of the roles of ideologies and beliefs, and of the cognitive–evolutionary view on policy-making has several implications for giving policy advice. Let me start by observing that there exists some degree of mutual discontent between economists and politicians. *Economists* complain that politicians lack sound economic knowledge, and accuse them of implementing policies that are inefficient or even irrational from an economic point of view. *Politicians*, on the other hand, seek economic advice, but find that economists are single-minded and do not understand politics. Also, for every economic expert opinion there appears to exist another exactly contrary expert opinion.

There are several reasons for this. First, economists and politicians live in different worlds that involve different beliefs, goals, means and restrictions (Section 4.1). Second, the advisory process cannot always deliver what politicians hope for. While they expect objective, scientific solutions to predefined policy problems, economists have to gauge the pros and cons of alternatives often without being able to provide an objectively best policy. Hence, the politicians' call for the 'single-handed economist'.[16] Economists typically work with statements that are contingent on certain assumptions and on developments of the economy or society (that is, scenarios). Politicians feel uneasy with these techniques since they do not provide definite answers. Overall, political decisions cannot be delegated to scientific procedures that produce objectively best solutions as some politicians would like to think. Therefore, economic advice should involve an *interactive process* that includes defining goals and developing solutions, both of which are subject to political, cognitive and economic restrictions (Section 4.2).Third, economic policy proposals are often incompatible or contrary to the rules, requirements and idiosyncracies of the politico-administrative system (Section 4.3).

4.1 The Two Worlds of Economists and Politicians

When trying to understand why professional economic advice is not taken up or sometimes completely ignored by politicians it seems crucial to have in mind that economists and politicians live in different worlds. For instance, the economist Joseph Stiglitz (1998), member and chairman of the US Council of Economic Advisors 1993–97, reports his own experience: 'When I arrived in the lawyer- and politician-dominated White House environment, I often felt that I had arrived in another world. ... It was that often another system of logic, another set of rules of reasoning, applied' (op. cit., 5). In both worlds there exist different goals, incentives, time-horizons, and restrictions as summarized in Table 6.2.

Behind this table is the unsentimental view of politicians as *political entrepreneurs* who are experts in the management of political processes. They are prone to pursue their personal aims and are subject to various restrictions that result from the actual political process and political constellations. The criteria for the achievement of goals are partly individual (based on personal regulative beliefs) and partly induced by the political system. Accord with accepted norms

Table 6.2   The two worlds of economists and politicians

		Economist	Politician
Orientation		• Explanation, prediction	• Political action
Goals	General goals	• Find general (empirical) regularities • Applications to specific problems	• Make or prevent binding decisions in order to – solve specific problems – establish organizational structures or procedures • Interpretation, explanation in ambiguous situations[17]
	Goals in advisory process	• Long-term 'rational' solutions • Efficiency of solutions	• Short-term problem-solving, s.t. various restrictions • Distributional effects of solutions
Criteria for achievement of goals		• Clear-cut notions, internal logic and consistency • Accord with paradigm of schools of thought	• Generally accepted norms and behavior • Accord with everyday intuition, dominant ideology, regulative beliefs
Restrictions		• Largely self-chosen, systematically varied, and abstract • No time pressure	• Mainly given; financial, personal, political support of organization, group, or citizens • Often time pressure

and tolerated behavior in politics may be as essential as correspondence with everyday intuition of citizens in democratic systems, or compatibility with ideology of parties.

Since the success of political entrepreneurship depends on attributes that are often considerably different from the criteria used in economic analysis, professional economic expertise is not always widespread among politicians. For instance, while economists are trained in analyzing the economic system, politicians are specialists in analysing the political system and in acting within this system. The politician's job requires not only analytical skills, but also communicative abilities and possibly a charismatic personality. This may explain why not many economists ever make it to leading political positions (see Frey, 2000, 22ff., for a list of economists in office).

What follows for economists as political advisers is the importance of being aware of 'the politician's world' described in Table 6.2. Typically, economists tend to overestimate the latitude for action available to politicians (and to even leading parties) in democratic systems at any given time. The point is that while economists may start from scratch when designing optimal or efficient policies, politicians must start from an already *existing set of policies* that (i) is associated with certain distributions of incomes, wealth or rights, that (ii) is embedded in an evolving political environment, and that (iii) is the result of bargaining, compromising and coalition formation in earlier stages of the process. Thus, in most cases the specific situation of an administration, politician or group who seeks advice has to be *taken as given*, and should be carefully analysed by the adviser. Hence, in addition to the conventional economic policy analysis, economists may benefit from examining the goals and restrictions of his or her client in order to match advice with the requirements of the political system and process. That is, the economic analysis is paralleled with a politico-economic analysis.

In sum, economic advice should not only be correct in terms of scientific standards but can be improved upon by fitting the situation and needs of the addressee. Therefore, economists' advice should *account for*

- compatibility with the regulative beliefs of the recipients and their relevant political environment, that is, with regulative beliefs of other (potentially opponent) actors;
- the existing political constellation, that is, the possibilities of interaction among actors with respect to their factual relative influence;
- the political restrictions – especially political support – the advised actor *and* the economists' proposals are subject to;
- familiar *symbols* that may be employed in support of proposals, customary *rituals* that have to be followed, and emotions of involved actors;
- the logical and practical interdependencies of ends and means in the political field.

4.2   Two Models of the Advisory Process

The view outlined so far contrasts with *traditional decisional concepts* of the advisory process where advisers only have to propose efficient means, that is, policies, with respect to *given* goals (see left side of Figure 6.4). In the 'decisionistic' approach to policy advice based on the Tinbergen tradition, the first step is that political goals are defined by politicians. Next, experts analyse

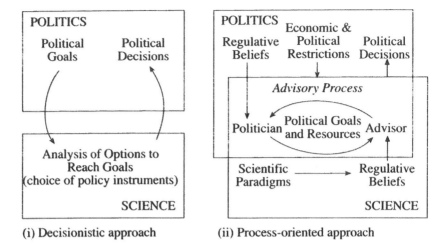

(i) Decisionistic approach   (ii) Process-oriented approach

Figure 6.4   Two approaches to economic advice

options and devise policies in order to achieve these pre-defined goals based on
scientific knowledge and evidence. The adviser's job is to design an optimal,
objectively best policy, or to compile a list of alternative policies for politicians
to choose from. Finally, the decision which policy to implement is taken in the
political realm. The decisionistic approach works smoothly only under the
rather ideal conditions that

- policy goals are fixed and defined unambiguously
- an objectively best (or second best) solution can be designed
- all pros and cons of all alternatives are/can be known
- the proposed policy is in harmony with the predominant ideologies and
  beliefs.

In practice, however, these requirements are rarely met, because:

- Policy goals are moving targets that are continuously redefined in the
  political process. Since they are the outcome of political bargaining and
  compromising, goals are often formulated at a level that is too general
  for being operational in policy design.
- There is not an objectively best solution to a policy problem that all
  experts (not to mention all politicians) can agree upon. Hence, in many
  areas of economic policy there is rarely general consensus among experts
  (at least not with regard to all details of a given policy proposal).

• Not all pros and cons of all alternative policies can be known. It is often difficult to gauge all (unwanted) side-effects of a policy. Scenario techniques and econometric analysis of past data do not deliver 'safe grounds' for policy decisions, and do open opportunities for political adversaries to fight over the details and probabilities of scenarios and estimates.
• Proposed policies may run counter to ideology and beliefs of influential politicians, parties, or (voter) groups.

The *procedural approach* to policy advice proposed here proceeds somewhat differently (see right side of Figure 6.4). In the same way that the political process involves the finding, defining, deciding, and implementing of collectively accepted goals *and* means to achieve them, the advisory process should also involve the discussion of ends *and* means of the actor or group seeking advice with respect to actual economic and political restrictions. In this view, it seems necessary to implement an *interactive advisory process* instead of simply delegating the finding of optimal solution to some experts.

It seems especially important to recognize that politicians bring their own beliefs and ideologies to this process that may conflict with the beliefs of academic advisers that are based on scientific paradigms and schools of thought. To acknowledge this potential conflict and dealing with it in a communicative process may considerably increase the likelihood for 'rational' advice to be successfully implemented.

4.3   Shortcomings of Policy Proposals

The political realm involves a system of logic and rules that are quite apart from the economists' world. I will now outline some basic obstacles that make it difficult for politicians to accept the economists' view and for economists to put forward their ideas in policy-making.

First of all one should keep in mind that many proposals in economic policy focus on increasing efficiency in one or the other way. Often the aim is to lower the costs (of the pension system, say) for reaching a given policy goal. One potential problem is that goals are not given, but defined in the political process; political goals are moving targets. A second problem is that reformed systems (for example pensions or health care) are, of course, organized differently (that is, more efficiently) so that they almost certainly also differ in terms of outcomes. Hence, in practice it is almost impossible to reach exactly the same goals as in the status quo with a new, more efficient system or policy.

Furthermore, in practice there are virtually always winners and losers from a reformed system or policy. Most frequently there is a potential for near-Pareto improvements where 'almost everyone' would benefit from changes and only a small, narrowly defined group would be hurt. However, Stiglitz (1998, 4) reports that '"almost everyone" was rarely sufficient in government policy-making and often such near-Pareto improvements did not occur'. The point – that economists tend to overlook – is that small groups can sometimes exert enormous political resistance (see Olson, 1965), and that it is often difficult to compensate losers. While in theory it may seem simple to compensate losers out of the efficiency gains of a new policy, in practice the compensation may be only monetary and does not include changes in non-monetary respects (such as political or social status) induced by a new policy.

How about strict Pareto improvements? Insofar as they exist in practice (in fact they are extremely rare), they are difficult to implement for several reasons that all relate to the dynamics and uncertainties of the political process (see Stiglitz, 1998).

- *Inability of government to make credible commitments*: a Pareto improvement is not a one-shot, static policy change, but part of a dynamic process of a sequence of policies. While a reform may be favorable to all groups in early stages of the process, this may not be true in later stages. The government usually cannot commit itself to ensure that the interests of some groups are not undermined in years (or decades) to come.
- *Coalition formation and bargaining*: actions that appear to be a Pareto improvement in the short run can look much riskier in a long-run, dynamic perspective, since new coalitions may be formed and policies may be renegotiated.
- *Uncertainty about the consequences of change*: whenever one aims to implement Pareto improvements by a policy that introduces competitive elements there is uncertainty about the precise consequences for certain groups. Also, political adversaries may not agree on what appear to be Pareto improvements because due to imperfect or asymmetric information they are suspicious about the adversary's 'true' and future intentions.[18]

As argued in Section 2.2, ideologies serve as a self-binding device that allow policy-makers to credibly commit to some rules or programmes by limiting the set of acceptable behavior or choice. Ideologies help to make coalitions more lasting and stable, and tend to reduce uncertainty about future policy-making. Hence, in the absence of ideology the above obstacles to Pareto improvements are likely to be even more pronounced.

Another problem is that economists' policy proposals typically aim to improve the efficiency of policies but tend to neglect the *distributional aspects*. It follows from the politicians view of the world, and from the incentives of the political system, however, that the efficiency of policies is only a secondary aspect. What matters more in politics, instead, are the distributional effects of policies. The true costs of policies are of minor importance as long as 'almost everyone' is 'not too unhappy', and (re)election is therefore not jeopardized. Many efficiency improvements alter existing distributions of incomes, wealth or rights, and are therefore difficult to implement. Especially unattractive are improvements that increase general welfare but do not account for distributional effects, since 'a policy that hurts five people and helps five people produces five enemies and five ingrates' (Verdier, 1984).

For instance, the privatization of social security may increase system efficiency and thereby general social welfare in the long run, that is in favor of future generations. Privatization, however, has to include compensation to initial generations since long-run gains come primarily at their expense (Kotlikoff, 1995, 30).[19] The big question, however, is *how* such compensation can be implemented and financed, and if voters can be convinced of the long-run gains in favor of future generations. In view of the problems and idiosyncracies of the political process discussed above – especially with regard to the government's lack of credibility and the problem of time-inconsistency in long term reform projects – voters may prove to be rather skeptical about such reform even if they generally believe in its long-run benefits.

Of course, no politician would ever admit that the efficiency of policies is only of secondary importance in policy-making. In order to *mask the real cost* of a policy or system, and to redistribute income, wealth or rights in favor of their respective electorate, politicians usually adopt a mixture of several ingredients that make it hard to implement efficiency-improving policies (see Slembeck, 1997b).

One ingredient is that policy instruments are designed such that several goals are achieved simultaneously. The ideal of having one policy instrument associated with only one goal (Tinbergen, 1956) is violated in a multi-stage bargaining process that merges the interests of various groups and coalitions. Typically, politicians strive to reach allocative *and* distributive goals with the same instrument. Although, this mixing may be economically inefficient in many cases, it is politically attractive in that it allows support to be gained by integrating a variety of (possibly opposing) interests. Therefore, reforms designed to disentangle the mixture of instruments with multiple goals are difficult to implement, because they break off existing coalitions resulting from log rolling.

Another aspect is that politicians aim to *keep transparency low* about who pays for what and who benefits from what in a policy field. This is to conceal the (re)distributive effects of policies agreed upon in political bargaining and compromising. Many economic reform proposals, however, increase cost–benefit transparency. For instance, *direct payments* to compensate farmers for positive externalities (such as taking care of the environment) are much 'more visible than price fixing, and thus more vulnerable to political pressure for cuts later on.' (Stiglitz, 1998, 10). Also, it may be impossible for the government to credibly commit itself to future direct payments. Various kinds of *hidden subsidies* – for instance in the form of charging electricity from government-owned plants at cost instead of market price – may suddenly become visible under a new and efficient regime, and therefore increase future political pressure.[20] In a public choice perspective, it should also be noted that increased transparency diminishes the politicians' potential for acquiring information rents from their role as political agents of their electorate. All this makes transparency-enhancing policy proposals extremely unattractive in many cases.

A third related ingredient to hide the real cost of a policy or system and to increase public spending in favor of one's own electorate is to ignore the 'principle of fiscal equivalence' (Olson, 1969). This principle basically stipulates that the level of provision of collective or public goods and services, or in fact of any political measure involving public spending or social cost, is optimal only if the three following groups or collectives are in congruence: (i) those who benefit from the measure, (ii) those who decide about the measure, and (iii) those who provide the necessary resources, that is pay for the measure (see Figure 6.5).

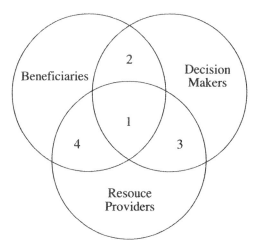

Figure 6.5   Fiscal equivalence

This equivalence is given in area 1 of Figure 6.5 where all three groups coincide. The level of public spending, for instance, is optimal since those who benefit are also those who decide and pay. For political decision makers, however, there is a strong incentive to design policies or systems (for example, tax systems) such that their own electorate is in the role of beneficiaries but does not have to pay for the costs involved (see area 2 in Figure 6.5), thereby causing inefficient allocations and over-provision of public goods.

Moreover, in economies that are organized by federalist principles there is a tendency to design policies or systems that involve several levels of government (from local to federal) so that the principle is violated simultaneously at several interwoven levels, making it all the easier to conceal who really pays for what and who benefits from what. In effect, reforms that aim to foster the efficiency-enhancing principle of fiscal equivalence typically also increase transparency, and run counter to the interests of leading politicians and parties.

In sum, there are (at least) the following obstacles to rational, efficiency improving policy reforms.

*   Achieving several goals with a single policy instrument is often inefficient but politically attractive.
*   Cost transparency is politically unattractive.
*   Fostering the principle of fiscal equivalence is politically unattractive.

5.   SUMMARY AND CONCLUSIONS

This chapter discusses several topics of economic policy-making in a cognitive–evolutionary view that economists have tended to neglect. While economists like to regard ideologies as obstacles to 'rational' policy-making, as argued in Section 2, they allow to form platforms and coalitions of shared beliefs needed for collective action in a democracy, they reduce information cost by making political actors or groups identifiable, and they allow actors to commit themselves to rules and behaviors in more credible and predictable ways. Therefore, in democracies ideologies are rational devices of self-commitment that increase credibility of policy-makers and tend to reduce problems of time-inconsistency and discretion in policy-making. In view of the literature on monetary and fiscal policy these features of ideology may indeed be desirable.

Normative beliefs are the value-laden building blocks of ideologies and enforce the functions just described. Positive beliefs have been found to differ significantly between economists and non-economists in many instances. Table 6.1 presents tentative examples of such 'economic fallacies' and their possible effects at behavioral and political levels. I have argued that taking such fallacies seriously may have several implications. First, given that beliefs guide behavior there may be a case for revising theory in areas where the beliefs of economic or political actors induce behavior to deviate from theory prediction. Second, policy-makers have to sort out which beliefs they share with economists and the public, and economists have to account for the beliefs of addressees when giving policy advice. That is, advancing 'rationality' in economic policy-making requires careful analysis of beliefs and adequate communication. Third, economic education, especially of politicians and journalists, may need to be improved upon.

In sum, understanding differences in positive beliefs is the first step towards 'more rational' policy-making in that it is a prerequisite for shifting policy debates from a purely normative or 'ideological' level to a positive level of analysis. However, little effort has been put into studying the actual economic beliefs of policy-makers and the public. Systematic empirical work is needed to substantiate the fallacies listed in Table 6.1 and their implications at behavioral and political levels. Such work will also need to include the analysis of the link between economic beliefs and economic or political behavior, since divergent beliefs may be relevant to economists only insofar as they induce certain types of behaviors. Overall, there appears to be a vast new area of research for economists to explore. Section 2.4. sketches the basic direction of a new research agenda along these lines.

In Section 3 the cognitive–evolutionary approach to policy-making is outlined. It models policy-making as a collective problem-solving process that evolves over four stages each of which functions a filter. The main point is that real-life political processes differ substantially from the puzzle-solving task of a social planner in that they involve elements of perception, cognition, and interpretation that bias processes and outcomes. Since political actors rarely agree on definition, explanation, and potential solutions of problems due to diverging beliefs and interests, processes of mobilization, collective interpretation, and negotiation are essential features of actual policy-making. The roles of regulative beliefs have been stressed for the emergence of problems at the level of the individual. They also play an important role at the collective level, since policies can be implemented successfully only if their characteristics and their expected effects are compatible with the dominant regulative beliefs of politically relevant or powerful actors and groups.

The process of policy-making evolves in time and involves several feedback loops that connect the stages of the process (see Figure 6.3). By continuous introduction of new issues and problems into the process, and by application of new beliefs and behaviors that challenge existing beliefs, rules, and routines the political system evolves. That is, the political process not only selects or solves collective problems, it also selects beliefs and behaviors, and preserves successful ones until they are newly challenged. Therefore, actual policy-making may better be described as a sequence of disequilibria than by the traditional equilibrium concept.

The regulative beliefs of political actors play an additional role in giving policy advice (Section 4). Since economists and politicians live in worlds that involve different goals, norms, and restrictions, it has been argued that economic advice is most effective when it is embedded in an interactive process that includes not only rational economic analysis and arguments, but also a politico-economic analysis of the political process as outlined in the cognitive–evolutionary approach. The main function of such additional effort is to account for political idiosyncrasies and restrictions, especially those restrictions based on the regulative beliefs of powerful political actors or groups, when designing economic policy proposals.

The discussion of some shortcomings of economic policy proposals (Section 4.3) has highlighted several cases of such peculiarities that render it difficult to implement efficiency improving proposals. First of all, the distributional effects of policies or systems appear to matter more in politics than their efficiency. Reforms, however, usually change existing distributions of income, wealth, or rights so that losers often need to be compensated. Such compensation may not be simple to implement due to problems of time-inconsistency, increased transparency, and the government's lack of credibility. Finally, efficiency-improving reforms tend to increase transparency about who pays for what and who benefits from what. Such reforms may break up existing agreements and coalitions that are the result of political bargaining and compromising. For this reason, reforms that aim to disentangle the usual mixture of goals and instruments or to foster the principle of fiscal equivalence tend to be politically unattractive.

NOTES

1. Author's address: Tilman Slembeck, Department of Economics. University of St.Gallen, Varnbuelstrasse 19, 9000 St.Gallen, Switzerland, *E-mail*: tilman@slembeck.ch.
2. According to Drucker (1974, 3) 'the word "ideology" was first used on 23 May 1797 by the French theorist Antoine Louis Claude Destutt de Tracy ... as the name of a newly conceived science – the "science of ideas". ... The new science of ideas was intended to be the basis of an entirely new social and political order. ... "Ideology" was seen as the modern answer to the unscientific past.' The aim was to attack the established institutions of French society, and to create new. 'scientific' institutions. '"[I]deology" soon came to stand for the theory of government an the programme of political action which the Idéologues built upon their science' (p. 6). The Idéologues are characterized as 'moderate republicans' who 'were all students of, and sympathizers with, the Enlightenment tradition' (p. 6). After de Tracy failed in reforming France according to his new science the term ideology was little heard of. It was Karl Marx who later used the term. however, in a rather different, pejorative way by 'condemning a characteristic of most social-political thought' (Drucker, 1974, 14). According to Marx, a theory is ideological when – by the way the theory functions – it serves the interests of some social class. 'De Tracy's "ideology" is the Enlightened replacement for the idols of the market-place: Marx's "ideology" is the idol of the market-place' (p. 14).
3. The reduction of transaction cost induced by rule-guided behavior is the core of modern Institutional Economics; see for example, Kasper and Streit (1998).
4. It should be noted that in a direct democratic system there may also be additional incentives for interest groups to provide information about the pros and cons of policy proposals (see Kirchgässner (2000, 166); and Schneider (1985) for empirical evidence for Switzerland).
5. It should be noted that other definitions of the term 'belief' have been used in economics. In game theory the term is employed in the sense of expectations about the behavior of other

players based on information about past behavior or outcomes. Hence, while in the game theoretic use beliefs are more like expectations, I will use the term positive beliefs in the sense of theories.

6. See, for example, the National Council on Economic Education's survey (NCEE, 1999) for evidence from the United States or Lüdecke and Sczesny (1998) for an international companion of economic literacy.

7. This reveals, of course, a main difference between natural and social sciences. While a physicist cannot influence his research object by talking to it, and there is no sense for a biologist to claim that birds are 'flying wrong' or to teach them how to efficiently construct nests, there is a distinct normative level to social sciences that involves the potential of scientists to influence the beliefs and behaviors of their own research object. In sum, people can behave in unpredicted ways and learn things that other animals cannot.

8. Shiller's study also suggests that economists may lack competence in communicating their ideas and knowledge about the economy which may result in misperceptions about what economists think: 'The communications gap is all the wider because many people think that the prominence given inflation in the news is due to the economists, while economists often feel differently' (op. cit. 46).

9. See Fudenberg and Levine (1998) for an overview of theories on learning in games, and Brenner (1999) for various formal models. A critical review of this literature can be found in Slembeck (1999) and Slembeck (forthcoming).

10. For a discussion of the roles of ideologies in the perspective of economic history see North (1981, Ch. 5) who advocates a *positive theory of ideology*.

11. The literature gives some empirical hints in this direction – see Blendon et al. (1997) who directly compare the 'beliefs' of economists and non-economists, and Caplan (2002) who analyses the same data set with regard to potential effects of self-serving biases, political ideology, and economic education – but these studies provide only *indirect* evidence on *positive beliefs* or mental models in that the used questionnaire involves only *normative questions* about factors that are thought to be 'good' or 'bad' for the economy, or factors of why the economy is 'not doing better than it is'.

12. For instance, many long debates in parliament may appear as inefficient and ideology-driven to a 'rational' outside observer. Such debates, however, serve the function of putting forward and exchanging ideas and beliefs in public. While private talk may be cheap, public talk is more binding and 'costly'. Also, these debates are used to rationalize and legitimize policy decisions.

13. For instance, Stiglitz (1998, 10) reports that US dairy farmers pushed forward a cartel-like arrangement of price fixing under the name of 'self-help' to prevent the government from introducing competitive markets for milk.

14. France provides an example where resistance 'on the street' has repeatedly led politicians to withdraw already decided policies (for example, on minimum wages).

15. A *political constellation* is the sum of possibilities of interaction among political actors with respect to their factual relative influence. Influence is based on personal, role-related, and political resources. The ways in which political actors interact and how they influence the political process are determined by formal and institutional arrangements, and by informal processes, especially by various kinds of personal communications (see Slembeck, 1997a, 239).

16. The story goes that politicians prefer 'single-handed economists' because they are unable to say that on one hand something is good, while on the other hand it has its down sides.

17. Since situations of ambiguity call for explanation, advisers' access to political actors is best in these situations. Search and need for explanation is the joint interest of the economist and the political actor. The latter demands explanation also to legitimize and strategically plan his actions; see Niskanen (1986), Verdier (1984).

18. Stiglitz (1998, 13) suggest that 'generalized skepticism' about proposals offered by an adversary may not only come from the fear that the adversary may benefit at one's own expense (due to asymmetric information), but 'also from the fact that many people lack the training or competence to understand the consequences of policies'.

19. See also Kotlikoff et al. (2001, 1): 'Social Security's privatization can substantially raise long run living standards. But achieving these gains will take a considerable amount of time and will entail some welfare losses to transition generations.'
20. Similar arguments may apply to policies aimed at reducing the number of working poor. While the costs of 'inefficient' minimum wages (for example, in the form of a higher risk of unemployment for low-skilled workers) are rather dispersed, the costs of 'efficient' direct subsidies or tax reductions to low-income families (for example, earned income tax credits) are more visible and vulnerable with regard to future budget cuts.

REFERENCES

Ajzen, I. and M. Fishbein (1980), *Understanding Attitudes and Predicting Social Behavior*, Englewood Cliffs: Prentice-Hall.

Arthur, W.B. (1992), *On Learning and Adaption in the Economy*, Institute for Economic Research, Discussion Paper No. 854, Queen's University.

Barro, R.J. (1985), 'Recent developments in the theory of rules versus discretion', *Economic Journal*, Supplement, 23–37.

Barro, R.J. (1996), *Getting It Right – Markets and Choices in a Free Society*, Cambridge, US and London, UK: MIT Press.

Blendon, R.J., J.M. Benson, M. Brodie, R. Morin, D.E. Altman, D. Gitterman, M. Bossard and M. James (1997), 'Bridging the Gap Between the Public's and Economists' View of the Economy', *Journal of Economic Perspectives*, 11 (3), 105–18.

Brenner, T. (1999), *Modeling Learning in Economics*, Cheltenham: Edward Elgar.

Buchanan, J.M. (1993), 'The triumph of economic science: is Fukuyama wrong and, if so, why?', *Journal of the Board of Audit*, 3 (7), 5–14.

Caplan, B. (2002), 'Systematically biased beliefs about economics – robust evidence of judgmental anomalies from the survey of Americans and economists on the economy', *Economic Journal*, 112 (479), 433–58.

Denzau, A.T. and D.C. North (1994), 'Shared mental models: ideologies and institutions', *Kyklos*, 47 (1), 3–31.

Downs, A. (1957), *An Economic Theory of Democracy*, New York: Harper.

Drucker, H.M. (1974), *The Political Uses of Ideology*, London: Macmillan.

Frey, B.S. (1998), Book review of: *Economic Socialization: The Economic Beliefs and Behaviours of Young People*, edited by P. Lunt and A. Furnham, *Economic Journal*, 241–3.

Frey, B.S. (2000), 'Was bewirkt die Volkswirtschaftslehre?', *Perspektiven der Wirtschaftspolitik*, 1 (1), 5–33.

Fudenberg, D. and D.K. Levine (1998), *The Theory of Learning in Games*, Cambridge, US and London, UK: MIT Press.

Henderson, D. (1986), *Innocence and Design – The Influence of Economic Ideas on Policy*, Oxford, UK and New York, US: Basil Blackwell.

Holland et al. (1986), *Induction: Processes of Learning, Inference, and Discovery*, Cambridge, US and London, UK: MIT Press.

Hutt, W.H. (1936), *Economists and the Public – A Study of Competition and Opinion*, London: J. Cape Ltd.: reprinted 1990, New Brunswick, US and London, UK: Transaction Publishers.

Kaiser, F.G. and U. Fuhrer. (in press), 'Ecological Behavior's Dependency on Different Forms of Knowledge', forthcoming in *Applied Psychology: An International Review*.

Kasper, W. and M.E. Streit (1998), *Institutional Economics: Social Order and Public Policy*, Cheltenham: Edward Elgar.

Keynes, J.M. (1936), *The General Theory of Employment, Interest and Money*, London: Macmillan.

Kirchgässner, G. (2000), 'Wirtschaftliche Auswirkungen der direkten Demokratie', *Perspektiven der Wirtschaftspolitik*, **1** (2), 161–80.

Kotlikoff, L.J. (1995), 'Privatization of Social Security: How It Works and Why It Matters', NBER Working Paper No. 5330, Cambridge, MA: National Bureau of Economic Research.

Kotlikoff, L.J., K. Smetters and J. Walliser (2001), 'Distributional Effects in a General Equilibrium Analysis of Social Security', in M. Feldstein and J.B. Liebman (eds), *The Distributional Aspects of Social Security and Social Security Reform*, Chicago: University of Chicago Press.

Kydland, F. and E. Prescott (1977), 'Rules rather than discretion: the inconsistency of optimal plans', *Journal of Political Economy*, **85** (3), 473–90.

Leiser, D., C. Roland-Lévy and G. Sevón (1990), 'Economic socialization', *Journal of Economic Psychology*, Special Issue, **11** (4).

Lewis, A., P. Webley and A. Furnham (1995), *The New Economic Mind – The Social Psychology of Economic Behavior*, New York, US and London, UK: Harvester-Wheatsheaf.

Lüdecke, S. and Ch. Sczesny (1998), 'Ökonomische Bildung im internationalen Vergleich', *Schweizerische Zeitschrift für kaufmännisches Bildungswesen*, **92** (6), 417–32.

Lunt, P. and A. Furnham (eds) (1996), *Economic Socialization: The Economic Beliefs and Behaviours of Young People*, Cheltenham: Edward Elgar.

Meier, A. and T. Slembeck (1998), *Wirtschaftspolitik – Ein kognitiv-evolutionärer Ansatz*, second edition, München und Wien: Oldenbourg publishers.

National Council on Economic Education (NCEE1999): http://www.ncee.net.

Niskanen, W.A. (1986), 'Economists and politicians', *Journal of Policy Analysis and Management*, **5** (2), 234–44.

North, D.C. (1981), *Structure and Change in Economic History*, New York: Norton.

Olson, M. (1965), *The Logic of Collective Action*, Cambridge, MA: Harvard University Press.

Olson, M. (1969), 'The principle of "fiscal equivalence": the division of responsibilities among different levels of government', *American Economic Review*, **59** (2), 479–87.

Persson, T. and G. Tabellini (1997), 'Political Economics and Macroeconomic Policy', NBER Working Paper No. W6329, Cambridge, MA: National Bureau of Economic Research.

Samuels, W.J. (1977), 'Ideology in Economics', in S. Weintraub (ed.), *Modern Economic Thought*, Oxford: Basil Blackwell, 467–84.

Schneider, F. (1985), '*Der Einfluss von Interessengruppen auf die Wirtschaftspolitik*', Bern und Stuttgart: Paul Haupt Verlag.

Schultze, C.L. (1996), 'The CEA: an inside voice for mainstream economics', *Journal of Economic Perspectives*, **10** (3), 23–39.

Shiller, R.J. (1996), 'Why Do People Dislike Inflation?', NBER Working Paper No. W5539, Cambridge, MA: National Bureau of Economic Research.

Shimp, S. and S. Sharma (1987), 'Consumer ethnocentrism: construction and validation of the CETSCALE', *Journal of Marketing Research*, **24** (3), 280–89.

Slembeck, T. (1997a), 'The formation of economic policy: a cognitive–evolutionary approach to policy-making', *Constitutional Political Economy*, **8** (3), 225–54.

Slembeck, T. (1997b), 'Probleme der Akzeptanz wirtschaftspolitischer Vorschläge', in H. Schmid and T. Slembeck (eds), *Finanz- und Wirtschaftspolitik in Theorie und Praxis, Festschrift zum 60. Geburtstag von Alfred Meier*, Schriftenreihe Finanzwirtschaft und Finanzrecht, Bd. 86, Verlag Paul Haupt, Bern/Stuttgart/Wien, 531–56.

Slembeck, T. (1998), 'A Behavioral Approach to Learning in Economics – Towards a Theory of Contingent Learning', Working Paper No. 316, Department of Economics, University of Pittsburgh, 1997, current version presented at the European Economic Association Annual Conference, Berlin, September 1998.

Slembeck, T. (1999), 'Learning in Economics: Where Do We Stand? – A Behavioral View on Learning in Theory, Practice and Experiments', Discussion Paper No. 9907, Department of Economics, University of St.Gallen, August 1999.

Slembeck, T. (forthcoming), 'Evolution und bedingtes Lernen', in C. Hermann-Pillath and M. Lehmann-Waffenschmidt (eds), *Handbuch der Evolutiven Ökonomik*, Band II, Berlin: Springer Verlag.

Stiglitz, J. (1998), 'The private uses of public interests: incentives and institutions', *Journal of Economic Perspectives*, **12** (2), 3–22.

Tinbergen, J. (1956), *Economic Policy: Principles and Design*, Amsterdam: North-Holland Publishing Company.

Triandis, H.C. (1971), *Attitude and Attitude Change*, New York: Wiley.

Tuchtfeld, E. (1983), *Bausteine zur Theorie der Wirtschaftspolitik*, Bern: Haupt.

Upmeyer, A. (ed.) (1989), *Attitudes and Behavioral Decisions*, Berlin, etc.: Springer.

Verdier, J.M. (1984), 'Advising Congressional decision-makers: guidelines for economists', *Journal of Policy Analysis and Management*, **3** (3), 421–38.

Williamson, M.R. and A.J. Wearing (1996), 'Lay people's cognitive models of the economy', *Journal of Economic Psychology*, **17** (1), 3–38.

Wood, G. (1997), *Economic Fallacies Exposed*, Occasional Paper 102, London: Institute of Economic Affairs.

7. Equilibrium and evolutionary foundations of competition and technology policy: new perspectives on the division of labour and the innovation process

J.S. Metcalfe

A country's eminence in a field of science is not a good guide to its economic strength and growth. (Carter and Williams, 1964, p. 197)

INTRODUCTION

The problem addressed in this chapter, the relationship between science, technology and economic performance, has a long history and an even more promising future. It is unlikely ever to fall out of fashion and it is unlikely ever to be entirely resolved. For it deals with two immensely complicated and interlocking problems, the nature of economic dynamics in capitalist economies, and the nature of the accumulation of practically valuable knowledge. A distinguishing feature of capitalism is the wide array of unco-ordinated efforts to innovate that are subsequently strongly co-ordinated by market processes. While market competition is an integrating co-ordinating process, innovation is directed at the production of micro diversity. It is this creative dimension, the evolution of business conjecture and market test that makes the operation of capitalism so complex and dynamic. The system is continually being transformed from within, and the essential element in all this is the accumulation of new practical knowledge. This adaptive, learning capability, we claim, rests very largely on the distinctive role of the firm within the system, and the complementary distinctive role of the market form of economic co-ordination. The firm is unique as an organisation in its role of having to acquire and combine many different kinds of knowledge and put them to practical effort. The market is unique as an instituted set of rules that evaluates rival uses of resources and in the process creates the incentives and the opportunities for innovation-based challenges to existing activities. The combination is an extremely powerful basis for economic transformation at all levels, from the industry to the nation state. History tells us this beyond doubt (Freeman and Louca, 2001).

This chapter treats this topic in terms of three connected themes. The first two involve a critical appraisal of two of the dominant post-war ideas in the field, the linear model of the knowledge–innovation relationship, and the market failure doctrine and its relation to public policy. The third theme is the systemic view of the innovation process and the implications this has for our understanding of the collaborative nature of the innovation process. I conclude with some brief observations on recent policy issues in the UK, particularly the Foresight programme and the matter of tax incentives for R&D.

My argument will be that an effective innovation policy requires recognition that science and technology are distinctive but interdependent branches of knowledge. They are jointly required as inputs into wealth creation, and their effective alignment requires the creation of appropriate technology support and innovation systems, systems which increasingly transcend national boundaries. The chief distinguishing characteristic of such systems is the collaborative involvement of industry (my shorthand for the major user of science and technology) and academia in the execution of knowledge development programmes so that all the relevant and vastly different advances in understanding required to develop innovation are brought together. For a crucial feature of the modern innovation process is the multidisciplinarity of knowledge inputs combined with multiple institutional sources of relevant knowledge. Very few firms can expect to innovate in isolation and the question of how the potential innovator is embedded within, and connects with, the wider matrix of knowledge-generating institutions becomes an issue of the first importance for policy. Distributed innovation systems become the context in which policies have their impact for better or for worse. However, innovation systems, like all institutions, are not natural givens, they have to be constructed and they develop over time in response to incentives and opportunities. The dynamics of the birth, growth, stabilisation and decline of innovation systems is addressed in the final part of our argument.

I shall suggest that the principal aim of technology and science policy from a systems perspective is to ensure the creation of effective knowledge support systems, which bridge between industry and the science and technology base. By contrast, the principal aim of innovation policy must be to combine the scientific and technological knowledge with knowledge of market opportunities and organisational opportunities. One must recognise that firms, universities and public research bodies are distinctively different kinds of institution each adapted to a specific purpose. It would be as foolhardy to make academic organisations overly commercial, as it would be to make private firms unduly non-commercial. The division of labour between them is not accidental and the central problem of policy is to work with this division of labour and to connect these different agencies together in a more productive fashion. In short, science, technology and innovation policy should be concerned with proper process and not directly with specific creative events, which are inherently unpredictable. The true nature of the problem is the need to accept that the links between science, technology and innovation are as much matters of organisational and institutional design as they are of R&D expenditure. It is this claim that contains the principal implications for innovation policy. In this perspective, the policymaker is no longer an optimising, Pigovian, bureaucrat correcting for the market divergence between private and social costs and benefits. Rather he or she is an adaptive policymaker severely constrained in terms of what is known and at most as boundedly rational as the private agents whose behaviour is to be influenced by policy. The learning abilities of policymakers in an experimental economic system are consequently of considerable importance (Teubal, 1996).

An important logical strand runs through the evolution of policy thinking in recent years. A strand which recognises that if science and technology are funded as national investments the crucial issue is to ensure that those investments yield an adequate return, a return ultimately reflected in enhanced competitiveness, wealth creating potential, and the quality of life. This thread has characterised innovation policy in the USA and Europe as well as in the UK. Indeed, to the extent that new institutional arrangements ensure a more effective return is obtained from science and technology; this of itself provides the most powerful of arguments for increased expenditure on research and development of all kinds. In short, science and technology have become a victim of diminishing returns to effort. Even before the end of the Cold War, their role in wealth creation was subjected to critical scrutiny. The case for spending more on science and technology depends on a greater effectiveness of innovation policies more generally, and with the prospect of greater budgetary stringency in the European monetary area this makes the case even more pressing.

In raising the question of the return to R&D, I cannot avoid introducing the closely related question of the relation between innovation and competition treated as coupled dynamic processes. The generation of practical knowledge is inseparable from the wider context of economic activity and this implies that innovation policy and competitive policy are complementary elements in the innovation process. In each case the deep issues relate to how activities premised upon the division of labour are to be appropriately co-ordinated.

THE LINEAR MODEL AND THE DISTINCTIVENESS OF TECHNOLOGY AND SCIENCE

We can begin by noting two possible justifications for the public support of fundamental research in science and basic technology. The first sees their output as a cultural, consumer good, which enlightens and entertains the public at large. This is, of course, a perfectly valid viewpoint: the discovery of a new star or a hitherto unknown species of plant are, in these terms, no less merit-worthy than the performance of a new symphony. They enrich and enliven the understanding of our world. Sadly but understandably, this is not a style of argument which is usually appealed to when justifying public support of science and basic technology.[1] Instead, a second view, an instrumental view, has dominated. Promoted and accepted by government and the science establish-ment, this argues that such fundamental knowledge is an investment which generates a more than compensatory return in terms of wealth creation or improved living standards via, for example, medical advances or better control of the environment. This is so even though the linkages may be impossible to pin down in an *a priori* fashion. This modern, science-based investment argument was a theme first made public by the Vannevar Bush report 'Science – The Endless Frontier' (1945) in which the strong claim was made that 'New products, new industries and more jobs require continuous additions to knowledge of the *laws of nature* ... essential new knowledge can be obtained *only* through basic scientific research' (my emphasis).

As Wise (1985) has suggested this is the original statement of the modern, linear or production line model of the innovation process.[2] And in the UK as late as 1968, the Central Advisory Council for Science and Technology was able to claim that basic science is the origin of 'all new knowledge without which opportunities for further technical progress *must rapidly become exhausted*' (my emphasis). This, by now discredited, view was nonetheless extremely influential for about two decades after 1945 as were its twin corol-laries that technology stood below science in a hierarchy of importance, that technology was merely applied science, and that the flow of new scientific knowledge would increase in proportion to the funds allocated to basic research (Wise, 1985; Keller, 1984).

It is perhaps worth pointing out that this perspective on science was articu-lated with some force by Alfred Marshall in the immediate period following World War I. In his *Industry and Trade* (1919), he argues as follows:

> History shows that almost every scientific discovery, which has ultimately revolu-tionised methods of industry, has been made in the pursuit of knowledge for its own sake, without direct aim at the attainment of any particular practical advantage: Uni-versities are the proper place for such pursuit of 'pure' science ... (p. 100)

Perhaps not surprisingly for an economist who understood the full signifi-cance of increasing returns and the division of labour, we find in Marshall's discussion an emphasis upon different classes of laboratories (pure science, technological, quality control) and of the importance of teamwork to combine different skills in the advancement of knowledge. In all but name, Marshall can be said to have described elements of an innovation system; he entirely understood the importance of the pure scientist 'keeping in touch with some of those industries, whose methods might be improved by increased knowledge of the properties of the products which he is studying' (p. 100). Within this perspective, Marshall clearly saw a role for research collaboration between firms, ideally with some state support to keep an eye on possible anti-competition abuses of the consumer, and, indeed, he was fully aware that expensive laboratories could hand a competitive advantage to larger firms. Marshall is amazingly modern in his treatment, *Industry and Trade* is full of references to the importance of national differences in the institutions of science and technology and to the theme that 'thought, initiative and knowledge are the most powerful implements of production'. Thus, it seems that the Baconian tradition of the utility of science has had a powerful sway on thought and policy long after it was first enunciated.[3] It is, however, a view with serious limitations.

The first and crucial point about this instrumental view is that at best it covers only a small fraction of the activities involved in the innovation process. The return in terms of innovation and wealth creation depends on a wide range of other non-scientific and non-basic technological activities and expenditures of a quite different kind, including those to achieve organisational change. Unless these activities are carried out effectively to transfer science and basic technology into exploitation, the economic return to extra scientific expenditure is likely to reduce very rapidly. Whether we take a 'demand pull' or a 'science push' approach to the linear model, the weaknesses remains the same, complementary assets of many different kinds have to be accumulated to turn fundamental knowledge into economic wealth. Innovation policy must necessarily have a broader focus than either science or technology policy.

The second flaw in the production line model concerns the failure to distinguish between the different attributes of science and technology. A wealth of recent research has established quite clearly that science and technology are largely independent but mutually beneficial bodies of knowledge, created by different processes of accumulation within distinctly different communities located in different institutional contexts (Layton, 1987; Vincenti, 1990; Keller, 1984; Faulkner, 1994). Both solve problems and are creative and imaginative, but the problems addressed are quite distinctly different and the communities that identify and solve those problems respond to different incentive mechanisms.[4] In broad terms, science is naturally academic, its legitimate output is additions to the existing stock of knowledge about natural phenomena for their own sake. Science is open, the outputs are widely diffused through an international publication culture and the primary incentives are in terms of priority in publication and the influence of ideas. Conversely, technology is naturally practical, its legitimate outputs are artefacts and the knowledge by which they are designed, constructed, operated, and intrinsic worth is to be judged not by the law-like truthfulness of the knowledge but by its practical utility. Moreover, while it is essential to the replicability of scientific results that they be codifiable, much of technological practice rests in a tacit realm only easily communicated through observation and trial, not publication. This is why one important dimension of technology concerns the people-embodied skills of the practitioners. An immediate consequence of this is to deny that technology is merely science applied. Rather technology is a distinctive body of knowledge, ranging from the basic to the applied, with its own operating principles and norms for design activity and its own distinct communities of practitioners; it is essentially local knowledge (Antonelli, 1998; Constant, 1980; Layton, 1987). Moreover, as many scholars have observed, technologists have designed and operated artefacts well in advance of a scientific understanding of the phenomena observed and their labours have directly stimulated the search for an understanding of the natural laws that underpin the operation of the artefacts. Equally, the technologies of instrumentation have played a major role in expanding the experimental boundaries of science.

There is another way of looking at the science–technology relationship which is illuminating. It is not difficult to see that if the choice of technological problems were decided randomly then there would not be much progress. The number of combinatorial possibilities is simply too vast and so individual dis-coveries do not have an impact unless they connect with other accepted facts and theories. So technological advance, like scientific advance, is necessarily cumulative, within a set of given design principles it proceeds along paths which, at least *ex post*, seem to involve their own inner logic. Technical advance involves guided variation in which knowledge of where to search in the set of possible options is absolutely crucial to rapid advance (Metcalfe and DeLiso, 1998). Here lies a key contribution of science, providing knowledge of where to look, and crucially where not to look in advancing technology, and in providing both tools for investigation and skilled practitioners (Vincenti, 1995; Pavitt, 1991). Better scientific understanding is a contributor to more effective technological search (Nelson, 1982; Gibbons and Johnson, 1974) and it reduces the cost of technological advance. It is not helpful, consequently, to claim that science leads and technology follows or *vice versa*. They are distinctive mutually supporting bodies of knowledge created for different purposes. That they illuminate one another is scarcely surprising, and the interesting question is how this process of division of labour and reciprocal enlightenment works and is institutionalised.[5]

It is this insight which lies behind the recent illuminating book by Stokes (1997). He argues that a great deal of the practice of modern science cannot be located at the mutually exclusive, extreme ends of the basic to applied spectrum. Rather much of what is called basic science is in fact a fundamental exploration into the properties of nature with an *explicit awareness* of their potential application in practical contexts. An unwillingness to accept this simple fact of application-directed, fundamental enquiry lies behind many attempts to develop overly simple taxonomies to record scientific activity (for example the distinction between curiosity-oriented and mission-oriented research), behind the ill-design of the organisations which carry out science, and in the ideology of the separation of the relative roles of public and private sectors in promoting science and technology. Indeed the OECD picked up this theme in a complementary fashion when it rightly argued for the importance of transfer sciences (engineering, pharmacology, agronomy, computing, medicine) bridging between fundamental work and application within the scientific enterprise (OECD, 1992).[6] There are two lessons to be drawn from this: many different kinds of knowledge have equal status in the innovation process, and the design of the institutions of science and technology is of great practical significance for the link between science and innovation. In this regard, Stokes's work is a devastating critique of the Bacon/Bush view but it leaves untouched two further and important issues in relation to the science–innovation relationship.

The first of these follows from the practical directedness of technological knowledge and its close interaction with economic and social stimuli. What technologists and engineers design and construct in the innovation process has to pass the test of economic viability and social acceptability. Design is ultimately normative: what is the best, read most profitable, combination of materials turned into components and linked into systems of varying scales of grandeur which reduce costs to a minimum or raise product value to a maximum.[7] Such an approach, dependent on the specific economic and social context, has no meaning when one is seeking for the timeless truth about a natural phenomenon.

Equally important is the fact that many technological advances flow from experience gained in using and producing specific artefacts. This dependence of technological advance upon practical experience gained in the diffusion and integration of artefacts into the economy is a quite distinctive feature of technological change which scientific advance does not share. One need hardly add that practical experience is accumulated by quite different processes than is scientific knowledge. Yet both are vital for the innovation process. Consequently, markets and technologies co-evolve and the way in which technology develops is strongly shaped by the rate and direction of market application. This is, of course, one of the key implications of the product/technology life cycle literature (Utterback, 1994) and the modern analysis of the diffusion of innovation. To know what consumers will be willing to pay for is no less significant a kind of knowledge than the scientific and engineering knowledge which underpins any particular artefact. Sadly, the role of this demand-related knowledge is almost entirely neglected in the current theory of innovation.

Now in putting these observations together we recognise that a number of scholars have found fault with the linear model for its failure to recognise the recursive, autocatalytic nature of innovative activity (Langrish et al., 1972; Kline and Rosenberg, 1986). I want to emphasise a different point. It is that quite different processes operating in quite different organisational contexts accumulate the different kinds of knowledge essential to the innovation process. Science and basic technology is guided by theory and experiment, and carried out primarily, but not exclusively, in universities and public research laboratories.

The nature of the knowledge and its mode of accumulation vary from discipline to discipline. Engineering and applied technology are relatively less theory driven, they depend more on trial and error accumulation in practical contexts, and failure in use is often a significant knowledge-generating event. Such knowledge is accumulated primarily but not exclusively in firms. Market knowledge is devoid almost entirely of theoretical foundation but depends on conjectures which are tested and revised in the far more amorphous market place. Naturally, the different kinds of knowledge are accumulated over different timescales and in institutions specialised to develop that kind of knowledge. It is this insight which underlies the increasing emphasis upon innovation systems. Many different kinds of knowledge are required to innovate and be competitive, and this requires some system of interaction and communication. Division of labour in producing knowledge implies co-ordination in putting knowledge to practical use, and co-ordination is a systemic instituted property (Coombs et al., 2001).

THE FAILURE OF MARKET FAILURE

The development of an economics of information and knowledge in the 1960s has paved the way for a particular rationale of innovation policy no less inaccurate and misleading than that embodied in the linear model of innovation. Central to this rationale is the idea that markets in relation to knowledge and information have an inherent tendency to produce socially inefficient outcomes, inefficiencies, which provide the justification for failure correcting public policies. This has proved to be a powerful set of ideas for shaping policy debate, particularly concerning the public support of university-based science and technology that are far from market application. I shall argue that it has been a far less useful means for designing specific innovation policies. The reason is clear, the idea of a perfectly competitive allocation of resources (the doctrine of Pareto optimality) on which the idea of market failure is premised is a distorting mirror in which to reflect the operation of capitalism. This doctrine seriously misreads the nature and role of competition in modern societies through its failure to realise that capitalism and equilibrium are incompatible concepts and that innovation precludes equilibrium. We can explore this claim in more depth by considering the phenomena advanced as types of market failure in relation to the production and use of knowledge in general.

The most transparent and unproblematic ones are imperfect property rights and genuine uncertainty. The former has long been recognised as a justification for patent and copyright systems, and rightly so, on the grounds that imitators derive economic benefit from unprotected new ideas without rewarding properly the creator of these ideas. It follows that the incentives to invest and innovate may be dulled by the existence of unrequited knowledge spillovers. In principal, the answer is to the affirmative but in practice, the issue is less clear-cut, and policy is about practice.

The problems here are twofold. It is not spillovers *per se* that damage the incentive to invest in knowledge production but a presumption of instantaneous and complete spillover, an unlikely state of affairs for reasons which become clear below.[8] Absent this, and the existence of many practical ways that firms have developed for protecting knowledge acquired privately, and it becomes clear that inventors and innovators may still gain an adequate return from their investments without patent protection. In some situations, patents and copyrights are important sources of provisional, temporary protection but these cases by no means cover the whole range of innovative activity.[9] Secondly, this doctrine is far too negative; not all spillovers are between direct competitors. Spillovers have positive benefits in stimulating the creation of new knowledge, which should not be underestimated, indeed, this is why patents are designed to put inventive ideas in the public domain. There is no reason why an alert firm should not gain more than it loses from the unplanned flow of information and so enrich its innovative capacity. In this regard, information spillovers are to be encouraged and one might expect firms to try to manage this process through links with other knowledge generating institutions, which is precisely what we observe in practice.[10]

What is interesting about the idea of property rights in commercially valuable knowledge is that they sit side by side with very imperfect property rights in economic activities more generally.[11] Copy my invention and I can pursue you in the courts. Make a better but unrelated equivalent and there is nothing I can do except compete. Indeed if it were otherwise, it is difficult to see how capitalism could have been the source of so much economic change and development. This means of course that competition is a painful process. Investors, whether their assets are in paper titles or human skills, are ever open to the erosion of their worth by innovations made by others. The fact that on average standards of living are enhanced by innovation should not blind us to this fact and to the inherently uncertain nature of innovation related economic processes. From a policy viewpoint, one immediate implication is that the scope of patents should not be drawn too broadly for this simply limits the ability of others to explore the design space with which any invention is associated. Thus, broad patents have the potential to damage the creativity of the capitalist model (Merges and Nelson, 1990).

Consider next the second broad source of market failure. In modern capitalism, genuine uncertainty is 'built in', as it were, and its consequences for the willingness to invest in innovation are far more difficult to cope with. However, the idea that innovation-related risks may be accurately computed, priced and used in actuarial calculations of expected costs and benefits is fanciful in the extreme. Innovations, like all discoveries, are unique events for which the probability calculus is an inappropriate method of analysis. Much decision making about knowledge creation is at root an act of faith, it is a matter of conjecture with necessarily unpredictable time delays between knowledge creation, application and market testing. Moreover, it is not at all obvious that the process of accumulation of scientific or technological knowledge is any less hazardous than the accumulation of market knowledge (Callon, 1994).

One immediate consequence of true uncertainty is what economists call asymmetric information, an imbalance of knowledge, for example, between firms and potential suppliers of capital or customers and between R&D managers and a firm's board of directors. Neither potential lenders nor customers nor, for that matter, civil servants, can accurately judge the credibility of innovative claims made by a firm nor can boards of directors always accurately evaluate the claims of technical personnel. Firms then find it difficult to get others to share the uncertainties of technology development; in short, it is difficult to trade the uncertainties associated with innovation projects. To some degree, this puts large firms at an advantage in that they can pool the indeterminacies from a portfolio of projects, and it helps us understand the pressures towards more collaborative work in R&D and towards mergers and acquisitions between complementary technology-based companies. One consequence of all this is that many knowledge transactions are mediated by a range of non-market methods, primarily involving networks and other forms of arrangement between organisations and individuals, procedures which build confidence and trust and work to limit the damaging consequences of uncertain asymmetric information.

However, this scarcely calls for the appellation 'market failure'. Quite the contrary, asymmetric information is an essential element in the working of a competitive, capitalist economy. The uncertainty which follows arises not from games with nature but from the very pursuit of innovation by rivals as a route to competitive advantage. It is simply perverse to label as market failures phenomena which are integral to the competitive market process and which give modern capitalism its unique dynamic properties. Nor is there any obvious way that policy could 'correct' for asymmetries, they are simply part and parcel of the process of innovation and economic change. The fundamental fact is that profits follow from the deployment of ideas that others do not have and so the whole system dynamic is premised on the generation of unquantifiable uncertainty. One cannot sensibly argue that the economy would perform better if innovation-related uncertainties were reduced, for the only way to reduce these uncertainties is to reduce the incidence of innovation and thus to undermine the mainspring of economic progress.

Consider thirdly, the so-called public good problem. All knowledge has the intriguing property that it is used but not consumed in its using, and that once discovered, it is in principle useable by any individual on any number of occasions to any degree. In the terminology of economics, there is non-rivalry and non-excludability of knowledge. So, runs the argument, the incentives for any one individual to reveal how much they value an item of knowledge are deficient, with adverse consequences for the willingness to pay and the establishment of predictable demand relationships. Of course, this links with the spillover argument, for it is the non-rival nature of knowledge that makes spillovers possible. Notice, however, that the public good dimension does not imply that the communication of information, that is to say the representation of knowledge in some message format, is costless. There is much more to the transfer of knowledge than the costs of communication in the narrow sense. In many cases the interchange of knowledge requires communication between 'like minds' only open to those who have acquired comparable abilities to understand the significance of new scientific and technological information. Knowledge is a public good in the sense of non-rivalry in use but it is not usually a free good and this is particularly true of complex scientific and technological knowledge. Hence the oft-remarked point that to benefit from the information generated by others one must make one's own substantial investment in scientific and technological capability (Mowery and Rosenberg, 1989; Rosenberg, 1990; Hicks, 1995; Veugelers, 1997).

Scholars interested in innovation have for many years drawn upon the useful distinction by Polanyi (1958) between tacit and codified knowledge, the former embodied in human skill and practice, the latter in material form. Tacitness is presented as a reason why information does not flow freely, while codification is seen as a means to make information public. Thus, Callon (1994) is quite right to point out that the limits to excludability depend upon the way in which information is embodied in different communication media, and that access to any particular knowledge depends upon complementary assets being accumulated to give the capability to maintain and use knowledge-based statements. However, it is important to recognise the point that the division of knowledge into mutually exclusive categories, codified and tacit, does not uniquely reflect properties of the knowledge itself. Rather, it is in part an economic decision dependent on the scale on which the information is to be used and the costs of codification. It is thus inextricably linked with the division of labour in the economy more widely, as I shall explain below (David and Foray, 1996). To summarise, the weakness of the public good model of knowledge is that it places the transmitter and recipient of knowledge on the same footing and ignores entirely the importance of mode and process of inter-communication. This is simply not helpful. It may be cheap to transmit information but the interpretation of information, its translation into practical knowledge, is never costless.

I turn now to a fourth broad class of market failures: those that relate to indivisibility and increasing returns to exploitation. Fundamental to the economics of knowledge production and dissemination is the fact that the exploitation of a discovery is subject to increasing returns: the fixed cost of producing an item of knowledge can be spread over a greater volume of output as it is used more widely and more intensively in the production process. This is an important consequence of non-rivalry. However, since one cannot innovate on the basis of a fraction of a technology or a quarter of a scientific fact, there is necessarily an indivisible cost of creating the knowledge behind an innovation. This fixed cost makes the ex ante valuation of knowledge virtually impossible since the scale of its application cannot normally be predicted and, incidentally, means that marginal cost pricing of innovations would prevent the costs of knowledge creation from being recovered. Furthermore, every investment in innovation now requires its own minimum scale of exploitation if an adequate return is to be achieved. The result of these considerations is the complete inability of the perfectly competitive model to provide guiding principles in a world where firms are required to innovate in order to compete (Stiglitz, 1994). The fixed costs they must incur unavoidably mean that such markets will at best be imperfectly competitive. The only way the fixed costs of knowledge production could be covered independently of prices and outputs would be for public laboratories to develop that knowledge or for all private research and development expenses to be fully subsidised from the public purse. This is not a model for innovation likely to commend itself outside of very special cases such as metrology and public technical standards in general.

The public support of university science is thought to constitute the best case for the market failure argument on grounds of uncertainty, appropriability and publicness. Even here, the matter is not clear-cut. For by no means all university research in science and technology is funded by government, and of that which is, a proportion is directed at meeting the mission objectives of government agencies in such areas as defence or health. Conversely, non-academic organisations carry out a substantial portion of work on fundamental science and technology; indeed firms can often boast far more advanced research facilities than can universities.[12] Moreover, it is not obvious that the primary motive for universities is the production of knowledge in the abstract. Rather, the production of scientific knowledge is an input into the production of qualified scientists and technologists, and if a 'market failure' is to be found it is with respect to the market for skills not the market for knowledge.

It is when we turn to innovation in practice that the difficulties multiply. Leaving aside the well recognised imperfections which governments can be subject to when they intervene, backing the wrong horse too quickly or maintaining programmes long after the evidence against continuation is conclusive (Walker, 2000), it is clear that market failure as a policy framework leaves much to be desired (Metcalfe, 1995a, 1995b). The logical underpinning it provides tells us nothing about the design of policy instruments or their appropriate method of implementation or the areas that are most appropriately in need of support in their attempts to innovate. Is the focus to be on new knowledge, new skills or new artefacts? Is it to be concerned with design, with construction or with operation? Is it to focus on the creation of innovation or upon the diffusion of innovation? The answers to these questions could generate very different policy initiatives. Yet, the information to provide the answers is simply not available to the policymaker or, for that matter, to anyone else. The policymaker cannot become the innovator and so the effective judgement of the relevant market failure is not possible. The market failure framework, despite its formal elegance, is an empty box.

WHAT IS MISSING: COMPETITIVE PROCESS AND INCREASING RETURNS

Competitive Process

If we reflect on why the market failure doctrine has produced little practical resonance with the world of science, technology and innovation, the answer is not difficult to find. A framework of thinking built on the idea of an efficient equilibrium in the allocation of *given* resources to *given* ends cannot come to terms with the essence of capitalism, its restless, unpredictable nature. Better to start from a different perspective, one that recognises economic activity as a cumulative struggle against ignorance, not as an unfortunate lapse from a world of perfect and perfectly foreseeable knowledge. This different perspective is consonant with evolutionary theories of economic change and with competition as a dynamic discovery process driven by rivalry between finely detailed differences in behaviour. In such a view, the roles of markets is to co-ordinate and evaluate the rival business conjectures and so guide the economic change we (partially) measure in raising standards of living. This involves adaptation to new opportunities, new needs and new resources and it is this function that market institutions perform: they are to be judged not by the canon of Pareto optimality but by their openness in stimulating and adapting to change (Metcalfe and Georghiou, 2000).

Thus, the central weakness of the market failure approach is not its lack of precision but its attempt to establish a policy perspective within the confines of the static equilibrium theory of markets and industry. Each of the market failure arguments identifies significant features of the production and use of knowledge but these features have their full impact only in relation to the dynamic nature of the competitive process. Economic progress depends on the ongoing creation of private, asymmetric knowledge which is sufficiently defensible to justify the original investment. How this works out is ultimately a matter of competition, and competition requires active not passive behaviour and the ability to gain access to privileged knowledge is at its core. Competition depends upon the search for competitive advantage, and the development of new products and processes is the principal way this is achieved in modern capitalism. The imperfections identified in the market failure approach are to be viewed in a different perspective, as integral and necessary aspects of the production and dissemination of knowledge in a market economy. From this perspective, it is surely perverse to call them imperfections or market failures. This is, of course, not a new point: for those who have studied Schumpeter they are the natural features of an economic process driven by creative destruction. Another way of putting this is to say that without asymmetries of knowledge and the correlated uncertainties and indivisibilities the competitive process has nothing with which to work. The quasi-public good nature of knowledge, indivisibility and increasing returns, the inherent uncertainties of creative, trial and error processes and the imperfect nature of property rights in knowledge are essential if market capitalism is to function. They are not imperfections to be eliminated by policy.

Several important themes now fit into place in a way that is impossible with the market failure doctrine. First and foremost among them is entrepreneurship, a phenomenon which has no meaning in economic equilibrium of any kind. Entrepreneurs introduce novelty into the economy, they disrupt established patterns of market activity, they create uncertainty, and they provide the fuel that fires the process of economic evolution. To act they need, and indeed create, privileged access to knowledge, entrepreneurship and asymmetric information are inextricably linked.

Secondly, the reward to entrepreneurship is the differential economic reward which comes from introducing economic improvements. Such abnormal rewards are not always the consequence of market imperfections, they do not necessarily reflect the undesirable use of market power; they are instead the rewards to superior performance and are to be judged as such. It is a view that abnormal profits are the socially undesirable consequences of market concentration that is the real Achilles heel of the market failure approach and which denies it anything useful to say in the appraisal of knowledge-based, innovative economies.

It is this perspective of competition and innovation as coupled dynamic processes, which provides us with a framework to formulate innovation policy. Innovations create the differences in behaviour which we identify as competitive advantages, and the possibility of competition provides the route and the incentives to challenge established market positions. Moreover, to the extent that market institutions function properly, firms with superior innovations will command an increasing share of the available scarce productive resources, the process which is the link between innovations in particular and economic growth in general.[13]

Lest this appear dangerously Panglossian we should add immediately that the market process is quite capable of putting barriers in the way of innovation. Firms may have every incentive to gain competitive advantage improperly by distorting the competitive process rather than by innovating. Through creating barriers to entry or by imposing constraints upon the freedom to choice of their customers, the market selection process may be distorted in undesirable ways. From this follows the importance of legislation on restrictive practices and competition policy more generally. Not in terms of a concern with price–cost margins or excessive (!) market shares but rather with the maintenance of open innovative and market conditions. The real danger of market concentration lies in creating barriers to potential innovative entrants and in concentrating the innovation process in too limited a range of organisations. There is no guarantee that the firms that have been successful innovators in the past are the most likely potential innovators for the future. An established market position is no guarantee of an ongoing capacity and willingness to innovate.[14]

This suggests that the role of innovation policy is to ensure that conditions remain in place for the continued creation and exploitation of asymmetries of knowledge. In truly competitive markets, all established positions are open to challenge and it is this link between innovation and competition, which has proved to be the reservoir of economic growth. Thus, capitalism is necessarily restless, occasionally kaleidoscopic, and competition is at root a process for diffusing diverse discoveries, the utility of which cannot readily be predicted in advance. The market mechanism is simultaneously a framework within which to conduct innovative experiments, and a framework for facilitating economic adaptation to those experiments.[15]

Increasing Returns and Roundaboutness in Knowledge Production

We have referred already to the inevitable presence of increasing returns in a knowledge-based economy, the fact that the returns to investments in innovation increase with the scale of their exploitation. That this rules out a perfectly competitive allocation of resources is well understood but there is much more to the phenomena than is suggested by this partial and static perspective. The point is a more general one. As Adam Smith understood so clearly, increasing returns applies to the generation of knowledge as well as to its exploitation precisely because of the increasing specialisation of bodies of knowledge and knowledge-generating institutions. What we are observing in modern innovation systems is the increasing roundaboutness of production, not of material artefacts but of knowledge in general (Young, 1928).

It can be argued that two features shape the modern innovation process; namely, increasing complementarity of different kinds of knowledge together with increasing dissimilarity of these bodies of knowledge, a reflection of an increasingly fine division of labour in knowledge production. Innovating firms need to draw on and integrate multiple bodies of knowledge, whether scientific, technological or market-based, produced in an increasing range of increasingly specialised contexts.[16] At the same time to understand the significance of and contribute to advances in these various kinds of knowledge is increasingly beyond the internal capabilities of the individual firm. Consequently, firms must increasingly complement their own R&D efforts by gaining access to externally generated knowledge and learn how to manage a wide spectrum of collaborative arrangements for knowledge generation (Coombs and Metcalfe, 2000). The consequences of this is that innovations take place increasingly in a systemic context with respect to the use of new technologies and their generation. How they do so is a question on the co-ordination of the division of labour in innovation systems.

THE SYSTEMIC CONTEXT

The focus of this perspective is best summarised in terms of the development of the science and technology infrastructure in the economy; an infrastructure that facilitates the intercommunication of existing research results and mutually shapes the future research agendas of different organisations. This infrastructure is a set of interconnected organisations to create, store and transfer the knowledge and skills that define technological opportunities (Edquist, 1997; Carlsson, 1997; Nelson, 1993). Many organisations are involved, private firms, universities and other educational bodies, professional societies and government laboratories, private consultancies and industrial research associations. Between them there is a strong division of labour and, because of the economic peculiarities of information noted above, a predominance of co-ordination by networks, public committee structures and other non-market mediated methods

(Tassey, 1992; Teubal, 1996). The division of labour is of considerable significance for the degree to which the different elements of the system are connected. Different organisations typically have different cultures, use different 'languages', explore different missions, operate to different timescales and espouse different ultimate objectives as our brief contrast between science and technology illustrated. As a consequence of these differences, knowledge is 'sticky', it is partially unintelligible, it does not flow easily between different institutions or disciplines. Thus, there is a major problem to be addressed in seeking to achieve greater connectivity.[17]

One strand of thinking in this area has been to emphasise the national domain of the science and technology infrastructure, and rightly so (Freeman, 1987, 1994; Lundvall, 1992; Nelson, 1993). Policy formulation and implementation is essentially a national process, despite an increasing range of policies at European level. However, there are good reasons to elaborate the national perspective both downwards and outwards. It is important to recognise that different activities have different supporting knowledge infrastructures so that a sectoral innovation system perspective becomes essential.[18] This is simply one way of recognising the specificity of the innovation opportunities facing firms (Carlsson, 1995). On the other hand, it is clear that the sectoral infrastructure frequently transcends national boundaries. Science and basic technology have always been understood as international systems and the same is increasingly true of technology more generally. Governments collaborate increasingly in major technology programmes, often in the defence area, and transnational companies typically have multiple technology development activities co-ordinated between different national infrastructures. Consequently, we begin to see the emergence of transnational technology development initiatives as exemplified by the European Framework Programme, which is now approaching its sixth stage, as well as much small-scale, inter-firm collaboration across national boundaries.

This strand of thinking has been explored further by Gibbons et al. (1994), who draw attention to the emerging characteristics of new models of knowledge production which fit exactly with the view that innovation requires many kinds of knowledge for its successful prosecution. What they term 'mode-2' knowledge is produced in the context of application, seeks solutions to problems on a transdisciplinary basis, is tested by its workability not its truthfulness and involves a multiplicity of organisational actors, locations and skills. Together this entails a distributed system for innovation with no necessary connection with traditional national or sectoral boundaries. Is it perhaps knowledge production for a global economy?

INNOVATION POLICY AND AN EXPERIMENTAL ADAPTIVE SYSTEM

The central thrust of the argument so far is that the dynamic features of modern capitalist economies depend crucially upon their capacities as experimental systems; systems which continually generate new varieties of behaviour to be tested, adopted or rejected in the economic and social spheres. Innovation *qua* variety generation combined with the properties of selective processes makes competition an adaptive, evolutionary process. What has this to say about innovation policy if we are not to be guided by market failure? It is obvious that many policies impinge on the innovation process, in particular macroeconomic policy, competition policy and education policy, the latter in relation to the supply of scientifically, technologically and managerially qualified individuals.[19] My concern here is with innovation policies proper.

The initial step is to recognise the adaptive nature of the policy process and to contrast that with the optimal policy framework which is the corollary of the market failure approach. In this latter, the private sector generates the wrong incentive signals, the wrong relation between values and costs, which the policymaker corrects to guide decisions to their socially optimal values. We have already noted that this would require an unseemly amount of detailed knowledge and make the policymaker indistinguishable from the agents whose behaviours are to be influenced. Adaptive policy takes a more modest stance. It recognises the complex nature of the innovation process, that economic systems are capable of more than one kind of response to a given set of signals and incentives, that the outcomes of innovation processes are inherently unpredictable, and that it is the non-average, 'deviant' behaviours that drive economic change. Its concern is the design and formation of institutional arrangements that promote business experiments and which generate a greater degree of connectedness between knowledge-generating and knowledge-applying organisations.

To explore this further it is helpful to distinguish four specific elements that make up the innovation process. These are, the opportunity to innovate, as defined by the range of knowledge (scientific, technological *and* market) which is brought to bear; the resources available to develop and exploit the innovation; the incentives to develop the innovation; and, the capability to manage all of the diverse elements involved in innovating in a timely manner. The market failure perspective has emphasised the incentive and resource issues. By contrast, the systems failure perspective places the attention on the innovation opportunities facing firms and upon their management capabilities, including the capability to access and integrate external information with internal knowledge. This reflects directly the importance of the division of labour in knowledge production and the increasingly transdisciplinary and combinatorial nature of innovation processes. As explained above, firms must increasingly look beyond their formal boundaries for complementary knowledge, and this explains the recent rapid growth of innovation webs at many levels, from bilateral collaborations, to research clubs, to the formation of large-scale joint research institutions involving universities, government laboratories, users and suppliers as well as the innovating firms. These linkages enhance the knowledge base of innovating firms, and enable them to produce superior innovations more quickly than would otherwise be possible (Katz and Martin, 1997).[20] They are essentially devices for generating as well as for managing spillovers. From this perspective collaboration reduces R&D costs, it creates benefits from combining complementary knowledge bases and generally enhances the profitability of innovation. However, it is equally important to recognise that collaboration not only enhances profits, it may also dissipate the potential profits from innovation; costs and profits may be shared alike (Metcalfe, 1992). Shared knowledge is knowledge that rivals can use to compete against each other. Several features of R&D collaborations now fall into place. Those arrangements that improve profit enhancement are the ones that combine organisations with strongly complementary but dissimilar knowledge bases. Those arrangements that minimise the risks of profit dissipation, include the involvement of non-commercial organisations (for example universities), of other vertically-related members of the supply chain including customer firms, and of horizontal rivals who will exploit the shared knowledge in different niches or localities. Only if the collaboration is sufficiently 'far from market', developing generic capabilities, are close horizontal rivals likely to be involved.

The Adaptive Policymaker

Innovation systems are neither natural givens in the economic process, nor do sets of knowledge-based organisations of themselves constitute an innovation system at any scale unless they co-ordinate their actions in the conduct of an innovation project, indeed, this is the insight contained in the quotation that starts this chapter. Innovation systems are constructed for a purpose, to solve particular problems. How is an innovation system created? I suggest that three principles are at work. First, the firms, universities and other research organisations in an economy, the components of specific innovation systems, constitute a latent innovation resource not an innovation system. Secondly, that the connections that form an innovation system have to be articulated and the principal organiser of these connections is the private firm, for only the firm is in the position to combine all the many kinds of knowledge into a specific innovation sequence. Thirdly, the focal thread around which the connections are made is the set of unsolved problem sequences associated with the innovations in question. These problem sequences not only involve the production of knowledge but also the utilisation of existing knowledge and the combination together of different kinds of knowledge produced in different contexts. Moreover, as this set of unsolved problems evolves so must the structure and composition of the relevant innovation system change. New problems may require new kinds of knowledge and connections with new organisations if a momentum of innovation is to be sustained. Thus, the organisational ecology of a country's knowledge system is capable of being shaped into a plethora of operating innovation systems that connect with similar ecologies in other nations. What are national are the organisational ecologies and their institutional context of law, tradition and polity. What is systemic is the process of combining different organisations in the solution of specific innovation problems.

It follows that many of the collaborative arrangements that define a distributed innovation system can be interpreted as the temporary outcome of a process of spontaneous order. The interpenetrating webs of market and non-market arrangements are formed from below, they do not arise by chance alone but rather because there is commercial merit in knowing what is happening beyond the boundaries of the firm. Does this mean that there are grounds for policy concern? Can there be situations where the spontaneous order of system formation will not produce appropriate innovation systems? To the extent that the answers are in the affirmative we are in a position to argue that a central concern of the adaptive policymaker is to facilitate the self-organisation of innovation systems.

From a systemic perspective, failures can be of three general kinds: the system boundary is drawn in the wrong way, the organisations within the boundary are not appropriate as defined by the knowledge that they command, and the connections are not functioning correctly. Each of these is a problem associated with the division of knowledge labour and the increasingly roundabout knowledge production processes, and their location in specialised organisations.

From the adaptive policy viewpoint, it follows that the principal task is to address these three kinds of system failure in order to stimulate the formation of innovation webs and to create bridging processes within those webs that better combine and utilise knowledge to further the innovation process.[21] First, missing components, the ecology of knowledge-based organisations may be deficient, important branches of knowledge may be missing from the national research effort. Here the appropriate response may be to set up research organisations to concentrate on the knowledge gaps. Second, missing connections, the incentives and opportunities may need to be created to encourage collaboration between different organisations. If innovation systems are to form spontaneously across public and private sectors, the policymaker has a role in enhancing mutual awareness of knowledge capabilities, and in removing barriers to collaboration that arise from differences in mission of different organisations. This is particularly so for research organisations located in the public sector and directed at public sector missions. These policies in relation to components and connections can only work through an understanding of the relevant communities of practitioners whether in firms, their suppliers or customers, higher education institutions or public and private research, development and design laboratories. A first policy requirement is to know this community, its institutions and the way they connect simply because it is through the community that policy effects will be channelled. A second policy requirement is to emphasise the guided nature of the growth of innovation-related knowledge. Its accumulation is neither random nor set in fixed channels but proceeds within the constraints of cognitive frameworks which underpin the knowledge acquisition process. These cognitive frameworks provide a natural focus around which governments can stimulate network formation. Moreover, when knowledge changes, existing frameworks of relations may become obsolete and may actively resist reformation. Here, policy has a role to facilitate the transition to new innovation systems.

Market mediated transactions also play an important role in the system perspective. The recent privatisation of public research laboratories in Europe has encouraged the emergence of markets for knowledge and problem solving expertise within innovation systems, so that the boundary between market and network is fluid (Georghiou, 1998). The market in QSEs, research contracts and consultancies between firms and universities, payments for licences and, at the other extreme, mergers and acquisitions, are all devices used by firms to bring more knowledge within their walls.[22] Indeed the market for corporate control is a central market in an experimental economy. It is not simply to be seen as a device for disciplining poor management but as a device for combining complementary assets and for decombining them when they prove to be incompatible. The low cost facilitation of business experiments is vital for a creative innovation process, and particularly relevant to the growth problems of the SME.[23] In the presence of limited supplies of entrepreneurial talent and substantial barriers to the growth of small technology-based firms, the acquisition process can allow the assets built up in small companies to be exploited and developed more effectively in a large firm.

There is an important additional lesson contained in these principles. Governments will increasingly be unable to make national innovation policy decisions in isolation, policies will have to be co-ordinated and compatible for fear of making their country an unattractive location for technology development activities (Carlsson, 1995). The trend towards higher research costs has encouraged greater collaboration and major multinational firms in these sectors make significant investments in the national innovation systems they consider most relevant to their needs. In so doing they influence the development of these different national systems and of the universities within them. The attraction of high quality R&D activities in several high technology areas, pharmaceutical/medical and information technology, provide salient examples of this policy problem.

Having dealt with some general principles of innovation policy from a system failure perspective, I turn now to some specific examples drawn from UK experience and debate. The first is the UK Foresight programme; the second is tax subsidies for R&D.

Technology Foresight

There is no more appropriate indication of the switch in policy from matters of resources and incentives to matters of opportunities and capabilities than the adoption of a Technology Foresight Programme by the UK Government and indeed other governments (Laat and Larédo, 1998). Foresight activities have been defined as:

> a systematic means of assessing those scientific and technological developments which could have a strong impact on industrial competitiveness, wealth creation and the quality of life. (Georghiou, 1996)

The process involved in conducting a large-scale foresight programme is precisely a matter of bridging and connectivity within a nation's science and technology base and between that base and its areas of application. Foresight is, from this view, a policy to encourage the self-organisation of multiple innovation systems. In particular, the crucial point about foresight proper is its inclusion of information about demand and market developments in its activity.

The process involved the creation of sectoral panels of 'experts' that consulted on a wide basis with the relevant communities in industry, academia and government through regional workshops, a major delphi survey and numerous other activities.[24] Each panel has produced a report indicating the main forces for change and the policy issues which flow from the analysis as well as identifying the likely constraints on change. Without question, this is the most extensive consultation of industrial and scientific opinion which has ever occurred in the UK. It is because the development of modern technology is so heterogeneous with respect to its discipline base and institutional context that makes the sounding of opinion in the broadest possible fashion extremely important.

It is too early yet to come to clear conclusions concerning implementation; indeed it is central to the exercise that the consequences may not be fully realised until a quarter century from now. It may also be that one outcome of Foresight will be a reallocation of resources within publicly funded science and technology in the UK. If so it will simply make transparent Weinberg's (1967) careful enunciation of external criteria for the support of science. Despite strong objections from the pure science lobby, the use of external criteria does not imply that pure science is to be transmuted into applied science (Vannevar Bush's demon it will be remembered) but rather the differential focusing of basic scientific work in relation to non-scientific objectives. Be that as it may, the principal lasting benefit of the exercise lies in the process and what the process does to the formation of commercial and academic strategies to promote innovation: to the creation of lasting networks between industry, government and the science and technology community, and to the emergence of coherent visions within those communities on complementary developments in science and technology. By a coherent vision is definitely not meant a consensus view about specific technologies or routes to innovation but rather an understanding of the breadth and interdependence between the uncertain opportunities open to a particular sector.

In summary, the Foresight Programme reflects an increasing concern with matters of systemic co-ordination in the innovation process: creating and supporting the technology support systems of particular groups of firms; and bridging between those formal and informal institutions which interact in a specific technological area for the purpose of generating, diffusing and utilising technology (Carlsson and Stankiewicz, 1991; Carlsson, 1997). To create effective webs the policymaker must know the relevant communities of scientists and practitioners, and possibilities for commercial exploitation. The sequence of innovations which emerge and the firms which are successful are the outcomes of the process and are not a specific concern of the policymaker. Winners and losers emerge; as in any experimental process they are not and cannot be pre-chosen.

TAX SUBSIDIES FOR R&D

The idea of providing general tax credits for R&D related activities is certainly not new (Metcalfe, 1995a) and has been adopted by several governments including those of Australia, Canada and the United States and most recently the UK. The general purpose is clear; the tax credit reduces the incremental cost of R&D spending and thereby provides incentives for private firms to spend more. As a policy, this certainly has the advantage that it focuses on the prime movers in the innovation process, and that does not involve governments in making market judgements about winners and losers. All that is necessary is that the company be profitable so that the tax credit has substance.[25]

All of this implies that the policy must be designed carefully. Within any one sector, the effectiveness of the policy will depend on the rate at which returns to R&D diminish and on the elasticity of supply of R&D resources; the less elastic they are the more the subsidy will be dissipated in rents to QSEs, not in real R&D outlays. In particular, there is little point in subsidising the generation of new technological knowledge without at the same time subsidising the generation of the market knowledge. Secondly, drawing on our distributed innovation systems perspective, any subsidy should apply to externally acquired as well as to internally generated knowledge. The tax credits can be fashioned to encourage the formation of collaborative arrangements.

Tax subsidies fit well with our dynamic perspective on markets and they are complementary to the emphasis on other bridging policies. The effects are broadly distributed and no attempt is made to second guess the market. However, unless firms have a minimum in-house innovation capability their ability to participate in innovation webs will be severely limited. Tax subsidies may help firms gain and sustain that minimum capability while, conversely, the efficient working of innovation webs increases the pay-off to the R&D subsidy.[26] The two kinds of policy are complementary.

The final point that has to be addressed with any general subsidy policy such as tax credits, is that it is bound to give rise to claims of waste and the misallocation of public revenues – even leaving aside the incentives for creative accounting. This is an important point because innovative, trial and error processes are inherently wasteful. Outcomes are not predictable *ex ante*, many projects fail and very few generate spectacular returns, as one would expect with any evolutionary process. There is no way to improve on this elemental indeterminacy and complexity of economic life. Our economics are adaptive experimental systems, increasing the rate of experimentation requires that more failures are to be accepted along with more successes.

CONCLUSION

In this chapter I have reviewed recent developments in innovation policy thinking and attempted to view them through the lens of new developments in thinking about the science, technology, competition relation. Here the fundamental insight is the experimental, evolutionary nature of a market and network economy. As Schumpeter aptly observed capitalism works by means of creative destruction, a process that is played out on a global scale. Patterns of international competition are ever changing and an advanced country must be ever aware of new opportunities and threats if its standard of living is to be sustained. Central to this must be the rate of innovative experimentation and I have suggested that a consistent thread to policy has emerged in the past twenty years based around a distributed innovation perspective. In this new approach, it is the institutional basis of innovation that is the focus of attention, rather than expenditure on research and development. I have called this the system failure perspective. From a political point of view this raises several interesting problems. Experimental economies have many failures as well as successes, blind variation means that a great deal of effort comes to nought and that patience is the sure companion to long-term success.

NOTES

1. Although, of course, there is widespread concern, in the UK at least, in relation to public understanding of science, and of science as an element in school curricula. I treat basic technology as equivalent to basic science in that both are concerned with the search for fundamental principles that help connect and classify different phenomena. Not all technology can be equated with knowledge of specific applications.
2. Branscomb (1993) also refers to this as the pipeline model of the science technology relationship.
3. Prior to the Industrial Revolution, one should note.
4. Faulkner (1994) provides a perceptive and thorough review of the more important aspects of the science–technology relationship, and the links with innovative activity.
5. See Narin et al. (1997) for evidence of the increasing citation of basic science papers in industrial patents. Notice carefully that a closer degree of interdependence between patents and scientific papers, particularly strong in the biomedical and chemical areas, does not establish that there is a closer link between science and economic growth. There is a missing link, namely the translation of patents into competitive innovations. As this chapter argues there is much more to innovation than scientific knowledge.
6. The transfer sciences are precisely the sciences which constitute Pasteur's Quadrant in Stokes's analysis and indeed they fit easily into the Gibbons et al. (1994) notion of mode-2 knowledge production. As the OECD report rightly emphasises their hybrid, bridging role does not imply that they lack coherence. The communities of practitioners involved are usually formed into distinctive professional associations (OECD, 1992, 35–7).
7. Petroski (1996) lists the following facets of engineering activity: design, analysis, failure, economics, aesthetics, communication, politics and quality control – to name but a few.
8. I note in passing that what is spilt is information (messages) not knowledge. The knowledge content of any information flow is, of course, notoriously unpredictable as any university examiner knows only too well. That this is so is essential to the emergence of novelty.
9. Those industries where other aspects of public regulation force innovative knowledge to be placed in the public domain well in advance of exploitation provide important examples. Health and safety legislation in relation to the pharmaceutical/medical industry is an obvious case in point. In regard to patent systems there is a longstanding debate on their merits and demerits, particularly in regard to the duration of patents and their scope.
10. Hence the increasing volume of work which points to the role of knowledge spillovers in productivity growth. Compare Griliches (1998) for an authoritative treatment.
11. It is worth noting that competition authorities in the UK have taken a dim view of firms which refuse to grant licenses to exploit their patents and of attempts to use licenses to distort the competitive process.
12. Narin et al. (1997) find that of the US scientific papers cited by US industrial patents only 50 per cent came from academic sources while 32 per cent came from scientists working in industry.
13. As an aside here, we note that competition is not to be judged by market structure. Two rivals may compete far more intensively than many. The way to judge the efficacy of competitive arrangements is to consider the degree to which rivals can gain market share at the expense of each other and the degree to which they are innovating in the pursuit of competitive advantage.

14. I am very conscious that this leaves an unanswered (unanswerable?) question as to how much competition is desirable. If 'red in tooth and claw' it may well destroy the longer-term ability to maintain innovative progress. If too benign it may stimulate indolence and the pursuit of the quiet life. The system needs some grit to presume sufficient incentives to innovation which will vary from context to context. Unfinished business I am afraid.
15. This theme of the experimental economy has been particularly important in Eliasson's work (1998). It has an inevitable Austrian hue, that markets are devices to make the best of our limited knowledge (Rosenberg, 1990).
16. Compare Grandstrand et al. (1997) for evidence that large corporations are increasingly diversified in the technological fields which they employ, and more diversified relative to their product fields. See also Kodama's work on technology fusion (1995).
17. Compare Andersen et al. (1998) and Green (1998) for further elaboration of the systems perspective. Also Edquist (1997) for a quite excellent overview of the current state of the art. Smith (1997) provides an excellent statement of an infrastructure perspective on innovation systems.
18. There is a growing literature on regional innovation linkages in which an attempt is made to correlate innovation clusters with the processes of university based scientific activity. See Varga (1998) for a review and empirical study of linkages in the USA.
19. The prospect of EMU is certain to have rather profound implications for all of these background policies.
20. An article in the *Times Higher Education Supplement* (25/9/98) writes of a collaborative venture between Rolls Royce, British Aerospace and three leading British university engineering departments to develop new design processes so that better aircraft can be brought to market more quickly.
21. The EC programmes beginning with ESPRIT in 1984 and culminating in the series of Framework programmes after 1987 fit exactly this model. They encourage collaborative research, pre-market in most cases, across national boundaries within the community. They are precisely policies for web formation.
22. Howells (1997) shows that contract research and technology organizations in the UK have doubled their share of business R&D performed in the UK in the past ten years. In 1995 they accounted for 10 per cent of total business expenditure on R&D.
23. See Autio (1997) on the growth problems of new-technology-based firms and the view that their economic role is not to be judged by their growth but by their providing linkages in innovation webs.
24. A delphi study takes repeated samplings of opinion within a target group with feedback of the results to the participants between each sample, providing the opportunity to revise their opinions.
25. This is particularly problematic for small companies at the start-up stage. A market in tax credit certificates would certainly help in this regard.
26. It is suggested that the Industrial Research Association model widely utilised in the UK between 1920 and 1983 failed because the relevant firms never developed sufficient internal capability to understand the research carried out on their behalf.

REFERENCES

Andersen, B., J.S. Metcalfe and B. Tether (1998), 'Innovation systems as instituted economic processes', in J.S. Metcalfe and I. Miles (eds), *Innovation Systems in the Service Economy: Measurement and Case Study Analysis*, Dordrecht, The Netherlands: Kluwer Academic Publishers.
Antonelli, C. (1998), 'The Italian way to innovation, state of the art and new perspectives', mimeo, University of Turin.

Autio, E. (1997), 'New technology based firms in innovation networks, sympletic and generative impacts', *Research Policy*, **26**, 263–82.

Branscomb, L.M. (1993), *Empowering Technology*, Boston: MIT Press.

Bush, V. (1945), Science: The endless frontier (*A report to the President by Vannevar Bush, Director of the Office of Scientific Research and Development*), Washington: United States Government Printing Office.

Callon, M. (1994), 'Is science a public good?', *Science, Technology and Human Values*, **19**, 395–424.

Carlsson, B. (ed.) (1995), *Technological Systems and Economic Performance: The Case of Factory Automation*, Dordrecht, The Netherlands: Kluwer Academic Publishers.

Carlsson, B. (ed.) (1997), *Technological Systems and Industrial Dynamics*, Dordrecht, The Netherlands: Kluwer Academic Publishers.

Carlsson, B. and R. Stankiewicz (1991), 'On the nature, function and composition of technological systems', *Journal of Evolutionary Economics*, **1**, 93–118.

Carter, C. and B. Williams (1964), 'Government science policy and the growth of the British economy', *Manchester School*, **32**, 117–214.

Constant, E.W. (1980), *The Origins of the Turbo-Jet Revolution*, Baltimore, MD: John Hopkins University Press.

Coombs, R. and J.S. Metcalfe (2000), 'Organizing for innovation: co-ordinating distributed innovation capabilities' in N. Foss and V. Mahnke (eds), *Competence, Governance and Entrepreneurship: Advances in Economic Strategy Research*, Oxford, UK: Oxford University Press.

Coombs, R., M. Harvey and B. Tether (2001), 'Analysing distributed innovation processes', CRIC Discussion Paper, No. 43, University of Manchester.

David, P.A. and D. Foray (1996), 'Information distribution and the growth of economically valuable knowledge: a rationale for technological infrastructure policies', in M. Teubal, D. Foray, M. Justman and E. Juscovitch, E. (eds), *Technological Infrastructure Policy: An International Perspective*, Dordrecht, The Netherlands: Kluwer Academic Publishers.

Edquist, C. (ed.) (1997), *Systems of Innovation: Technologies, Institutions and Organizations*, London: Pinter.

Eliasson, G. (1998), 'On the micro foundations of economic growth', in J. Lesourne and A. Orléan (eds), *Advances in Self-Organization and Evolutionary Economics*, London: Economica.

Faulkner, W. (1994), 'Conceptualizing knowledge used in innovation: a second look at the science-technology distinction and industrial innovation', *Science Technology and Human Values*, **19**, 425–58.

Freeman, C. (1987), *Technology Policy and Economic Performance*, London: Pinter.

Freeman, C. (1994), 'The economics of technical change', *Cambridge Journal of Economics*, **18**, 463–514

Freeman, C. and F. Louca (2001), *As Time Goes By*, Oxford, UK: Oxford University Press.

Georghiou, L. (1996), 'The United Kingdom technology foresight programme', *Futures*, **28**, 359–77.

Georghiou, L. (1998), 'Global cooperation in research', *Research Policy*, **27**, 611–26.

Gibbons, M. and R. Johnson (1974), 'The role of science in technological innovation', *Research Policy*, **3**, 220–42.

Gibbons, M., C. Limoges, H. Nowotny, S. Schwartzman, P. Scott and M. Trow (1994), *The New Production of Knowledge*, London: Sage.

Grandstrand, D.. P. Patel and K. Pavitt (1997), 'Multi-technology corporations: why they have "distributed" rather than "core" competences'. *California Management Review*, **39**, 8–25.

Green, K., R. Hull, V. Walsh and A. McMeekin (1998), 'The construction of the techno-economic: networks vs paradigms'. CRIC Discussion Paper, No. 17. University of Manchester.

Griliches, Z. (1998), *R&D and Productivity: The Econometric Evidence*, Chicago: Chicago University Press.

Hicks, D. (1995), 'Published papers, tacit competencies and corporate management of the public/private character of knowledge', *Industrial and Corporate Change*, **4**, 401–24.

Howells, J. (1997), 'Research and technology outsourcing', CRIC Discussion Paper, No. 6, University of Manchester.

Katz, J.S. and Martin, B. (1997), 'What is research collaboration?', *Research Policy*, **26**, 1–18.

Keller, A. (1984), 'Has science created technology', *Minerva*, **22**, 161–82.

Kline, S.J. and Rosenberg, M. (1986). 'An overview of innovation', in National Academy of Engineering, *The Positive Sum Strategy: Harnessing Technology for Economic Growth*, Washington: National Academy Press.

Kodama, F. (1995), *Emerging Patterns of Innovation*, Cambridge. MA: Harvard Business School Press.

de Laat, B. and Larédo, P. (1998), 'Foresight for research and technology policies: from innovation studies to scenario configuration', in R. Coombs, K. Green, A. Richards and V. Walsh (eds), *Technological Change and Organisation*, Cheltenham, UK and Northhampton, MA: Edward Elgar.

Langrish, J.. M. Gibbons, W. Evans and F. Jevons (1972), *Wealth from Knowledge*, London: Macmillan.

Layton, E.T. (1987). 'Through the looking glass, or news from lake mirror image'. *Technology and Culture*, **15**, 594–601.

Lundvall. B.A. (ed.) (1992), *National Systems of Innovation: Towards A Theory of Innovation and Interactive Learning*, London: Pinter.

Marshall, A. (1919), *Industry and Trade*, London: Macmillan.

Merges, R.P. and R. Nelson (1990), 'On the complex economics of patent scope', *The Colombia Law Review*, **90** (4), 839.

Metcalfe. J.S. (1992), 'Competition and collaboration in the innovation process' in A. Bowen and M. Ricketts (eds), *Stimulating Innovation in Industry*, London: Kogan Page.

Metcalfe. J.S. (1995a), 'The economic foundations of technological policy: equilibrium and evolutionary perspectives', in P. Stoneman (ed.), *Handbook of the Economics of Innovation and Technological Change*, Oxford: Blackwell.

Metcalfe. J.S. (1995b), 'Technology systems and technology policy in an evolutionary framework', *Cambridge Journal of Economics*, **19**, 25–46.

Metcalfe, J.S. and N. DeLiso (1998), 'Innovation, capabilities and knowledge: the epistemic connection', in R. Coombs, K. Green. A. Richards and V. Walsh. V. (eds), *Technological Change and Organisation*, Cheltenham, UK and Northhampton, MA: Edward Elgar.

Metcalfe, J.S. and L. Georghiou (1998), 'Equilibrium and evolutionary foundations of technology policy', in *Science, Technology Industry Review*, OECD, **22**, 75–100.

Mowery, D.C. and N. Rosenberg (1989), *Technology and the Pursuit of Economic Growth*, Cambridge, UK: Cambridge University Press.

Narin, F., K.S. Hamilton and D. Olivastro (1997), 'The increasing linkage between US technology and public science', *Research Policy*, **26**, 317–30.

Nelson, R. (1982), 'The role of knowledge in R&D efficiency', *Quarterly Journal of Economics*, **97**, 453–70.

Nelson, R. (1993), *National Innovation Systems*, New York: Oxford University Press.

OECD (1992), *Technology and the Economy*, Paris: OECD.

Pavitt, K. (1991), 'What makes basic research economically useful', *Research Policy*, **20**, 109–19.

Petroski, H. (1996), *Innovation by Design*, Cambridge, MA: Harvard University Press.

Polanyi, M. (1958), *Personal Knowledge*, London: Routledge.

Rosenberg, N. (1990), 'Why firms do basic research (with their own money)', *Research Policy*, **19**, 165–74.

Smith, K. (1997), 'Economic infrastructure and innovation systems', in C. Edquist (ed.), *Systems of Innovation: Technologies, Institutions and Organizations*, London: Pinter, pp. 86–106.

Stiglitz, J.E. (1994), *Whither Socialism*, Oxford, UK: Oxford University Press.

Stokes, D.E. (1997), *Pasteur's Quadrant*, Washington: Brookings Institution Press.

Tassey, G. (1992), *Technology Infrastructure and Competitive Position*, Dordrecht, The Netherlands: Kluwer Academic Publishers.

Teubal, M. (1996), 'R&D and technology policy in NICs as learning processes', *World Development*, **24**, 449–60.

Utterback, J.M. (1994), *Mastering the Dynamics of Innovation: How Companies Can Seize Opportunities in the Face of Technological Change*, Cambridge, MA: Harvard University Press.

Varga, A. (1998), *University Research and Regional Innovation*, London: Kluwer Academic Publishers.

Veugelers, R. (1997), 'Internal R&D expenditures and external technology sourcing', *Research Policy*, **26**, 303–15.

Vincenti, W.G. (1990), *What Engineers Know and How They Know It*, Baltimore, MD: John Hopkins University Press.

Vincenti, W.G. (1995), 'The technical shaping of technology: real world constraints and technical logic in Edison's electrical lighting system', *Social Studies of Science*, **25**, 553–74.

Walker, W. (2000), 'Entrapment in large technology systems: institutional commitment and power relations', *Research Policy*, **29** (7–8), 833–46.

Weinburg, A.M. (1967), *Reflections on Big Science*, London: Pergamon Press.

Wise, G. (1985), 'Science and technology', *Osiris*, **1**, 229–48.

Young, A. (1928), 'Increasing returns and economic progress', *Economic Journal*, **38**, 527–42.

8. Institutional evolution, regulatory competition and path dependence

Wolfgang Kerber and Klaus Heine

1. INTRODUCTION

After several decades of intensive research on the impact of institutions on economic performance, it is widely accepted that the institutional structure of a society does not only 'matter' but seems to be the decisive factor for economic development. But economic history does not lend support for the proposition that institutional evolution implies a clear mechanism that institutions will improve over time. North (1990) showed that in many periods of economic history societies have been stuck with inefficient institutional structures leading to economic stagnation or decline instead of economic growth. Therefore, theories on institutional evolution which are able to contribute to the explanation of those phenomena are necessary. North suggested 'path dependences' of institutional change as an important explanation, why societies might be 'locked in' in an inefficient institutional setting. If the present institutions are shaped to a great extent by the past ones, institutional trajectories can emerge that impede the evolution of superior sets of rules for society.

In economics two different groups of theories for the emergence and change of the institutional structure of a society can be differentiated:[1]

(1) Most theoretical approaches analyse institutional change as the outcome of processes within one society, as for example theories of the emergence of property rights (Demsetz 1967; Libecap 1989; Knight 1992), the rent-seeking approaches of Public Choice (Mueller 1989) and Chicago Political Economy (Posner 1998) or the analysis of institutional change by North (1990).[2]
(2) Another group of approaches tries to take into account processes of interaction and competition between different societies as an additional and perhaps important determinant for institutional evolution. In the context of his more general theory of cultural evolution Hayek (1973) developed the notion of competition among groups with different sets of rules, suggesting the controversial proposition that in such a process of variation and selection of

rules the more effective would prevail. Although this optimistic notion of an evolutionary process of ever-improving institutions was correctly criticized on methodological grounds (Vanberg 1994), the basic idea that a competition-like process among different states or institutions may lead to a process of institutional evolution through the innovation and imitation of institutions (Vanberg 1992) might be a promising starting-point for further research on institutional evolution.

Independent from contributions to the theory of institutional evolution, this evolutionary approach of institutional competition plays an increasingly important role in the debate about the feasibility of locational competition and its impact on economic policy.[3] Here the question arose whether competition among states (or more general, jurisdictions), which increasingly can be observed as a consequence of rising factor mobility, will lead to an improvement or deterioration of public goods and services supplied by jurisdictions. An important part of this discussion refers to the more specific question of the feasibility of competition among rules or regulations (regulatory competition). From the perspective of legal scholars competition among legal rules or systems of legal rules is discussed both on the global level and on the level of the European Union. Within the European Union this discussion is particularly important for the policy question, whether regulations/legal rules of the European Union member states should be harmonized or remain decentralized.[4] Therefore research on regulatory competition can be seen both as research on policy questions and as contributions to a positive theory of institutional evolution.

Despite using the recent literature on regulatory competition, the focus of our chapter is on the positive explanation of institutional development. Therefore we investigate a specific question concerning the working of competition among legal rules. Without negating other potential deficiencies of regulatory competition, we want to pick up the idea of North that path dependences might be an important cause for the emergence or persistence of inefficient institutions. According to North (1990) the potential institutional path dependences can be explained by political-economic factors, subjective models of reality (mental models) and the increasing returns characteristic of institutions. But in contrast to North, who analysed institutional path dependence without taking processes of interaction and competition between states into account, we want to analyse whether path dependences can also emerge in processes of regulatory competition among different states (or jurisdictions). Can path dependences lead to selection problems in processes of competition among legal rules through lock-in effects, which means that inferior institutional solutions might succeed over superior ones? For a more thorough analysis of potential path dependences in regulatory competition we apply the concept of technological paradigms and technological trajectories (Dosi 1982), which is well-established in innovation economics, to institutions. This implies the development of the new concept of legal paradigms and legal trajectories, which will be used for analysing the example of the evolution of corporate law.

Our chapter is organized as follows: after introducing the theory of regulatory competition (Section 2) and the presentation of the basic ideas of the concept of technological paradigms and its implications of potential lock-ins for technological competition (Section 3), it will be shown how legal paradigms and trajectories can be defined and integrated into a theoretical framework of regulatory competition and which conclusions on potential failures of regulatory competition can be drawn from this perspective (Section 4). Then the attempt is made to substantiate our theoretical considerations on the causes of path dependence by applying the theoretical framework to the analysis of the well-known competition among the state corporation laws in the United States. A short comparison to the path dependence problem in regard to European corporate laws will suggest some important implications for the policy question of introducing competition among corporation laws within the European Union (Section 5). Finally, some conclusions will be drawn about the importance of path dependences in regulatory competition for the explanation of institutional evolution (Section 6).

2.   REGULATORY COMPETITION AS INSTITUTIONAL EVOLUTION

In the last years an intensive discussion on locational competition has developed which also was called institutional competition, competition among governments or interjurisdictional competition.[5] The basic idea is that through technological progress and liberalization the mobility costs for individuals, firms and factors of production (especially financial capital) have been considerably reduced, which leads to an increasing competition among states, regions or municipalities. If we apply the market paradigm to these processes of locational competition, then the jurisdictions correspond to firms, the governments to the management of firms, and the individuals, firms and factors represent the customers of the services supplied by jurisdictions. The combinations of products and prices that firms offer to their customers correspond to the complex bundles of public goods, services and taxes which are offered by the jurisdictions. The provision of a legal order with an appropriate set of legal rules (institutions, regulations) is one of the most important tasks of these jurisdictions and therefore a crucial part of their public good–tax bundles. From a normative point of view we can interpret legal rules as social tools for solving problems of interaction and cooperation within a society and therefore – similar to other public goods – they should be designed for the fulfilling of the preferences of the citizens.

In the Tiebout approach on the competitive provision of local public goods (Tiebout 1956) a neoclassical concept of competition (perfect competition) is used, that assumes perfect knowledge of the agents. But the assumption of perfect knowledge about the optimal quality and quantity of public goods does not stand critical scrutiny. In contrast, we have to accept the existence of Hayek's knowledge problem (Hayek 1945), that is the governments have no perfect knowledge which public goods or legal rules are the best to solve the problems of a jurisdiction's citizens. From this point of view regulatory competition should be seen as a 'discovery procedure', in which jurisdictions compete with different legal rules. This implies a process of parallel experimentation, in which new rules are generated and tested in regard to their problem-solving capacity, and in which we hope that the superior legal rules might be found out and spread by imitation. From this perspective legal rules should be seen as hypotheses, how problems of interaction and coordination in society could be solved best. Consequently, in the concepts of interjurisdictional competition – or more specific, regulatory competition – an evolutionary concept of competition should be used, which is based upon central ideas of Hayek (competition as a discovery procedure) and Schumpeter (competition as a process of innovation and imitation). Such an evolutionary concept of knowledge-generating competition makes it possible to employ the rich theoretical and empirical insights of innovation economics also for the analysis of regulatory competition.[6]

An analytical approach to regulatory competition calls for a careful analysis of the potential meanings of 'regulatory competition'. In the first place we have to differentiate between competition among jurisdictions as locations for individuals, firms and investments on one side, and competition among legal rules/regulations on the other. In interjurisdictional competition the innovation of superior legal rules can be one possibility to improve the locational conditions and to get a competitive advantage over other jurisdictions. So institutional/regulatory innovation is a competitive action within interjurisdictional competition. But we can also focus on the population of legal rules which are applied in jurisdictions. Consequently we can speak of competition among legal rules, if we mean the processes of generating, spreading or elimination of legal rules. Therefore competition among legal rules could be seen in analogy to competition among different products in ordinary markets.

After differentiating interjurisdictional from regulatory competition, also several basic types of regulatory competition might be distinguished. A useful criterion for this taxonomy is the extent of mobility (see in a more elaborated form Kerber 2000a).

To start with, even in the extreme case of isolated countries, in which there is no mobility of goods or factors, an experimental process with legal rules in different jurisdictions with the possibility of mutual learning from their experiences is possible, if at least the legal rules in other countries and their impact can be observed. Although we have no direct competition among jurisdictions, due to the mobility of ideas (and therefore legal concepts) we can speak of competition among legal rules which is based upon the experiences in the various countries. This sort of regulatory competition is called 'yardstick competition' (Salmon 1987).

A different situation arises, if (a) goods and services and additionally (b) individuals, firms and factors of production are mobile between jurisdictions. We may call this a *type A-regulatory competition*. A *type A-regulatory competition* leads to a more direct competition between different jurisdictions and might force governments to improve the locational conditions of their jurisdictions by offering attractive public good–tax bundles. In that case the legal rules of a jurisdiction are part of the entire bundle and therefore influence the locational decisions of individuals, firms and factors. But competition among different legal rules is hampered by being only a small part of a complex bundle of services and it requires a complete entry/exit decision (voting by feet).

A third basic type of competition among legal rules arises if the individuals or firms can choose between legal rules of different jurisdictions without having to change their location. This sort of regulatory competition we will call a *type B-regulatory competition*. In this kind of regulatory competition 'choice of law' rules determine under what conditions individuals are allowed to 'opt out' and to use legal rules from other jurisdictions. Whereas in the case of 'yardstick competition' the decisions on legal rules can only be made collectively for whole jurisdictions and in a *type A-regulatory competition* the individual choice of legal rules is only possible by changing the whole bundle of services by migration, the individuals in the third case have the right to directly choose single legal rules. This allows for an individual combination of legal rules from different legal orders. Such a differentiated choice of legal rules might enhance competition among single rules considerably. But the question arises, to what extent the possibility to choose legal rules freely might lead to deficiencies in the working of these rules. These deficiencies might lead to the necessity to restrict the 'choice of law' and maintain the mandatory character of legal rules.

What can be the potential advantages of regulatory competition?[7] Since we cannot assume that the optimal rules have already be found, regulatory competition as a parallel process of experimentation with different legal rules might lead to a much greater capability of finding superior rules and might imply consequently a higher rate of legal innovations and a greater adaptability to all kinds of exogenous shocks than in centralized legal systems, in which only sequential experimentation and learning is possible. Interjurisdictional and regulatory competition might also be employed to control political power, because governments lose their monopoly power and are put under competitive pressure (Sinn 1992). In other words, regulatory competition might help to limit rent-seeking behavior, since firms and individuals can avoid those legal rules or jurisdictions better, which shift rents to certain groups. A third advantage of regulatory competition can be seen in the heterogeneous supply of regulations, which is able to fulfill the preferences of a heterogeneous population with different problems better.

In the literature on regulatory competition many arguments can be found why regulatory competition may suffer from deficiencies, leading to a suboptimal supply of regulations (for example Sinn 1997). One of the most prominent examples refers to the possibility that competition among legal rules leads to a 'race to the bottom', which means the jurisdictions try to outperform one another by reducing the standards of regulation to an inefficient low level. Although this assertion still lacks empirical support (Sun and Pelkmans 1995), the question has to be taken very seriously whether regulatory competition might jeopardize the aim of a certain regulation. Therefore, whether regulatory competition really leads to the selection of superior legal rules has to be analysed in detail and cannot simply be assumed.

Another group of potential problems have their cause in incentive problems (Wegner 1998). In many applications it is not easy to see which incentives politicians have to improve regulations, because in situations of inter-jurisdictional/regulatory competition there are usually no incentives that are comparable to profits and losses in market competition (for these problems see in more detail Tirole 1994). If these incentives are missing or do exist only in a very indirect way, important preconditions for continuous processes of innovation and imitation are lacking. Another important problem, which up to now has not been analysed to a greater extent, might be the existence of path dependences, which – in analogy to corresponding problems in technological competition – can lead to legal 'lock-ins'. This would imply the possibility that less efficient rules can dominate, despite the fact that more efficient rules are available.

3.   TECHNOLOGICAL PARADIGMS, TECHNOLOGICAL COMPETITION AND LOCK-INS

3.1   Technological Paradigms

The concept of technological paradigms is part of the evolutionary branch in innovation economics. The concept tries to explain and – as far as possible – to prognosticate the technological development of industries. Different levels of analysis can be identified: on the one hand, competition among firms to establish a new technological paradigm; and on the other hand, competition between firms within an established technological paradigm.[8] For example at the beginning of the century there were different technological paradigms for the development of an automobile: electric motor, steam engine and combustion engine. After the combustion engine had become generally accepted, innovations essentially took place in the context of this technological paradigm, like four-stroke engine, compressor or water cooling.

The concept of technological paradigms uses the ideas of the science theoretician Thomas Kuhn (1970) for the analysis of innovation processes. Kuhn assumes that scientific progress is determined by scientific paradigms. Scientific paradigms dominate for a certain time the direction and the intensity of the scientific progress. The research within a paradigm is called 'normal science'. The dominant paradigm shifts, if the dominant paradigm supplies no more solutions to actual problems in science.

Dosi (1988a, 1127) transfers Kuhn's concept of scientific paradigms to the development of technology as follows:

> (A)s modern philosophy of science suggests the existence of *scientific paradigms* ...., so there are *technological paradigms*. Both scientific and technological paradigms embody an *outlook*, a definition of the relevant problems, a pattern of enquiry. A 'technological paradigm' defines contextually the scientific principles utilized for the task, the material technology to be used. In other words, a technological paradigm can be defined as a 'pattern' of solution of selected technoeconomic problems ... A technological paradigm is both an *exemplar* – an artifact that is to be developed and improved ... – and a set of *heuristics* (e.g., Where do we go from here? Where should we search? What sort of knowledge should we draw on?).

Thus, a technological paradigm selects both the area in which an industry becomes innovative, and the method with which one looks up for innovations. This directs the technological progress into a corridor that can be called 'base-design' (Elsser 1993, 114).[9] The development of the base-design can be observed by the modifications of its most important technoeconomic characteristics. From the observation of these modifications the path of the technological development (technological trajectory) can be derived.

3.2   Stabilizing Factors

In connection with the 'revolutionary' shift of paradigms the question arises about the historic course or time path of paradigmatic shifts. More exactly: it is conceivable that paradigms become detached very rapidly or that paradigms are hardly destabilized by competitors. The temporal process of the paradigmatic shift in a single case is surely a fact that has to be clarified by empirical research.

However, experience shows that paradigms are often stable for a long time. For that reason certain factors must exist, which stabilize paradigms. These factors can be divided into four groups (Elsser 1993, 118; Schilling 1999): (1) sunk costs, (2) uncertainty, (3) dynamic economies of scale and (4) complementarities.

(1) Sunk costs concern the costs of specific investments. After a specific investment has been done, the costs of the investment cannot be capitalized, because there is only one possible use of the investment. So, technology-specific investments stabilize a paradigm, since a shift in the paradigm would devalue the investments and additional switching-costs would occur. On the other hand, a shift of the paradigm seems to become more probable the smaller the specific investments are.

(2) Most decisions concerning innovations are decisions under uncertainty. The reason for this lies in limited information or the lack of sufficient cognitive resources to process all relevant pieces of information adequately. A possibility to deal with this problem is the use of routines or judgement heuristics (Simon 1976; Heiner 1983). A technological paradigm leads to the preferred reduction of complexity, because the technological paradigm builds a guiding structure that directs the decision-maker to where he should search for innovations and which was the appropriate method to overcome a technological barrier. Therefore, a technological paradigm is stabilized by the fact that in the decision process the same routines for problem-solving are used again and again.

(3) The most important examples of dynamic economies of scale are learning effects and network externalities. Learning effects stabilize a paradigm, since learning effects are specific to a certain technology. A decision-maker who has to select between an established technological paradigm or a new technology might usually choose the established technological paradigm, because the decision-maker can profit from the experiences of the former users. This is different in the case of a new technological paradigm, even if the learning potentials may exceed those of the old technological paradigm by far. By the adoption of the established technological paradigm the cumulative learning will be fostered, making the decision for the new technological paradigm more and more unattractive for the future. A technological paradigm is stabilized also by network externalities. The stabilization of a technological paradigm by network externalities always occurs if an increase in the number of users increases the value of a technology to each single user (for example telephone, video-cassettes, keyboards of typewriters and so on). In this case competitors are forced to increase their number of participants in their own network in order to become competitive. But this might not be an easy task for newcomers, since there are high requirements of capital and high switching costs for the users. So there might be lock-in effects in favor of established technological paradigms.

(4) The problem of complementarity refers to the fact that the efficiency of one technology is frequently influenced by related technologies. The quality of a photograph not only depends on the optics of the lenses, but also on the mechanics of the camera and the chemical composition of the film. The more technologies are complementary to each other, the more difficult it is to separate a single technology from the entire technological product. The total performance of the entire technology can increase in such a case only by the coevolution of all involved technologies. For the stability of a technological paradigm the existence and organization of the technological complementarities is very important. In the case of complementarities no technology can be altered without consideration of the other technologies. This can lead to a stabilization of technological paradigms.

3.3   Technological Competition and Lock-ins

The term 'technological competition' means that technologies compete to be used by firms for their production processes. In an unhampered technological competition those technologies are selected by the criterion of the lowest costs of production. Therefore technological competition is welfare-increasing. But from the perspective of the concept of technological competition, the stabilizing factors can lead to market failures, because they may cause path dependencies which can prevent the selection of the efficient technologies. This can be clarified by Figure 8.1 (Klodt 1995, 103; Arthur 1994, 13).

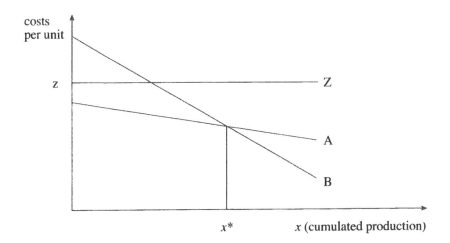

Figure 8.1   Technological competition and lock-in (compare Klodt 1995, 104)

Firms may apply technology Z, that has constant costs z per unit. Now, a new technology A may be developed that allows a common use of dynamic economies of scale, which lower the costs per unit for all firms. When the output increases on the industry level, all firms within the industry can lower their costs, which means learning by doing takes place on the industry level. Since the costs per unit are lower if technology A is used, the producers switch to technology A. But the change to A represents an inefficient technological selection, if a technology B exists, and a quantity greater than x^* can be sold, because beyond x^* the technology B has lower costs per unit than technology A. But a switch to B does not occur, because the producers are captured in a technological lock-in. A single firm which is willing to switch to B faces the problem that it cannot be sure that its competitors also select B. Up to the quantity x^* the adopters of B have a disadvantage in manufacturing costs against the adopters of A. Since no firm will run the risk to be outperformed, all firms choose technology A.

4. LEGAL PARADIGMS AND REGULATORY COMPETITION

4.1 The Concept of Legal Paradigms

For the analysis of potential path dependences in regulatory competition we now try to apply Dosi's concept of technological paradigms – including technological trajectories and the possibility of 'lock-ins'.[10] Despite many differences the analogy between technologies and legal rules is not so far-fetched as it may seem at a first glance, because we can interpret legal rules (as other kinds of institutions) as 'socio-technological instruments' that attempt to solve problems of human interaction in societies. Both technologies and legal rules are more or less successful in attaining their aims, so both kinds of problem-solving devices usually can and should be improved by innovative solutions. The latter are important, too, if during the process of economic development new problems emerge that have to be tackled by the legal system. In the following we want to outline how a transfer of Dosi's concept of technological paradigms to legal rules would look like. Can we define 'legal paradigms' and 'legal trajectories' in a similar way?

It is most interesting that one of the most famous legal scholars, Oliver Wendell Holmes (1897, 1899), had developed ideas in his contributions to legal development which seem to be similar to the concept of technological paradigms. According to him today's legal concepts – as for example in contract law – are the outcome of a process of 'competing ideas', which he modeled –

following Spencer and Darwin – as a variation-selection process, in which original legal variety is transformed into the dominance of certain legal concepts. But such 'generalizing principles', which we now can call 'paradigms', can also lose influence and be superseded by other paradigms (Holmes 1899, 449). Holmes even described certain mechanisms that stabilize such paradigms. An important factor, for example, is the common notion of problems legal scholars learn from the dominant legal paradigm. That leads to the application of common routines for solving legal problems and therefore to the stabilization of a path of legal development (Holmes 1899, 451, 1897, 468).

In analogy to Dosi's transfer of the concept of scientific paradigms to technologies, 'legal paradigms' can be seen as embodying an outlook, a definition of the relevant problems, and a pattern of enquiry. The outlook consists of the specific perspective that legal scholars use to grasp the central problems of specific kinds of human interaction. For example, in antitrust law the outlook of the efficiency paradigm of the Chicago School always begins with the assumption of efficiency explanations for all kinds of firm behavior or market structures. In contrast to that the competing paradigm of the Harvard School starts with the basic assumption that the existence of and the striving for market power is the decisive perspective that should be used to assess the behavior of firms and the structure of markets. The legal paradigms also define which problems are relevant and what kinds of trade-offs are important that legal rules as instruments for solving problems should help to solve. The Chicago School only knows the trade-off between allocative and productive efficiency (trade-off analysis of Williamson) and rejects the additional trade-offs of the multi-goal approach of the Harvard School.[11]

The common perspective of a problem that is generated by a legal paradigm also encompasses a common set of heuristics how to deal with new problems. What phenomena are problems at all? And if they are problems, in what way should they be solved? Which legal instruments should be used and which be avoided? Legal scholars using the efficiency paradigm of the Chicago School use entirely different heuristics from those that start from the market power paradigm. The example of the controversy between Harvard and Chicago School can be interpreted as competition between the two legal paradigms 'efficiency paradigm' and 'market power paradigm', and the transition from the dominance of the market power paradigm to the efficiency paradigm was generally interpreted as a 'revolution' in US-antitrust policy. This characterization matches completely into Kuhn's (Dosi's) notion of scientific (technological) progress as a sequence of revolutions by substituting one scientific (technological) paradigm by another.

Decisive for the suitability of the transfer of Dosi's concept of technological paradigms to legal rules is the question whether we can observe factors that stabilize legal paradigms and therefore might lead to path dependences. From the considerations mentioned above it seems obvious that legal scholars using different legal paradigms will search in different directions for solving problems. This implies the possibility of different paths of legal development. In this chapter we suggest that also in legal evolution stabilizing factors for legal paradigms can be very important. In Section 5 we want to show that those stabilizing factors that have been emerged as relevant in the concept of technological paradigm (sunk costs, uncertainty, dynamic economies of scale, network externalities) can also be important for stabilizing legal paradigms in the realm of corporate law. We will suggest that one factor is particularly relevant for the stabilizing of legal paradigms: the complementarity to other (sets of) legal rules.

Before asking for potential consequences of those path dependences that might follow from these stabilizing factors for regulatory competition, it is necessary to make two methodological remarks:

(1) The concept of 'paradigm' is a heuristic concept. It depends on the problem how we should apply the concept of paradigms to specific legal concepts. We can speak of the whole Anglo-Saxon Common Law system as a paradigm in contrast to the alternative paradigms of Continental Law in Europe (German BGB, French Code Civil, Scandinavian Law). But we can also define different paradigms in US-antitrust law, although both are part of the Anglo-Saxon law system. Depending on the problem the term 'paradigm' can be applied to different levels of the legal system, that is on the whole legal system, a specific part of the legal system (as corporate law) or on specific subsets of legal rules, as for example legal concepts dealing with insider trading. This heuristic interpretation of the paradigm concept should not be seen as an indicator for the vagueness of the concept, but for allowing a flexible use of the concept on different levels of legal evolution.

(2) If we speak of legal rules and their development it is not sufficient to limit our attention on the legal rules in form of the statutory law. Not only in Common Law systems but also in Continental Law legal development to a large extent takes place through the judgments of the supreme courts of a legal system, as for example the US Supreme Court or the European Court of Justice. So legal evolution and therefore also competition among legal rules is possible without having to change laws in the form of statutory law by parliament.

4.2   Regulatory Competition and Legal Lock-ins

How can the concept of legal paradigms with its consequence of potential path dependences be integrated into the notion of regulatory competition? As technological competition can be seen as a part of competition among firms which generate technological innovations or imitate them for improving their performance for customers, also jurisdictions can try to improve their legal rules in order to solve problems of human interaction in a better way. In Section 2 it was shown that in a multi-jurisdictional system a parallel process of experimentation with whole legal systems, subsets of legal rules or even single rules is possible, in which the jurisdictions are able to learn mutually from the experiences of other jurisdictions with legal rules. Depending on the degree of mobility between jurisdictions, that is whether (1) the jurisdictions are only able to observe one another, or (2) individuals, firms, factors of productions and goods/services are mobile between jurisdictions, or (3) even the individuals or firms can decide themselves which legal rules they want to use (choice of law), different types of competition processes between jurisdictions or legal rules develop.

In the concept of technological paradigms technological competition between firms can take place as a competition between different technological paradigms or as a competition between different technologies (design configurations) within the same technological paradigm, which might be used by the whole industry. The same differentiation can be applied to competition among legal rules. As far as different jurisdictions use the same legal paradigm for solving certain problems, it is still possible to have competition among legal rules as an experimentation process with mutual learning on a lower level of the legal system. We can call this a competition among legal rules within a legal paradigm. The other form of regulatory competition would be competition among legal paradigms, if different jurisdictions use different legal paradigms as hypotheses how to solve specific kinds of problems best. Both regulatory competition between legal paradigms and regulatory competition within a legal paradigm are processes of experimentation, in which different sets of rules are tested and experiences are made, from which other jurisdictions might learn in form of imitating the superior rules.

If we analyse the potential impact of path dependences on the efficacy of regulatory competition, it can be suggested that also the problem of a legal 'lock-in' can occur. Stabilizing factors can lead to the problem that superior legal paradigms will not be chosen by the jurisdictions, because the costs of switching from one paradigm to the other are too large to be worthwhile. In particular if dynamic economies of scale exist, situations as in Figure 8.1 can occur: if we interpret the horizontal axis as the time for accumulating experience with a certain legal paradigm, then learning implies an improvement of the problem-solving capacity of this legal paradigm leading to decreasing costs. From the starting-point of a legal rule Z without such learning effects, the jurisdictions (in *type A-regulatory competition*) or the firms/individuals (in *type B-regulatory competition*) can choose between the additional legal paradigms A and B. Whereas the adoptors each have incentives to switch from the paradigm Z to A, triggering off the learning effects of cumulative experience within the legal paradigm A, the jurisdictions or firms/individuals have no incentives to choose the ultimately superior legal paradigm B. The cause for the wrong selection of legal paradigms can be a prisoner's dilemma, because the superiority of legal paradigm B only emerges if a certain threshold of experience is exceeded, which requires the simultaneous adoption of B by several jurisdictions. But the lock-in of inferior legal paradigms (or legal design configurations) can also have other reasons beyond dynamic economies of scale. In our example of competition among corporate laws, which will be discussed in the next section, we will explain potential causes in more detail.

5. COMPETITION AMONG CORPORATE LAWS: AN APPLICATION

5.1   An Example: Competition Among US Corporate Laws

The question about the workability of competition of corporate laws has been discussed broadly in the United States.[12] In the United States companies must select a charter for running business. But the companies can choose freely between all charters that are provided by the fifty Federal States. The decision for a specific charter is independent from the place of production and managerial decisions. From the perspective of choice of law this means the application of the so-called 'incorporation theory'. The counterpart to the incorporation theory is the 'real seat theory', which requires that the place of incorporation and the place of business operations is identical. The real seat theory, for example, is applied in Germany and France.

The Anglo-American discussion about the workability of corporate chartering has its historical origin in the second half of the last century. Between 1870 and 1890 powerful monopolies had been formed in many industries, which were legally fought by the single states and finally on the federal level by the Sherman Act in 1890. In this situation the government of New Jersey got the idea to stabilize the state's budget by giving monopolies and trusts a new home. The means for this was to allow special business forms that were able to circumvent the antitrust laws. The price for this was the payment of a 'franchise tax', that is a tax for using the corporate law (Grandy 1989). So it was fiscal interests which led New Jersey to develop a corporate law that fulfilled the needs of the companies. But the company-friendly legislation had not been seen as having only welfare-enhancing effects. And when Woodrow Wilson was elected as governor of New Jersey in 1910 he took steps against the company-friendly legislation. Because of these corporate law reforms it was no longer attractive to incorporate in New Jersey. But from 1913 on Delaware took over the role of New Jersey. Delaware's simple competition strategy was the exact copying of the corporate law of New Jersey (Bebchuk 1992, p. 1443), in order to make the reincorporation to Delaware as cheap as possible. Since that time the majority of the limited liability companies has been incorporated in Delaware (308,492 corporations on 31 December 1999). In the course of time the other states tried to 'out Delaware' Delaware, but they failed again and again, because Delaware introduced many legal innovations throughout the entire corporate law, such as for example: election of the executive committee, amendments of the by-laws, rights of the general meeting, payment of dividends, mergers, fiduciary duties or possible measures against hostile takeovers (Bebchuk 1992, 1444).

A state's incentive to engage in charter competition is the raising of the 'franchise tax'.[13] Whether this competition leads to a 'race to the bottom' or to a 'race to the top', is vehemently disputed. Followers of the 'race to the bottom' hypothesis (for example Cary 1974; Eisenberg 1983) argue that charter competition would lead systematically to a degradation of corporate law. The cause for the degradation would be that the states make only legal offers to those managers which are relevant for the incorporation decision. But especially the managers are looking for protection from the checks of investors. The result of this are corporate laws which intensify managerial problems (manageralism), for example establishing rules that prevent hostile takeovers (poison pills). Consequently, the market for corporate control is no longer able to sanction mismanagement. In short, competition in the market for corporate law is seen to increase inefficiencies.

The followers of the 'race to the top' hypothesis (for example Winter 1977; Easterbrook and Fischel 1996) do not deny that competition in corporate law had forced a liberalization of corporate laws in the last decades. They deny, however, that this development runs against the interests of the investors. On the contrary, the legal innovations were in the interest of the investors. Competition among legal rules is the means to fight the interests of the investors against the management (Bebchuk 1992, p. 1445). This argument is supported by empirical investigations about the development of the firm value of corporations, which are incorporated in Delaware. It is shown that corporations which are incorporated in Delaware have a higher firm value and higher net returns than firms incorporated outside of Delaware (Dodd and Leftwich 1980; Daines 2001). The conclusion can be drawn that competition among corporate laws leads to the selection of efficiency-increasing rules.

Romano (1985) made a third point. She did not ask about the normative implications of competition in corporate law but what factors were responsible for the lasting success of Delaware. The attractiveness of Delaware is attributed to the fact that it won the 'race for predictability and stability' (Bebchuk 1992, p. 1446), because corporations are primarily looking for a stable legal system.

Delaware can signal this stability reliably: on the one hand the revenues of the small state of Delaware depend on the 'franchise tax' substantially, on the other hand Delaware commits itself on the constitutional level, as modifications of the corporate law can be made only with two-thirds majority in both chambers. Additionally, in Delaware's courts and bar specific knowledge has been accumulated, which is used to solve complicated judicial conflicts. This specialized legal knowledge is hardly imitable by the other states and therefore offers a sustainable competitive advantage.

5.2   Legal Paradigms in Corporate Law

A legal paradigm in corporate law consists of all rules which govern the relation between the shareholders and the relation between the shareholders and the management. A corporate law paradigm structures solutions for all questions, which can become important in governing the corporation. For example, answers must be given to the following problems: set-up and closing of business, rights and duties of the management and the shareholders, accounting or procurement of capital.

For example, the functions of the organs of a company can be considered as of paradigmatic importance. In the German legal family one finds the strict separation of the executive board (Vorstand) and its check by the supervisory board (Aufsichtsrat). This constellation is called a two-tier system. On the other hand in the legal family of Common Law the one-tier system is adopted widely, in which only one board exists that directs and controls the business simultaneously (Weimer and Pape 1999). These different features in the design of governance lead to certain trade-offs, which must be solved with consideration of the entire institutional setting of the corporate law paradigm. The German system of specialized supervisory boards interacts with the so-called Universalbankensystem (a bank which is investor and creditor simultaneously). The interaction leads to the consequence that an effective corporate financing can take place by 'house banks'. House banks are banks which organize all financial services for corporations for a long period of time. A house bank gets specific knowledge which can reduce agency costs enormously. As a consequence supervisory boards are frequently house bank dominated. But such a connection of the banks with the industry by investment and credits can entail specific clashes of interests, which can undermine the basic logic of the German supervisory board system.

One possibility to overcome the trade-off between interests in financing and control is the inclusion of outside experts into supervision. In Germany this was done via co-determination and participation of unions in the supervisory board. Possible problems of manageralism are thereby reduced. Surely, the intention of the legislator, when co-determination in German governance was introduced, was primarily not to overcome a perceived trade-off between financing and control in a corporate law paradigm. The legislator intended to introduce democracy on the firm level. But this is exactly a paradigmatic act of the legislator, because the German legislation is framed by the political paradigm of 'Social Democracy', that intends to amplify the voices of the members of corporate actors, as firms, universities and other institutions. On the other hand the US legislation is framed by the political paradigm of 'Check and Balances', which leads to a sort of governance, that is dominated by 'exit'. If exit is possible, the checks take place by 'voting by feet' (Roe 1999, see also Gerum 1998).

In the United States the one-tier board system in interaction with the separation of investment banks and commercial banks implies another solution of the trade-off between the interests of finance and control. Since corporate finance via credits and simultaneous holding of securities in the same corporation was forbidden till 1999 by the Glass-Steagall Act, corporate finance is essentially made by the stock market. The consequence is that most corporations are publicly held and the executive directors (CEO) enjoy a strong position. The position of the CEO is hardly monitored by the shareholders, because there seldom exists a dominant shareholder (blockholder) who has the capacity to control the management permanently. The trade-off between financing and control is solved by the mobility of the shareholders on the capital market. The shares of a corporation that does not perform well are sold. If the share price declines, the possibilities for corporate finance diminish and the management becomes under pressure. In the case of a hostile takeover the management faces the sanction of dismissal and being marked as a poor performing manager.

The German and the US governance system each have their pros and cons. So the question which of the systems might be the more efficient, cannot be answered easily (Schmidt and Spindler 1999). From the perspective of the concept of corporate law paradigms the normative question needs not be the crucial one. It is important that in each system a path was taken on which relevant trade-offs have been overcome. Since in the United States the success of monitoring depends strongly on the efficiency of the capital markets, major improvements were made in the past on the capital markets to increase the mobility of shareholders by exit-decisions. In Germany the development of governance is different. Here the focal point of interests was the improvement of voice via the supervisory board (Jürgens et al. 2000).

Another example how differently corporate law paradigms develop is the protection of investors and creditors. A corporation can raise its capital in two ways: selling shares or taking debt. Investors and creditors will only be willing to invest if their capital is secured against the opportunism of the transaction partners. Therefore rules are needed that protect investments. Both in Germany and in the United States such rules exist. But the quality of investor-protection and creditor-protection is different in both countries (La Porta et al. 1998). In the United States the trajectory of the investor protection begins with the Securities Exchange Act (1934), which means a paradigmatic shift from the traditional self-regulation of securities markets to mandatory regulation on the federal level. Further, major improvements were made by the Investor Protection Act (1970), the Insider Trading Sanctions Act (1984) and the Private Securities Litigation Act (1995). All these regulations have the aim to strengthen the legal position of the investors and to guarantee the external check of the management through the capital market. In Germany also good legal rules exist that protect investors, but in comparison to the United States the protection is poorer (no proxy by mail, right of banks to vote proxies and so on). Conversely, in Germany a better protection of creditors exists. So the conclusion may be drawn that the legislation in the United States and Germany develops and refines those protecting rules, in which comparative advantages already exist.

5.3 Stabilizing Factors in Corporate Law

5.3.1 Sunk costs

A corporate law paradigm is stabilized if costs exist that are connected with the establishment of a new corporate law paradigm, but that do not occur by running the old corporate law paradigm. Sunk costs particularly arise in connection with the building of human capital in regard to law. On the supply side, the creation of corporate law implies sunk costs. Specialists have to be consulted, ministries have to work out sketches and the law must pass the political system. Special qualifications are required whose value is preserved only with a specific corporate law paradigm. A German ministerial official who is a specialist in the German two-tier supervisory board system can become the same specialist in the US one-tier board system only after substantial efforts and training. So if the official has to solve a trade-off in regard to managerial supervision, he will use his already accumulated knowledge of the German two-tier system instead of suggesting a new construction, even if this would be the superior one in the long run.

On the demand side, human capital is also confronted with the problem of sunk costs, particularly lawyers, who are specialized in a certain corporate law. A fundamental modification of the corporate law would devalue their knowledge, or they might be forced to bear substantial costs in order to get expertise in the new corporate law. Therefore the lobby of the lawyers has a great interest to preserve a uniform corporate law, implying that the market for judicial advice remains as large as possible and the switching costs are kept small (Kobayashi and Ribstein 1996). The lawyers can carry out such a strategy if they have access to the legislation via the function as political advisors. An example is the American Bar Association (for detail see Carney 1998).

5.3.2 Uncertainty

Uncertainty stabilizes a corporate law paradigm by the fact that problems in corporate law are often solved by the use of routines that have been tested in the past successfully. The use of routines reduces complexity and gives a pattern of solutions. New solutions are usually regarded as too complex and uncertain and might be not adopted, even if the new solution would offer substantial advantages in the long run. A striking example is the selection of the legal form as 'stand-alone corporation' that is widely adopted by high-tech start-ups in Silicon Valley. The selection of this legal form has fiscal disadvantages, which do not occur in partnerships. The explanation for the inferior choice of law is that risky high-tech firms attract specific human capital usually by stock options. However, this routinized form of payment ('plain vanilla') is not the only solution to pay specific human capital for doing jobs in risky enterprises. Equivalent option plans could be set up also in the legal form of partnership. But the workers would have to be convinced in an atmosphere of trust (Klausner 1995, p. 821). The establishment of such an atmosphere and the discussions with potential workers increase the transaction costs that are connected with the setup of the business. Because the entrepreneurs often want to save these costs, they take the wrong legal form. The following of legal routines leads to the choice of standard corporate law (herding effect).

Apart from the herd behavior other reasons can play a role as to why routines are applied in the choice of corporate law. One reason is that the use of a different corporate law code puts uncertainty on potential investors, since they cannot measure easily what influence the new code might have. The uncertainty of the investors and financial analysts leads to the consequence that the value of the firm decreases. Since a smaller firm value reduces the financial scope of the management (Klausner 1995, 785; Daines 2001), the management has a large interest in choosing standard corporate law.

5.3.3 Dynamic economies of scale and network externalities

Learning effects occur within a corporate law paradigm if corporations make experiences with a corporate law and pass on these experiences to other corporations. This is the case if, for example, an indistinct regulation becomes sharper and sharper by litigation. Corporations, which are not legal prime movers, can decide on corporate law with lower uncertainty. The same applies to lawyers, who become more competent the more they participate in similar litigation (Klausner 1995, p. 786) – so early adopters produce positive external effects to latter adopters. The learning effect does not stem from the simultaneous use of a legal rule, but from the temporal accumulation of experiences that are made with the rule. This means that the comparative advantage of old against new rules is a result of the continuous adoption of the rules of an established paradigm. This pattern of adoption lasts even if there are new rules that could be in the future more workable than the old ones, but that have still to be developed by legal learning.

Contrary to the learning effects network externalities result from the simultaneous use of a regulation. The value of a regulation rises if (1) by future litigation the rule is improved and adapted, (2) the regulation is open for implementation of common practices, and (3) a specialized legal service is available (Klausner 1995, 774). All three reasons lead to stabilization and path dependence of the corporation law paradigm.

(1) Some regulations are unmistakable, for example that a two-tier supervisory board has to be formed. But there are also regulations which need intense interpretation, especially for fiduciary duties. The more corporations adopt such an 'open' regulation, the more probable it becomes that litigation will occur. The litigation leads to a common interpretation that adjusts to single cases. So the simultaneous adoption of a regulation produces a positive external effect, which is based upon the fact that a substantial improvement of the rule will be realized in the future. In other words: if a corporation wants to benefit from future legal improvements, it should take the corporate law which is selected by the majority of the corporations. Since the learning effect has its cause in the intertemporal accumulation of legal knowledge, the positive external effect of network externality stems from the simultaneous implementation of the rule.

(2) If regulations are open for implementation of common commercial practices, positive external effects occur, too. In this case it can benefit from future experiences and the implementation of common practices into judicial decisions.

(3) Network externalities exist also in the area of legal advisors. The more legal advisors specialize on a certain corporate law, the larger is the potential of future improvements and the higher the quality of the legal advice.

5.3.4 Complementarities

Institutional complementarity is an additional important stabilizing factor. The fact that complementarities can produce path dependences in corporate law has already been discussed by Roe (1994, 1996, 1998), Bebchuk and Roe (1999) and stressed particularly by Schmidt and Spindler (1999). The difference that is made here does not lie in details, but in the application of the concept of legal paradigm, which implies an explicit innovation perspective. Complementarity in regard to corporate law means that the institution of 'corporate law' gets its value not only from the addition of single corporate regulations, but also from the specific mixture of the single rules and its mutual effects. Complementarities lead to the fact that the system of 'corporate law' is worth more than the addition of its rules. One can call such a system 'consistent' (Schmidt and Spindler 1999, p. 9).

The consequence of complementary institutions is path dependence in the institutional development and the stabilization of the corporate law paradigm. Single elements of a corporate law paradigm can only be altered after consideration of the interdependences to other elements in the corporate law paradigm. Without considering the other elements, disturbances in the entire system will occur. Therefore complementarities can prevent regulatory competition on the level of single rules. If complementarities are present, no general institutional optimum might be achieved by the addition of locally optimal rules. It follows that competition among legal rules might perform its role of selecting optimal rules only on the level of whole consistent systems but not on institutional subsets.

The French system of governance offers an example of the loss in efficiency by institutional inconsistency (Schmidt and Grohs 2000, 175). The French corporate law paradigm in particular puts attention on a strong position of the PDG (président directeur général), who can determine the business policy of a corporation almost autocratically. The PDG is controlled sufficiently neither by a supervisory board nor by the capital market (for details see Charkham 1994; La Porta et al. 1998). In the past the supervisory function was taken by the bureaucratic elite. The bureaucracy controlled the PDG by a close network of complex interdependencies. Public orders could be refused, credits by the national banks could be denied or nationalization could be threatened. Beyond this the French elite was united by a common attitude: all economic concern has to serve the purpose of strengthening the position of France in the world. In the course of European integration the influence of the French state decreased due to deregulation and liberalization, simultaneously centralization on the European level took place. The consequence is a substantial loss of influence by the French bureaucracy on corporations. A bureaucratic vacuum has developed, because the European regulations (concerning for example capital market and auditing) are largely incompatible with the French system of governance.

5.4 Competition Among Corporate Law Paradigms and Lock-ins

The previous paragraphs showed that in corporate law legal paradigms exist, which stabilize and channel the path of legal evolution in corporate law. The path dependence in corporate law can prevent the taking place of unhampered competition among corporate laws.

Therefore the question arises under which circumstances a corporate law paradigm is destabilized in such a manner that the transition to another – possibly more efficient – regime becomes probable.

Generally a paradigm changes if a new paradigm promises better problem-solving. The probability of such a situation increases if corporations have the freedom to choose between different corporate laws. Therefore the probability for a paradigmatic shift increases if the set of institutional alternatives is enlarged. In respect to dynamic economies of scale this situation can be illustrated graphically (Figure 8.2).

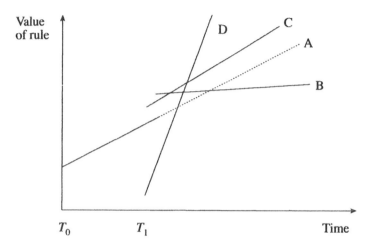

Figure 8.2   Competition among legal paradigms and lock-ins in corporate law in the case of dynamic economies of scale (compare Klausner 1995, p. 810)

It is assumed that at point T_0 only one corporate law paradigm exists. Now let us assume that in T_1 it becomes feasible for a corporation to switch its entire corporate law or a fraction of corporate law rules. The consequence is that we now have the possibility of choice of law between the old and the new corporate law rules. This means an increase in the intensity of competition between legal rules. But the path dependences which result from the corporate law paradigm can be a cause for serious deficiencies of regulatory competition. This becomes clear by the following considerations.

Consider a new corporate law paradigm C that forms in T_1. C has a higher value than A, hence the corporations switch to the corporate law paradigm C. This switch increases efficiency, since C possesses a superior potential of future legal improvements. If only legal improvements of type C would exist in regulatory competition, no problem of path dependence would occur, since regulatory competition would lead to sustainable legal improvements. However, apart from the type C corporate law paradigms of type B might emerge. In T_1 type B paradigms are superior to the established corporate law paradigm A. The consequence is that the corporations switch to type B. But the potential of legal improvements is smaller than that of A. From a normative point of view it would have been better not to introduce regulatory competition by an enlargement of choice of law. Finally, the situation might occur that in T_1 a new corporate paradigm of type D is created, which has a substantial potential of legal improvement in the future. However, D is not adopted, because presently the established corporate law paradigm has higher returns. Even if the corporations face the chance of corporate law paradigm D, they do not turn to D, because they are captured in a prisoner's dilemma. In this case an intervention by the government, which for example can prescribe or subsidize the adoption of corporate law paradigm D, would allow corporations to escape the lock-in. But it is doubtful whether the government can have sufficient foreknowledge for solving those problems.

In sum, paradigmatic shifts are favored by an extension of choice of law. But one cannot conclude that an enlargement of the freedom in legal choice necessarily increases welfare. Competition among legal paradigms can suffer from path dependences, which leads to the problem that the selection of the most efficient legal paradigms can fail. This implies that inefficient legal paradigms can sustain, although superior legal paradigms exist (lock-in).

But regulatory competition is not only hampered by the existence of dynamic economies of scale in the production of legal rules. As we have mentioned earlier, legal complementarities are playing an important role in stabilizing a legal paradigm. The legal complementarities may weaken the workability of regulatory competition considerably. In the next section we will take a look at this by a rough comparison between the corporate laws in the United States and the European Union.

5.5 Competition Between Corporate Laws in the United States and the European Union: a Suggested Interpretation

The US corporate law has been called an excellent example of regulatory competition. Independent from the discussion whether this competition is regarded as efficiency-enhancing or not, it is emphasized that the US corporate laws are similar in their basic configurations and the Delaware code is the undisputed leading corporate law. From the perspective of the concept of corporate law paradigms this can be explained by the 'incorporation theory' and the working of path dependences.

The 'incorporation theory' as a legal rule for the choice of law permits the free selection between the corporate laws of the US states. However, the choice of corporate law and the production of corporate law is restricted by certain protocols at the interfaces to complementary institutions.[14] Such protocols are set up by the uniform capital market law, by the stock exchanges which require certain publicity requirements for the 'listing', or exist by the interlocal private law (inter-state law). Additionally, the American Bar Association updates the Model Business Corporation Act (Modelact), which serves as a (noncommittal) pattern for corporate law reforms. Together, the interfaces and the corporate laws of the United States form the corporate law paradigm of the United States; therefore one can speak of a corporate law paradigm of the United States and the single corporate laws of the federal states can be better understood as legal design configurations of the US corporate law paradigm.[15] Central characteristics of the base-design in US corporate law are: shareholder orientation, one-tier board system, outside control through capital market and a low owner concentration (Weimer and Pape 1999; Roe 1994). Below and within these general features the single states develop legal design configurations in the context of predefined interfaces. The conclusion may be drawn that there exists no competition on the level of whole corporate law paradigms, but a competition on the lower level of legal design-configurations within the base-design of US corporate law.

To sum up, it is suggested that the observed processes of competition among US corporate laws can be understood as competition among legal design configurations within the common US corporate law paradigm, which is on the whole characterized by strong path dependences. But since in the United States the incorporation theory is in order and institutional complementarities are kept small through common interfaces on the federal level, competition among US corporate laws still exists despite certain path dependences due to other stabilizing factors. Although the latter help to stabilize the dominance of the corporate law of Delaware, other states are able to attack this dominant position and to force Delaware to improve its corporate law permanently.

In the European Union we have another situation, because there are not only corporate laws that are different on the level of legal design configurations, but also on the level of the entire corporate law paradigm.[16] The reason for this difference lies in the initial condition under which the corporate laws have developed in Europe and the United States. When in the second half of the nineteenth century the need for corporate laws as a special complex contract arose, we had different political situations in Europe and the United States. In the United States a federation has formed in which an internal market assures the freedom of establishment up to now. In this federation the 'incorporation theory' was the preferred meta-rule from the beginning of the legal evolution of corporate law. In the nineteenth century Europe corporate laws were formed, too, but there was no internal market that assured the freedom of establishment. So the European countries widely adopted the real seat theory as the guiding meta-rule.[17] After this initial choice of the meta-rule, different corporate law paradigms with different legal basic features have formed, which have directed different paths of legal evolution.

The fact that there are consistent corporate law paradigms with strong complementarities which are closely related to their national legal orders, does become fully clear if one considers that the European corporate laws belong to quite different legal families (Common Law, French Code Civil, German BGB, Scandinavian Law; La Porta et al. 1998, Zweigert and Koetz 1996). As long as the differences in the European corporate legal base designs remain, it seems to be improbable that a regulatory competition unfolds, which achieves the intensity of that in the United States. This does not mean that no regulatory competition will exist at all, but it will be more like a *type A-regulatory competition* than a *type B-regulatory competition*. Surely, it could be claimed that in the last decade a harmonized capital market law and accounting standards have been developed. Beyond that the already famous Centros judgment (C-212/97 ECJ) of the European Court of Justice in 1999 opens up the possibility of substituting the real seat theory by the incorporation theory within the European Union.[18]

Despite these institutional adaptions in the legal framework of the European Union we assume that competition between corporate laws in the European Union will remain clumsy. One implication of this reasoning is that inefficient corporate laws may prevail, although the 'incorporation theory' is in order, because strong legal complementarities are building strong legal blocs.[19]

6. CONCLUSIONS

This chapter intends to contribute to the positive theory of institutional evolution. Having shown from economic history that the claim that institutional evolution leads to an ever-improving development of institutions cannot stand critical scrutiny, North (1990) argued that institutional path dependences might be responsible for the fact that societies can be 'locked in' in inefficient institutional settings. But the theoretical approach of North belongs to the group of theories of institutional change that emphasize primarily internal determinants for the development of the institutions of a society. In our chapter we have used a different perspective, which also takes into account processes of interaction and competition between different societies as one important additional determinant for the institutional development of societies. Based upon seminal ideas of Hayek's theory of cultural evolution and his ideas of 'competition as a discovery procedure', we claim that institutional change in societies might be partly also explained as the outcome of interjurisdictional competition, in which different jurisdictions (states) experiment with new institutions and learn mutually from each other. From this perspective we have used the recent policy-oriented discussion about the feasibility of institutional or regulatory competition for the positive explanation of the development of regulations or, more generally, institutions. Therefore our approach to the problem of path dependence in institutional evolution is characterized by the question whether path dependence can also be a cause for failures in processes of regulatory competition, leading to similar 'lock-in' effects in institutional evolution as North described them in his work.

For the analysis of this problem we introduced a general evolutionary framework for regulatory competition among jurisdictions and the concept of technological paradigms (Dosi) with its possibility of 'lock-ins' in technological competition. Based upon these approaches we developed a theoretical framework for investigating potential lock-in effects in regulatory competition by introducing the concept of 'legal paradigms' and 'legal trajectories'. In the second half of the chapter this theoretical framework was applied to the analysis of the evolution of corporate law, which in the US is dominated by the well-known regulatory competition among the corporate laws of the US federal states. It was shown (1) that the concept of legal paradigms can be applied to corporate law and (2) that also in corporate law sunk costs, uncertainty, dynamic economies of scale, network externalities and particularly complementarities to other legal rules and institutions are empirically important stabilizing factors. Therefore it is possible that corporate law paradigms can lead to path dependences and therefore to legal trajectories, which might lead to the possibility of 'lock-in' effects in regulatory competition.

For competition among US corporate laws the conclusion can be drawn that despite the existence of stabilizing factors which help to maintain the dominance of the corporate law of Delaware, competition among the corporate laws of the federal states seems still possible. The reason might be that one important stabilizing factor, that is complementarities to other parts of the legal system, plays a minor role in the United States, because there exist many common legal rules on the federal level, which mitigate the problems of switching corporate laws. In the European Union the situation seems to be different: here legal complementarities between the national corporate laws and other national legal rules have led to substantial path dependences and therefore we face the possibility of considerable lock-in effects in regulatory competition, even if in the European Union the transition is made from the 'real seat theory' to the 'incorporation theory' as relevant choice of law rule.

NOTES

1. For a careful taxonomy of different approaches in the theory of institutions see DiMaggio and Powell (1991).
2. For a comprehensive survey on economic theories of legal evolution see Eckardt (2001).
3. For an overview see the seminal contribution by Tiebout (1956) and the following works by Oates and Schwab (1988), Siebert and Koop (1990), Kenyon and Kincaid (1991), Vanberg and Kerber (1994), Frey and Eichenberger (1995), Sinn (1997), Bratton and McCahery (1997), Kerber (1998), Apolte (1999) and Streit and Wohlgemuth (1999).
4. See Sun and Pelkmans (1995) and Streit and Mussler (1995).
5. See the literature in note 3.
6. See Hayek (1978) and Schumpeter (1934); for an integrated evolutionary concept of knowledge-generating competition see Kerber (1997). For an application of an evolutionary concept of competition to interjurisdictional competition and regulatory competition, in which the legal innovations are emphasized, see Vanberg and Kerber (1994), Streit and Mussler (1995) and Kerber (2000a). For a first outline of an evolutionary concept of federalism see Breton (1987).
7. See especially Streit and Mussler (1995), Gatsios and Holmes (1998), Trachtman (2000) and Kerber (2000b).
8. See for example Dosi (1982, 1988a, b), Nelson and Winter (1982), Sahal (1985), Elsser (1993), Freeman (1992), Andersen (1994).
9. Beyond the base-design it is also possible to identify so-called design configurations. Design configurations are technical features within a base-design (Elsser 1993, 116). Design-configurations can have their own paradigmatic shape, so we could say that design-configurations are technological paradigms on a lower level, for example it would be possible to say that the otto-engine and the diesel-engine are design configurations within the technological paradigm of the internal combustion engine.
10. The idea to apply Dosi's concept of technological paradigms to legal evolution was introduced by Eckardt (2001).
11. For a highly competent and entertaining analysis of the Harvard–Chicago controversy see Adams and Brock (1991).
12. See Cary (1974), Winter (1977), Dodd and Leftwich (1980), Ramseyer (1998), Romano (1985, 1993), Kübler (1994), Easterbrook (1994), Buxbaum and Hopt (1988), Bebchuk (1989, 1992), Macey (1993); a more general analysis is given by Buxbaum (1986). For an overview see also Heine (2003).
13. In 1970 nearly 25 per cent of Delaware's budget was due to the franchise tax (Romano 1985, p. 242). In 1998 the corporation revenues were approximately $400 million, still a quarter of the state's budget (Kenton 1999).
14. A first conceptual outline to analyse the constitution of the firm with the help of 'institutional interfaces' and 'institutional modules' is given by Schanze (1986).
15. For the notion of legal design configurations see the definition of technological design configurations that is given in note 9.
16. An outline of the British, German and French governance systems is given by Schmidt and Grohs (2000) and Charkham (1994).
17. For a closer look on the different legal evolution of corporate laws in Europe and the United States see Shughart and Tollison (1985).
18. In Centros the European Court of Judgment examined the question whether the EC Treaty enforces the application of the incorporation theory, because Article 43 EC Treaty guarantees persons or firms to set up in another Member State (freedom of establishment). An excellent overview of the Centros judgment and its controversial reception by legal scholars is given by Halbhuber (2001a, b). For a policy-oriented analysis of the perspective of regulatory competition between European corporate laws due to potential problems of path dependences after the Centros judgement see Heine and Kerber (2002).
19. From our point of view the main reason for this is the lack of appropriate institutional interfaces which have to be seen as prerequisites for a workable regulatory competition between the

different corporate law paradigms. From a policy view institutional interfaces are the devices which are able to connect the different legal modules which are supplied by the member states. It becomes clear that the definition and shape of the appropriate institutional interfaces is a political task that has to be undertaken on the meta-level.

REFERENCES

Adams, Walter and James W. Brock (1991), *Antitrust Economics on Trial. A Dialogue on the New Laissez-Faire*, Princeton: University Press.
Andersen, Esben S. (1994), *Evolutionary Economics. Post-Schumpetrian Contributions*, London: Pinter.
Apolte, Thomas (1999), *Die ökonomische Konstitution eines föderalen Systems: dezentrale Wirtschaftspolitik zwischen Kooperation und institutionellem Wettbewerb*, Tübingen: Mohr Siebeck.
Arthur, W. Brian (1994), 'Competing technologies, increasing returns, and lock-in by historical small events', in W. Brian Arthur (ed.), *Increasing Returns and Path Dependence in the Economy*, Ann Arbor: University of Michigan Press, pp. 13–32.
Bebchuk, Lucian A. (1989), 'The debate on contractual freedom in corporate law', *Columbia Law Review*, 89, 1395–415.
Bebchuk, Lucian A. (1992), 'Federalism and the corporation: the desirable limits on state competition in corporate law', *Harvard Law Review*, 105, 1435–510.
Bebchuk, Lucian A. and Mark J. Roe (1999), 'A theory of path dependence in corporate ownership and governance', *Stanford Law Review*, 52, 127–70.
Bratton, William W. and Joseph A. McCahery (1997), 'The new economics of jurisdictional competition: devolutionary federalism in a second-best world', *The Georgetown Law Journal*, 86, 201–78.
Breton, Albert (1987), 'Towards a theory of competitive federalism', *European Journal of Political Economy*, 3, 263–329.
Buxbaum, Richard M. (1986), 'Federal aspects of corporate law and economic theory', in Terence Daintith and Gunther Teubner (eds), *Contract and Organisation*, Berlin: de Gruyter, pp. 274–92.
Buxbaum, Richard M. and Klaus J. Hopt (1988), *Legal Harmonization and the Business Enterprise*, Berlin: de Gruyter.
Carney, William J. (1998), 'The production of corporate law', *Southern California Law Review*, 71, 715–80.
Cary, William L. (1974), 'Federalism and corporate law: reflections upon Delaware', *Yale Law Journal*, 83, 663–705.
Charkham, Jonathan P. (1994), *Keeping Good Company: A Study of Corporate Governance in Five Countries*, Oxford: Clarendon Press.
Daines, Robert (2001), 'Does Delaware law improve firm value?', *Journal of Financial Economics*, 62, 525–58.
Demsetz, Harold (1967), 'Towards a theory of property rights', *American Economic Review*, Papers and Proceedings, 57, 347–59.
DiMaggio, Paul J. and Walter Powell (eds) (1991), *The New Institutionalism in Organizational Analysis*, Chicago: University of Chicago Press.
Dodd, Peter and Richard Leftwich (1980), 'The market for corporate charters: "unhealthy competition" versus federal regulation', *Journal of Business*, 53, 259–83.

Dosi, Giovanni (1982), 'Technological paradigms and technological trajectories. A suggested interpretation of the determinants and directions of technical change', *Research Policy*, **11**, 147–62.

Dosi, Giovanni (1988a), 'Sources, procedures, and microeconomic effects of innovation', *Journal of Economic Literature*, **26**, 1120–71.

Dosi, Giovanni (1988b), 'The nature of the innovative process', in Giovanni Dosi et al. (eds), *Technical Change and Economic Theory*, London: Pinter, pp. 221–38.

Easterbrook, Frank H. (1994), 'Federalism and European business law', *International Review of Law and Economics*, **14**, 125–32.

Easterbrook, Frank H. and Daniel R. Fischel (1996), *The Economic Structure of Corporate Law*, Cambridge, Mass.: Harvard University Press.

Eckardt, Martina (2001), *Technischer Wandel und Rechtsevolution. Ein Beitrag zur ökonomischen Theorie der Rechtsentwicklung am Beispiel des deutschen Unfallschadensrechts im 19. Jahrhundert*, Tübingen: Mohr Siebeck.

Eisenberg, Melvin A. (1983), 'The modernization of corporate law: an essay for Bill Cary', *Miami Law Review*, **37**, 187–212.

Elsser, Stefan (1993), *Innovationswettbewerb*, Frankfurt: Lang.

Freeman, Christopher (1992), 'Innovation, changes of techno-economic paradigm and biological analogies in economics', in Christopher Freeman (ed.), *The Economics of Hope*, London: Pinter, pp. 121–42.

Frey, Bruno S. and Reiner Eichenberger (1995), 'Competition among Jurisdictions: The Idea of FOCJ', in Lüder Gerken (ed.), *Competition among Institutions*, London: Macmillan, pp. 209–29.

Gatsios, Konstantine and Peter Holmes (1998), 'Regulatory competition', in Peter Newman (ed.), *The New Palgrave Dictionary of Economics and the Law*, vol. 3, London: Macmillan, pp. 271–5.

Gerum, Elmar (1998), 'Organisation der Unternehmensführung im internationalen Vergleich – insbesondere Deutschland, USA und Japan', in Horst Glaser, E.F. Schröder and A. Werder v. (eds), *Organisation im Wandel der Märkte*, Wiesbaden, pp. 136–53.

Grandy, Christopher (1989), 'New Jersey corporate chartermongering, 1875–1929', *The Economic Journal of History*, **49**, 677–92.

Halbhuber, Harald (2001a), *Limited Company statt GmbH? Europarechtlicher Rahmen und deutscher Widerstand*, Baden-Baden: Nomos.

Halbhuber, Harald (2001b), 'National doctrinal structures and European company law', *Common Market Law Review*, **38**, 1385–419.

Hayek, Friedrich A. v. (1945), 'The use of knowledge in society', *American Economic Review*, **35**, 519–30.

Hayek, Friedrich A. v. (1973), *Law, Legislation, and Liberty*, vol. I: *Rules and Order*, London: Routledge.

Hayek, Friedrich A. v. (1978), 'Competition as a discovery procedure', in Friedrich A. v. Hayek (ed.), *New Studies in Philosophy, Politics, Economics and the History of Ideas*, London: Routledge, pp. 179–90.

Heine, Klaus (2003), *Regulierungswettbewerb im Gesellschaftsrecht*, Berlin: Duncker und Humblot (forthcoming).

Heine, Klaus and Wolfgang Kerber (2002), 'European corporate laws, regulatory competition and path dependence', *European Journal of Law and Economics*, **13**, 47–71.

Heiner, Ronald A. (1983), 'The origin of predictable behavior', *American Economic Review*, **73**, 560–95.

Holmes, Oliver W. (1897), 'The path of the law', *Harvard Law Review*, **10**, 457–78.
Holmes, Oliver W. (1899), 'Law in science and science in law', *Harvard Law Review*, **12**, 443–63.
Jürgens, Ulrich, Katrin Naumann and Joachim Rupp (2000), 'Shareholder value in an adverse environment', *Economy and Society*, **29**, 54–79.
Kenton, Glenn C. (1999), 'A modern, efficient division of corporations', *Corporate Edge*, Spring, quarterly newsletter published by the Delaware Department of State.
Kenyon, Daphne A. and John Kincaid (eds) (1991), *Competition Among States and Local Governments. Efficiency and Equity in American Federalism*, Washington: Urban Institute Press.
Kerber, Wofgang (1997), 'Wettbewerb als Hypothesentest: eine evolutorische Konzeption wissenschaffenden Wettbewerbs', in Karl v. Delhaes and Ulrich Fehl (eds), *Dimensionen des Wettbewerbs: Seine Rolle in der Entstehung und Ausgestaltung von Wirtschaftsordnungen*, Stuttgart: Lucius & Lucius, pp. 29–78.
Kerber, Wolfgang (1998), 'Zum Problem einer Wettbewerbsordnung für den systemwettbewerb', *Jahrbuch für Neue Politische Ökonomie*, **17**, 199–231.
Kerber, Wolfgang (2000a), 'Rechtseinheitlichkeit und Rechtsvielfalt aus ökonomischer sicht', in Stefan Grundmann (ed.), *Systembildung und Systemlücken in Kerngebieten des Europäischen Privatrechts. Gesellschafts-, Arbeits- und Schuldvertragsrecht*, Tübingen: Mohr Siebeck, pp. 67–97.
Kerber, Wolfgang (2000b), 'Interjurisdictional competition within the European Union', *Fordham International Law Journal*, **23**, S217–S249.
Klausner, Michael (1995), 'Corporations, corporate law, and networks of contracts', *Virginia Law Review*, **81**, 757–852.
Klodt, Henning (1995), *Grundlagen der Forschungs- und Technologiepolitik*, München: Vahlen.
Knight, Jack (1992), *Institutions and Social Conflict*, Cambridge: Cambridge University Press.
Kobayashi, Bruce H. and Larry E. Ribstein (1996), 'Evolution and spontaneous uniformity: evidence from the evolution of the limited liability company', *Economic Inquiry*, **34**, 464–83.
Kübler, Friedrich (1994), 'Rechtsbildung durch Gesetzgebungswettbewerb', *Kritische Vierteljahresschrift für Gesetzgebung und Rechtswissenschaft*, **77**, 79–89.
Kuhn, Thomas (1970), *The Structure of Scientific Revolutions*, 2nd ed., Chicago: University of Chicago Press.
La Porta, Rafael, Florencio Lopez-de-Silanes, Andrei Shleifer and Robert W. Vishny (1998), 'Law and finance', *Journal of Political Economy*, **106**, 1113–55.
Libecap, Gary D. (1989), *Contracting for Property Rights*, Cambridge: Cambridge University Press.
Macey, Jonathan R. (1993), 'Corporate law and corporate governance, a contractual perspective', *The Journal of Corporation Law*, **18**, 185–211.
Mueller, Dennis C. (1989), *Public Choice II*, Cambridge: Cambridge University Press.
Nelson, Richard R. and Sidney G. Winter (1982), *An Evolutionary Theory of Economic Change*, Cambridge, Mass.: Harvard University Press, Belknap Press Cambridge.
North, Douglass C. (1990), *Institutions, Institutional Change and Economic Performance*, Cambridge: Cambridge University Press.
Oates, Wallace E. and Robert M. Schwab (1988), 'Economic competition among jurisdictions: efficiency enhancing or distortion inducing?', *Journal of Public Economics*, **35**, 333–54.

Posner, Richard A. (1998), *Economic Analysis of Law*, 5th ed., Boston, New York: Aspen Law & Business.

Ramseyer, J. Mark (1998), 'Corporate law', in Paul Newman (ed.), *The New Palgrave Dictionary of Economics and the Law*, vol. 1, pp. 503–11.

Romano, Roberta (1985), 'Law as a product: some pieces of the incorporation puzzle', *Journal of Law, Economics, and Organization*, 1, 225–83.

Romano, Roberta (1993), *The Genius of American Corporate Law*, Washington: AEI Press.

Roe, Mark J. (1994), *Strong Managers, Weak Owners*, Princeton: Princeton University Press.

Roe, Mark J. (1996), 'Chaos and evolution in law and economics', *Harvard Law Review*, 109, 641–68.

Roe, Mark J. (1998), 'Comparative corporate governance', in Paul Newman (ed.), *The New Palgrave Dictionary of Economics and the Law*, vol. 1, pp. 339–46.

Roe, Mark J. (1999), 'Political preconditions to separating ownership from control: the incompatibility of the American public firm with Social Democracy', Discussion-Paper Columbia University, Center for Law and Business.

Sahal, Devendra (1985), 'Technological guide-posts and innovation avenues', *Research Policy*, 14, 61–82.

Salmon, Pierre (1987), 'Decentralization as an incentive scheme', *Oxford Review of Economic Policy*, 3, 24–43.

Schanze, Erich (1986), 'Potential and limits of economic analysis: the constitution of the firm', in Terence Daintith and Gunther Teubner (eds), *Contract and Organisation*, Berlin, pp. 204–18.

Schilling, Melissa (1999), 'Winning the standards race: building installed base and the availability of complementary goods', *European Management Journal*, 17, 265–74.

Schmidt, Reinhard H. and Stefanie Grohs (2000), 'Angleichung der Unternehmensverfassung in Europa aus ökonomischer Perspektive', in Stefan Grundmann (ed.), *Systembildung und Systemlücken in Kerngebieten des Europäischen Privatrechts*, Tübingen: Mohr Siebeck, pp. 145–88

Schmidt, Reinhard H. and Gerald Spindler (1999), 'Path dependence, corporate governance and complementarity – a comment on Bebchuk and Roe', *Working Paper Series: Finance & Accounting*, University of Frankfurt.

Schumpeter, Joseph A. (1934), *The Theory of Economic Development. An Inquiry into Profits, Capital, Credit, Interest, and the Business Cycle*, Cambridge, Mass.: Harvard University Press.

Shughart, William F. and Robert D. Tollison (1985), 'Corporate chartering: an exploration in the economics of legal change', *Economic Inquiry*, 23, 585–99.

Siebert, Horst and Michael J. Koop (1990), 'Institutional competition. A concept for Europe?', *Aussenwirtschaft*, 45, 439–62.

Simon, Herbert (1976), 'From substantive to procedural rationality', in Spiro J. Latsis (ed.), *Methods and Appraisal in Economics*, Cambridge: Cambridge University Press, pp. 129–48.

Sinn, Stefan (1992), 'The taming of Leviathan: competition among governments', *Constitutional Political Economy*, 2, pp. 177–96.

Sinn, Hans-Werner (1997), 'The selection principle and market failure in systems competition', *Journal of Public Economics*, 88, 247–74.

Streit, Manfred E. and Michael Wohlgemuth (eds) (1999), *Systemwettbewerb als Herausforderung an Politik und Theorie*, Baden-Baden: Nomos.

Streit, Manfred E. and Werner Mussler (1995), 'Wettbewerb der Systeme und das Binnenmarktprogramm der Europäischen Union', in Lüder Gerken (ed.), *Europa zwischen Ordnungswettbewerb und Harmonisierung*, Berlin: de Gruyter, pp. 75–107.

Sun, Jeanne-Mey and Jaques J. Pelkmans (1995), 'Regulatory competition in the Single Market', *Journal of Common Market Studies*, 33, 67–89.

Tiebout, Charles M. (1956), 'A pure theory of local expenditures', *Journal of Political Economy*, 64, 416–24.

Tirole, Jean (1994), 'The internal organization of government', *Oxford Economic Papers*, 46, 1–29.

Trachtman, Joel P. (2000), 'Regulatory competition and regulatory jurisdiction', *Journal of International Economic Law*, 3, 331–48.

Vanberg, Viktor (1992), 'Innovation, cultural evolution, and economic growth', in Ulrich Witt (ed.), *Explaining Process and Change. Approaches to Evolutionary Economics*, Ann Arbor: University of Michigan Press, pp. 105–21.

Vanberg, Viktor (1994), 'Cultural evolution, collective learning and constitutional choice', in David Reisman (ed.), *Economic Thought and Political Theory*, Boston: Kluwer, pp. 171–204.

Vanberg, Viktor and Wolfgang Kerber (1994), 'Institutional competition among jurisdictions: an evolutionary approach', *Constitutional Political Economy*, 5, 193–219.

Wegner, Gerhard (1998), 'Systemwettbewerb als politisches Kommunikations- und Wahlhandlungsproblem', *Jahrbuch für Neue Politische Ökonomie*, 17, 281–308.

Weimer, Jerome and Joost C. Pape (1999), 'A taxonomy of systems of corporate governance', *Corporate Governance*, 7, 152–66.

Winter, Ralph K. (1977), 'State law, shareholder protection, and the theory of the corporation', *Journal of Legal Studies*, 6, 251–92.

Zweigert, Konrad and Hein Koetz (1996), *Einführung in die Rechtsvergleichung*, 3rd ed., Tübingen: Mohr Siebeck.

9. The German *Neuer Markt* as an adaptive institution

Helge Peukert

1. INTRODUCTION

Continental European economies are often criticized for their moderate growth (between 2 and 3 per cent) and high unemployment rates (slightly below 10 per cent). In the case of Germany, one reason was seen in the underdeveloped equity culture and a modest and rather risk-averse venture capital market to finance start-ups and innovative entrepreneurship (Heitzer and Sohn 1999). At the end of 1998, Germany ranked fourth compared with other stock markets with regard to market capitalization, but this was only half the size of Japan and the UK. In 1996, one year before the *Neuer Markt* (NM) was started, only 14 companies went public in Germany, but 100 in Japan, 350 in the UK, and over 900 in the US. 'More companies went public on NASDAQ in 1996 (598 companies) than in the whole German market from 1949 to 1996 (374 companies)' (Johnson 2000, 13). The going public of the German Qiagen at NASDAQ in 1996 was a signal for reform to the German finance community.

In March 1997 the new market segment was introduced in Germany to raise sufficient equity capital to finance the growth of companies with innovative ideas for new products, new services and new markets (Rödl 1999; Plückelmann 2000, and the profound study by Knips 2000). The *Neuer Markt* recently celebrated its fourth birthday as a success story in terms of more than 340 listed companies. They are divided into the ten segments of biotechnology (20), industrial and industry services (17), IT services (39), technology (67), financial services (6), software (49), telecommunications (20), internet (67), medtech and health care (11), media and entertainment (42 companies in February 2001; a description of the segments can be found in Beike et al. 2000, 63, and Plötz 2001). The volume of new emissions was 12 billion Euro and 133 IPOs (Initial Public Offering) in 2000 with a total market capitalization of 120 billion Euro (NASDAQ: 5.5 trillion US Dollars).

The function of the new market segment is mentioned in the first paragraph of the rules and regulations of Neuer Markt on the scope of applicability: 'Issuers are, in particular, innovative enterprises which develop new sales markets, utilize new methods of, for example, procurement, production or distribution, or offer new products and/or services, and whose activities can be expected to generate high turnover and profits in the future' (www.exchange.de, rules and regulations, March 2001, 2). This functional description exactly coincides with Schumpeter's concept of the introduction of productive new combinations: '(1) The introduction of a new good ... or a new quality of a good. (2) The introduction of a new method of production ... (3) The opening of a new market ... (4) The conquest of a new source of supply of raw materials of half-manufactured goods ... (5) The carrying out of the new organisation of any industry' (Schumpeter 1951, 66). In Schumpeter's influential evolutionary concept, 'credit [by bankers] is primarily necessary to new combinations' (1951, 70, elaborated in ch. 3, 95) to finance entrepreneurs with initiative, authority and foresight and their only partially rational motives like the dream and will to found a personal kingdom, the sensation of power, snobbery or social ambition, the will to conquer, spiritual ambition, the joy of creating, and so on (1951, 93) – the NM offers illustrious examples of Schumpeter's list which fascinate the German public. Entrepreneurs need credit 'to produce at all, to be able carry out ... new combinations, to *become* an entrepreneur' (1951, 102).

For Schumpeter as well as for the organizers of the new market the importance of new combinations lies in their importance for economic development and growth, discussed by Schumpeter as the upswing of a business cycle due to innovations (1951, ch. 6, 212) which normally leads to the disappearance of unemployment, at least in the case of non-regulated labor markets (1951, 249–51). Two differences between the situation at the NM and Schumpeter's setting may be mentioned. On the one hand, even in his early book Schumpeter assumes that the entrepreneurial function is exerted 'as is becoming the rule, [by] "dependent" employees of a company, like managers' (1951, 75). In many companies of the NM the entrepreneurs hold a considerable percentage of shares and in fact take the major decisions, they are real captains and the company's story and investor's fantasy depend essentially on them. A second difference is that Schumpeter holds an insider- and banking-driven model (credit by banks), whereas the NM exemplifies a capital-market-oriented outsider-driven model (equity capital by shares, for the resulting different corporate governance structures see Schmidt and Grohs 2000).

In the following we will describe the institutional framework of the new market in an evolutionary perspective. We will especially show that (1) the NM is a new third type besides the traditional public law/private contract distinction, and (2) that its well functioning needs a dense regulatory framework. Further, we will give some explanations for the crash since March 2000 and briefly point out some alternatives to efficient market hypotheses. Finally, we will try to derive some concrete policy reform proposals and confront them with the recent reforms realized by Deutsche Börse AG.

2. DEVELOPMENT AND STRUCTURE OF THE *NEUER MARKT*

In March 2001 more then 340 companies are listed at the NM which started in March 1997 with just two companies (Bertrandt and MobilCom). Almost none of these companies were listed at another exchange before going public. About 40 companies are domiciled outside of Germany and about ten also have a listing at NASDAQ. The success of the NM goes hand in hand with a change of the German equity culture; the best example is the run on shares of the Deutsche Telekom IPO in autumn 1996. In 1999 78 per cent of all companies going public have chosen the NM and a remarkable increase and change of composition (younger, smaller, more technology-oriented) can be observed after 1997 (Kukies 2000). The average age of German stocks in general is 55 years, the average age of the NM firms is 11 years (Plückelmann 2000, 123), with an average turnover of 150 mio. DM. Firms have on average 300 employees, the spread is from less than ten up to more than 1500. This shows that the NM is not a homogenous market, it is dominated by middle-sized (mid-caps), but also small-sized companies (small-caps) and blue chips like T-online exist.

The employment effects are undeniable, the number of employed in the NM companies is about 200 000 (see the study by Schaible and Thielbeer 2000). The NM is more successful then its European counterparts, for example the French Nouveau Marché or the EASDAQ in Brussels. The market capitalization of the NM corporations has increased from 26 billion at the end of 1998 to about 200 billion Euro in mid-2000. On July 1, 1999 the Nemax 50 was launched. It covers the 50 largest stocks in terms of market turnover and capitalization (80 per cent of the total segment). To make the increasing number of companies more transparent, sector indices were introduced. As mentioned, younger companies in an early stage of their life cycle to carry through innovations with above-average sales and earnings prospects and an international orientation are the target of the NM. When NASDAQ, the American counterpart (see the comparison in Beike et al. 2000) for high-technology companies where more than 6000 companies are listed today, was established in 1971 its main characteristic was the automatic system. It slightly developed into the role of the high-technology segment with listings like Microsoft, Intel, and so on.

Start-up corporations require sufficient equity capital to finance their future growth. For these companies, a bank-oriented system is less adequate because banks are reluctant to finance companies with a low proportion of fixed assets which could serve as collateral and a high proportion of intangible assets like ideas, R&D knowledge and projects and highly skilled employees, that is human capital. A natural rate of bank credits for these firms should be around 30 per cent (Niquet 2000, 32–3) if we also take the risky nature of their investments into account. Two major problems for these companies are that they do not satisfy the usual creditworthiness criteria as mentioned and that outside capital is too expensive for new companies. Further, the loan interest would damage their cash flows. In general, the capital resources of German companies are extremely low (20 per cent) compared with the US (60 per cent) or GB (50 per cent). The significant lower number of IPOs and publicly traded firms relative to the population in Germany and France (La Porta et al. 1997, 1998, and 1999) turned out to be a structural impediment for innovations in the new growth markets. So a natural drift exists to transform the German bank-oriented system into a market-oriented system.

The demand side for equity capital is matched by the supply side. In Germany private financial assets are about DM 5.4 trillion. Especially the younger generation does tend to higher risk and return investments. Relatively low interest rates for bonds, which are partly due to the balanced budget philosophy in the European Union, the demographic change which fosters increasing investments to achieve high returns for retirement (the target to establish private pension plans is backed by the German government), and the increasing claims for inheritance lead to a highly liquid supply side.

3.   THE *NEUER MARKT* AS AN EXAMPLE FOR THE EVOLUTION OF ECONOMIC INSTITUTIONS

From an evolutionary viewpoint it is interesting to ask who the institutional reformer of the NM was. In the old and new institutional and evolutionary literature two main answers have been given. On the one hand, old institutionalism including the German historical school stressed (Commons 1924; Schmoller 1989/1884) that successful institutional reform depends on state intervention and a highly motivated public regulator, or to put it in the Rutherford dichotomies i., iv., and v.: social institutions mold individual behavior, deliberate design is a primordial condition for success and government intervention should play an important role. Modern evolutionary economics would argue instead that individual behavior molds social institutions, that institutions are the result of spontaneous or individual-hand processes and that government intervention should as a rule of thumb be more limited.

It is interesting to note that we have the same cleavage in the more narrow debate on corporate governance reform (Johnson 2000). On the one hand we have those who argue in favor of changes in public law (legal rules matter) and a highly motivated regulator (La Porta et al. 1997, 1998). On the other hand we have the market-based view of, for example, Easterbrook and Fischel (1991). They argue that firms should at best conclude private contracts with investors.

These contracts are beneficial for both sides and the Coasian neutrality principle holds as a rule. From a practical policy point of view it can be argued further that the degree of disclosure in accounting standards should be left to the negotiations between firms and investors so that they choose the optimal degree of disclosure from case to case, invest in reputation building, promote voluntary codes of conduct and let independent agencies monitor the firms. This may be called the Smith and Hayek positive laissez-faire solution where the net result for economic structures is the unplanned outcome of the economic agents who enter into private contracts.

In fact, the NM was established as a private law entity which is similar to NASDAQ, launched by the Deutsche Börse Group, a stock company (80 per cent of the stocks are held by German and foreign banks, 10 per cent by brokers, and 10 per cent by the German regional stock exchanges, see Gruppe Deutsche Börse 2001, 26). There were neither initiatives by public institutions nor by private companies to establish the NM! Companies which want to enter the new market segment must – after the admittance to the *geregelter Markt* – comply with Deutsche Börse rules and sign a private contract with Deutsche Börse without a *per se* right to be accepted at the NM even if all conditions like an innovative profile are fulfilled (about 20 per cent of the applications have been rejected in the last years, see *Financial Times Deutschland*, 9/5/2000, 21). If firms break the rules, they can be punished in various ways (for example penalties up to 100 000 Euro since March 2001), including the delisting from the NM (two examples are Lösch Umweltschutz and Sero for wrong financial information). As we will see below, the (for example transparency) rules are very strict and higher than the rules in the three other segments: the *amtlicher*, the *geregelter Markt* and the *Freiverkehr*. The listing rules for the first two market segments are directly governed by public law, and Deutsche Börse cannot refuse admission if the requirements are met. But it can introduce specialized segments and impose and enforce rules which are not enforceable by the securities regulator or judges. The latter is the case for the *Freiverkehr* and the NM.

The regulatory mode of the NM can be interpreted in Lachmann's dichotomies of inner and outer institutions (Lachmann 1963). The first refer to the necessary explicit framework which must be given and established ex ante and in principle by some political authority before a market economy can evolve. From these we have to distinguish the inner institutions which develop slowly in the process of real market developments and which accompany the evolution from primitive to higher market forms. In this typology the NM is an example for inner institutions and the learning process of the economic agents inside the economic system and the self-regulation of a segment of this system.

The NM as an internal institution can further be described as a specific type of institution. It is not specifically market-based in the sense that the firms have to comply to the Deutsche Börse rules. The contract is a contract between two independent private parties but one party sets the rules and the other party has to accept them. At the same time it is not the result of a public or governmental reform accompanied by changes in public law as it is in the United States where the Securities and Exchange Commission (SEC) as a public institution sets the major rules and strictly enforces them (*Deutsche Börse* 2001b, 9 and 55). Instead, it is run by a private body and not the result of government intervention.

If we have a look into the history of economics and institutional reform we can find some examples for this third type of institutional arrangements. Good behavior of the members was, for example, enforced by the Maghribi traders in the medieval Mediterranean, also the Champagne fairs of the early Middle Ages and some merchant guilds had mechanisms to enforce compliance and settle disputes (for more detailed analyses see Milgrom et al. 1990; Greif 1993; and Greif et al. 1994). In all of these cases clear behavioral standards were defined by an intermediate private institution, access was voluntary and the right to be punished in case of misbehavior accepted.

From a modern evolutionary point of view the reason for the reemergence of this third type could be that a private body can react more flexibly to the rearrangement of rules and that it does not need changes for firms that were already listed. On the other hand, it cannot be ruled out that the private regulators may change the rules in their interest. In the following we will see how far self- and external regulation interact and if and how far the internal self-regulation also reaches some limits.

4.   *LAISSEZ-FAIRE* OR A STRONG REGULATORY FRAMEWORK OF INNER INSTITUTIONS?

Hitherto we have analyzed the institutional and evolutionary origin of the NM. Now we will have a closer look at the regulatory framework to give an inside explanation for the success of the NM. To understand the specifics of the NM we have to compare it with the other German market segments. At the *amtlicher Handel* about 600 well-established and bigger stocks are listed. The rules are enforced by the public Federal Securities Supervisory Commission (BAWe). The index of the 30 blue chips is the Deutsche Aktienindex (DAX), comparable to the American Dow Jones Industrial Average. The importance and volume of the segment is underlined by the fact that the DAX stocks alone cover 80 per cent of the overall turnover at the Frankfurt stock exchange (75 per cent nationwide, see Gruppe Deutsche Börse 2001, 19). The listing standards are high (companies must exist for at least three years before listing, business reports must be published, shareholder controlling thresholds must be disclosed, and so on).

The *geregelter Markt* was established in 1987, especially for medium-sized companies. The policy was to attract new companies by lowering the admission and regulatory standards. But on average less than ten IPOs per year were listed. Today only 100 companies are listed and the turnover is less than 1.5 per cent of the turnover at the *amtlicher Markt*. The less regulated segment is the *Freiverkehr*, about 1500 companies are listed but most of them are (dual) listings of foreign companies. Neither segment is a success story in terms of liquidity, turnover and new listings so that the closing of one of the segments is under discussion (see Beike and Schlütz 1999 for the details).

A closer look at the rules of the NM shows that it shares less restricted listing requirements with respect to size (minimum capital resources of 1.5 mio. Euro, minimum of emitted stocks 100 000) and profitability records with *geregelter Markt* and *Freiverkehr*, but that it differs in terms of, for example, strict transparency and information disclosure rules. The interesting point is that they seem to be attractive both for investors *and* emitting companies. Rigorous information disclosure can be interpreted as an answer to overcome the structurally unavoidable high degree of asymmetric information, that is, investors have to evaluate new firms with a low substance value and no history (information asymmetries are also the starting point of the market microstructure theory, see O'Hara 1995). The exceptionally high degree of information serves as a signal to outsiders of the true quality of the firm and therefore attracts investors.

These requirements include the publication of a very detailed listing prospectus, quarterly reports, annual analyst meetings and the acceptance of the International Accounting Standards or the US-GAAP. This implies a more detailed and international comparable disclosure compared with the German HGB which emphasizes the interests of creditors (for a comparison see Born 1999). The obligation of ad-hoc publicity on relevant issues (§15 WpHG) should also be mentioned here. Besides transparency specific rules for investor protection hold, for example only voting shares can be issued by IOPs. The credibility of a long-term commitment of the management is enhanced by the rule that pre-IPO stock-holders must hold their shares for at least six months (lock-up period) with the side-effect that they cannot influence the share price in this time period negatively and cash-out. The free float should be 25 per cent, the minimum is 20 per cent, 50 per cent of the new stocks must be an increase of capital, the minimum emission volume of stocks is 100 000. The book-building spread is fixed by an agreement between the company and the emission bank. It should represent the real value of the firm. Objective reference numbers and the perceptible interest of prospective (institutional) investors play a role (for the details see Rödl 1999, 255–96). The so-called greenshoe has the function to regulate the demand price and quantity for new stocks. It consists of 10–15 per cent of the stocks of pre-IPO stockholders which are given to the emitting bank (lead-manager). If oversubscription takes place, the lead-manager puts the greenshoe on the market, if the opposite takes place, the stocks are returned to their initial holders.

Another aspect is provisions for liquidity. A listing condition is a probable market value of at least 10 mio. DM. A further rule is that the companies must choose two designated sponsors (usually the investment banks) for the automated XETRA system. They must offer stocks at regular bid-ask spreads (maximum spread 4 per cent, in practice the designated sponsor spreads are approximately 2 per cent). Their offers are combined with a central order book system so that a hybrid market maker system exists (for the details see Plück-elmann 2000, 95). The sponsors are rated by the stock exchange four times a year in terms of engagement and spread. A further protection for investors is the obligatory acceptance of the takeover codex. It says that companies must not countervail takeover activities which are usually combined with the offer of higher stock prices (see Deutsche Börse Group: Rules and Regulation, download www.exchange.de).

The German market segments show that – contrary to a simplistic laissez-faire intuition – market performance is enhanced and more firms go public when a dense regulatory framework exists. This can be deduced from the fact that considerably more firms want to be listed at the NM instead of the *Freiverkehr* or *geregelter Markt* (for a comparison of their regulatory framework with that of the NM see Heitzer and Sohn 1999), or for example the premium segment at the regional Munich stock exchange (we will leave out the SMAX here).

Let us note that a high degree of regulation does not imply the rule: the more regulation the better. It is *not* possible to develop an armchair optimal degree and structure of regulation because trade-offs have to be taken into consideration (Knips 2000, 218, especially 256–8). This is interesting for evolutionary economics and its understanding of market and institutional processes and the mechanisms of variation and selection. In fact, the best degree of (non)regulation can only be found out by some sort of empirical Popperian trial and error process and experimentation. One trade-off for firms is that tight information disclosure may enhance firm liquidity by attracting venture capital and realizing an advance price for being listed at the NM, but at the same time it may put firms at a disadvantage because they have to disclose information to their competitors. It may also be mentioned from an Austrian viewpoint that a high degree of disclosure may increase the general overload of decision makers, that information processes always have subjectivist components and that information *per se* is not helpful for understanding but must be put in an interpretative frame. The more information we get the more difficult this necessary framing may become. Another trade-off exists between transparency and price continuity.

If informational efficiency is enhanced and information leads to immediate price changes, volatility will increase. It can also be argued that there will exist a composite effect of all regulations which strangulates the innovative animal spirits of entrepreneurs and their motivation. As Sombart noted, entrepreneurship implies a delicate balance of the spirit of order and calculation and the spontaneous Faustian drive (Sombart 1987, vol. 1, 327–9). If one side of this characteristic mix is deprived by over-regulation (compare Knips 2000, 88) this may impede innovative activities. A further aspect are the costs which are incurred on companies by all informational requirements.

5.   WHY HAVE SO MANY FLOWERS GONE?

In the evolutionary–dynamic dimension a tremendous international downturn at the stock markets, especially in the technological and innovative segments, can be noticed since the middle of the year 2000. The peaks of the respective indexes were reached in March 2000. In a one year perspective from March 2000 to March 2001 the Nemax indices of the NM lost more than 80 per cent, the Nasdaq 100 lost 60 per cent and, for example, the French Nouveau Marché more than 70 per cent (*Wall Street Journal Europe*, 13 March 2001, 1). As a consequence the IPO stream runs dry. In Germany, only eight new companies have been listed since March 2001 (Dr. Hönle, Sunways, Condon and so on). In September 2001, the Nemax all share and the Nemax 50 with 750 points even went below the initial 1000 points at the inception. Due to insolvency four companies disappeared (Gigabell, Sunburst, Refugium and Teldafax), seven companies disappeared because of a takeover and two changed to the *Geregelter Markt* (Deutsche Börse 2001b, 25–6).

Some companies reduced during the book-building process the selling spread for the new emissions to a maximum of 50 per cent of its fair value (for example OHB Teledata, see *Handelsblatt*, 6 March 2001, 49) and the chart analysts see no turning point (*Going Public*, No. 3, 2001, 56–8.). One year ago, about 250 billion Euro were invested in the NM segment, in March 2001 it was less then 90 billion Euro, despite 133 new emissions with a volume of 13 billion Euro fresh money. Empirical studies have shown that the underpricing of IOPs depended on the fact that the investors were strongly influenced by the general drift of the economy and the market segment and less by the real performance of the firms (Löffler 2000). It can be argued that an ex post correction solves the problem but for a single firm an overpricing and the following downswing makes a new increase of capital very difficult and insofar has long-reaching negative effects. This coincides with the criticism that many investors simply did not read the prospectus where the risks have often been disclosed (*Handelsblatt*, 11 August 2000, 35).

If we ask for the reasons for the negative bias in the investor community we first of all have to consider the real and mental dependence of the private and especially the professional investors of the American economy and NASDAQ. Maybe 50 per cent of the decline in stock prices at the NM depends on the American development and in fact the growth of the US economy slackens (a 50 per cent US influence is also the estimate in the series of the *Financial Times Deutschland*, see 12–16 March 2001, always 21). In our view this influence is far from self-evident because at the NM mainly German firms are listed, the sales dependence of the new firms from the American market is not excep-tionally high, and the reaction of the Fed with a remarkable decrease in the American interest rates is in general good for the stock markets. But the subjective and mental component has to be stressed here as well as the fact that a fundamental change in the composition of investors took place: at the beginning of the NM private investors dominated, but since 1999 – and with an increasing tendency – 2/3 of the turnover at the NM is executed by institu-tional investors, half of them foreign investors. They take international market developments like the American growth rate, interest rate changes, and so on strongly into account (*Börsen-Zeitung*, 1 July 1999). They also concentrate on the large caps of the Nemax 50 which may increase the low trading volume and rising volatility of the smaller caps (the so-called orphan stock problem, that is stocks with no research coverage).

From the supply side it can argued that the general rise of the share prices is due to over-liquidity, that is billions of DM have no attractive alternatives like bonds due to low interest rates and even the rational fund managers have to put the success cards on the table every three months and therefore must participate in the NM boom. Bottlenecks emerged and focused in the NM segment because the NM was strongly marketed by Deutsche Börse and the media and no limits existed for the free float of stories and visions, but the real free float of stocks is only 20 per cent, since June 2000 it must only be 10 per cent if the emission volume is higher then 100 mio. Euro.

This argument can be combined with the observation that the companies became younger and younger, and the product ideas more and more ambitious, that is less competent companies went public to profit from the general boom. One possibility is that these firms had no real innovative ideas, another that they missed the necessary business structures like accounting, another the sheer incompetence of the management. In all these cases, they were not adequately controlled by the respective Deutsche Börse committee. One explanation for this neglect may be that all involved parties of the financial community make money with the going public, for example the emitting banks and their analysts (plus the frontrunning problem). The costs for the IPO to go public are after all between 10 and 15 per cent of the emission value. Often the chartered accoun-tants lack expertise in this fast growing business. The Deutsche Bank, for example, is the major stockholder of Deutsche Börse AG, often the bank is also an important stockholder and the bank of emission, so that interest conflicts are unavoidable (for the thesis of an exploitative investment cartel see Ogger 2001). For their services as designated sponsors the banks receive about 30 mio. DM per year. It can be argued that the interest of the investment community to list companies is so compelling that they alone have strong incentives to produce a positive bubble loop.

Another channel of this positive bubble loop can be seen in the interest of the banks to have a high emission volume with a minimum of 40–50 mio. Euro because they get a percentage of this volume and the effort is almost constant from 30 mio. upwards. To get a serious emission bank and designated sponsor the companies must be very ambitious to be attractive. This may also explain the high number of return and profit warnings, in the software segment for example almost 50 per cent of the companies listed published warnings in 2000 (*Going Public*, No. 3, 2001, 100–103). Maybe all parties have been infected by the gold rush atmosphere (*Financial Times Deutschland*, 1 Feb 2001, 22), so that the details, for example the correct prospectus, were neglected (see the notice by Deutsche Börse, dated 29 August 1999, on their low quality). On the side of the companies the competition between the banks (beauty contest, pitches) to become the emitting bank sometimes depended on the highest proposal for the stock price.

A separate point is obviously unfair and sometimes illegal behavior and fraud by the management which massively shake the confidence of investors. On the one hand, many companies revised their profit and growth targets in such a short time from positive to outright negative that this cannot be explained as a result of the unpredictability of the market forces. On the other hand, the insider problematic is evident in many companies: when insiders like pre-IPO stock-holders, friends and family and so on plan to sell their shares after the lock-up period the market is flooded beforehand with non-precise but positive infor-mation, often misusing the ad-hoc publicity rules (for numerous examples see *Capital*, No. 9, 2000, 283–9). A side-effect is the whole lot problem, when for example some technology stocks revise their plans drastically, this also strongly influences the stocks of serious and fundamentally sound companies (for example IDS Scheer).

In some companies, especially small caps, very few large stockholders (for example Consumer Electronic has two large investors) can also influence the stock price with clever selling and buying tactics which may irritate other investors and undermine general confidence. Another facet is the breaking of the lock-up period of six months or not to accept the self-commitment to hold the stocks more than six months (Haffa/EM.TV). It is not important that most managers behave this way, but that some do so. These cases become a media focus and the surprised public realizes that they can do it without penalties.

Another point is the book-building price. It can be argued that it was on average too low so that an accelerating bubble was unavoidable in the sense that the low prices provoked excess demand which fueled the overshooting cascades.

The counter argument is that the book-building price was correct and the public was wrong and that we now experience the end of the bubble and the return to adequate prices and, for example reasonable price–earnings ratios. Besides the argument of a general readjustment of the price level it can also be pointed out that we are in the process to sift the chaff from the wheat. This is a painful process with a combined short-term general downswing. It implies delistings and bankruptcies, on the NASDAQ on average 20 per cent of the companies disappear every year. But it must also be noted that many companies which are listed at the NM still have a considerable performance record; the 15 most successful performers per annum had an increase in their stock price between more than 500 per cent and more than 120 per cent related to their emission price in February 2001 (*Going Public*, No. 3, 2001, 12). Even the scandal-company EM.TV has a performance per annum of + 160 per cent.

A further crash explanation hints at the necessary learning process of the hitherto non-experienced public which no longer continues to react to any positive message but learns to distinguish unimportant good news from important good news like realized and not only projected growth rates, a voluntary extension of the lock-up period, and so on. A persistent information problem for the public is the sometimes low quality of the quarterly reports, the ad-hoc information policy of companies, and so on so that they can only rely on more general, soft and sometimes spectacular news. This may also depend on the informational two-class system because private investors usually have no access to the professional research reports of the banks.

Another rationalization could be the extreme risky orientation of many (not only private and penny-stock?) speculators at the NM which leads to unpredictable behavior and extreme volatility of some stocks. One day before Micrologica went bankrupt as expected, the share price rose by 50 per cent (*Handelsblatt*, 6 March 2001, 64), maybe as a reaction to the unexpected survival credits for Letsbuyit.com in February 2001, where the stock price rose by 350 per cent in one day.

Finally it can be argued that more or less natural rates of return exist. If the price–earnings ratio (P/E) of DAX stocks in the long run were between 11 and 25, some listings of the NM had three-digit P/Es (for example RTV Family Entertainment: 438). But the counter argument was that for fast-growing companies more dynamic valuation standards like the price–earnings to growth should apply where the P/E is divided by the expected growth rate. The expected growth rates have often been exaggerated. And does even a maximal optimistic outlook justify that, for example, the market capitalization of Intershop was temporarily 20.370 per cent of the firm's capital resources (*Die Welt*, 29 January

2001,15)? EM.TV (media, with Kermit the frog and Quack the duck) had a twenty-thousand-fold increase in value until May 2000, an investor in October 1997 made 3 mio. DM in March 2000 with an investment of 10 000 DM in 1998. These figures resemble the outraged tulip mania in the seventeenth century. The NEMAX All Share rose from 1998 to June 2000 by 500 per cent, the growth of the German economy was between 2 and 3 per cent. It is not easy to describe in neutral words the manic atmosphere of the first years of the NM (but read Deibert and Serrar 2000). As a further example, the giant Telekom, was evaluated at 60 billion DM in the process of due diligence. In March 2000 the value was 640 billion, in July 2000 it went down to 290 billion DM, an up and down for which no reasonable explanation exists. Where the US economy is concerned it is also hard to see if the real economy justified the NASDAQ crash, since there were no wars, no crisis and still an above average growth rate. In fact, only some companies presented warnings and in May 2000 Boo.com. went bankrupt.

It is hard to give an efficient market explanation for this international change of winds. It can be argued that the risk–earning prospects are very unsure so that every signal or information has a high impact and consequently causes extreme volatility. In our view, the situation is more reminiscent of the main messages of the subjectivist tradition in economic thought. In Shackle's (1992) approach, human knowledge and evaluation is kaleidoscopic in the sense that a small change in the economy changes the whole picture or pattern of cognition like a kaleidoscope, where a slight change rearranges the same parts and presents a completely different picture (for the theoretical implications see Streit and Wegner 1989). This must have happened in March 2000 worldwide, beginning with the changing analysts' views in major American stock market centers and cities like New York. Before March 2000 they were optimistic and saw the growth potentials, then they asked for the proof of the pudding in terms of short-term real earnings. Before, the glass was half full, then it become half empty.

One of the few economists who predicted the crash was Shiller (2000). He puts the emphasis on the thesis of a speculative bubble, comparing the development of the rocketing stock prices and the rather normal trend in earnings. Not fundamentals but cultural precipitating factors like the renaissance of materialist orientations, the breakdown of communism, the personal experience of the Internet, the general increase in gambling institutions caused the take-off. It was accelerated by a ponzi-process bandwagon-effect induced by increasing stock prices. Their increase and following decrease is explained by epidemic models where first more and more people become infected and then the rate of infection necessarily must decrease. So Shiller offers two sides of herd behavior, a subjective cultural and an epidemic objective aspect. Soros (2000) pointed out another positive feedback: the fundamentals cannot be distinguished from the sphere of financial markets because both interact – for example high share prices arouse consumer confidence and change the firm's growth and profit prospects – so that the real or fair price depends on the general stock price trend and the mental attitudes of investors.

A third valuable approach to understand the dynamics and euphoria on the German NM is behavioral finance as a relatively new method of capital market analysis (Goldberg and Nitzsch 2000) where non-rational psychology, emotions, decisions under stress, motives like Knight's instinct to play, situations in which many err in the same direction, and informational overload play a role. Overload makes the reduction of complexity by diverse heuristics necessary. In a certain sense, behavioral finance is the opposite to the neoclassical rational, fully informed, risk-averse economic agent with stable preferences.

The double high euphoria and depression in Germany compared with the US is explained by the fact that many German private investors lacked an availability heuristic (no experience with crashes). Another observation is that in Germany stories like fraud by managers and so on played a central role and influenced the investor climate strongly, which coincides with the behavioral finance observation that affective, surprising and colorful news is often more important then abstract data. A further aspect is affective congruence, the reduction of cognitive dissonance and so on which implies that agents select the good information in the upswing and the bad information in the downswing and repress countervailing evidence or interpret it in the desired way (unemployment can mean no rise of interest rates or a bad economic outlook). This includes the contrast effect: even if firms make further profit, a slight slack in the increase after many increases in the past attracts negative attention. Many investors also seem to have a strong anchoring and think in reference points of, for example, a normal rate of return (sometimes triple digits in 2000 as we saw above).

The conjunction fallacy is a major problem for many sound companies in the new market: if one firm in a market segment does not perform as expected, the stock price of all companies listed in the segment may be negatively affected. In the crash we can also observe overconfidence and the control illusion in the reports of those who give retrospective explanations (why their forecasts from yesterday were wrong).

Before we come to some policy reform proposals, let us summarize the mentioned factors of influence: the influence of the American environment, low or high book-building prices, the fundamental change of real growth and earnings perspectives, the normal sift the chaff from the wheat process, the hitherto uneducated public, high-risk speculators, overliquidity (much money, much less innovative ideas), companies not fit to go public or overstretching, managerial and organizational incompetence and unproductive anarchy, an investment-community bias for positive bubble loops, fraud/cash–out/insider exploitation (confidence), kaleidoscopic change due to minor information signals, and herd behavior (cultural and epidemic).

6. SOME EVOLUTIONARY ECONOMIC POLICY PROPOSALS

We have already seen that no theoretically optimal structure of capital markets can be derived because different groups with different interests and trade-offs are involved. Some theories like the micro market structure approach have mainly one group in perspective (the investors) and can nevertheless hardly define optimal structures. A way out could be Soros's view: unregulated capital markets lead to downturns and crashes; to prevent them a tight regulatory framework and state intervention is necessary (Soros 2000). From an evolutionary point of view, this opinion is not convincing.

If the evolution of an economic system depends on change, novelty, surprise, and innovations, the other side of the coin must be included, namely that there is a boom before the crash. Schumpeter argued that the main function of the boom is to introduce new combinations. This necessitates flexibility, free space for experiments and animal spirits and their fascinating stories and visions, a playground to introduce innovative mutations and select the fit from the unfit. As a pattern prediction we may say the more regulation the less we can get in terms of spontaneous mutation and selection. A basic insight of evolutionary economics is that the market-setter and leader of the future cannot be predicted. So the stock prices are bets on the future with high risk and return potential. Those who bet on Microsoft in the past had a triple-digit profit rate, many others could wipe their bets off.

On the other hand, the volatility and crash of the stocks and indices at the NM of about 80 per cent is out of the necessary and beneficial corridor. We do not know what the maximal beneficial spread of the corridor is. but we can guess that with 80 per cent the negative impacts for investors, companies and the innovative régime at large prevail. In the following we will make some economic policy proposals for regulatory reform and take the trade-off between the risk of surpassing the beneficial corridor and the necessary space and flexibility for spontaneous innovative evolution into account.

As a measuring rod a dichotomy of orientations, introduced by T. Veblen, one of the early founding fathers of evolutionary economics, can be introduced here. He distinguished between the two basic orientations of creative workmanship and the production of new goods on the one hand, and wastemanship, emulation and making money on the other hand (Veblen 1923). In an evolutionary framework, (stock) markets should encourage the productive instead of the pecuniary interests. Agents in the innovative workmanship orientation also want to make money – but by means of innovative products and not. for example, by tricky cash-outs. We will see in the following how far the Veblen criteria may be helpful.

Let us now come to the criticisms of the institutional setting of the NM and the proposals for reform in more detail. One criticism was that the pre-IPO book-building prices set by the banks were (either too high or) too low. To prevent over-subscription it may be asked why the market should not give the answer so that an auctioning system (Wallmeier and Rösl 1999) to fix the emission price should be obligatory (Trius AG was auctioned in 2000). It would disclose the real willingness to pay of investors. The counter arguments are that in this case the selling price depends much more on the general stock market atmosphere, less on the company's fundamentals and that the firms have no calculable basis of the new financial resources (Knips 2000, 250). In our view these arguments are not convincing because the price rise after an over-subscription reflects the general market atmosphere anyway and the fixing of a minimum price could drastically reduce the uncertainty of the emitting companies. The market is also a neutral force and the allegations of conscious under- or overvaluation will end.

Another point was the over-stretching problem, that is that companies have to exaggerate in terms of growth and the emission volume to attract first class emitting banks which may be motivated primarily by Veblen's pecuniary interest. It can in fact be asked if the requirements with respect to size are not too demanding for small start-up firms. From an evolutionary viewpoint, these little garage firms in particular need venture capital with realistic exit options like going public. Today, these firms have only the disadvantageous options to list at regional stock exchanges or at the *Freiverkehr* with a rather undemanding regulatory framework. Therefore, the proposal would be to establish a new segment especially for small-caps.

Another problem was the extreme volatility of indices and the bottlenecks of many stocks. This could be changed by an increase of the free float. When it is agreed that the interest of the public to buy shares is positive for a general investment culture, and functional for an innovative evolution of the economic system, it is hard to see what the advantage of all the family and friends programs are. Also questions of the insider and cash-out confidence problem come into play here. In addition, the criteria for the dissemination of stocks are mostly unclear and not made public. Therefore we opt for the definition of a much lower maximum share for institutional investors and insiders, the rest should be given to the interested public. For example, a 50:50 per cent rule and in both categories a pure auction model could be set up. The trend should be to reduce the pecuniary short-term interest of the owner of firms which Veblen castigated. Real Schumpeterian entrepreneurs are not motivated by giving gifts to friends and family members.

A special question is the lock-up period of six months (Korfsmeyer 1999). In our view a lock-up period of two years does not turn back real innovative entrepreneurs but those who want to cash-out and walk away. They can even buy a put option on their stocks so that they are insured against a price decline. The incentive for short-term pecuniary motives to go public is reduced significantly. Another possibility to reduce unproductive pecuniary maneuvering and information asymmetry would be the public disclosure of the selling of stocks by insiders like old stock holders, managers, but also friends and family. For investors, it is relevant to know this *ex ante* instead of being informed *ex post* why the own stocks eventually lost value. We suppose that the disclosure of relevant stockholders would reduce asymmetry and the invitation to pecuniary maneuvering further without the implication of a weakening of the competitive position of the firm.

To balance the positive heuristics of analysts and institutional investors the research reports should be available on the internet, as well as the analyst conferences so that all interested investors can follow with low transaction costs.

Another point concerns the sudden loss of confidence by the fraudulent behavior of insiders like the selling of stocks in the lock-up period or the illegal exploitation of insider information before they have been made public. In the US the SEC exerts a tight control and follows the movements of stock prices closely. In Germany three completely understaffed institutions (among them the Bundesaufsichtsamt für den Wertpapierhandel, see their publication on the German laws against insider-trading, Frankfurt, 1998) with overlapping functions have only an alibi function in this respect. Not even one example of many obvious cases exists where real penalties and not only minor fines were imposed. This is an open invitation for Veblen's wastemanship activities. It increases the volatility of the company's stock prices, and reduces investors' confidence and market liquidity.

At this point we see the limits of a private regulation of the stock exchange because the persecution of potential criminal acts (for example by the interception of telephone calls) is for good reasons forbidden for non-governmental institutions. We have here an example of the limits of self- or internal regulation. The learning process of economic agents and the establishment of inner institutions and rules reaches a certain limit or boundary which cannot be surpassed in the existing legal framework and therefore necessitates a complementary activity of the legal and public system. The interaction of outer and inner institutions (Lachmann) leads to a mutual adaptive upgrading which can also be observed in other spheres of public policy (Grimm 1996).

Managerial and organizational incompetence should be detected in the process of due diligence. Here the chartered accountants play the central role. They should be encouraged to seriously check the companies. It is an open question how the interest cartel including the media in too optimistic forecasts could be balanced. In our opinion also public and non-profit institutions should step in here. At the moment public TV does not understand its potential role as *advocatus diaboli*. Maybe we also need a German analyst's *Stiftung Warentest*.

It is hard to say how the investment community bias and the positive bubble loop can be controled. Besides an eventual loss of reputation they make money with sound as well as with unsound companies (the profit after taxes of Deutsche Bank increased by more then 100 per cent in 2000). Maybe a control instrument would be a tax of a certain percentage of the bank's emission profit if the company goes bankrupt; also the prohibition of gratis stock gifts in the pre-IPO phase is worth considering. Some people argue that this is a necessary cross subsidy for their unprofitable role as designated sponsor. It could be asked if this role at XETRA could not be performed much cheaper by a public body. A side-effect would be a reduction of the dependence of companies from their emission banks.

Let us ask now, how did the Deutsche Börse as the private regulating agency react to the crash? In the first months the need for change was more or less rejected (*Financial Times Deutschland*, 11 August 2000, 17; *Frankfurter Allgemeine Zeitung*, 11 August 2000, 23). But according to an economic German magazine, even 4/5 of the listed companies supported a tougher regulation (*Die Welt*, 11 August 2000, 21) Finally, since the beginning of 2001 the following changes were decided: the information of the quarterly reports has been standardized and extended and since March 2001 members of the board of directors and the supervisory board have to declare their buying and selling of the company's stocks after three days. They have to give notice in the quarterly reports, further they have to make their initial shares transparent in the firm's prospectus (disclosure of directors' dealing). The fines have been extended from 10 000 to 100 000 Euro (see for the details Förschle and Helmschrott 2001; Deutsche Börse AG 2001a). These new rules can be interpreted as the result of a learning process of those who organize the inner institution NM and its rules. Internal regulations were increased as a result of a temporary malfunctioning of this stock market segment. It is a piecemeal economic engineering and evolutionary adaptation to enhance the functionality of the NM.

The mostly reasonable criticism of organizations like the *Deutsche Schutzvereinigung für Wertpapierbesitz* was that the declaration of stock dealings by insiders is only an *ex post* rule, potential insiders are not concerned (family and friends), major investors have not to be notified, no published rules for the buying and selling policies of large investment companies exist, the inclusion of emitting banks in company stocks is not transparent, the lock-up period has not been extended, the public enforcement and control machinery is still weak and the maximum fine is extremely moderate compared with the millions of eventual profit from irregular conduct motivated by Veblen's pecuniary motive.

The argument that all these regulations may deceive potential new IPOs is invalidated by the fact that many of these rules are practiced in the US and do not at all discourage new companies from going public. One interesting counter argument of the Deutsche Börse is that in the case of *ex ante* announcements and majority stockholder publicity a problem arises due to the private character of the NM segment. Only the public legislator is empowered to take these decisions (see the interviews with V. Potthoff in *Börsen-Zeitung*, 21 December 2000, and *Handelsblatt*, 10 January 2001). We see here that the potential of the NM to acquire capital for innovative entrepreneurs seems not only to depend on relatively extended regulations set by the Deutsche Börse AG as the originator of the NM as an internal institution but must also be supplemented by public law so that a reciprocal upgrading between internal and external institutions can take place. Where the public authorities are concerned, the fourth law to strengthen the financial markets (*Viertes Finanzmarktförderungsgesetz*), which cannot be discussed here in detail, will increase market transparency and punish illegal behavior.

Also the *Deutsche Börse* as the organizer of the NM as an internal institution has changed the regulations again and introduced the possibility of a delisting of pennystocks, a new standard which will start in October 2001. A delisting can take place if for 30 consecutive trading days the value of a stock is below one Euro and the market capitalization is below 20 mio. Euro. The rule can be enforced if both values are below this minimum for the next 90 days and will not be above the minimum for 15 consecutive trading days. Companies can also be delisted if insolvency is declared (*Deutsche Börse* 2001b, 74).

Together with the investment bank Dresdner Kleinwort Wasserstein, Roland Berger Consultants and the solicitor's office Shearman and Sterling the *Deutsche Börse* has published a report (*Deutsche Börse* 2001b) on the NM which can be interpreted as a summary of their learning process in the last year and the consequences they draw from the crash. Especially on the part of Shearman and Sterling the question is asked if the German laws of the capital markets are sufficient or not. Further rules are considered absolutely necessary and in their view the public legislator must also play an important role. The proposed regulations concern *inter alia* a simplification of the control institutions of the stock market, a new definition of price manipulations, for example in the context of family and friends programs and so on, a drastic increase of the penalties, a tightening of the liability standards with respect to irregular ad-hoc information, the quarterly and annual reports, and so on (*Deutsche Börse* 2001b, especially 9. 80 and 105). We can therefore observe that a continuous learning process takes place on the side of the internal and the external (public) institutions, that the regulations can be complementary and that both sides may even ask for accompanying regulations of the other side.

7. CONCLUSION

In this chapter we first identified the NM as the segment of the German stock market which comes closest to fulfilling the function of providing liquidity to Schumpeter entrepreneurs. After a brief description of the market we asked who initiated the new institution and how did it evolve, also in a comparative theoretical context. We saw that the NM is an example of Lachmann's internal institutions and a new third type besides the traditional public law/private contract distinction. Further, we saw that the road to success for the NM and for NASDAQ was not a broad *laissez-faire* policy but a dense regulatory framework. Then we gave some explanations for the crash since March 2000 and briefly pointed out some alternatives to efficient market hypotheses (Shackle's subjectivism, Shiller's cultural and epidemic herd behavior and some results of behavioral finance). Finally we tried to derive some concrete policy reform proposals and confronted them with the recent learning processes and reforms realized by the *Deutsche Börse*.

POSTCRIPT

After this volume had gone to press, the German Stock Exchange Company (Deutsche Börse) decided to close down the *Neuer Markt* with effect from January 2003. Thereafter, the German stock market will be divided into a General and a Prime Standard segment. The latter imposes stricter conditons of access on companies than the former. It will include the former Dax (the 30 major blue chips), the mid-cap segment MDax with 50 companies (formerly 70) and the SDax with 50 smaller companies. The Nemax 50 will be listed until the end of 2004 in order to give issuers of Nemax certificates time to conclude dealings in this market. A new segment, the TecDax 30, will be launched in March 2003. It will be comprised of 30 technological issues and can, to a certain degree, be looked upon as a substitute for the *Neuer Markt*. Many companies hitherto listed on the *Neuer Markt* will in future fall under the General Standard segment with less stringent rules regarding information disclosure, no designated sponsors etc.

REFERENCES

Beike, R. and J. Schlütz (1999), *Finanznachrichten*, Stuttgart: Schäffer-Poeschel.
Beike, R. et al. (2000), *Neuer Markt und Nasdaq*, Stuttgart: Schäffer-Poeschel.
Born, K.(1999) 'Neue Offenheit: Die Rechnungslegung des mittelständischen Unternehmens nach HGB, IAS und US-GAAP im Vergleich', in W. Koch and J. Wegmann (eds), *Mittelstand und neuer Markt*, Frankfurt, pp. 311–38.

Bundesaufsichtsamt für den Wertpapierhandel (1998), *Insider Trading Prohibitions and Ad Hoc Pursuant to the German Securities Trading Act*, Frankfurt.

Commons, J.R. (1924), *Legal Foundations of Capitalism*, New York: Macmillan.

Deibert, V. and K. Serrar (2000), *Besser anlegen am Neuen Markt*. Munich: FinanzBuch-Verlag.

Deutsche Börse (2001a), *Reporter: Der Informationsdienst für die Kunden*, Frankfurt, February.

Deutsche Börse (ed.) (2001b), *Neuer-Markt-Report: Zugang zum europäischen Kapitalmarkt-Schlüssel für Wachstum*, Frankfurt.

Easterbrook, F.H. and D.R. Fischel (1991), *The Economic Structure of Corporate Law*, Cambridge, MA: Harvard University Press.

Förschle, G. and H. Helmschrott (2001), 'Neuer Markt: Rückblick auf Veränderungen im Jahr 2000 und Ausblick'. *Finanz-Betrieb*, 3, 111–17.

Goldberg, J. and R. Nitzsch (2000), *Behavioral Finance*, Munich: FinanzBuch-Verlag.

Greif, A. (1993), 'Contract enforceability and economic institutions in early trade: the Maghribi traders' coalition', *American Economic Review*, **83**, 525–48.

Greif, A. et al. (1994), 'Coordination, commitment, and enforcement: the case of the merchant guild', *Journal of Political Economy*, **102**, 745–76.

Grimm, D. (1996), *Staatsaufgaben*, Frankfurt: Suhrkamp.

Gruppe Deutsche Börse (2001), *Die Gruppe Deutsche Börse*, Frankfurt.

Heitzer, B. and C. Sohn. (1999), 'Zur Bedeutung des Neuen Marktes für die Venture Capital-Finanzierung in Deutschland', *Finanz-Betrieb*. **1**, 397–405.

Johnson, S. (2000), 'Private contracts and corporate governance reform: Germany's Neuer Markt. Mimeo, Cambridge, MA.

Knips, S. (2000), *Risikokapital und Neuer Markt*, Frankfurt: Lang.

Korfsmeyer, J. (1999), 'Die Bedeutung von lock-up agreements bei Aktienemissionen', *Finanz-Betrieb*, **1**, 205–12.

Kukies, J. (2000), 'The effect of introducing a new stock exchange on the IPO process', Paper delivered to the Euroconference on the Design of Primary Equity Markets, Capri, 16–18 June.

Lachmann, L.M. (1963), 'Wirtschaftsordnung und wirtschaftliche Institutionen', *Ordo*, **14**, 63–77.

La Porta, R. et al. (1997), 'Legal determinants of external finance', *Journal of Finance*, **52**, 1131–50.

La Porta, R. et al. (1998), 'Law and finance', *Journal of Political Economy*, **106**, 1113–55.

La Porta, R. et al. (1999), 'The quality of government'. *Journal of Law, Economics and Organization*, **15**, 222–79.

Löffler, G. (2000), 'Zeichnungsrenditen am Neuen Markt: Gleichgewicht oder Ineffizienz?', Mimeo, Frankfurt University.

Milgrom, P.R., D.C. North, and B.R. Weingast (1990), 'The role of institutions in the revival of trade: The law merchant, private judges, and the Champagne fairs', *Economics and Politics*, **2**, 1–23.

Niquet, B. (2000), 'Old versus new economy', in Bundesverband der Börsenvereine an deutschen Hochschulen (ed.), *Börsenperspektiven 2001*, Munich: FinanzBuch-Verlag, pp. 29–36.

O'Hara, M. (1995), *Market Microstructure Theory*, Cambridge MA: Blackwell.

Ogger, G. (2001), *Der Börsenschwindel*, Munich: Bertelsmann.

Plötz, W. (ed.) (2001), *Who's who Neuer Markt*. Frankfurt: Frankfurter Allgemeine Zeitung Buchverlag.

Plückelmann, K. (2000), *Der Neue Markt der Deutsche Börse AG*, Frankfurt: Lang.
Rödl, B. (1999), *Going Public*, Frankfurt: Frankfurter Allgemeine Zeitung Buchverlag.
Schaible, S. and M. Thielbeer (2000), 'Der Beitrag der am Neuen Markt gelisteten Unternehmen für die Beschäftigung in Deutschland, Roland Berger und Partner GmbH', Mimeo, Berlin.
Schmidt, R.H. and S. Grohs (2000), 'Angleichung der Unternehmensverfassung in Europa aus ökonomischer Perspektive: Eine Bestandsaufnahme', in S. Grundmann (ed.), *Systembildung und Systemlücken in Kerngebieten des Europäischen Privatrechts*, Tübingen: Mohr-Siebeck, pp. 145–88.
Schmoller G. (1989/1884), *The Mercantile System and its Historical Significance*, Fairfield: Kelley.
Schumpeter, J.A. (1951), *The Theory of Economic Development*, Cambridge, MA: Harvard University Press.
Shackle, G.L.S. (1992), *Epistemics and Economics*, New Brunswick: Transaction Publishing.
Shiller, R.J. (2000), *Irrational Exuberance*, Princeton: Princeton University Press.
Sombart, W. (1987), *Der moderne Kapitalismus* (3 Vol.), Munich: Deutscher Taschenbuch Verlag.
Soros, G. (2000), *The Crisis of Global Capitalism*, New York: Public Affairs.
Streit, M.E. and G. Wegner (1989), 'Wissensmangel, Wissenserwerb und Wettbewerbsfolgen', *Ordo*, **40**, 183–200.
Veblen, T. (1923), *Absentee Ownership*, New York: Huebsch.
Wallmeier, M. and R. Rösl (1999), 'Underpricing bei der Erstemission von Aktien am Neuen Markt (1997–1998)', *Finanz-Betrieb*, **1**, 134–42.

10. Understanding and the mobilisation of error – eliminating controls in evolutionary learning

Hansjörg Siegenthaler

I

Adequate opinionmaking is at the root of all successful politics. It matters most where it is particularly difficult to achieve: in periods of rapid institutional change with highly uncertain outcomes of decisions to be made, in processes of what we came to call, during the last decade, social transformations, in the 'American Revolution' of the eighteenth century, for example, in the beginnings of modern British democracy, in the quest for modern statehood in Switzerland during the 1930s and 1940s, in the transition of the Republic of Weimar to National Socialism in Germany, in the transition of the Soviet Union to capitalist Russia. In all these cases political goals were heavily contested and, more important, it was a moot question just which goals one had to fight for in order to achieve a truly useful result: individual actors were quite conscious of what it means to be stricken by 'bounded rationality' without depending in the least on Herbert Simon's pertinent insights. How did they come to grips with the cognitive problems of decision making when, simultaneously, grave institutional problems were at stake and the attribution of long-run consequences to decisional options was exceptionally difficult? As an economic historian I share with traditional history a primordial interest in developing satisfactory answers to this question. And as an economist I share with evolutionary economics a keen interest in learning theories that could throw some light on individual and social behaviour in the borderline case of learning under conditions of uncertainty.[1]

What are the conditions of adequate opinionmaking in such a situation? If we start from the triple assumption that (1) opinionmaking is the outcome of communicative processes,[2] that (2) these processes follow the rules of an evolutionary interplay of factors of variation and factors of selection,[3] and (3) that in politics as well as in science the quality of the final result tends to depend on the ability of the system to mobilise counterevidence, that is 'error-elimi-

245

nating controls' which are able to falsify our erroneous beliefs, *then we want to understand the conditions under which this mobilisation of contradictory evidence is likely to get produced.*

The mobilisation of error-eliminating controls can take on many different forms. It results from individual action wherever it is possible to attribute to this action some observable outcomes. But to wait for such outcomes can be an extremely wasteful learning strategy. People who devote large amounts of resources to projects they are likely to depend upon for years are well advised to look for error-eliminating controls in advance. Knowledge contained in available texts or conveyed by interface communication can provide such controls. Unfortunately, the learning individual may be tempted to look for useful knowledge in those quarters where error-eliminating evidence is most unlikely to be mobilised: in literary traditions he is particularly well acquainted with or within carefully delineated social groups of people who share his beliefs and prejudices. In order to get rid of erroneous beliefs he should devote time and patience on texts and utterances that he finds difficult to understand, because they alone tend to deviate in what they tell from the routine of his own argumentation. But of course he profits from texts and utterances only to the extent that he is able to grasp their message. In order to mobilise error-eliminating controls he has to cross cultural barriers; he must be able to make sense of signs and sounds he is not familiar with. He is faced with the *task of understanding* strange people and their equally strange ways of talking. This is not an easy task to be fulfilled. Some authors would bluntly deny the possibility of meeting it adequately. We try to show that *successful penetration of cultural barriers – adequate interpretation of texts and their authors – depends upon adequate heuristics, that is upon elements of a specific institutional framework.* And we will treat this framework as an element of a particular *metaculture,* which started to spread through the Western World since the beginnings of the age of enlightenment.[4] *Rationality presumptions make up the core of this metaculture.* The application of rationality presumptions adds decisively to the efficiency of communicative learning processes in which the penetration of language barriers contributes to the mobilisation of error-eliminating controls. It steps in where semantic differentiation seems to prohibit intercultural communication.

We develop our argument in three steps: Section II highlights problems of mutual understanding and intercultural communication. It puts these problems in perspective by addressing the pronounced scepticism prevailing among present day language theorists with regard to the possibility of transgressing intercultural boundaries. Section III confronts this scepticism with a definition of those conditions that would allow for successful intercultural communication, if they were realised. It refers to Donald Davidson's theory of 'radical interpretation'; we present some elements of this theory in order to substantiate our belief in the crucial importance of rationality presumptions. Section IV applies these theoretical preliminaries to history, that is to processes of evolutionary learning in the emergence of the United States and its modern constitution. Section V draws some conclusions.

II

In order to get rid of prejudice and error we ought to address those people who deviate in their knowledge and beliefs from our own. But in private or public debates we are likely to deny all counterevidence the weight it deserves because it tends to be framed in a language with which we are not familiar, or because it tends to be presented by people we perceive to deviate somehow from standards according to which we tend to judge the reliability of authors and speakers. On very special and rather rare occasions we are spared these difficulties. An intradisciplinary discussion among professionals follows neatly designed rules that seem to be designed exactly to alleviate the problems of mutual understanding.[5] Such a discussion makes use of a language with well-defined terms. It usually addresses a well-defined problem. It excludes outsiders at its 'ports of entry', so that those engaged in the debate are assumed with good reason to comply with the basic rules of the game and tend to be treated as insiders whom one can trust. But most other debates deviate from this case of intradisciplinary scientific discourse in many respects. A discussion among parliamentarians cannot rely on well-defined terms. Problem definitions are hotly disputed. Ports of entry are loosely defined if they are defined at all. Members of a democratically elected parliament are not a 'Denkkollektiv' in the sense in which Fleck (1994) used the term. As a consequence parliamentary communication tends to be loaded with problems of mutual understanding, and participants are not likely to waste their time on a careful scrutiny of strange arguments put forward by their opponents in order to learn from them.

It is true of course that 'freedom of speech' prevailing in western societies goes a long way to familiarise participants with the very idea of a debate as a process of communicative learning; John Stuart Mill provided a justification of this idea.[6] But they are nevertheless strongly tempted to deny their adversaries – and the arguments of them – the attention they would have to pay if they were to search for truth. A special kind of 'rational ignorance' seems to be involved: Why bother with strange views of strange people if it takes time and effort to bridge the gap between specific cultural groups? Economists might stress heterogeneity of interests among participants as an obvious reason for the reluctance to listen to one's adversaries. One suspects the opponent to blend his arguments with all kinds of 'dirty information'. To get wiser in a debate with representatives of well-specified interest groups is probably not the most obvious goal to be pursued. But it should be emphasised that controversy with regard to an issue dividing participants along the lines of economic advantages and disadvantages is not at the root of the difficulties involved in cross-cultural communication. These difficulties go deeper. They concern the basic question of interest definitions and the language barriers that make it so difficult to reach agreement with regard to these definitions.

If economists might find it irrational to pay much attention to people one is not familiar with because it is costly to pay attention, they find strong support for their convictions among adherents of language theories which stress the basic difficulties involved in the penetration of boundaries among cultures. In its most radical version this scepticism amounts to agnosticism pure and simple: it does not make sense at all to raise the question of successful communication as a process in which participants get access to beliefs of others. We interpret the words we are confronted with according to cognitive structures of our own. These structures are the result of inherited dispositions and individual histories. They are not conveyed with words, although words may be able to change them. And wherever words affect structures, they do this unintentionally and by chance, so that anything may happen, be it a closing down of gaps between cognitions of participants or a widening of these gaps. Luhmann (1995) thus recommended a shift in emphasis away from inquiries into the possibility of intersubjectivity to the study of evolutionary achievements in terms of cultural artefacts, that is new texts that refer to some given utterances and that gain their usefulness not through authenticity of interpretation but through the impact they might have on ideas and actions.

Some German philosophers tried to justify the idea of successful communication, that is adequacy of mutual attributions of meanings to texts and beliefs to authors, by referring to some 'common ground' which participants come to share as individuals who belong to rather loosely defined social entities. Such entities may be treated as the result of common or similar histories of people involved. Husserl introduced his concept of a 'Lebenswelt' which we may, for the sake of brevity, define as a space of experience available to participants.[7] The concept of 'Lebenswelt' points again to both conditions and to limitations of successful communication. It may lead rather inadvertently to cultural relativism; to the idea that reality perceptions depend upon mental structures which differ with cultural preconditions in ways which defy all efforts at bridging cultural gaps. Public debates going on today point to the political relevance of these philosophical concepts. 'Multiculturalists' not only teach the lessons of hampered communication within the multiethnic laboratories of modern societies; they want us to believe that we have to accept ethnic pluralism, cultural relativism, and the coexistence of multiple truths as a result of reality perceptions differing with cultural preconditions. They not only deny the possibility of basic agreement on politically relevant facts and their interpretation as something to be developed among people of different ethnic groups, different sexes, and different social strata. They also reject the idea of mutual understanding, that is the accessibility of meanings and beliefs for cultural outsiders.

III

How is it possible to meet such scepticism and to get rid of it? Which are the means – beyond philosophical argument – by which people help themselves to, and actually do, cross cultural boundaries? If we accept the basic idea of radical constructivists, according to which nobody is able to emancipate himself from mental dispositions that control to the last item whatever he does with a text and its meaning: how is it possible to justify nevertheless the very idea of 'understanding' in our sense of the word?

The route to be taken has been thoroughly explored by Donald Davidson. He devoted many decades of his life to problems of 'radical interpretation'. The term refers to a communicative situation in which participants do not share a common language of well-defined semantics. It responds very closely to our problem just defined. Davidson started as an experimental philosopher well acquainted with methods and achievements of cognitive science as they presented themselves in the 1950s. Thus the idea of 'mental schemes' governing cognitive processes of individual actors was familiar to him. When he questioned the wisdom of cultural relativism he certainly did not discard the very idea of schemes; he simply remained faithful to his basic belief in our ability to bridge cultural gaps nevertheless.[8] What is the stuff from which our intercultural bridges are built?

Let me present some elements of his pertinent theory.[9] Paramount among them is the belief that the solution has to be looked for not in the characteristics of cultural differentiation but in the attitudes of people who are devoted to the task of understanding what appears to be inaccessible. These attitudes themselves make part of culture. They step in where Husserl's 'Lebenswelt' fails to provide the common ground alluded to before. I try to summarise Davidson's basic ideas in six points:

1. Davidson's treatment of processes of 'radical interpretation' does not imply any assumptions with regard to the language that an interpreter tries to understand. Take the case of somebody who is confronted with a sequence of strange sounds for which there is no lexicon, no thesaurus of words or expressions. The confrontation entails nothing but the experience of human beings who live in the same world. In such a situation observation and inference must of necessity play a most important part. Step by step the

sounds reveal some of their meaning as soon as they become associated with observable behaviour and observable features of the environment. Inference then proceeds from things already understood to things still to be interpreted. The modalities of this inference obviously deserve close attention.

2. These modalities follow the rules of an interpretation that is devoted not to decoding a sequence of sounds or words pure and simple but to understanding the meaning of what a fellow being tries to say and the beliefs this fellow being wants to express. The interpreter cares[10] for his alter ego, and his interpretation of language does full justice to cognitive structures to which the language relates. It does so if the interpreter applies a holistic approach, that is an approach that tries to identify not only the meaning of words, but also the propositional attitudes of people to whom the words can be attributed.[11] Wherever an interpreter fails to pay attention to propositional attitudes of an author he of necessity fails to grasp the meaning of his words. There are no unambiguously defined semantic rules followed by an author outside the sphere of his subjective world of beliefs and preferences: economists will be pleased to find that Davidson shares their devotion to *preferences* and *beliefs* as those propositional attitudes that should command our attention in the first place.

3. Davidson relates his theory of radical interpretation to a theory of truth in ways which captured the attention of critical observers for years. Rather late in his life he tried to make explicit what his earlier essays implied in terms of truth theories (Davidson, 1990). And what he made explicit remains open to debate. I present a rather personal variety of an interpretation which seems to be compatible with what he says and which does justice to my objectives. The point of departure is an explicit truth theory developed by Tarsky.[12] Tarsky tried to define that structure of a sentence, which makes the sentence true. We may address as an example the following sentence: '(Der Satz) "Schnee ist weiss" is true (in German) if and only if snow is white' (Davidson, 1990, p. 288). It is quite obvious that the second part of this sentence uses the metalanguage of an observer well acquainted with snow, whereas the first part makes use of an object-language to be interpreted by the outside observer. Davidson tries to put the formal definition of this truth-sentence to good advantage by turning the construct upside down: truth is no longer the issue; the issue shifts from truth to the actor's belief and the meaning of his words (Davidson, 1984, essay 9, p. 134). Let us assume that he wants to tell the truth and that he is able to tell the truth because his reality perceptions are adequate to the task. Assume he is observing snow in its whiteness and says: 'Ganz herrlich, wie weiss dieser Schnee doch ist': we might fall quite easily on the idea that he believes snow to be white, and that his words are somehow related to this belief. To

live in the same world and to perceive the world in the same way contributes decisively to mutual understanding.[13]

4. A holistic approach to the process of interpretation obviously is a highly demanding job for an interpreter. He must attribute meanings to a text and beliefs and/or preferences[14] to authors on the basis of one single piece of evidence, namely words. This looks very similar to the situation of a mathematician confronted with the task of identifying more unknowns than the available equations allow him to determine. How is one to proceed in such a situation? The most obvious strategy to be applied is to introduce some assumptions. If we have to identify the unknowns we cannot afford to hesitate and to avoid a decision in favour of this or that assumption even if we fail to find the evidence which could justify the decision. The theory of radical interpretation suggests at this point of the argument the introduction of a generalised rationality presumption.[15] This presumption implies two different hypotheses with which an interpreter approaches the author of the words he wants to understand. It implies a consistency assumption, and it implies a coherence assumption. Coherence means relatedness in ways that make it possible to judge the consistency of doings with words in particular or of behaviour in general.

5. If a rationality assumption serves the purpose of making sense out of words which would otherwise remain inaccessible, it quite obviously finds its justification not in any characteristics of texts and authors. Its heuristic value does not depend on observable rationality of texts and authors. There is no substitute available for a rationality assumption in a situation in which irrationality seems to prevail. A presumption of irrationality adds to the indeterminacy of meanings and attitudes to be attributed to words and authors. It means nothing else but resignation with regard to the task of interpretation. It denies an author the goodwill one is obliged to offer as long us one remains interested in mutual understanding.[16] But this does not mean of course that an interpreter should not be impressed by a particularly recalcitrant text that refuses to comply with ordinary standards of rationality. An author may produce intricate riddles and present them, not without delicacy, on the surface of his texts, provoking the verdict of irrationality quite irreverently. How should we meet such a provocation? Richard Rorty paved the way to an answer that should satisfy even the economist: whenever a text fails to meet rationality standards on the surface of it the interpreter has to dig a little bit deeper, look for circumstantial evidence, go into the biography of the author, even follow the recommendations of Sigmund Freud and decode the symptoms of unconscious elements hidden beyond the seemingly contradictory evidence. This fascinating suggestion reminds us of those representatives of hard-core neoclassics who stick to the rationality presumption to the limit, and who react to a behavioural change

that many other people might treat as evidence for irrationality with the recommendation to look for some hidden costs or to invent some new
categories of costs: reality never turns against the rationality presumption
as a heuristic device. It demands of us that we mobilise our creativity.[17]

6. The rationality presumption restricts the space of options within which an
interpretation as a mental construct is likely to be developed. As a heuristic
device the rationality presumption turns against voluntarism in interpretation.[18] It helps the author to impose his intentions on the reader. It helps the
reader to enter the world of the author. It makes for successful communication. Above all, it makes it hard for the reader to escape the cognitive
controls that a text is able to exercise on erroneous beliefs. *It makes it hard
for the reader to escape the error-eliminating controls a text implies.*

IV

All our doings with words are shaped by institutional arrangements in a similar
sense in which our actions are constrained by institutional rules, by an 'institutional matrix' to use the term suggested by North (1989). These arrangements
concern both semantics and hermeneutics. They attribute meaning to words,
and they tell the alter ego how to handle a text. Together they constitute *constraints of verbal communication.*[19] They may be treated as a topic of empirical
research just as those rules of behaviour that matter most in institutional
economics.

This empirical research serves the purpose, within the context of the present
chapter, to identify a particular subset of constraints, namely those rules that
foster cross-cultural mobilisation of contradictory evidence, of 'error-eliminating controls'. In a world in which Babylon still commands widespread
influence and in which cultural differentiation both in time and space makes for
semantic heterogeneity, cross-cultural mobilisation of error-eliminating controls
depends on adequate heuristics of interpretation. These heuristics are adequate
to the task if and only if they help people to cross semantic barriers, be it in
their endeavour to learn from history or to learn from outsiders they find difficult
to understand. *Semantic homogeneity is not the most desirable objective to be
pursued, and intertemporally it is out of the question anyway; but institutional
arrangements in terms of hermeneutic rules seem to be adequate substitutes
for semantic homogeneity if properly designed. Analytical philosophy prepared
us for this particular design.*

It enables us to discover a strong relationship between the emergence of
particular heuristics on one hand, and adequacy of social learning on the other
hand. It points to historical developments that show how some relevant social
groups deal successfully both with problems of mutual understanding and with

problems of institutional change. And of course it draws attention to the opposite, the covariance of defective heuristics and pathologies in processes of evolutionary learning. Cross-cultural studies covering large areas of historical experience in time and space are called for.[20] We concentrate in what follows on one particularly well documented case, *that is on the new design of communicative constraints in the American colonies that proved to be so eminently successful in the process of constitutional change by the end of the eighteenth century.*[21] We take it for granted that the new institutional framework turned out to be adequate to the multitude of problems related to economic and social modernisation for decades. We also assume that new communicative constraints were able to sustain a process of evolutionary learning in which the mobilisation of error-eliminating controls made it easier to avoid grave mistakes. With this double assumption in mind *we want to show that communicative constraints thought to be suitable to the task on theoretical grounds emerged during the last decades of the eighteenth century. A culture of rationality presumptions was in the making in the old American colonies very early in the eighteenth century.* At least three elements of such a culture can be discovered: (1) a new public sphere which encompassed culturally different quarters of American society started to manifest itself; (2) a growing legitimisation of individual interests or preferences testified a holistic concern for propositional attitudes; (3) new procedural rules guiding individual behaviour in doings with words made it easier to penetrate cultural barriers.

(1) *Public debates* were important in the colonies as early as the beginning of the eighteenth century, although by then the decision-rules of communities did not tie them very closely to the output of political systems. A pamphlet literature started to flourish; an American press addressed a growing readership despite censorship and other obstacles. A growing awareness of the political relevance of public debates motivated explicit statements on basic rules of a discourse considered to be adequate to the task of cross-cultural communication. By 1727 one pamphleteer was able to stipulate the idea that, ideally, public communications should be purged of 'private views or ends' (Warner, 1990, p. 38). Michael Warner took this recommendation as evidence for a general 'impersonality of public discourse' and for the acceptance of what he called the 'principle of negativity': the exclusion of individual idiosyncrasies from public utterances;[22] the reader was taught to rely not on the merits of an author but on the merits of an argument. He got involved in a routine of critical scrutiny without concern for the origins of a text, and he was supposed to devote time and energy on an article before he got an opportunity to discriminate against ideologies of outsiders, innovators or even adversaries; he had to presume, with charity, that the text deserved attention and careful interpretation without concern for its origin.

(2) Notwithstanding this presumption people and the social strata to which they belonged were explicitly represented and *treated as individuals driven in what they said or did by specific interests*.[23] In the heated atmosphere of the debate over the new federal Constitution during the years 1787–1790 it became very hard to overlook the fact that people differed in what they thought according to social and economic conditions.[24] This prepared the ground for liberal attitudes towards party politics and ideological diversity without, however, fostering an economic interpretation of political action as it became so tremendously important under the influence of the writings of Charles Beard (1913) at the beginning of the twentieth century. It was well understood that beliefs step in between social and economic conditions observable from without or from historical hindsight and actions that are meant to serve an individually useful purpose; otherwise it would be very difficult to understand the immense amount of intellectual resources the protagonists of all political factions invested in their quest for support. To presume the universal dependence of performance in words and deeds on personal interests was nothing else but an implication of a generalised rationality presumption; it helped to make sense out of what people said and did; it was a prerequisite of 'radical interpretation' and of a general readiness to treat even the enemy as somebody who deserved to be treated as a reasonable human being. To refer to material interests was not, in the age of enlightenment, the first step towards sociology of political decision making, rather it was a hermeneutic device (Schenk, 2000, 31) devoted to the art of mobilisation of contradictory evidence.

(3) Hermeneutics in politics includes *procedural rules* that make for successful communication. One should look at observable measures taken by protagonists of the political debate to the effect of creating and safely securing the conditions under which a routine of rationality presumptions is likely to prevail. Such measures played an outstanding role in the definition and enforcement of procedural codes that disciplined the behaviour of 55 well-bred, nevertheless rather ruthless and restless delegates to the constitutional convention of 1787 in Philadelphia. For three months a remarkable lot of individualities were thrown together in one place with the not very modest mandate of inventing and mediating the institutional framework of a society yet to come. The codes wanted the delegates to express their opinions freely. The debates were sheltered from outside pressure. But the codes wanted the delegates also to be good listeners. They were expected to follow the debates. They were not allowed to exchange their opinions with friends during the presentations of a speaker. Neither were they allowed to read newspapers (Ferrand, 1911, 8). Old George Washington himself, the hero of the War of Independence, presided over the assembly and personalised the rules he was charged to enforce. According to the records the convention

followed the rules very closely, resembling an orderly university seminar more than a modern parliament. And to the codes of conduct corresponded a level of argumentation that appealed to the closest attention and perseverance of those who followed the debate: speakers assumed their audience to be able to grasp the message and to turn it to good advantage. The procedural arrangement very effectively mobilised whatever evidence was collectively available.

It would be most rewarding to look at some of the judgements produced by historical actors themselves on the characteristics of the process of social learning they were involved in. James Madison, one of the truly outstanding 'founding fathers', was very conscious of the potential merits of procedures likely to lead to the rejection of erroneous views. He was a devoted adherent of falsificationism, and he was quite explicit in his pertinent testimony. He was well aware of the fact that he and his compatriots were on the way to draft a constitution without precedent for a society yet to come. Nevertheless he devoted a good deal of his time to the study of history. How did he relate what he learned from history to the visions he had to design? In a way he was able to anticipate anxieties that were later formulated by Hegel and Tocqueville with regard to the relevance of historical experience in the context of fundamental institutional change (Koselleck, 1967): in a phase of dramatic change in which the lessons of history might be in high demand, historical experience tends to become obsolete and to lose its role as an authority in guiding thoughts and actions. But finally he came to convince himself and his readers that there was a way out of the dilemma: history teaches its lessons even in situations of fundamental change. It throws light on a scene of transition. But this light is 'no other light than that of beacons, which give warning of the course to be shunned, without pointing out that which ought to be pursued'.[25] The routes are something to explore or even to invent; in the evolutionary process they belong to the realm of variation. The cliffs are there to be observed; they have an impact upon the selection of the route one finally wishes to take. Obviously Madison generalised what he followed as a set of rules in public debates anyway with regard to history. He spent a good deal of his time on the scrutiny of dissenting opinions, and he hoped to discover in historical traditions as he did in the views of political opponents a particular brand of 'error-eliminating controls' that could help him to get rid of prejudice and error.

V

To conclude we would like to refer to a basic idea of evolutionary economics. Individual rationality is bounded, and the individual actor finds it difficult to make an optimal choice among alternative options in a world that defies reliable descriptions in all its relevant traits. So he is likely to depend on behavioural rules that help him out of the impasse he confronts. These rules have an impact on what he does and, according to the language theories we are working with, they also have an impact on what he says, that is on what he does with words.

The emergence of rules may be treated as an evolutionary process, in which factors of variation and factors of selection both work together without anybody anticipating or controlling the result. If we want to understand this process we have to look at the mechanisms of selection. In the very long run some restrictions set by nature may be decisive. But we are, even as historians, not exclusively interested in the rhythms set by nature. Centuries, decades, even days may matter. In the short run of centuries man-made rules definitely belong to the set of relevant selective forces. And man-made rules decide on emergence and modification for the rules themselves. I have tried to highlight a special set of such rules, the rules that make us apply specific strategies in our endeavour to understand our fellow beings, semantic and hermeneutic rules. And I have tried to show that these rules decide on the prospective outcome of learning processes in everyday life no less than they do in science. They help, if properly designed, to mobilise error-eliminating controls, that is evidence contained in texts and verbal utterances of other people. This evidence becomes available to the extent that we are able to interpret these texts and utterances. It may help to get rid of prejudice and error. So the rules add, if they are adequate to the task, to the efficiency of opinion-making procedures. A routine of rationality presumptions commands a very prominent role among them.

NOTES

1. The examples given for such borderline cases are taken from the field of political or institutional economics. We claim, however, for our arguments some relevance also for the field of organisational learning as referred to by Witt (1998).
2. Wohlgemuth (1999) adequately presented arguments in favour of this assumption.
3. Popper (1987, p. 151) introduced in his falsificationist perspective the concept of 'imagined or vicarious trial-and-error behaviour' which can replace 'real trial-and-error behaviour'; this is exactly what we are referring to with our treatment of communicative processes as evolutionary ones. Campbell (1987, p. 54) reminds us of an earlier contribution of Popper to our topic (Popper 1966), in which he spoke of 'error-eliminating controls ... that is controls which can eliminate errors without killing the organism'; 'it makes it possible, ultimately, for our hypotheses to die in our stead.' Our term 'contradictory evidence' may be replaced by Popper's concept of 'error-eliminating controls'. See also Siegenthaler (1997).
4. This hypothesis comes close to pertinent concepts of Jürgen Habermas (1981).
5. This is true a fortiori for natural sciences. Markus (1987) gives a highly elaborate analysis of pertinent rules uniting authors and readers in a tightly knit scientific community since the end of the nineteenth century. And he relates these rules very convincingly to the goal persued by such a community to solve problems of mutual understanding.

6. Mill (1859/1956), chap. 2: Of the liberty of thought and discussion, pp. 19–55. Mill anticipated falsificationist perspectives in his first justification of freedom of opinion: unless we
assume our own fallibility, we are never entitled to deny an opponent's opinion the potential
of containing the truth; and this truth may be able to falsify our beliefs: man 'is capable of
rectifying his mistakes, by discussion and experience' (p. 23).

7. Gadamer (1990), p. 251, defines 'Lebenswelt' (lifeworld) as 'the world which we inhabit in
the natural attitude, the world which as such can never be objective, but which represents the
pre-given ground of all experience' (our translation).

8. Davidson (1984), essay 13: 'On the very idea of a conceptual scheme', pp. 183–98.

9. I rely on his own texts as far as I feel able to grasp them. The very extensive literature on the
theory of 'radical interpretation' and the ongoing debate on many rather moot questions will
hardly be touched upon. However I will take advantage of the German philosophers and representatives of analytical philosophy Oliver Scholz (1998, 1999a, 1999b) and Hans Rott
(2000a, 2000b).

10. The crucial term suggested by Davidson is the venerable notion of 'charity', as it has been
used by classical hermeneutics of the eighteenth century. We hesitate, however, to refer to this
concept, because it evokes attitudes of altruism that are clearly misplaced in the present
context. John Stuart Mill was eager to show that good conduct in public debates involved
'giving merited honour to every one, whatever opinion he may hold' (Mill, 1859/1956, 55);
his justification for this normative statement fits Davidson's argument quite well.

11. Davidson (1995, 12: 'The Unified Theory is holistic through and through'. See Scholz (1999a,
1999b, 205–10 and passim) for a thoroughgoing discussion of the concept. A holistic approach
seems to be appropriate for very different reasons in a structuralist perspective that attributes
meanings to words according to their position within a semantic field, that is a network of relationships between meanings of words (Fehr, 1997, 153).

12. See Scholz (1999b, pp. 105–9), for a careful treatment of Davidson's reception of Tarski's truth
theory.

13. See, for a pertinent elaboration of this point Davidson (1984), essay 13, 183–98, particularly
196.

14. 'Preferences' may be defined as mental dispositions that allow the individual actor to make
a choice between options as soon as these options are adequately defined on the basis of
beliefs.

15. See Scholz (1999b, part II, chap. 2): 'Eine Theorie der Präsumption', 148–58.

16. Davidson (1984, essay 9, 137): 'If we cannot find a way to interpret the utterances and other
behaviour of a creature as revealing a set of beliefs largely consistent and true by our own
standards, we have no reason to count that creature as rational, as having beliefs, or as saying
anything.'

17. Rorty (1993, 96, 97, 102). An institution (a heuristic device, for example) may fail its purpose.
It may have unintended consequences. But to ask whether it has empirical content is beside
the point. Interestingly enough adherents of analytical philosophy tend to approach rationality presumptions in exactly the same way as hard-core neo-classical economists used to
approach them. Economics after all used to be, in the eighteenth century, a field among others
within the humanities rather than without. It would be appropriate to look at Max Weber in
this context. His suggestion to differentiate between 'Zweckrationalität' and 'Wertrational-
ität' seems to be an application of the rationality presumption to the problem of understanding
the behaviour of decision-makers who are led to behavioural change by a change in their
propositional attitudes. See Swedberg (1998, 146–72). The relevant empirical question does
not address the text or the behaviour one tries to understand; it concerns the heuristic practised
in a given historical context. Dennett (1990) goes to the limit in his application of rationality
presumptions to justify everything we could possibly want to understand.

18. Eco (1996) very convincingly tries to show, in the role of a literary critique, in what ways a
text may be able to constrain an interpretation, even if it never imposes something like a
genuine one. And he provides a very strong motivation for his search for constraints. In full
sympathy with Popper he points to the pragmatic importance of constrained interpretation:
'Unsere Spezies hat bisher überlebt, weil sie Hypothesen aufstellte, die statistisch betrachtet
erfolgreich waren. Erziehung bedeutet nur, den Nachkommen zu erklären, welche der

Hypothesen sich als fruchtbar erwiesen haben' (p. 155). And such an explanation serves its purpose only if it is able to state the explanandum and the explananda in question rather unambiguously. It should be added that Eco was among those authors who, very early, wanted an artistic artefact to be treated as a text open to different interpretations (Eco, 1990). But this openness does not, according to his argument, preclude rigid restrictions.

19. Albert (1994, p. 119) reminds us of the fact that hermenutics originally was a 'Kunstlehre', a professional practice, which can be treated as a kind of 'technology'.
20. In Siegenthaler (1995) we tried to delineate the problem area just alluded to.
21. The remaining passages of this section are heavily indebted to Heideking (1988a, 1988b) and Widmer (1998). My acknowledgements also go to Peter Rasony and Jan Baumann, who helped me to prepare and direct a seminar on the topic in 1996/97, and to the students of that seminar.
22. Warner (1990) introduced the term in order to designate 'a ground rule of argument in a public discourse that defines its norms as abstract and universal' (p. 38); referring to the fact that 'several publications under fictitious names ...' (were able) 'by means of their fictive personae, ... to avoid the resistance of "Personal Prejudice"' (43). On anonymity of authors see Heideking (1988b, pp. 193 and 202–5).
23. It should be added that 'American Republicanism' of the eighteenth century seemed to start with the explicit rejection of any allowance for individual interests, as Warner (1990) is eager to show. But as a major achievement in the evolution of public discourse at the time of the foundation of modern United States it came to be an accepted fact that understanding involves attribution of individual preferences.
24. Heideking (1988b), particularly chap. III: Parteien und Parteienverständnis im Übergang zum Bundesstaat, 93–104, and chap. VII: Das literarische Medium: Bücher, Flugschriften und Zeitungen, 192–239.
25. *The Federalist* No. 37, January 11, 1788. In Cooke (1961, p. 177).

REFERENCES

Albert, H. (1994), *Kritik der reinen Hermeneutik. Der Antirealismus und das Problem des Verstehens*, Die Einheit der Gesellschaftswissenschaften, Bd. 85, Tübingen: Mohr.

Beard, C. (1913), *An Economic Interpretation of the Constitution of the United States*, New York: Macmillan.

Campbell, D.T. (1987), 'Evolutionary epistemology', in Gerard Radnitzky and W.W. Bartley (eds), *Evolutionary Epistemology, Rationality, and the Sociology of Knowledge*, La Salle: Open Court, pp. 47–89.

Davidson, D. (1984), *Inquiries into Truth and Interpretation*, Essays, Oxford: Clarendon Press.

Davidson, D. (1990), 'The structure and content of truth', *The Journal of Philosophy*, 87 (6), 279–328.

Davidson, D. (1995), 'Could there be a science of rationality?', *International Journal of Philosophical Studies*, 3 (1), 1–16.

Dennett, D.C. (1990), 'The interpretation of texts, people and other artefacts', *Philosophy and Phenomenological Research*, 1 (Supplement), 177–94.

Eco, U. (1990), *Das offene Kunstwerk*, Frankfurt: Suhrkamp.

Eco, U. (1996), *Zwischen Autor und Text. Interpretation und Überinterpretation, mit Einwürfen von Richard Rorty, Jonathan Culler, Christine Brooke-Rose und Stefan Collini*, München: Deutscher Taschenbuch Verlag.

Fehr, J. (1997), *Ferdinand de Saussure. Linguistik und Semiologie, Notizen aus dem Nachlass: Texte, Briefe und Dokumente*, Frankfurt a.M.: Suhrkamp.

Understanding and the mobilisation of error 259

Ferrand, M. (ed.) (1911). *The Records of the Federal Convention*, vol. I, New Haven: Yale University Press.

Fleck, L. (1994), *Entstehung und Entwicklung einer wissenschaftlichen Tatsache. Einführung in die Lehre vom Denkstil und Denkkollektiv*, Frankfurt a. M.: Suhrkamp.

Gadamer, H. (1990), *Wahrheit und Methode. Grundzüge einer philosophischen Hermeneutik*, Tübingen: Mohr.

Habermas, J. (1981), *Theorie des kommunikativen Handelns*, 2 Bde., Frankfurt a. M.: Suhrkamp.

Heideking, J. (1988a), 'Verfassungsgebung als politischer prozess. Ein neuer Blick auf die amerikanische Verfassungsdebatte der Jahre 1787–1791', *Historische Zeitschrift*, **246**, 47–88.

Heideking, J. (1988b), *Die Verfassung vor dem Richterstuhl. Vorgeschichte und Ratifizierung der amerikanischen Verfassung, 1787–1791*, Berlin and New York: de Gruyter.

Koselleck, R. (1967), 'Historia Magistra Vitae. Über die Auflösung des Topos im Horizont neuzeitlich bewegter Geschichte', in H. Braun and M. Riedel (eds), *Natur und Geschichte, Karl Löwith zum 70. Geburtstag*, Stuttgart: Kohlhammer, pp. 196–219. Reprinted in Koselleck, R. (1989), *Vergangene Zukunft. Zur Semantik geschichtlicher Zeiten*, Frankfurt a. M.: Suhrkamp, pp. 38–66.

Luhmann, N. (1995), 'Intersubjektivität oder Kommunikation', in N. Luhmann (ed.), *Soziologische Aufklärung, 6, Die Soziologie und der Mensch*, Opladen: Westdeutscher Verlag, pp. 169–88.

Markus, G. (1987), 'Why is there no hermeneutics of natural sciences? Some preliminary theses', *Science in Context*, 5–51.

Mill, J.S. (1859), *On Liberty*, republished 1956, Indianapolis and New York: The Liberal Arts Press.

North, D.C. (1989), 'Institutional change and economic history', *Journal of Institutional and Theoretical Economics*, **145**, 238–45.

Popper, K.R. (1966), *Of Clouds and Clocks. An Approach to the Problem of Rationality and the Freedom of Man*, St. Louis: Washington University Press.

Popper, K.R. (1987). 'Natural Selection and the Emergence of Mind', in G. Radnitzky and W.W. Bartley, *Evolutionary Epistemology, Rationality, and the Sociology of Knowledge*, La Salle: Open Court, pp. 139–53.

Rorty, R. (1993), 'Heidegger, Kundera und Dickens', in R. Rorty, *Eine Kultur ohne Zentrum, vier philosophische Essays*, German translation by Joachim Schulte, Stuttgart: Reclam, pp. 72–103.

Rott, H. (2000a), 'Two dogmas of belief revision', *The Journal of Philosophy*, 503–22.

Rott, H. (2000b), 'Rationalitätsunterstellungen im Dienst der Interpretation von Texten', working paper (unpublished).

Schenk, G. (2000), 'Hermeneutik und Vernunftlehre aus pietistischer Sicht', in M. Beetz and G. Cacciatore (eds), *Die Hermeneutik im Zeitalter der Aufklärung*, Köln, Weimar and Vienna: Böhlau, pp. 31–48.

Scholz, O.R. (1998). 'Wahrheitshintergrund und Interpretation', *Studia Philosophica*, **57**, 27–51.

Scholz, R.O. (1999a), 'Verstehen und Rationalität. Untersuchungen zu den Grundlagen von Hermeneutik und Sprachphilosophie', *Philosophische Abhandlungen*, **76**, Frankfurt a.M.: Klostermann.

Scholz, O.R. (1999b), 'Wie versteht man eine Person? – Zum Verhältnis von Alltagspsychologie und wissenschaftlicher Psychologie, Projekt Erklärungskohärenz, DFG –Forschergruppe "kommunikatives Verstehen"', manuscript.

Siegenthaler, H. (1995), 'Wege zum Wohlstand. Das Beispiel der USA, der Schweiz und Brasiliens', in W. Fischer (ed.), *Lebensstandard und Wirtschaftssysteme*, Frankfurt a. M.: Knapp, pp. 173–212.

Siegenthaler, H. (1997), 'Learning and its rationality in a context of fundamental uncertainty', *Journal of Institutional and Theoretical Economics*, **153** (4), 748–61.

Swedberg, R. (1998), *Max Weber and the Idea of Economic Sociology*, Princeton: Princeton University Press.

Warner, M. (1990), *The Letters of the Republic. Publication and Public Sphere in Eighteenth-Century America*, Cambridge, MA: Harvard University Press, pp. 34–72.

Widmer, B. (1998), 'Kollektive Lern- und Entscheidungsprozesse im Kontext der amerikanischen Bundesstaatsgründung, Lizentiatsarbeit der Universität Zürich', manuscript, Zürich.

Witt, U. (1998), 'Imagination and leadership – the neglected dimension of an evolutionary theory of the firm', *Journal of Economic Behavior & Organization*, **35**, 161–77.

Wohlgemuth, M. (1999), 'Democracy as a discovery procedure. toward an Austrian economics of the political process, Max-Planck-Institut zur Erforschung von Wirtschaftssystemen', Discussion Paper 17, Jena.

Index

Adams, W. and Brock, J. 217
Adamovich et al. 127
adaptive policy 164, 179, 180, 181
Ajzen, I. and Fishbein, M. 138
Akerlof, G. 43
Albert, H. 78, 84, 99, 258
Alchian, A. 23
allocation 28–9, 39, 46, 49, 50, 53, 56, 61, 65. 104–5, 155, 169, 174, 177, 183
Alexy, R. 76
Andersen, B. et al. 187
Andersen, E. 217
Antonelli, C. 167
Apolte, T. 217
Arrow, K. 12, 19, 96, 98, 102
Arrowian Social Choice 96
Arthur, W. 42, 137, 199
Arthur, W. et al. 42
Austrian economics 40, 90, 96, 121, 187
Autio, E. 187

bankruptcy 24
Barro, R. 132, 138
Barry, N. 73, 89
Baumol, W. 111
Beard, C. 254
Bebchuk, L. 205, 217
Bebchuk, L. and Roe, M. 210
Beike, R. and Schlütz, J. 229
Beike, R. et al. 223, 225
beliefs 9, 10, 17. 79, 101, 108, 117–18, 121, 128–31, 135–8, 140–51, 155–8, 248–52, 254, 256–7
Blaug, M. 68
Blendon, R. et al. 158
Boettke, P. 123
Born, K. 229
Boulding, K. 99, 100, 107, 110, 118, 123
Boyd R. and Richerson, P. 24
Branscomb, L. 183

Bratton, W. and McCahery, J. 217
Brennan, G. and Buchanan, J.M. 78, 89
Brenner, T. 158
Breton, A. 217
Buchanan, J.M. 35, 41, 47–8, 58, 64, 79–81, 89, 96, 99, 102, 123, 136
Buchanan, J.M. et al. 35
Budzinski, O. 74
Bundesaufsichtsamt für den Wertpapierhandel 239
bureaucratic procedure 145
Bush, V. 165, 168, 184
Buxbaum, R. 217
Buxbaum and Hopf, K. 217

Campbell, D. 256
Cary, W. 205, 227
capital 106, 171, 193. 198, 206–7, 223–6, 229–31, 234, 238, 241
capital: human capital 208–9
cartels 49–50, 53
Carlsson, B. 177, 178, 182, 184
Carlsson, B. and Stankiewicz 184
Carney, W. 209
Carter, C. and Williams, B. 162
Cassidy, J. 68
choice 5–11, 13, 22, 29, 35, 47–8, 51–2, 58–9, 74, 77–82, 86, 88, 90, 96, 98, 101–2. 104–5, 111, 115–16, 121, 123, 129, 150, 152, 154, 167, 176, 191, 195, 203–4, 209, 212–16, 255, 257
cognitive-evolutionary approach 11, 89, 128, 138, 140, 142–3, 146, 155–7
Commons, J. 226
competition 4. 9, 10, 11, 13, 23–4, 26, 29, 30–31, 34–6, 39. 42, 46, 49–51. 53, 56–7, 63, 70, 73, 81–3, 85–6, 88–9, 96–8, 102–14, 107, 108–12, 115–16, 119, 121–4, 132–3, 162, 164, 166, 169–70, 147–76, 178,

185–7, 191–6, 199–206, 211–17.
233
competition policy 48–50, 53, 56, 57.
179
complementarity 123, 177, 199, 202, 210
Constant, E. 167
constitutional policy 48
consumption 8, 23, 26, 30–31, 80, 101,
106–7, 115, 123, 139
Coombs, R. and Metcalfe, J. 177
Coombs, R. et al. 169
Cordato, R. 64
custom 19, 24, 149

Dahl, R. 107
Daines, R. 205, 209
David, P. 32, 53
David, P. and Foray, D. 173
Davidson, D. 246, 249, 250, 257
Deibert, V. and Serrar, K. 235
democracy 11, 80, 85, 87, 89, 96–104,
106, 108–10, 113–17, 119–23, 129,
131–3, 155, 207, 245
Demsetz, H. 4, 18, 39, 110, 123, 191
Dennett, D. 257
Denzau, A. and North, D. 128, 130, 137
Deutsche Börse 13, 224, 227–8, 230–33,
240–42
development 3, 5, 15, 24, 28, 41–2, 48,
53, 55, 68, 72–3, 101, 111, 114,
142–3, 147, 163–4, 169, 171, 173,
175, 177–8, 182–5, 191–3, 196,
200–202, 205, 207, 211, 215–16,
222, 224–5, 232, 252
see also evolution
Dewey, J. 84, 85, 87, 90
discovery procedure 4, 81, 83–4, 97,
120, 122, 194, 216
distributional policy 46, 52
DiLorenzo, T. 123
Di Maggio, P. and Powell, W. 217
Dixit, A. 87, 90
Dixon, W. 123
DiZerega, G. 117, 123
Dodd, P. and Lettwich, R. 205, 217
Dosi, G. 53, 192, 155, 200–201, 216–17
Downs, A. 9, 109, 132
Downsian 96, 101
Drucker, H. 157
Dye, T. 90

Easterbrook, F. 217
Easterbrook, F. and Fischel, D. 205, 226
Eco, U. 257
economic fallacies 136, 140, 155
economic policy 1, 3–7, 9, 11–12, 18,
24, 46–52, 54–6, 59–60, 63–5,
67–73, 76–7, 82, 85, 87–90,
128–30, 134–6, 138–43, 145–9,
150–51, 155–7, 192, 237
economic policy, theory of 47, 64
economic freedom,
see liberty 48–9
economic performance 55, 113, 162, 191
economies of scale 198, 200, 202–4,
209, 212–13, 216
economy
German economy 54, 235
Eckardt, M. 217
Edquist, C. 177, 187
efficiency 18, 21, 29–31, 33–7, 42, 78,
148, 151–3, 155, 157, 198, 201,
205, 207, 211–13, 231, 246, 256
allocative efficiency 23–30, 42, 67
evolutionary efficiency 18, 29, 30, 32,
42
Pareto-efficiency 78
election 11, 23–4, 26, 36–7, 43, 48, 85,
90, 97, 101, 105–6, 109, 120, 133,
153, 205
Eisenberg, A. 65
Eisenberg, M. 205
Eliasson, G. 43, 187
Elsser, S. 197–8, 217
Engel, C. 61
Entrepreneurs 7, 9–10, 12, 31, 36, 77,
96–7, 101, 108–10, 113, 119, 122,
175, 209, 224, 231, 238–9, 241, 243
entrepreneurship 10, 30–31, 109–10,
112, 121–2, 139, 148, 175, 223
entrepreneurship: government entrepre-
neuship 27
environmental policy 48, 50, 52, 56–7,
65
equilibrium 1–2, 9–10, 12, 15, 41–43,
72–4, 78, 96, 102, 156, 162, 170,
174–5
equilibrium analysis (*see also* static
market theory) 1, 2, 10, 15, 41
Erdmann, G. 53

error (eliminating) 13, 246, 252–3,
    255–6
ethics
    business 27
Eucken, W. 68–70, 72–4, 76–8, 89
evolution 2–4, 8–9, 12, 20, 22–8, 30–36,
    42–3, 58, 71–5, 78, 85, 107, 111,
    115, 137, 140, 145–6, 162, 164,
    202, 211, 214–17, 227, 237–8, 258
evolution of technologies 18
    economic evolution 23–4. 52–4, 59,
        175
    institutional evolution 12, 191–3,
        215–16
evolutionary economics 1–3, 23, 43, 68,
    97, 101, 121, 123, 226, 230, 237,
    245, 255
evolutionary market processes 97
experimental economic policy (Eucken)
    69, 70, 73
exploitation 102, 166, 173, 176–7, 184,
    186, 236, 239

Faulkner, W. 166, 186
federalism 81, 88, 217
Fehr, J. 257
Fernandez, R. and Rodrick D. 80
Ferrand, M. 254
firms, 1–2, 19, 21–8, 30, 35–7, 41–3, 53,
    57, 61–3, 86–7, 108, 112–13, 115,
    118, 129, 163, 166, 169–71, 173,
    176–80, 182, 184–7, 193–7,
    199–205, 207, 209, 217, 225–32,
    235–6, 238
    see also organisation
Fleck, L. 247
formal / informal institutions 27, 65, 80,
    184
formal political decision process 145
Forte, F. 43
Foss, N. 90
Foster, J. 123
Freeman, C. 178, 217
Freeman, C. and Lovea, F. 163
Friedman, M. 16–17, 25, 39
Frey, B. 9, 64, 68, 90, 122–3, 137, 149
Frey, B. and Eichenberger, R. 90, 217
Frey, B. and Oberholzer-Gee 64
Fudenberg, D. and Levine, D. 64

Gadamer, H. 158
Gatsios. K. and Holmes. P. 217
Georghiou, L. 182–3
Gerber, D. 89
Gerum, E. 207
Gibbons, M. and Johnson, R. 167
Gibbons, M. et al. 178, 186
Goldberg, J. and Nitzsch, R. 236
Good 9, 22–3, 30–31, 49, 61, 89, 97, 99,
    103–4, 106–7, 109–10, 122–3, 139,
    195, 224, 237
    common good, public good, collective
        good 5, 25, 29, 34–5, 48, 50, 60,
        63, 67, 154–5, 172, 175, 192–4,
        203
    private good, market good 105
governance 22, 67–70, 76–7, 86–8,
    206–7, 211, 217, 224, 226
    self governance 60–63
government 1–3, 6, 10, 16, 18–22, 24,
    26–9, 31–9, 41, 43, 49, 61, 69, 72,
    74, 79, 81, 84, 86, 99, 106, 109,
    111, 115–17, 121, 123, 130, 132–4,
    139, 152–5, 157–8, 165, 173, 177,
    180, 183–4, 204, 213, 226, 228
governmental failure 6, 7
Grandstrand, D. et al. 187
Grandy. C. 204
Granovetter, M. 117–18
Green, K. et al. 187
Greif, A. 228
Greif, A. et al. 228
Griliches, Z. 186
Grimm, D. 239
Gruppe Deutsche Börse 227–8

Habermas, J. 66
Halbhuber, H. 217
Hayek, F.A. 2–4, 8, 10–12, 20, 24, 33–5,
    37, 42–3, 46–7, 49–52, 54, 58, 64,
    68–72, 74–8, 80, 82, 84–6, 88–90,
    96, 98–100, 102, 104, 111–13,
    115–16, 120–23, 191, 194, 216–17,
    227
Hegmann, H. 79
Heideking, J. 258
Heinemann, F. 81
Heiner, R. 28, 198
Heitzer, B. and Sohn, C. 223, 230

Helmstaedter, E. 86
Henderson, D. 136
hermeneutic(s) 252, 254, 256–7
Heuss, E. 83
Hicks, D. 172
Hippel, E. 87
Hirschman, A. 100, 120
historical school 226
Hodgson, G. 123
Hodson D. and Maher, I. 88
Holland et al. 137
Holmes, O. 67, 76, 82, 89, 200–201
Homann, K. 79
Howells, J. 187
Huckfeldt, R. and Sprague, J. 119–20
Hume, D. 116, 123
Hutt, W. 128, 135

ideologies 11, 128–35, 138, 140–41,
    148, 150–51, 155, 158, 253
imperfection 18, 26, 29, 31, 33–4,
    37–40, 101, 174–5
  market imperfection (*see also* market
    failure) 10, 26, 31–3, 39, 43
implementation 69–70, 73, 78, 143, 145,
    174, 178, 183, 210
impossibility theorem 76–7, 89, 98
incorporation theory 204, 213–17
increasing returns 32, 165, 173–7, 192
industry 30, 33, 57, 60–61, 65, 134, 163,
    165–6, 175, 183–4, 186, 197, 200,
    203, 206, 223–4
information, asymmetry 239
infrastructure 87, 173, 178, 187
innovation 1, 4, 7–8, 12, 23, 38, 42, 47,
    51–9, 62, 72, 83–4, 97, 111,
    113–14, 119, 162–166, 168–74,
    176–87, 192–8, 203, 205, 210, 217,
    224, 226, 237
innovation, institutional 80
innovation policies 164, 169, 179
innovation, political 97, 111, 113–14
innovation, technological 30, 202
innovativeness 47, 54–5, 57–9, 64
institutions 4, 11–12, 18–19, 22, 24, 27,
    33, 41, 43, 47–63, 65, 68, 72, 77,
    79–81, 83–4, 86, 88, 114, 121, 130,
    132, 136, 146, 157, 163, 166,
    168–70, 175–8, 180, 182, 191–3,

200, 207, 211, 214–17, 226–8, 235,
    239, 241–2
  adaptive institution 12, 223
  external institution 62–4, 241
  formal institution 27, 65, 80, 184
  informal institution 27, 65, 80, 184
  institutional framework 4–5, 12, 79,
    84, 224, 246, 253–4
  internal institution 60, 65, 227, 241–2
institutional/system competition 12, 46,
    81–3, 86, 89, 192–3
institutional choice 59, 78–81, 88
institutional design 20, 41, 48, 51, 89
institutional evolution 12, 191–3, 215,
    216
instruments 9, 25–9, 41, 58, 61, 154,
    157, 200–201
  policy instruments 20, 25–7, 140, 142,
    150, 153, 174
interventionism 7, 48–9, 72, 74

Johnson, S. 223, 226
Justice 70, 73, 250

Kaiser, F. and Fuhrer, U. 138
Kasper, W. and Streit, M. 157
Katz, J. and Martin, B. 180
Keller, A. 165–6
Kenton, G. 217
Kenyon, D. and Kincaid, J. 217
Kerber, W. 59, 83, 88–9, 112, 194, 217
Kerber, W. and Heine, K. 12, 43, 191
Keynes, J.M. 1, 10, 15, 16, 68, 135
  Keynesian policy 43
Kirchgässner, G. 157
Kirzner, I. 53
Klausner, M. 209–10, 212
Klein, D. 107
Kline, S. and Rosenberg, M. 169
Klodt, H. 199
Knight, F. 85, 90
Knight, J. 49–50, 84, 101
Knips, S. 223, 230–31, 238
knowledge 3, 5–7, 9–11, 17, 19, 24, 28,
    34, 36, 40–41, 46, 56, 58–60, 62,
    64, 67–72, 75, 77, 79–90, 96–8,
    102–8, 110–12, 116–18, 120–21,
    128, 130, 132, 136, 147, 150, 158,

162–82, 185–7, 194, 197, 206, 208, 216–17, 225, 235, 246, 247
knowledge production 9, 17, 47, 170, 173, 176–9, 181, 186
Kobayashi, B. and Ribstein, L. 208
Koch, L. 74
Kodama, F. 187
Korfsmeyer, J. 238
Kotlikoff 153
Kotlikoff et al. 159
Kuhn, T. 67, 197, 201
Kukies, J. 225
Kydland, F. and Prescott, E. 132
Kuran, T. 99, 101, 109–10, 118–20, 123

Lachmann, L. 60, 227, 239, 242
Ladeur, K. 75, 86
laissez-faire 20, 69, 70, 85, 89, 227–8, 230, 242
Langrish, J. et al. 169
La Porta, R. et al. 208, 211, 215, 226
law 12, 20, 22, 24, 27–28, 33–4, 40, 43, 48–50, 53, 56–7, 61, 64–5, 68, 70–72, 74–6, 89, 100, 102, 104–5, 107, 109, 111–12, 114–16, 122, 139, 146, 165–7, 181, 193, 195, 201–17, 239, 241
  formal laws 19, 22, 24
  public law 71, 75, 112, 224, 226–8, 241–2
Layton, E. 166–7
legal development 200–202
legal paradigms 193, 200–204, 206, 213, 216
Lehmann, M. 63
Lehmkuhl, D. 60, 65
Leiser, D. et al. 137
Lewis, A. et al. 137
Libecap, G. 191
Liberty 48, 75, 256
Loasby, B. 84, 90, 106, 114, 123
locational competition 192–3
Lowell, A. 115
Luedecke, S. and Sczesny, C. 158
Luhmann, N. 49, 248
Lundvall, B. 178
Lunt, P. and Furnham, A. 137

Macey, J. 217
Mantzavinos, C. 89

Majone 62, 65
market
  market agents 12–13, 53–4, 56–7, 63
  market competition 4, 13, 23–4, 26, 35–6, 39, 83, 86, 97, 103, 107–8, 110, 162, 196
  market failure *see also* politicants
    political 3–5, 7, 12, 46, 49–50, 54, 60, 63–4, 163, 169–71, 173–5, 179, 199
  market order 9, 11, 47–8, 51–2, 55, 60, 70–71, 73
  market outcomes 32, 46–9, 51, 55, 59
  market participants 4, 6, 7, 33, 50–52, 56–9, 64, 106, 139
  market performance 46–51, 61, 230
  market sphere 4, 10, 11, 47–8, 55
  contestable market 111
  financial markets, capital markets 33–4, 36, 37, 207–8, 211, 214–15, 223–4, 235–7, 241
  Neuer Markt, new market 12, 65, 223, 225–6, 242
Markus, G. 256
Marris R. and Mueller, D. 42
Marshall, A. 165–6
Meier, A. and Slembeck, T. 131, 138, 140
merger laws 56
mergers 49–50, 53, 57, 171, 182, 205
Metcalfe, J. 3–5, 12, 43, 77, 162, 167, 174–5, 177, 180, 184
Metcalfe, J. and Georghiou, L. 77, 175
Milgrom et al. 228
Mises, L. 7, 9, 49, 77
Mitchell, W. and Simmons, R. 123
motivation 34, 39, 64, 142, 231, 257
Mowery, D. and Rosenberg, N. 172
Mueller, D. 42, 191

Narin, F. et al. 186
NASDAQ 12, 65, 223, 225, 227, 231–2, 234–5, 424
nation state 12, 46, 59, 88, 163
Nelson, R. 167, 177, 178
Nelson, R. and Winter, S. 2–3, 24, 217
Nemax 225, 231–2, 235, 242

neoclassical 98–9, 102, 111, 116, 122, 194, 236
neoclassical economics 98, 121
network externalities 198, 202, 209–10, 216
new institutional economics (NIE) 24, 47
Niquet, B. 225
Niskanen, W. 35, 158
Noelle-Neumann, E. 119
Noll, R. 64
nomos 71, 74, 76–7
normative beliefs 130, 135, 142–3, 155
norms 1, 22, 24, 27, 33–4, 60–61, 75–6, 147–8, 156, 167, 258
    moral norms 27
North, D. 2, 19, 24, 40–43, 50, 68, 83, 128, 158, 191–2, 215–16, 252
novelty 9, 19, 22, 41, 73, 74, 77, 98, 115, 123, 175, 186, 237
    see also innovation

Oates, W. 81–2, 88, 90
Oates, W. and Schwab, R. 217
OECD 168, 186
Ogger, G. 43
O'Hara, M. 229
Okruch, S. 11, 67, 74–6, 88
Olson, M. 152, 154
order
    economic order 51–3, 55, 69, 72, 73, 76
    market order 9, 11, 47–8, 51–2, 55, 60, 70–71, 73–4, 76, 86, 89, 98
    order of actors 20, 85–7, 89
    spontaneous order 3, 70–71, 75–6, 96, 181
Ordnungstheorie/Freiburg School/ordoliberalism 68–9, 72–3, 77–8, 89
Ormerod, P. 68
organization 60, 71, 87, 97, 111, 162, 178, 183, 224

Parkinson, C. 43, 56
path 9, 53, 72, 197, 201, 207, 211
path dependence 12, 32–3, 191–3, 196, 200–203, 210–17
path dependencies 53, 112, 199
Pavitt, K. 167
Pelikan, P. 1, 4–5, 10, 15, 40–43, 106

Perelman, M. 68
Persson, T. and Tabellini, G. 133
Petroski, H. 186
Peukert, H. 12, 62, 65, 223
Plötz, W. 223
Plueckelmann, K. 225
Polanyi, M. 41, 172
policy makers (political agents or entrepreneurs) 6–11, 25, 27, 16–51, 54–9, 61–4, 70, 132, 133, 136–8, 145, 152, 155–65
policy-making 2, 5–7, 11, 15, 17–18, 24–5, 39, 41, 43, 47–8, 128–33, 135–6, 138, 140–42, 146, 151–3, 155–6
policy prescriptions/advice 16, 128–30, 135–6, 146, 149, 151, 156
policy, rational 8, 11, 128–9
policy recommendations 4, 12, 67
policy, institutional; top down, bottom up 47–8, 51, 59–60, 62
political competition 10–11, 96–8, 103–4, 108–13, 115–16, 121
political entrepreneurs 9, 77, 96, 101, 108–10, 112–13, 119, 122, 148
political failure 46–7, 58–9, 64
political system 67, 105, 107, 112, 118–22, 124, 147–9, 152, 156, 208, 253
politics 9, 11, 65, 84–5, 96, 98, 100, 107, 113–14, 122–3, 128–30, 140–42, 145, 147–8, 150, 152, 157, 186, 245, 254
politics, political sphere 9–10, 47, 58, 69
Popper, K. 83–4, 88, 99, 230, 256–7
positive beliefs 130–31, 135–8, 140, 143, 144, 155–6, 158
pragmatism 69, 84, 87, 90
preferences 6, 8–9, 17, 21, 61, 63–4, 78–9, 81, 96, 98–100, 102, 104–5, 107, 109–10, 116–19, 122–3, 130, 135, 142–3, 194, 196, 236, 250–51, 253, 257, 258
price system 70, 104, 108, 122
product regulation 49–50, 54
profit 7, 104, 108–9, 114, 139, 168, 172, 175, 180, 186, 233, 235–7, 239–40
property rights 1, 20, 24, 29, 33, 49, 104–5, 107, 121, 170, 175, 191

public choice 9–11, 35, 86, 90, 96, 98,
  105, 110–11, 116, 121, 123, 129,
  154, 191

QWERTY 32–3

Rabin, M. 80
Ramseyer, J. 217
R & D 37, 40, 86, 163–4, 171, 177, 180,
  183–5, 187, 225
rationality 13, 21, 64, 129–30, 156,
  246–7, 251–2
reform 13, 26, 27, 34, 42, 47, 81, 88, 90,
  115, 152–3, 223–4, 226, 228,
  236–8, 242
  institutional reform 1, 19, 226, 228
  political reform 13, 122
regulation 12, 50, 61–5, 74–5, 186, 196,
  208–10, 228, 230, 237, 239, 240
regulatory competition 12, 191–6, 200,
  202–3, 211–13, 215–17
resources 4, 8, 19–21, 29–32, 42, 50, 56,
  97, 104–6, 108–9, 130–31, 141–2,
  144, 150, 154, 158, 162, 169, 174,
  176–7, 179, 183–4, 198, 226, 229,
  234, 238, 246, 254
Roe, M. 207, 210, 214
Roedl, B. 223, 229
Romano, R. 205, 217
Rorty, R. 251, 257
Rosenberg, N. 169, 172, 187
Rott, H. 257
Rowley, C. 123
Rule-based behaviour 133
rule of law 70, 72, 102, 107, 116, 122
rules 1–2, 4, 8, 11–13, 19–20, 22, 30,
  33–4, 41–3, 47–52, 54–5, 57, 63,
  70–76, 78–80, 84–6, 89–90, 104–5,
  111–12, 114, 117, 123, 128, 132–3,
  139, 145–7, 151–2, 155–6, 162,
  177, 191–6, 200, 202, 205–8,
  210–13, 216, 223–4, 226–30, 233,
  239, 240–42, 245, 247, 250, 252–6
  rules of just conduct 70–72, 74–6
  legal rules 74, 192–6, 200–203, 205,
    208, 211–13, 216, 226
  negative rules 11, 49, 51–2
  rule setting 47, 49, 53, 55, 62–4
Ryle, G. 80

Sabel, C. 87, 88, 90
Sahal, D. 217
Samuels, W.J. 129–31
Sartori, G. 106
Schaible, S. and Thielbeer, M. 225
Schanze, E. 217
Scharpf, F. 49, 79, 81, 89
Schenk, G. 254
Schilling, M. 198
Schmidt, R. and Grohs, S. 217, 224
Schmidt, R. and Spindler, G. 207,
  210–11
Schmoller, G. 226
Schneider, F. 157
Scholz, O. 257
Schumpeter, J.A. 20, 23, 42, 64, 97–8,
  100, 102, 113, 123, 175, 185, 194,
  217, 224, 237, 242
Schultze, C. 136
science 12, 67, 75, 82–3, 85, 136, 150,
  157, 162–9, 173–4, 177–8, 183–6,
  197, 245, 249, 256
selection, market selection 23, 26, 106,
  176
self-organisation 181, 183
Shackle, G. 235, 242
Shiller, R. 136–7, 158, 235, 242
Shughart, W. and Tollison, R. 217
Siebert, H. and Koop, M. 217
Siegenthaler, H. 13, 245, 256, 258
Silverberg, G. 87
Simon, H. 198, 245
Sinn, H. 196, 217
Sinn, S. 196
Slembeck, T. 10–11, 90, 128, 130–31,
  137, 138, 140, 145–6, 153, 158
Smith, A. 6, 177, 227
social system 47, 141
social use of knowledge 96
social welfare function 98, 102
Socialist 1, 15, 38, 41, 106, 118, 132,
  136
Sombart, W. 231
Soros, G. 235, 237
spontaneous co-ordination 104, 106
state 1, 3–4, 6, 11–12, 19, 22, 27, 28, 32,
  46–7, 49, 51, 59, 60–61, 63–4,
  69–70, 72, 84–5, 87, 107, 110, 163,

166, 193, 204–6, 211, 217, 226, 237, 257
state action/intervention 69, 70, 72, 226, 237
static 1–3, 10, 10–11, 30, 40–41, 46, 54, 56, 58, 67–9, 96, 98–100, 116, 121, 131, 140, 152, 175, 177
Steiner, J. 76
stock exchange, 65, 214, 227–8, 230, 238, 239, 242
see also Neuer Markt
Stiglitz, J. 136, 152, 154, 158, 173
Stokes, D. 167–8, 186
Streit, M. and Mussler 217
Streit, M. and Wegner, G. 103–4, 108, 225
Streit, M. and Wohlgemuth, M. 89, 217
Sugden, C. 107
Sum, J. and Pelkmans, J. 196, 217
sunk costs 198, 202, 208, 216
Sunstein, C. 109
Swedberg, R. 257
system 1, 9, 19, 24, 42, 47, 66–7, 69–70, 75, 76, 79–81, 84, 86, 88, 98, 99, 104–5, 107–8, 114, 118, 120, 122–3, 129, 131, 134–6, 140–41, 146, 149, 151–4, 157, 162, 166, 169, 172, 178–83, 185, 187, 200, 202–3, 205–7, 211, 214, 225–7, 230, 234, 238, 245
economic system 1, 20, 76–7, 83, 100, 129–30, 135, 148, 164, 179, 227, 237–8
systems of ideas 130

Tassey, G. 178
tax subsidies 183–5
technological paradigms 192–3, 196–201, 203, 216–17
technology 12, 76, 162–9, 171, 173, 177–8, 182–7, 198–200, 225, 258
technology foresight 183
technology technological trajectory 53, 197
thesis 71, 74, 76–7
Tiebout, C. 194, 217
Tinbergen, J. 47, 64, 142, 149, 153

Tirole, J. 196
transaction costs 27, 60, 163–4, 209, 239
Triandis, H. 138
Tuchtfeld, E. 130
Trute, H. 75
Tullock, G. 35

uncertainty 9, 80–81, 132, 137, 152, 170–71, 173, 175, 198, 202, 209, 216, 238, 245
Upmeyer, A. 138
US-GAAP 229
Utterback, J. 168
Utility 21, 80, 98, 101, 119, 123, 166–7, 176

Vanberg, V. 24, 40, 43, 55, 76, 78–81, 111, 115, 122, 192
Vanberg, V. and Kerber, W. 59, 88–9, 99, 217
Vanberg, V. and Buchanan, J.M. 88
Varga, A. 187
variation 84, 90, 112, 114, 146, 167, 186, 191, 201, 230, 245, 255–6
Verdier, J. 153, 158
Vihanto, M. 89
Vincenti, W. 166–7
"voice" / "exit" 82
Voigt, S. 78, 89
voter 9, 96, 99–100, 105, 109, 114, 133, 151
voters 8–9, 29, 97, 101, 103–110, 112–14, 123, 131–2, 144–5, 153
voting 96, 100, 105–8, 114, 119, 132, 145, 195, 207, 229

Wagner, R. 123
Wallmeier, M. and Roesl, R. 238
Walker, W. 174
Warner, M. 253, 258
Watkins, J. 82
Weber, M. 56, 107, 257
Wegner, G. 1, 4, 7, 10–11, 33, 40, 42–3, 46, 59, 63–4, 76, 113, 196, 235
Weimer, J. and Pape, J. 206, 214
Weinberger, O. 75
welfare, economic 2, 4, 46–7, 139
welfare, state 1, 27

Weizsaecker, C. von 68
Widmer, B. 258
Williamson, J. and Haggard, S. 123
Williamson, M. and Wearing, A. 136
Williamson, O. 41
Winter, R. 205, 217
Wise, G. 165
Wiseman, J. 123
Witt, U. 40–41, 89, 123, 256
Wittman, D. 109, 111

Wohlgemuth, M. 10–11, 40, 59, 88–90,
    96, 98, 108, 110, 113, 122–3, 256
Wolf, C. 39
Wood, G. 136

Young, A. 177

Zaller, J. 109
Zumbansen, P. 75
Zweigert, K. and Koetz, H. 215